Alien Encounters

Mimi Thi Nguyen *and* Thuy Linh Nguyen Tu, *editors*

Alien Encounters

Popular Culture in Asian America

Duke University Press

DURHAM & LONDON 2007

© 2007 Duke University Press

Printed in the United States of America on acid-free paper ∞
Designed by Jennifer Hill. Typeset in Dante by Keystone Typesetting, Inc.

Library of Congress Cataloging-in-Publication Data appear on
the last printed page of this book.

Contents

3. Consuming Cultures

4. Troubled Technologies

Acknowledgments

We would first like to thank the contributors to this volume for their insightful essays, for their willingness to engage our queries and occasional odd questions, and for their patience during the process of bringing the manuscript to publication. We would also like to thank Ken Wissoker, our editor at Duke University Press, for his guidance and confident encouragement (especially when this project was a mere notion), and Anitra Grisales, who provided both humor and unimpeachable editorial aid. Our anonymous reviewers helped us to clarify our arguments about, and investments in, popular culture in Asian America, for which we are grateful. We are pleased to acknowledge as well the University of California, Berkeley; the University of Illinois, Urbana-Champaign; the University of Michigan; New York University; the Ohio State University; Vassar College; and Cornell University (and all our friends and colleagues at those institutions) for research, financial, and intellectual support at various stages of this project. Finally, we are grateful to Logan Hill and Mark Murrmann for reminding us to watch television, listen to music, go to the movies, and always have fun with our work.

Introduction

Mimi Thi Nguyen and
Thuy Linh Nguyen Tu

We love *The Goonies* (1985). This Hollywood studio adventure (produced by the movie mogul Steven Spielberg) features a ragtag band of teenage outsiders who go in search of a pirate treasure to save their "Goondocks" from foreclosure by country club developers. Set in a small town in the Pacific Northwest, *The Goonies* is populated by recognizable types: the sometimes cowardly fat kid (wearing both plaid pants *and* a Hawaiian shirt), the wise-cracker (appropriately nicknamed "Mouth"), the rich and arrogant jock (with the equally rich and arrogant father), the ditzy cheerleader and her bespectacled best friend, and the shy, stuttering boy whose unwavering belief in the impossible guides their unlikely quest. We rooted for them all, but Data, the Asian immigrant kid exhibiting tendencies toward both the mad inventor and the secret agent, was our childhood favorite. Endearingly portrayed by Jonathan Ke Quan, Data made us believe that injustice could be overcome with a Schwinn and some smarts.[1]

The Goonies joined dozens of other 1980s teen films—from *The Breakfast Club* to *The Outsiders*—that seemed to champion the misfit and misunderstood. To be sure, not all of them featured the likes of Data. A product of their times, many betrayed the anti-Asian sentiments of their Reagan era origins. In the absurdist film *Better Off Dead* (1985), a pair of Japanese exchange students, whose pitch-perfect mimicry of television sportscaster Howard Cosell seemed to suggest a robotic inability to innovate, are put in their place by John

Cusack's souped-up Camaro and his good ole' American ingenuity (aided and abetted by a French tomboy). In *Sixteen Candles* (1984), a kooky and lecherous Chinese exchange student named Long Duck Dong provides "comic relief" in his supposedly misplaced desire for the masculine female jock over the more appropriately feminine (and annoyingly petulant) heroine Samantha. In a number of these films, we witnessed fears of an "Asian invasion" in U.S. financial, territorial, cultural, and technological spaces managed by the lovable and comical, threatening and humiliating Asian images onscreen.

Against this cinematic roll call, it is possible to interpret Data as just another racist caricature—the heavily accented model minority who is also a source of comedic relief and whose slapstick inventions seem to succeed in spite of his gadget-minded genius. But it seems to us that the predictable demand for a more "positive" image would diminish and subordinate the possibility for a misfit, if necessarily flawed, identification to an oftentimes simplistic conception of the political, as well as ignore the aesthetic and narrative turns of the film's championing of its awkward misfits. Though it does bear questioning the racial breakdown of these stereotypes, that Data was tied, by virtue of his ethnicity, to the more conventional collection of weirdos—the fat kid, the smart-ass, the wimp, the "trash," the intellectual—made sense to us as we also "recognized" these outcasts among our own childhood affinities. (Indeed, in the universe of the Goonies, the "perfect" teens—tall, handsome, WASP-y, popular, and rich—are villains on par with murderous robbers.) The film trades in broad strokes and even broader humor (the kids force fat kid Chunk to do the Truffle Shuffle and glue a miniature David's broken penis on upside-down), within which Data, with his cartoonish gadgetry and dreams of super-spydom, fits right in.

In considering our childhood rapport for Data, we are confronted with the complexity of our affections, a complexity that comes to bear upon our intellectual preoccupations—stereotyping and the politics of representation, the queering of the look, cultural appropriation, fantasy, the meaning (and value) of identification, race in narrative and visual images, and the mass consumption and industrial production of popular culture among them. For instance, as scholars we could query what exactly qualifies as "proper" identification, or "accurate" representation, and through which measure we might categorize these. If Data is a stereotype, we nonetheless found that he was very much like us, an "us" composed of geeky Asian immigrants foundering in isolated American small towns. The fact that we were girls didn't stop us from seeing ourselves in Data. And we also might ask if the James Bond soundtrack

accompanying Data's front-door arrival (by way of Wings of Flight) necessarily functions to diminish him as a wannabe—less suave and more spastic—
or whether it instead acknowledges the critical role of fantasy in our adolescent utopian longings. Or both?

Inspired by these and other possible queries, as fans *and* critics, we are wary
of claiming that "internalized racism" is the ground for our "misguided"
affections, even as we acknowledge the conventional—and sometimes con-
stricting—contours of Data's Asian geek image. (The circulation of Data as a
"type" in excess of the film's triumphant narrative is important to consider
here.) The possible implications of this seeming contradiction forced us to
move away from the binary of condemnation (popular culture corrupts) and
celebration (audiences resist) and inspired us to think about the critical, political, and affective challenges posed by Data and other forms and figures of
popular culture.

Few of us are immune to popular culture's intimate address or to its pleasures and affirmations, frustrations and denials.[2] In beginning with this "problem" of Data, we hope to draw attention to the new, productive directions in
Asian American cultural studies represented in part by the contributions to
this collection. *Alien Encounters* moves to take stock of contemporary popular
culture in "Asian America," with all the affection and uneasiness that characterizes our relationship to our childhood hero. As such, this collection begins
with the obvious, though often unacknowledged, assertion that Asian Americans are not "outside" of popular culture—whether or not we are imagined by
it—and that popular culture is important to the ways in which Asian Americans move (or are not allowed to move) through the world. *Alien Encounters*
aims to track specific moments of uneven engagement that might manifest
themselves as complicity, confrontation, or both, and that differentially inter-
polate Asian Americans as consumers and in some cases producers and
workers. It considers the ways in which Asian Americans have responded to
popular culture in their intellectual and cultural work and the different needs,
affects, and motives these responses perform or fulfill. Ultimately, it seeks to
contribute to a broader, ongoing, and necessary dialogue about the meanings
of culture for a progressive political imaginary.

In editing this collection we were interested in how Asian Americans have
chosen to engage the idiom of the popular, particularly at a time when ideas
about culture, the images and conversations circulating through and manufactured as culture, and the "wars" waged about culture occupy the intersection
of the social and political in our everyday lives—from how architects design

downtowns to how curators display artwork, from how audiences listen to music to how they watch television, and from how nations fight wars to how they imagine peace. We can learn much about ourselves in our interactions with what Stuart Hall calls "the theater of popular desires."[3] Given this, we also look to our own childhood affinities in order to emphasize an optimistic note in our inquiries. Themselves flawed, obnoxious, cowardly, proud, imaginative, and brave, the misfit Goonies fueled our hopes for the impossible— that we could save the Goondocks, stop the developers, find the pirate treasure, and otherwise imagine a new world of utopian possibilities. It is in this spirit of need and adventure, in spite of our missteps, that we pursue the question of popular culture in "Asian America."

Defining Our Terms

Asian American and *popular culture* are unwieldy terms, overflowing with significance and import and yet empty of indexical certainty. Full of conflict and contradiction, they elude any hope of accurately and comprehensively describing what lies within their parameters. In order to introduce our object, then, we begin with an inquiry into the first half of this equation, the designation *Asian American*.

Over thirty years of scholarship has demonstrated that *Asian American* is an ever-changing and intrinsically relational term; it is a "racial formation," as Michael Omi and Howard Winant named it in a Foucauldian nod, that derives its various historical effects as a racial category from institutional apparatuses, discursive practices, and political mobilizations.[4] The specific construct of "Asian America" emerged during the late 1960s as both a census category and a defining principle of a coalition-building effort to group the diverse populations of Asian descent in the United States. But even in its emergence as a conceptual entity, the term's coherence was continually troubled by an influx of heterogeneous Asian populations that resulted from wars in Southeast Asia, transnational labor demands, changes in immigration policies (most notably the Immigration and Nationality Acts of 1965), and other geopolitical forces. In the intervening years, this coalition-building principle has been subject to criticism for too often privileging certain narratives and experiences (particularly those of East Asian heterosexual males) and eliding differences of gender, class, sexuality, religion, and national affiliation inherent to such a diverse range of populations.

Given this vexed history, many scholars and activists have cautioned that

4   Nguyen and Tu

Asian American, as a strategic political term born of a particular moment of cultural nationalism, should not be fixed lest dangerous essentialisms about Asian American subjects be reproduced. Important interventions in this regard have hailed from Asian American and diasporic feminist scholars such as Lisa Lowe, Laura Kang, and Rey Chow, who are interested and invested in the insights of poststructuralism and other postfoundationalist theories. Such insights informed a 2003 collection of short essays published in the *Journal of Asian American Studies* on the constitution of the Korean "comfort woman" in academic literary studies, art making, and movements for redress. Collectively, those essays decentered violation as the foundational component of a coherent identity, questioned the desire to extract "authentic" testimony, examined the historical discursive processes and material practices that make *Asian American* matter, and ultimately intervened in debates about Asian American subjectivity in ways that mirror our own intellectual interests.

Expanding on those insights in her recent *Imagine Otherwise*, the literary scholar Kandice Chuh argued that the Asian American construct should be retained as a self-reflexive term rather than a normative one. She called for reformulating Asian American studies as a "subjectless discourse." "Subjectlessness, as a conceptual tool," Chuh wrote,

> points to the need to manufacture "Asian American" situationally.... If we accept a priori that Asian American studies is subjectless, then rather than looking to complete the category "Asian American," to actualize it by such methods as enumerating various components of differences (gender, class, sexuality, religion, and so on), we are positioned to critique the effects of the various configurations of power and knowledge through which the term comes to have meaning.

This is not an abandonment of the political project of Asian American studies, she insists, but a "redefinition of the political, an investigation into what 'justice' might mean and what (or whose) 'justice' is being pursued."[5]

Drawing on these ideas, in this collection we approach the concept *Asian American* as an object of study and mode of analysis or, to use Chuh's terms, a form of critique rather than a given entity. Approaching our objects in this way, we believe, helps us to avoid the pitfalls of authenticity and essentialism and, perhaps more important, allows us to expand our terms of inquiry. It moves us beyond the strictly ethnographic or autobiographical mode—beyond asking "What is Asian American about this popular text?"—and enables us to address a range of other questions. Just what does an Asian American cultural text look like? What does it mean to "be" (or be recognized as) an

Asian American cultural form? Is Asian Americanness always the constitutive or primary site of subject formation or identification in Asian American cultural production? What specific practices of representation are important to understanding the subject of race and popular culture? Shifting our attention in this way allows us to see, as Wendy Hui Kyong Chun's essay in this volume shows, how those who may not be considered Asian American, such as members of the London-based, multicultural artist collective Mongrel, can produce works that pose an Asian Americanist critique.

In this sense, we argue that *Asian American* can be conceived as a marker of historical subjects, an axis of subordination, and a strategic coalition without presuming that it functions as a foundational property of our "selves." This does not mean that we cannot speak of the experiences of Asian Americans, but that we must account for the ways in which these political and cultural activities are linguistically managed, socially constructed, and tactically deployed. It is this important tension that we raise, if not resolve, in our own invocation of *Asian American* and in particular its marriage to the popular. In doing so, we hope to reveal how Asian American as a category of analysis can offer new insights into various social problems and cultural desires that, as we elaborate below, are given voice in popular culture.

If popular culture is the battleground for fantasies of desire and identification, as well as anxieties about alienation and incursion, the question of what to make of its economies (of signs or capital) has inspired many, often heated debates. Asian American studies has long taken part in those discussions, generating its own critical language for talking about cultural politics and political economies. For decades, Asian American scholars have turned their attention to American popular culture in order to examine, and often condemn, its mobilization and amplification of stereotypes at particular historical moments of war, crisis, and moral panic. As phantasmic constructs of Asia and Asian America, over a century's worth of dragon ladies, lotus blossoms, enigmatic assassins, black-clad guerillas, rapacious drug addicts, and sex-starved nerds have entered the American popular imaginary, often in a discordant cacophony of sounds and images. By examining these images in the historical specificity of their production, circulation, and consumption, scholars and critics have demonstrated the salience of popular culture as a realm of political conflict and an important force in shaping the material and social realities, but also the imaginative inner lives, of Asian Americans.[6]

This "tradition" of querying "images of Asians" in Asian American cultural criticism, along with the interventions enabled by cultural studies in general, has demonstrated to us the critical role of popular culture in delineating possible, and impossible, racial and political identities.[7] More recently, scholars have also begun to examine the range of Asian American cultural productions in film, literature, and performance, among other venues, that have responded (implicitly or explicitly) to these images, often in the hope of altering both the medium and the message of American popular culture.[8] Our collection emerges from the multiple junctures figured in these diverse projects, from the interrogation of "images of Asians" to the Asian American production of images in the American cultural and political landscape.

As editors we originally defined our second critical term, *popular culture*, quite broadly as those cultural practices and productions people encounter and inhabit in their everyday lives. However, we soon realized that the category *popular culture* should be subject to as much contest and conflict as *Asian American* in our project and as it is in cultural studies writ large. The question of what constitutes the "popular" is always a source of tension in this collection, as the debates that define it—whether about mainstream success ("selling out" or "being real"), the "corrupting" influences of the West on gender or sexual "traditions," the practices of self-orientalizing by "native" entrepreneurs, or the mass mechanical or digital production of "authenticity"—are formed in relation to the material and ideological conditions that shape changing ideas of Asian America. The pertinent questions then become not what is popular culture but how do Asian Americans "get to" participate in it and how might their participation shape its contours?

These questions must be answered by firmly situating Asian American cultural practices within their specific historical moments. In editing this volume, we limited our examination of Asian American popular cultures to the contemporary moment while reading them against and alongside the changes wrought in the last three decades. In the thirty-odd years since the term's genesis, the cultures and cultural productions of Asian America have contended with some profound political, cultural, and economic changes. In an essay outlining the epistemological demands of the contemporary moment for this racial formation, Lisa Lowe enumerates some of these shifts, which include the "post-Fordist" restructuring of global capitalism through "mixed production" and "flexible accumulation"; the creation of localized "free trade zones" in Asia and the United States; the altered demography of Asian American populations after 1965, which included diverse South Asian, Southeast Asian, Korean, and Filipino groups and communities; and the colonial and neocolonial relationship of the United States to the states from which many of these new groups emigrated.[9] And much more has changed since our Reagan era youth. The fears of a Japanese financial takeover, for instance, have been replaced most recently with renewed anxieties not only about immigration but also about transnational networks of capital and information in the wake of the Wen Ho Lee "spy" scandal and 9 / 11.[10]

What these changes mean for Asian American popular cultures is unpredictable if undeniable. For instance, during the political battles over the Public Broadcasting Service (PBS) and its program content in 2005, congressional Republicans drastically cut the network's funding in an explicit protest over its "left-leaning bias." No doubt this will have deleterious effects on the production and distribution of Asian American independent films and documentaries, many of which are sponsored in conjunction with groups such as Independent Television Service (ITVS) and the Center for Asian American Media (formerly known as the National Asian American Telecommunications Association), which receives "minority funding" from PBS. In the following chapters, we hope to begin to unravel the ways in which these historical changes—economic and cultural globalization, technological developments, and market restructuring—have shaped, and could shape, the production and consumption of Asian American cultures.

In this way, the essays in this collection are meditations on American and Asian American contemporary cultures as seen through the lens of the popular. Here readers will find subcultures consuming and engaging popular technologies of mechanical and digital production, including Japanese import cars and music videos; producers challenging and transforming "high" and "low" forms of culture in content (skewering noir conventions in pulp novels) and form (infiltrating galleries and museums); and arbiters of "authenticity" and innovation policing and challenging the boundaries of jazz, hip hop, and "native" cultures. At the same time, many of our contributors are also grappling with historical shifts as these occur in "real time." Examples include the "mainstreaming" of import car culture as major auto manufacturers begin to recognize this subculture as a source of "cool" and capital and the increasing advertising presence of telecommunications giants such as AT&T in Vietnamese diasporic videos as the normalization of relations between the United States and Vietnam continues apace. Through these various sites, our contributors demonstrate that it is through culture, and particularly popular culture, that persons are taught how to be *kinds* of citizens—how to dress, listen, shop, love, desire, and behave. As such, many of the essays in this collection approach popular culture as an index for appraising the historical discourses and practices that produce certain populations (whether racial, national, or sexual) as differently invested with multiple registers of citizenship (whether cultural, political, or diasporic) and its privileges or deprivations.

In raising the issue of the relationship between popular culture and politics, we do not seek to prescribe or predict how, why, or when this interaction might appear. In our next caveat, we are wary of defining such an encounter, which, while not totally "alien," is nonetheless rife with complicated possibilities and problems. Cultural studies (and its disciplinary cousins) has long grappled with this relationship, whose contours are mutable and unpredictable, and the strategies with which audiences and consumers negotiate between popular culture and politics. Here we are critical of the binarisms that often plague cultural critique, some of which we address later in the introduction, including readings that assign "resistance" and "accommodation" to motives or effects or separate "oppositional" from "stereotypical" images. This is not to say that we lack interest in the potential for pleasure as a source of political motivation or, as Wahneema Lubiano suggests, in what popular culture might tell us about how to construe politics as pleasurable.[11] We do believe that the desire to imagine a better world must include a place for the value and practice of pleasure. Critical scholarship on popular cultures, and here Asian American ones, can help us theorize the politics of affect and appeal that enable or constrain particular attachments to commodities and communities, to certain desires and dreams of personhood. However, our theorizing must also warn against understanding affect as raw materials, as libidinal or protopolitical energies, that are the potential source of resistance separable from the popular forms to which they are attached. We do not believe that popular culture "defuses" or "diverts" affect and attachment as much as it produces and creates them.

A second relationship we seek to examine, then, is that between affect and aesthetics. As editors, our concern lies less with situating this intellectual project within the parameters of a genre than with what an examination of such taxonomies might reveal. That is, we hope to productively interrogate the operations and mobilization of images, the construction of narratives, and the specificities of particular cultural forms in our critical inquiries about popular culture in Asian America. When and how are generic conventions mobilized to inspire particular affects and potentially shore up or undermine structures of feelings about the state, sex, or citizenship? How do filmic narratives contain or undermine types, from Asian martial artists to geeky inventors, within their internal structures and how might these escape into the realm of stardom's excess—fan magazines, celebrity interviews, and studio promotions? What arguments about cultural authority and racial authenticity (e.g., about hip hop or jazz practitioners) are attached to such conventions? In pursuing such questions, many of the essays in this collection ask, broadly, how we learn to feel about our world, and our place in it, through the aesthetics of its popular forms of representation. As such, the changing relationship between popular culture and the political must be analyzed not only in terms of the exchanges of culture and capital but also in terms of the linkages between affect and aesthetics. The important lesson for our critical work is therefore much more specific here; it is not that popular culture distracts us, seducing our more utopian longings away from the arena of politics, but that politics must also learn to produce and create affect effectively.

At the same time, as scholars we are wary of the insistence that popular culture is only meaningful insofar as it generates or services political and intellectual work, only valuable if it alleviates suffering or offers directions for its potential redress. This, too, is a familiar conflict in cultural studies' histories. Demands are made on both popular cultures and the scholarship about them to demonstrate their usefulness to social justice or "real" people. We argue that no one can guarantee that Asian American popular cultures will contain subversion let alone predict the specific nature of it. Furthermore, the imaginative reach of cultural work is too often foreshortened by the demand that it redress political, economic, or social inequities (and even more persistently within the time frame of "right now"!). What can this do to address structural poverty or racism? How does this reverse anti-immigrant sentiments? Can it tell us what is to be done? These types of questions tend to ignore the ways in which cultural work might address these very real problems in other manners—to perhaps act as a release for the anxieties engendered by everyday struggles, to act as a balm for one's complicity, to provide a dream of another world, or to piece together an armored body able to withstand, for a while, such slings and arrows. The demand that popular culture, and our inquiries into it, must offer some sort of utilitarian reference for political transformation thus refuses to take cultural work as a meaningful activity in and of itself, as deserving of nuanced and oftentimes open-ended inquiry.

While resisting such a demand and its limited imagination, as editors we note that this collection maintains that Asian Americans' engagements with popular cultures can be interpreted as political endeavors (though neither the shape and content of these politics nor their effects can be assumed); that these are historically constituted within ideological, social, and economic conditions; and that they require sustained analyses if scholars hope to expand their critical understanding of the interpenetration of the cultural and political in our everyday lives. The essays in *Alien Encounters* vary by form, style, and object of analysis, but they all share an investment in this intellectual project. They suggest that Asian American popular cultures are wide ranging and free of a univocal approach or vision and that encounters with them are critical sites of articulation, invention, consolidation, and exchange. In examining recent and contemporary Asian American writing, musicking, customizing, performing, filming, working, dragging, and imagining, this collection attempts to highlight the centrality of popular culture to Asian American lives, loves, and labors.

Culture in Context

To begin that discussion, it is important first to reiterate that Asian American representations are always framed and conditioned by historical, cultural, and political forces, even (and especially) when they appear to be at odds with them. The last few decades have provided us with many such studies in contrast. The appearance of an independent Asian American cinema, for example, occurred alongside the racism, nationalism, and xenophobia of popular Hollywood films such as *Year of the Dragon* and the historical revisionisms of the Reagan era *Rambo (First Blood)* (1982) and more recently *The Last Samurai* (2003). In the mid-1990s, the brief ascendancy of Margaret Cho to *All-American Girl* status took place in conjunction with legislative efforts to criminalize immigration and restrict immigrant rights. The sporadic revival of "Eastern" influences in fashion and the rise of Asian American designers such as Vivienne Tam have been accompanied by the continued, and increasing, exploitation of immigrant laborers in "flexible" industries such as garment production and restaurant and domestic work. And the unexpected success of the British import *Bend It Like Beckham* (2002) and the short-lived prominence of "Bollywood-inspired" productions such as *Bride and Prejudice* (2004), coexists with the post–9 / 11 creation of new racial categories such as "Muslim looking" (encompassing, among other groups, South Asians) and the detention and deportation of some Asian immigrants.

These apparent contradictions reveal much about the nature of Asian Americans' participation in the popular. They suggest, for instance, that there are firm if not always clear distinctions between cultural and political representation—that ideas permissible in the realm of culture are not always acceptable in the realm of politics. Moreover, they indicate that the structures that have enabled some Asian Americans to participate in popular culture have not ensured rights and protections for Asian Americans as a heterogeneous (and precariously grouped) population and have at times contributed to their political and economic disenfranchisement. Witness, for instance, how the growth of Asian Americans' involvement in fashion design has emerged not in spite of but because of the exploitation of Asian workers in the garment industry.[12] Or consider, as Sukhdev Sandhu's essay in this collection suggests, how a diasporic South Asian cinema must consistently turn a blind eye toward working-class South Asian immigrants in its appeals to wealthy Non Resident Indians (NRIS).

There are, in other words, material conditions that govern Asian Americans' participation in popular culture and limit the ways in which they "get to" be included, the hopes they can have, and the worlds they can imagine. What are these conditions? And what, ultimately, are their costs? We'd like to begin to address these questions by examining some of the specific processes through which Asian Americans encounter the popular in the current moment.

In the last few decades, Asian Americans have gained greater access to technologies of cultural production, which has enabled them to produce and disseminate their own works with greater ease, efficiency, and independence. This has been accomplished in part by the increased availability of production technologies, the cost of which decreases the longer they are on the market and the more users they have. Perhaps most profoundly, the emergence of digital technologies, including the Internet, and various software products such as Photoshop, Dreamweaver, and GoldWave have led to the establishment of legions of e-zines, Web blogs, and other self-produced cultural artifacts.

These technological changes occurred in tandem with cultural changes within Asian America. In the last few decades, there has been an emergence of what we might call an Asian American creative class, as Richard Florida has named it. In his influential book *The Rise of the Creative Class and How It's Transforming Work, Leisure, Community, and Everyday Life,* Florida defined the creative class as composed of the so-called bohemians who comprise 12 percent of the workforce and the creative professionals who support their work. It is the creative class that, according to Florida, spurs on technological and cultural innovation and subsequently economic growth. Historically strong in the science and technologies fields, a critical mass of young (usually second-generation) Asian Americans with both the interest and the means to pursue the creative arts came of age during the 1980s and 1990s.[13] This burgeoning group of creative workers joined the ranks of Florida's bohos, infiltrating the culture industries in a variety of capacities and fields from advertising, entertainment, and technology to publishing, design, and fashion. Their presence and access to means of production (both within and outside of the "mainstream") helped to make Asian American cultural productions both more pervasive and more visible.

This Asian American creative class was helped along in those years by the development of a global / multicultural market that valued Asian goods and aesthetics insofar as they could improve American lives and styles and that embraced Asian communities insofar as they could be reconstituted into a unified "Asian market." This was evidenced, as we elaborate below, by the well-publicized rise of "Asian chic" and the popular appetite for all goods Asian in both the United States and the West more generally. One needs only to think of the widely circulated image of Princess Diana in a *salwaar-kameez* and the booming "ethnic dress" industry to see one example of this dynamic.[14]

At the same time that signs of Asianness were being greedily consumed, Asian Americans were being courted by the corporate marketplace. By the early 1980s, advertisers were already heralding the emergence of the "post mass-market" era—a time when savvy businesses could no longer (if they ever could) speak of a single mass market but only of segments or niches. A 1987 article in *Quarterly Review of Marketing* highlighted the major challenges facing marketers in this era.

> How do we develop strategies to market mass-produced goods and services to a market which is rapidly fragmenting? How do we segment our markets and target economically viable groups of consumers who arc apparently behaving unpredictably? Even if we can understand the market behavior of these consumers, how do we locate them?[15]

In this context, young people, urban dwellers, gays, "Hispanics," women, and other social groups all became "segments." Thanks to the 1990s census, which hailed Asians as the "fastest growing ethnic minority" and, more important, the wealthiest, Asians in the United States became a "hot market" in the 1990s. Asian marketing firms emerged during this decade to locate, analyze, and target this new market, often by employing Asian faces in advertising or by sponsoring Asian American cultural events and products. One such firm, the iw Group, counts among its clients AT&T Wireless, the Bank of America, the California Department of Consumer Affairs, the *Los Angeles Times*, Nike, the U.S. Postal Service, and most recently McDonald's.[16] A 2004 campaign intended to attract Asian and Pacific Islander Americans to McDonald's saw the launch of a Web site called "I-am-asian.com," a phrase McDonald's also claims to have trademarked as an intellectual property, and a national effort to participate in events such as San Francisco's Chinese New Year Parade and Asian American Heritage Month celebrations. Accompanying a slide show of smiling Asian Americans engaged in a variety of activities with their fast food close at hand, the Web site cheerily declares in the "tossed salad" language of corporate multiculturalism, "Whether we're celebrating one of our cultural holidays or enjoying a Big Mac sandwich, we're helping make the magic mix called America become even richer. And McDonald's is right there with us, everyday!"

Certainly for years Asian American artists had worked to expand their cultural networks on their own by building community arts organizations such as the Center for Asian American Media (formerly the National Asian American Telecommunications Association), the Asian American Writer's Workshop, the Kearny Street Workshop, and the East-West Playhouse, to name just a few. These organizations, and the alternative structures and spaces they engendered—film festivals, theaters, publishing houses, and others—have expanded opportunities for Asian Americans to produce and present works "by and about" themselves. Bolstered by such community support and its resulting networks, Asian American media protests (against the film *The Year of the Dragon* and the Broadway production of *Miss Saigon*, for instance) have also challenged colonial discourses of orientalism and exoticism and opened up more spaces for Asian Americans in "mainstream" culture.[17] Nonetheless, the increase in corporate investment (made apparent by the presence of AT&T, Hennessey, and other corporate banners at community events and by bilingual advertisements in diasporic videos or on local cable broadcasts) helped to expand the arenas and resources through which Asian Americans could produce and distribute their work.

But even as the unprecedented corporate interest in Asian communities increased the circulation of Asian American cultural productions within and beyond Asian American audiences, participation in this new multicultural marketplace came with some new demands. The most pressing of these was the demand to produce palatable and thus saleable visions of Asianness—typically those images, icons, and ideas that have more market value than personal or communal resonance (such as dragons on dresses to cite just one example). As Nathan Huggans has argued, this multicultural marketplace trades on culturally "other" goods—whether Indian novels, Thai films, or "primitive" fashion—which must highlight rather than diminish signs of cultural difference in order to satisfy the appetites of Asian and non-Asian consumers for the new and the exotic. As such, some Asian American cultural producers have had to confront the conflict between their "oppositional" practices, which attempt to break down discourses about their inherent exoticness, and the transmission of these practices in a market that capitalizes on those very ideas of otherness.[18] Additionally, in the post–9/11 era cultural producers have had to face a new (or renewed) demand, articulated through informal and formal mechanisms such as the Patriot Act, to silence oppositional voices regardless of consumer desires.

These, we suggest, are some of the historical and material conditions that have made Asian Americans' engagement with popular culture both possible and limited. Whether they address those conditions directly or not, we hope that the essays in this anthology will be read within this context. Doing so will make even more evident our earlier suggestion that Asian American cultural practices come with no guarantees. Our aim in this project is neither to search for political assurances nor to announce the arrival of a cultural moment in which those assurances are no longer necessary. Rather, it is to draw attention to the ways in which Asian Americans have imagined themselves within multiple public spheres and in particular to consider how their recent access to various representational apparatuses has shaped their aesthetic and political choices. The essays collected here recognize that in order to grasp more fully the relationships between popular forms of representation and political ideologies, between self-imagining and social critique, scholars need to pay very careful attention to these choices and their effects. In doing so, we hope to reveal how *Asian American* as a category of analysis can offer new insights into the various social problems and cultural desires that are given voice in popular culture.

Part 1: Sounds Authentic?

It is perhaps obvious to note that Asian Americans have long engaged in practices of representation, even at times when they've had little access to modes of cultural production. History bears reminders that Chinese bachelors once scribbled protest poems on the walls of Angel Island;[19] Filipino men defiantly donned zoot suits;[20] and women, such as Edith Eaton (Sui Sin Far), wrote trickster stories.[21] In the last few decades, however, there has been an unprecedented increase in the presence of Asian and Asian American cultural productions in so-called mainstream culture—evidenced, for instance, by the recent success of such films as *Bend It Like Beckham* and *Better Luck Tomorrow* (the latter having earned the fierce partisanship of Roger Ebert). Films and filmmakers have had the most impact and success (though this is relative), from Wayne Wang (*The Joy Luck Club*) and Ang Lee (*The Wedding Banquet; The Ice Storm; Sense and Sensibility; Crouching Tiger, Hidden Dragon; The Hulk*) to Mira Nair (*Mississippi Masala, Monsoon Wedding*). But this is also true in literature, where a number of Asian American writers, including Chang-Rae Lee, author of *Native Speaker* (which won the Booker Prize) and *A Gesture Life*, and Jhumpa Lahiri, author of *Interpreter of Maladies* and *The Namesake*, have enjoyed commercial and critical acclaim. Recognition has also come in music, where artists such as Jin Au-Yeung, the so-called Chinese Eminem, have drawn the industry's attention to Asian American lyricists.

These flirtations and fights with mainstream acceptance have challenged the terms of Asian American cultural production in radical and, for some, unnerving ways. The sheer volume of cultural criticism centered on Wayne Wang's adaptation of *The Joy Luck Club* and other commercially successful ventures suggests that audiences inside and outside of Asian America continue to be anxious about what it might mean to be truly "popular." One sees this most clearly in the Asian American and entertainment press, where actors are often scrutinized (and condemned) for their choice of roles; Lucy Liu, for instance, has fielded many questions about the sexy, sometimes ruthless character she portrayed on Fox's mid-1990s drama *Ally McBeal*. One also sees it, albeit more subtly, in the debates about both mainstream success and subcultural credibility that haunt the work of Asian American music critics such as Todd Inoue, Sylvia Chan, Hua Hsu, and Oliver Wang, who find themselves responding again and again to suggestions that Asian Americans don't listen to or are not "able" (or "real" enough) to make indie rock, punk, or hip hop music.[22]

These ongoing debates about the appearance of Asian American cultural work in the mainstream suggest that there are still questions to be asked about the nature of commercial success, the meaning of "independence" and accountability, and the parameters of what is "sayable" or visible in these spaces of consumption—questions that have a long history. But what strikes us as particularly interesting about their manifestation in the current moment is their reliance on discourses of authenticity, that is, on discussions of cultural purity, originality, and reality.[23] Audiences now often ask of representations: Does it look like me? Does it feel like me? What can it do for or to me? Underlying these questions is an implicit desire to "look good" or to be "well represented" at a time when they know that "the whole world is watching."

In these discussions, however, there is little consensus about what it means to be well represented.[24] As such, one might suspect that this language of authenticity can do scant more than simply sanction certain identities and deny the "heterogeneity, hybridity, and multiplicity," as Lisa Lowe put it, of Asian American cultural practices (e.g., to draw boundaries around what or who is authentic or inauthentic).[25] And, indeed, the decades-long desire to generate "positive images" or more "authentic representations" has done little to undermine the power of stereotypes or ultimately to free Asian Americans from them. In fact, they have sometimes saddled them with other unjust norms. Witness, for instance, how protests against the "feminization" or "sexual disfigurement" of Asian American masculinity in the works of writers such as Frank Chin can ultimately reproduce discourses about the nonvalue of the feminine and reiterate other heterosexual norms.[26]

Yet the ethical impulse behind these types of debates has always been (at least in part) to highlight the political function of the popular—to force scholars to consider seriously how cultural representations can affect Asian Americans' political power, social realities, and life chances. Such an impulse has successfully helped to make popular culture more accountable for its practices and images. As such, these types of claims cannot be simply dismissed as cultural gatekeeping alone for at their best they can serve as an attempt to link the imaginative and the social. At their most generative, as the cultural theorist Coco Fusco put it, they can work to critique the common myth that "life looks more like a movie" or "we would prefer to live in one."[27]

At the same time, however, we cannot assume that an aesthetic representation must also be politically representative—that its obligations always and necessarily lie with a preestablished "community." We had to accept that Asian Americans also trade in fantasies and denials and that we (perhaps all critics) must find a language in which to talk about the methods and madness of their creative expressions. Without it, we cannot hope to account for such productions as the raunchy, "fag hag," queer comedy of Margaret Cho or the millennial noir of *Better Luck Tomorrow* (2003), a film distributed by MTV that depicts the Asian American straight-A student as an edgy underworld criminal. We could not see the critical possibilities of nonmimetic or disidentifying works such as *Terminal USA* (1993), Jon Moritsugu's satirical video, which skewers privileged idioms in Asian American filmmaking as well as the desire for self-affirmation. We could not understand the queer aspirations of Asian Americans who, as Mimi Thi Nguyen's essay in this volume details, yearn to be not "just human" but larger than life.

To begin to address some of these concerns, we have brought together two essays that highlight the problematics of authenticity, especially in those increasingly common intersections when and where national, cultural, and subcultural boundaries cross. Kevin Fellezs and Oliver Wang, in their respective examinations of jazz and hip hop, consider the conditions enabling and constraining Asian American participation in popular expressions most often understood as black vernacular cultures. Both emphasize the ways in which audiences, promoters, artists, and critics have mobilized discourses of authenticity to regulate cultural membership and assign value to an artist's work. In these instances, Fellezs and Wang demonstrate how popular notions about "talent" and "marketability" are articulated and understood through discourses of racial authenticity. In a recent *New York Times Magazine* article on the lyricist Jin Au-Yeung, the journalist Ta-Nehisi Coates makes this clear when she writes that "he knows he isn't black, but he has chosen a medium defined by blackness. Which means that whether he's rapping about sweatshops, ladies, Tiananmen Square or partying, Jin is always dancing on the color line."[28]

Jin is not the only one "dancing on the color line." In these times, "sophisticated fusions," to use George Lipsitz's term, are constantly being generated by artists and audiences in part because these fusions reflect their lived experiences in an intercultural society.[29] And, as reflected in the chapters in part I, such intercultural relations are multidimensional, involving much more than a non-Asian versus Asian binary, the former term too often signifying "white" or "mainstream" too simplistically. Over the last thirty years, cultural exchanges and affective politics between marginalized populations have produced the particularly rife site of Afro-Asian relations—from the iconic fighter Mohammed Ali's principled political stance against the war in Vietnam ("No Vietnamese ever called me a nigger," he said) to Bruce Lee's underdog popularity with black working-class audiences, both of which can be understood (at least partially) in the historical context of the Vietnam War but also in that of domestic liberation struggles. In the contemporary moment, these exchanges can be seen in hip hop music videos and MTV's Japanese and Korean thrillers, which feature the dubbed voices of African American hip hop artists. Yet, despite these histories of entanglement, claims of cultural authenticity are frequently generated to police legitimacy, to limit aesthetic influences, and often to disavow Asian Americans as cultural producers and innovators. And this type of border policing, as Fellezs's essay notes, also takes place within Asian American communities, as when musicians are accused of betraying their "roots" or "selling out" for experimenting with new cultural forms or reaching out to new audiences.

Certainly these types of concerns pervade more than just musical cultures. Similar alarms have been raised over the rise of "fusion" food, the proliferation of Hollywood-style kung fu films (inspired by the use of "wire fu" in *The Matrix*), and so on. Martin F. Manalansan's essay in this volume, for instance, details how some Asian immigrant consumers have expressed similar fears about the "corruption" of their "authentic" cultures by "mainstream" America—though in this instance this figure is represented by a Chinese American chef. By focusing on music in part 1, we do not mean to suggest that conflicts over authority and authenticity bear no relevance to discussions of other cultural forms. Rather, we mean to highlight their importance at one particularly resonant and evocative site through which racial relations beyond a simple "white" (a designation that often stands in for mainstream or non-Asian) versus Asian binary are complicated by multiple points of affiliation and alienation and where the nuanced performance of "being real" leads not just to cultural membership but to economic success.

It is important to note, as well, that if border-crossing anxieties are often expressed by artists and audiences, they are forcefully managed by marketers, promoters, critics, and producers. These actors play a crucial role in governing the circulation and reception of musical products, setting the context for understanding intercultural performances. Scholars and critics, therefore, cannot take the success or failure of Asian American musicians' participation in jazz and hip hop as an indication of Asian Americans' ability (or lack of ability) to build community or forge alliances with African Americans. These sorts of social yearnings (if they do indeed exist) can never be fully articulated in an industry based on packaging and profits. Nonetheless, as our authors show in part 1, an examination of these musical cultures can help expand our critical understanding of the nature of cultural circulation, the anxieties over cultural ownership and boundaries, and the new cultural practices and communities that emerge when such boundaries are crossed. Wong's and Fellezs's essays historicize the conditions that make a discourse of authenticity both necessary and dangerous, and in doing so offer a glimpse of what is at stake in forging links—culturally and politically—between Asian and African Americans and between the imaginative and the social more generally.

Part 2: Popular Places

In recent years, Asian America, as an imaginative and social construct, has been increasingly informed by the presence of "Asia" in U.S. culture. For nearly two decades, Saturday morning cartoons have featured serials imported from Japan, some of which became more popular than their (seemingly) stateside creations—including *Robotech*, *Voltron*, multiple series of *Power Rangers*, *Pokemon*, *Sailor Moon*, and *Hamtaro*.[30] In the last decade, anime and manga have become staples of comics' conventions, art house theaters, and Asian American film festivals (with the financial and cultural capital of Pixar Studios and Walt Disney, Nayao Miyazaki's animated features, most notably *Spirited Away* [2002], have found wider release and critical acclaim in the United States). The Japanese "kitchen stadium" of the *Iron Chef* has for several years been a cable hit (inspiring the 2004 Food Network remake *Iron Chef America*). And, as mentioned earlier, acrobatics in the Hong Kong style have infiltrated and come to dominate the visual languages of Hollywood. Trends in fashion have often turned "East," and modified cheongsams and mandarin collars now appear in both high-fashion spreads and suburban malls, and, "eastern spirituality" and its multiple "holistic" accoutrements, cited as "life changing" by pop stars and actors, have enjoyed a booming market.[31]

Although few popular accounts of this "Asianization of America," as these cultural shifts are often named, delve much into the issue, there are of course links between the circulation of Asian goods and practices and the presence of Asians and Asian Americans within U.S. borders. Many of these goods were first transported, adapted, and shared within immigrant communities; before sarongs and cheongsams appeared in the local mall and anime videos and kung fu films at Blockbuster, enthusiasts found them on the shelves of "oriental" markets. Even now, as these goods become more readily available, Asian Americans often act as cultural brokers, facilitating both their transmission and their reception. Here one needs only to think of the powerful influence of the California-based publication *Giant Robot*, which has for a decade acted as the purveyor of "cool" Asian culture and an arbiter and translator of its value and meaning.

To highlight these types of relationships is not to deny that marketing and other activities of the culture industries play a major role in the circulation of these goods—in, for instance, shaping consumer desires for them. It is rather to suggest that there are some important links between Asian cultures and those of Asian America—though the precise nature of those relationships certainly varies among communities and contexts—and that in this age of accelerating globalization it is often difficult to differentiate Asia from Asian America. For instance, one would be hard pressed to characterize the work of transnational artists such as Shu Lea Cheang, who, as the former associate director of the annual San Francisco International Asian American Film Festival, Marie K. Morohoshi, has noted, is "a lesbian from Taiwan, who grew up in New York where she started making videos, and has gone on to Tokyo and produced videos with the Japanese dykes there. Her *Fingers and Kisses* features Japanese dykes, and it's funded by Japanese money, but that's not Cheang's home." "How," Morohoshi asks, "do you begin to regionalize a filmmaker and [his or her] works?"[32]

In certain ways, a transnational framework can help to account for the increasingly globalized ways in which people produce and consume culture. As Inderpal Grewal has argued, "Transnational theories not only account for bicultural [and multicultural] rather than unicultural perspectives of the immigrant, but they also include how, for instance, the consumer lifestyles of those within one nation-state become transnationalized across many national boundaries."[33] A transnational approach can help scholars to see how the actions of the nation-state can shape the circulation of culture itself. It would reveal, for instance, the ways in which industrializing Asian nations have actively participated in the production and distribution of Asian culture—from Hong Kong couture to Thai cinema—in order to compete in a globally connected cultural market. Or, equally important, it would reveal the ways in which U.S. elites have directed the terms of global exchange by selecting and regulating the circulation of cultural goods to fit their own capitalist (for profit), philanthropic (for "cultural preservation"), or educational (for liberal multiculturalism) ends.[34]

Yet a diasporic framework can often diminish the extent to which Asian Americans have always had a fairly complicated relationship with the transnational. On the one hand, historical Asian communities in the Americas have consistently maintained ties to their homelands through modes of communication, travel, business relationships, and familial remittance, among others. In other words, they have always practiced a form of transnationalism. On the other hand, they have also been situated as always and necessarily foreign, as indistinct from or perpetually tied to their "native homelands," as evidenced during World War II with the Japanese American internment, the Wen Ho Lee spy scandal, and the federal shift that transferred immigration control—and the detention of thousands of Arab and Asian persons—to the Department of Homeland Security after 9 / 11. Such constructions have historically worked to prevent the understanding of Asians as "real Americans" and to limit their access to the rights, privileges, and responsibilities of citizenship. In this regard, categorical uncertainties between Asia and America are a cause for concern not celebration.[35]

As such, there is always a tension between the local and the translocal within Asian America, and Asian American cultural producers have articulated these tensions in often spectacular ways. Christopher A. Shinn's study of pulp fiction in this volume reveals how Asian American writers have used the genre's elaborate plots and formulaic devices—including the imagining of the "third-world" city as a criminal underbelly—to dramatize the narrative of "ethnic subjects in pursuit of social equality, law, order, and economic rationality, rendering grotesque an invisible global network of discipline that enacts violence akin to the torturing of the body under the ancien régime." In doing so, Shinn suggests, his Asian American authors have used pulp fiction to effectively expose the murderous excesses of globalization itself. In a similar way, Joan Kee argues that the artists Paul Pfeiffer and Nikki S. Lee use visually seductive images in order to wage a "tactical" or strategic critique of the demands of globalization. These Asian American cultural producers, as our authors demonstrate, are not naively resistant to the processes of globalization; their interests lie in making those processes more just.

These critiques of globalization have often entailed reasserting the persistent resonance of local places and the disciplinary aspects of mobility. Indigo Som's photo essay on Chinese restaurants in the Midwest offers a thoughtful meditation on these uneven exchanges of bodies and images in documenting how, in areas where Chinese communities are few and far between, the idea of Chineseness is imagined. Her photographs depict restaurants with pagoda-style exteriors, gilded lions, slithering dragons, and other signs of "the Orient." These commercial sights refer to no particular time or place; instead they constitute a conglomeration of the easily transportable signs that have come to signal "Chinese." Yet, if these images could be from anywhere, the predominantly male, Chinese restaurant staff members feel their sense of localness acutely. Transported to small towns in the Midwest from urban areas in the United States and in China, the cooks and waiters talk about their feelings of social isolation, their lack of marriage partners, and their desire to build sustainable communities in ways that echo the concerns of Chinese bachelors of the last century. They are, in other words, bounded by the conditions of these particular places for, unlike the goods and images that these restaurants sell, their bodies are far less mobile.

Sukhdev Sandhu also argues for the importance of "placefulness." Many South Asian American films, he suggests, jettison treatments of local places and textures in ways that empty their images and narratives of any on-the-ground political force. Ironically, he finds in such sentimental mainstream films as *The Guru* (2002)—a multinationally produced, Indian musical comedy featuring a young Indian dancer who finds himself catering to the "spiritual" and sexual needs of New York's upper crust—a more vivid representation of urban immigrant life and placefulness.

By highlighting the enduring significance of place in their critiques of globalization, the authors in part 2 demonstrate that Asian American lives are still conditioned by their local circumstances, even as transnational forces constantly alter those circumstances. These essays assert that culture is created and imagined most often in the spaces of daily life and provide a caution about the injustices that can be made more widespread by globalization's reach.

Part 3: Consuming Cultures

Just as critical as activities of production, activities of consumption have particular resonance for our project, in part, as noted earlier, because Asia is so often an object to be consumed in America and in part, as our authors observe, because it is often Asian Americans who consume such representations of "home" and objects of "tradition." In other words, diasporic subjects are engaged in facilitating or negotiating transnational exchanges as intermediaries, translators, or consumers. Building on the previous discussions about authenticity and placefulness, the study of consumption raises many questions. Can we assume that Asian Americans are the "rightful" (or "authentic") consumers of such goods or might they also reproduce essentialized notions of an "ancestral home" in their glances eastward? If so, for what purposes or effects? How do such commodities and images "travel" and through which circuits of signs and capital? How might tracking historical practices of consumption challenge formulations of authenticity and artifice? What operations of value, meaning, and belonging are mobilized in arbitrating these distinctions? What dynamic roles do such practices of consumption fulfill in identity and community formations as codes of cultural citizenship? And, furthermore, what ideological or material functions might "self-orientalism" perform in the global market?

In this vein, cultural studies scholarship has a rich tradition of querying audience reception against the often more deterministic models of the culture industry. Indeed, the departure from the understanding of the consumer as dupe has often acquired additional urgency when the audience is marked as somehow "other," whether through gender, nation, class, race, or sexuality. Against denunciations of popular culture and its consumers as estranged from their "real needs" and authentic selves, these other studies of consumption, informed by numerous theoretical and methodological interventions by scholars of black and feminist cultural studies in particular, argue that such assumptions of manipulation and alienation fail to recognize that all needs and selves are constructed and interpreted through culture.

This approach is at once more intellectually, and we think politically, compelling than theories of passive consumption, but it runs the risk of assuming that the various pleasures, negotiations, or outright refusals of the would-be consumer can be understood to constitute an oppositional standpoint. As Peter X. Feng argues in his fan meditations on Nancy Kwan, the star of the film *The World of Suzie Wong*, "if all readings are negotiated, then negotiated readings are not inherently resistant. . . . Further, the very notion of contestatory uses implies that readers are always aware that their interpretations of the text are at variance with its intended effects."[36] That is to say, audience, reader, or consumer agency is multidirectional and unpredictable; its political effects remain horizons of possibility. As such, the potential celebration of the resistive agency of the Asian American consumer, in what might be understood as a revisionary myth of the "model minority," is just as dangerous for our purposes. Some of our authors find possibilities for an albeit limited agency within contemporary conditions for popular culture, but they also find that these agentive possibilities are "dense transfer points for relations of power."[37]

We begin then, with a definition borrowed from Daniel Miller, who understands consumption as "a use of goods or services in which the object or activity becomes simultaneously a practice in the world and a form in which we construct our understandings of ourselves in the world."[38] Practices of consumption are also technologies of the self in that they, as Michel Foucault suggests, "permit individuals to effect by their own means or with the help of others a certain number of operations on their own bodies and souls, thoughts, conduct and way of being."[39] In other words, consumption emerges as a specific set of dynamic practices through which subject positions are inhabited by individuals within fields of power and knowledge production.

In part 3, our contributors address a number of consuming, shopping, and grooming activities through which Asian Americans perform or interact with often conflicting notions about who they (think they) are in relation to Asia and America. While consumption practices are important in all of our contributions (just as discourses of authenticity and placefulness are), the essays brought together in this section focus on the uses of consumption practices to "construct our understandings of ourselves in the world." Our authors explore the effects of producing identities and communities through consumption in and against multiple imaginaries of Asia and America, "home" and home away from home. Furthermore, these imaginaries are often bound to particular disciplinary technologies of the self—whether manifest in the public comportment of an Asian immigrant in an American restaurant, Vietnamese female singers gauging the register of "appropriate" femininity against contemporary conventions of pop performance, or the facilitation by South Asian American "third-wave" feminists of the consumption of bodily practices of bindi and mehndi (henna painting) by non–South Asians. In all the essays, the disciplined body is approached as a critical site for transmitting and reading the meanings that consumption activities mobilize and engage about our preceding thematics, authenticity and place. For some, the America in Asian America is a foreign, unfamiliar presence, one that must be guarded against and policed for its falsifying intrusions. In Martin F. Manalansan's essay, for instance, the Asian immigrant viewers of a nationally televised cooking show featuring a Chinese American chef with no discernable Asian accent and a perceived white posture take issue with the cultural exchanges trafficked under the rhetoric of "fusion," in cuisine and culture. Informed by their diasporic displacements, they understand "home" and "away" as sensory structures of feeling and thus comprehend these supposedly glib "East meets West" productions as a "dissonant" experience. Positing a sensuous approach to popular culture, Manalansan documents the embodied responses of a segment of Asian immigrant populations to the both strange and familiar fusion of Asia and America.

As Nhi Lieu similarly reveals in her study of the production and circulation of popular Vietnamese music variety shows, a diasporic consciousness can be used to reassert claims to an authentic culture and to police the gender, class, and political identities of immigrant, or in this instance so-called exile, populations. Located in the contentious political history of the South Vietnamese remaking of "nation" in the United States after the Vietnam War, Lieu traces the emergence of a multi-million-dollar industry from the particular ideological and material conditions of Vietnamese migration. Focusing on a concert and video series known as *Paris by Night*, the cultural form of the musical variety show, Lieu argues, does not "reflect" an image of the overseas Vietnamese as much as it constructs a new, bourgeois diasporic subject in the seemingly contradictory spectacle of luxurious excess and morality plays. Simultaneously, these diasporic acts of consumption trade on nostalgic images to create a "phantasmic Vietnam," reaffirming what Louisa Schein observed in her study of Hmong American cultural practices: diasporic subjects are not immune to the romantic commodification of their "homeland" culture, particularly as it is sold by "native" producers.[40] In this diaspora, as Lieu demonstrates, consumption practices become both pedagogical and disciplinary acts through which Vietnamese cultural citizenship is measured and "new" membership in the United States is forged.

A similar order of questioning—the measure of appropriation and authenticity, assimilation and authority, in this case between South Asia and America—begins Sunaina Maira's account of the circulation of *mehndi* (henna) in American popular culture in the 1990s, particularly its uses by such diverse groups as pop stars, South Asian undergraduates, "global" feminists, and female entrepreneurs. Under conditions wrought by globalization, Maira suggests, South Asian American subjects necessarily engage in a range of consumption practices that challenge a limited and static notion of culture. Examining the mainstream marketing of mehndi at the turn of this century, Maira suggests that an embrace of the global can often exacerbate uneven exchanges and work to produce new forms of orientalism that often turn on particular notions of the body as a site for identity and community formation. For Maira, the critical issue finally becomes not the negotiation of who has a right to produce or consume, or the adjudication of the content of authentic culture, but who profits from doing so.

Part 4: Troubled Technologies

While the essays in part 3 illustrate that practices of consumption are also technologies of the self, the last set of contributions to this collection pays close attention to the mechanical and digital technologies of production, circulation, and reception involved in such practices of culture-making and self-making.

Just as the cinematic apparatus transformed the popular idiom in the early twentieth century, the last few decades have been marked by changes to the culture industries wrought by new media technologies. The 1970s video-cassette recorder (VCR) revolution ushered in the death of the porn theater and its semipublic space of erotic exchanges. Television, as an organizer of both private and public spaces, was transformed when cable and satellite subscriptions introduced narrowcasting, beginning with MTV but extending to the International Channel and local cable access stations, both of which bring a variety of programs and films from diasporic and "homeland" stations to migrants abroad. In 2005, the International Channel became the "all Asian all the time" AZN Channel—a spelling of *Asian* that emerged from Asian youth digital subcultures—which features campy redubbed 1970s martial arts films, anime serials, contemporary short films and "lifestyle" programs stocked with Asian American actors and comedians. The implications of the International Channel's decision to offer exclusively Asian content are wide ranging and significant, especially in terms of the reach of Asian transnationalism as culture and capital. And of course the digital revolution heralded new forms of connectivity across oceans and war zones, providing "community" spaces such as message boards and networking sites for the selling, trading, and buying of commodities (including undubbed films from Hong Kong), images (file photographs from film openings in Bollywood), and information (personal data for dating, or "friending," purposes).

These new technologies emerged in tandem with what we alluded to earlier as a particularly Asian cybernetic imaginary. Beginning in the 1980s, the threatening specter of the mechanistic, and supposedly "soulless," Japanese (on whom, of course, the "greatest" technological weapon of World War II was unleashed by the United States in the form of the atomic bomb) began to cast its shadow on American culture. Apparent admiration for "Japanese efficiency" slid easily, and quietly, into fears of a hyperrationalized, corporate empire of the rising sun. Within popular culture, these fears appeared in a spate of novels and films that pitted an all-American hero, with his rugged frontier skills, against a yuzuka-style, Japanese machine monolith. Such themes resonated, for instance, throughout the phenomenon of cyberpunk, a sci-fi retelling of the noir staples Christopher A. Shinn describes and analyzes in his essay in part 2. In these tales, the "third-world" underbelly of the criminal world is often paired with the hyperdisciplined space of a Japanese corporate empire above ground, both of which serve as the backdrop for the hero's adventures. Perhaps the most obvious, and enduring, example of these multiple orientalisms (of an overpopulation of Chinese bodies in the undercity and the specter of Japanese financial dominance figured by the electronic billboard of a geisha drinking Coca-Cola) is Ridley Scott's iconic science fiction film *Blade Runner* (1982).

As the American automobile industry fell behind in sales and technology, this fear of an Asian empire manifested itself in domestic resentment of Japanese automobiles and produced the toxic atmosphere that was in part responsible for the 1982 beating death of Chinese American Vincent Chin. In films such as *Gung Ho* (1984), ostensibly a comedy about the "culture clash" between Japanese factory owners and Detroit autoworkers, the inflexible hypermodernity of the Japanese is opposed to, and eventually tempered by, the "do-it-yourself" adaptability of their American counterparts. Following (and against) the bifurcated opposition of Asian bureaucratic efficiency and American idiosyncratic creativity in the Reagan era, as so modeled in *Gung Ho*, Robyn Magalit Rodriguez and Vernadette Vicuña Gonzalez discuss the contemporary customizations and innovations of Asian American masculinities through the technological apparatus of what they call the "auto/biography." Locating their arguments in the West Coast "import car" subculture, they argue that Japanese import car enthusiasts contest the racial rhetorics of racing and public space, creativity and masculinity. At the same time, they note that while "rice boys" and their "rice toys" have inserted an Asian presence into both the cultural mythology of the American love affair with the automobile and contemporary urban subcultures, it is a presence that is both masculinist and heteronormative in its assertions of "pride" and "difference." Import car cultures thus serve as particular (and differential) forms of public participation, and identity and community formation, for young Asian American men and women.

Similarly, digital technologies often promise a similar form of interactivity (as Rodriguez and Gonzalez note, many import car enthusiasts also discuss and display their machines on Web sites and online forums). Seeming to foreshorten both geographic and imaginative distance, as well as facilitating access to multiple registers of information and image, digital technologies have produced discourses and practices of identity and community, culture and capital. Such technologies offer the hope, possibility, and sometime illusion of (telepresent) intimacy with the objects of our desires—sometimes with a homeland, a potential lover, or one's beloved musical or cinematic stars. Digital technologies have also encouraged more creative endeavors by providing easier access to both production tools and potential audiences, resulting in fan-composed fiction that reimagines television series or literary characters, MP3s of independently produced music (including "mash-ups" and other forms of borrowing and innovation[41]), and digital films viewable through programs such as Flash or Quicktime. These multiple uses of digital technologies converge in Mimi Thi Nguyen's essay about JJ Chinois, the international superstar (wannabe) persona of drag performer and video maker Lynne Chan, in which she examines the ways technologies of the self and technologies of the star mediate the intimacy of pop forms of the music video and online presence. In examining these technologies of the self and the star, Nguyen reflects on the specific social histories and material conditions that shape the creation of a desirable commodity body and the ascent to superpersonhood in American and global popular culture.

Finally, and in a different, more dangerous sort of encounter with superpersonhood and the erotics of technologically enhanced intimacy, Wendy Hui Kyong Chun fulfills the promise of a "subjectless discourse" in Asian American studies in her exploration of high-tech orientalism and the logics of abstraction and disembodied agency. Examining an array of cultural notations, from Ted Chiang's science fiction and Greg Pak's cinematic collection *Robot Stories* (2003) to the British artist collective Mongrel, Chun highlights the critical possibilities of cross-racial (but also cross-human-machine) collaborations to critique the superagent escape from "race." Working both with and against the dominant logics of cybernetic and cyberspatial relations, Chun argues that these artists' endeavors make transparent the racial (and often racist) metaphors and processes operating throughout our everyday encounters with technologies, whether in our present or looming in our future. In an era of war and globalization, in which technologically enabled traffic in finance and information also fuels the neoimperial ambitions of the lone remaining military-industrial superpower, Chun's essays, like the others in part 4, make clear that technological practices have increasingly become practices of culture and citizenship.

Conclusion

By way of a conclusion, we'd like to elaborate on our choice of a title for this collection, which again takes its cue from the cinematic imaginary of our youth. In most science fiction tales, the alien encounter is that part of the story that manifests both threat and promise—the threat of imminent invasion, takeover, or control and the promise of adventure, transformation, and exchange (consider the "other" 1980s Steven Spielberg blockbuster *E.T.*). At these moments the balance of the strange and the familiar is uncertain, and the encounter is rife with suspicion, excitement, terror, and joy. In choosing the name *Alien Encounters*, we propose that popular culture holds out some very familiar and tired narratives but also new and exciting promises. With this collection, we hope to show that Asian Americans' meeting with the popular has been, and continues to be, one of fascination and worry—an experience of affective intensity and political complexity, of expressive pleasure and deep ambivalence, that in any case has irrevocably transformed our imaginations.

The authors gathered here take the threat and promise of popular culture seriously. Together they show how these encounters between the foreign and the familiar can help us to understand the constitution and negotiation of Asian American identities, communities, and histories. They demonstrate that if we, as scholars, are to imagine a different, more democratic future we must be able to account for the ways in which people participate in political and cultural life and imagine their affective relationships with such abstract notions as history, identity, and belonging. Popular culture often lies at the heart of these imaginings, and such imaginative acts can help us envision another world, one in which, as *The Goonies* had us believe, the impossible might be made real.

Notes

1   After graduating from the University of Southern California's School of Cinema Television, Jonathan Ke Quan (the actor who portrayed Data) is now working as a martial arts actor and assistant fight coordinator in Hollywood and Hong Kong.

2   There is an entire body of scholarship dedicated to the study of popular culture, much of it contending that, for better or worse, popular culture is a pervasive (and often seductively pleasurable) part of our everyday lives. To cite one recent and impressive example, see Jenkins, McPherson, and Shattuc, *Hop on Pop*.

3   Hall, "What Is This Black in Black Popular Culture?"

4   Omi and Winant, *Racial Formations in the United States*.

5   Chuh, *Imagine Otherwise*, 9, 11.

6   See, for example, Hamamoto, *Monitored Peril*; Marchetti, *Romance and the Yellow Peril*; and Lee, *Orientals*.

7   In addition to the work of scholars in the field of Asian American studies, this tradition includes the groundbreaking work of cultural critics such as Loni Ding, Valerie Soe, Wayne Wang, Maxine Hong Kingston, and Russell Leong among many others.

8   See, for example, Leong, *Moving the Image*; Hamamoto and Liu, *Countervisions*; Feng, *Identities in Motion*; Shimakawa, *National Abjection*; Maira, *Desis in the House*; Kondo, *About Face*; Lee, *Performing Asian America*; Ling, *Yellow Light*; Yoshida,

Reminiscing in Swing Time; Reyes, *Songs of the Caged, Songs of the Free*; Wong, *Speak It Louder*; and Lee and Wong, *Asian America.Net.*

9 Lowe, "Epistemological Shifts," 270.

10 Kim and Lowe, "Guest Editors' Introduction."

11 Lubiano, "A Symposium on Popular Culture and Political Correctness," 11.

12 Tu, "Outside In."

13 Although they do not use the term *Asian American creative class*, Amy Ling's and Sunaina Maira's work suggests that a second generation with a particular interest in the arts came of age during the last few decades. See Ling, *Yellow Light*; and Maira, *Desis in the House.*

14 Jones and Leshkowich, "Introduction."

15 Marti, "Context Marketing," 7–12.

16 Some of this information comes from http://www.theregister.com/2004/05/13/mcdonalds_iam_asian (accessed October 15, 2004).

17 Yoshikawa, "The Heat Is on Miss Saigon Coalition," 41–56.

18 Graham Huggan calls this contradiction a condition of the "postcolonial exotic." See his *The Postcolonial Exotic*, 28.

19 Wong, "The Politics and Poetics of Folksong Reading."

20 Espana-Maram, "Brown 'Hordes' in McIntosh Suits."

21 White-Parks, *Sui Sin Far/Edith Maude Eaton.*

22 Inoue, "The Stealth Asian Shall Inherit the Earth"; Wang, "Between the Notes," 439–65; Wang in this volume.

23 We don't mean to suggest that questions of authenticity are unique to this period, just that they have become much more prevalent.

24 We can see clear parallels in the discussions around Mira Nair's *Mississippi Masala*, in which both critics and defenders of the film used discourses of "the real" to measure the extent to which the film succeeded or failed to represent South Asians. For further analysis, see Bose and Varghese, "*Mississippi Masala*, South Asian Activism, and Agency," 137–69.

25 Lowe, *Immigrant Acts.*

26 In their seminal (and oft-cited) essay "Racist Love," Frank Chin and Jeffrey Paul Chan write: "The white stereotype of the Asian is unique in that it is the only racial stereotype completely devoid of manhood. Our nobility is that of an efficient housewife. At our worst we are contemptible because we are womanly, effeminate, devoid of all the traditionally masculine qualities of originality, daring, physical courage, creativity. We're neither *straight* talkin' or *straight* shootin'" (65–79). Here Chin (and his fraternal compatriots) use problematic intimations of homosexuality to describe a humiliated posture of racial and masculine inferiority. In the process of "recovering" or idealizing an Asian American claim to normative masculinities, cultural strategies employed by Asian Americans such as Chin can too often rely on the assertion of a vigorous (even predatory) heterosexuality against a despised faggotry. As Daniel Y. Kim writes, "What's pernicious about the analyses offered by these writers is that they *appear* to uncover how stereotypes of race, gender, and sexuality impinge upon one another, but, in fact, they merely

deploy the terms 'feminine' and 'homosexual' as misogynistic and homophobic epithets. . . . Women and gay men consequently bear the collateral damage of this strategy" ("The Strange Love of Frank Chin," 272).

There has been much discussion of Frank Chin and his cohorts—as well as the imagined opposition between cultural nationalism and feminism—elsewhere, most notably by Elaine H. Kim, King-kok Cheung, and Leslie Bow. For an overview of these arguments, and the often problematic binaries they construct, see Laura Hyun Yi Kang's "Generic Fixations: Reading the Writing Self" in her *Compositional Subjects*.

27 Fusco, "At Your Service," 200.

28 Coates, "Just Another Quick-Witted, Egg-Roll-Joke-Making, Insult-Hurling Chinese-American Rapper," 55–56.

29 Lipsitz, *Dangerous Crossroads*.

30 At the same time, other animated series that seem to be produced in the United States, including *The Simpsons*, farm their animation out to Asian illustrators.

31 Lau, *New Age Capitalism*.

32 Han with Morohoshi, "Creating, Curating, and Consuming Queer Asian American Cinema," 87.

33 Grewal, "Traveling Barbie," 801.

34 For a fascinating look at the changing uses of culture, see Yudice, *The Expediency of Culture*.

35 Many scholars have noted these contradictions. See Sau-ling Cynthia Wong's cautions in "Denationalization Reconsidered," 1–27. See also Chuh, *Imagine Otherwise*; Chuh and Shimakawa, *Orientations*; and Dirlik, *What Is in a Rim?*

36 Feng, "Recuperating Suzie Wong," 47.

37 Foucault, *The History of Sexuality*, 1:103.

38 Miller, "Consumption and the Vanguard of History," 30.

39 Foucault, *Technologies of the Self*, 18.

40 Schein, "Forged Transnationality and Oppositional Cosmopolitanism."

41 A mash-up combines (through digital means) the music from one song with the *a capella* vocals from another.

© Sounds
Authentic?

one

Rapping and Repping Asian: Race, Authenticity, and the Asian American MC

Oliver Wang

The first song recorded by a rapper of Asian American descent was the 1979 single "Rap-O, Clap-O" by the Latin soul singer Joe Bataan. Born to a Filipino father and African American mother, Bataan was a veritable giant in New York's Latin scene, having been at the forefront of Latin soul in the late 1960s and then scoring a crossover hit with his 1975 cover of Gil Scott-Heron's "The Bottle." That single appeared on an album (also in 1975) entitled *Afro-Filipino*, thereby settling any ambiguity as to how Bataan self-identified. The album's version of Bataan's best-known composition, "Ordinary Guy," changed the lyrics to reflect his ethnic state of mind: "I'm an ordinary guy . . . Afro Filipino . . . ordinary guy."

Produced by Arthur Baker—a seminal hip hop figure who later produced Afrika Bambataa's "Planet Rock" and other old-school rap hits—"Rap-O, Clap-O" was Bataan's first foray into hip hop, recorded at the very beginning of the music's recorded history. In fact, Bataan himself has claimed that the song was recorded prior to the release of both the Fatback Band's "King Tim III (Personality Jock)"—recognized as the first rap record—and the Sugarhill Gang's "Rapper's Delight," the first breakout rap hit. However, Bataan was unable to release the song first, and in the end, "Rap-O, Clap-O" failed to make much of an impact in the United States, although it did become a high-charting hit in Europe.[1] For the next twenty-five years, Bataan would be one of the first and last Asian American rappers to find such a popular welcome. Although

Asian Americans have taken leading roles throughout the rest of the hip hop industry—as disc jockeys, producers, journalists, designers, and so on—within the ranks of recorded rappers they remain a scant presence.[2]

Becoming a rapper, like any professional musician or entertainer, is a highly competitive process. Out of thousands of aspirants, only a handful will see a recording contract, let alone a commercially produced and distributed album. However, Asian American rappers face more than the challenge of climbing up through a corporate meritocracy—race is also a force that can hamper their efforts. Throughout the 1980s and 1990s, almost no rappers of Asian American descent were signed to any of the recording industry's major labels despite numerous success stories by Latino (Cypress Hill, Big Pun) and white (Beastie Boys, Eminem) rappers.[3]

The common excuse given is that "it's a matter of talent," meaning that there are no Asian Americans of recording caliber. "Talent" is an ill-defined and ambiguous concept most often deployed after the fact (i.e., success supposedly confirms the existence of talent, yet not every talented artist is successful). In the past, this red herring of talent has been used to explain the relatively poor sales of female rappers rather than to acknowledge that sexism may play a role.[4] As with women, in the case of Asian American rappers it is unlikely that their relative invisibility is a result of a lack of talent. Rather, it comes down to the issues of marketability and, intimately related to that, how racially *inauthentic* Asian Americans are in a social world of fans, artists, media, and industry, where blackness is normative.

Although the concept of authenticity girds most Western music cultures, from classical to pop, the idea finds its apotheosis within hip hop.[5] "Realness," even more than lyrical acumen or musical talent, is often praised and rewarded, whereas "fakeness" can discredit an artist beyond redemption.[6] There are various kinds of authenticity based around social identities such as class, gender, and race. For Asian American rappers, their racial difference creates a crisis of racial inauthenticity that supersedes other factors. As noted, this reflects the ways in which blackness is a normative reality in hip hop, though not one that goes uncontested.

In Imani Perry's *Prophets of the Hood: Politics and Poetics in Hip Hop*, she writes about hip hop's indelible relationship to blackness.

The assertion that hip hop is a form of black American music is in some ways radical (and unpopular) given current trends in hip hop scholarship that emphasize the multiracial origins of the music, in particular the significant contributions of Caribbean, white, and Latino communities and artists. Many critics have resisted the description of hip hop as black American music because they quite appropriately contest any suggestion that it is "100 percent black" given the active participation of other groups in the world of hip hop since the nascent days of the music. Critiques of the description of hip hop as black music also often stand as critiques of racial essentialism, or critiques of the way in which culture is marketed through race at the same time that it is fundamentally hybrid.[7]

However, Perry argues that despite hip hop's syncretism the music and culture must still be understood within the context of American blackness: "Even with its hybridity, the consistent contributions from nonblack artists, and the borrowings from cultural forms of other communities, it is nevertheless black American music."[8] Like others, Perry cites the roots of hip hop in cultural practices created by disenfranchised black and Puerto Rican youth within the postindustrial urban ghettos of 1970s New York.[9] Few dispute this history or the power of its narrative. The idea of black and brown youth crafting a vibrant subculture from the burned-out streets of urban America has helped hip hop fuel the imaginations of marginalized youth across the world as they come to identify hip hop with their own alterity.[10] However, this origin myth can lead to an authenticity paradigm in which African Americans are normative while other ethnic groups find their presence marginalized if not entirely missing.[11]

The absence of hip hop's hybrid histories is not a deliberate act of erasure—though some have argued otherwise[12]—but it is certainly a by-product of how powerfully hip hop's Afro-diasporic roots dominate conversations around rap and race. Scholars have raised concerns over this phenomenon, notably those writing on the Latino contribution to hip hop.[13] Others challenge the centrism that posits the United States as the sole country with a legitimate hip hop narrative.[14] Despite these attempts to diversify hip hop within scholarly discourse,[15] consumption habits by mainstream rap consumers,[16] which are often cited as the rationale behind industry decisions,[17] are still vastly tilted toward African American artists.[18] Nonblack rappers, especially Asian Americans, face a dilemma since their racial difference does not meet the standard of black authenticity held by rap fans and music executives alike.

This challenge poses a paradox to Asian American artists. There are few Asian American rappers in the mainstream because most record labels are wary of signing them out of concern for their commercial viability. However,

Asian American artists are unlikely to attain commercial viability until more record labels are willing to put their marketing and promotions resources behind them. In the meantime, the continued absence of Asian American rappers within mainstream media contributes to the perception of their inauthenticity, which further hinders their chances of finding commercial support. In this instance, the marginalization of Asian Americans within the hip hop recording industry becomes a self-perpetuating cycle that is difficult to break.

The following pages explore how select rappers of Asian American descent have dealt with their racial difference through self-conscious deployments of racial and ethnic signifiers in their lyrics, videos, and press material.[19] On one level, I am engaging what I perceive to be these artists' identity politics, that is, the kind of ethnic and racial identities they take on themselves and what their motives are for doing so. At the same time, I am also interested in looking at the wider issue of hip hop and its politics of identity and how racialized bodies fit into a matrix of power within the hip hop industry and fan community.

While I cover a span of approximately fifteen years, my intent is not to present a traditional, narrative history of Asian American rappers. Instead, I historicize one particular aspect—how they position a politics of racial identity within their music. The essay examines if, how, why, and to what ends Asian American rappers deploy ethnic and racial identities in their songs. The choice to express these identities is an individual one, but I argue that there have also been larger trends in the way Asian American rappers choose to deal with race in their marketing and music.

In quick summary, I chart how Asian American rappers in the early 1990s made race a central part of their image production and songwriting. In the mid-1990s, race and ethnicity became much more muted and were replaced with a rhetoric of universalism. In the early 2000s, race was deployed publicly again but as a strategic, "preemptive strike" against potential critics rather than an explicit, politicized embrace of racial identity. I suggest that these changes are reflective of both individual perceptions of race and identity and a general consciousness of racial difference within American hip hop culture at large.

"The Afrocentric Asian": Negotiating Blackness and Asianness

In *New York Ricans from the Hip Hop Zone*, Raquel Z. Rivera's exceptional history and analysis of Puerto Ricans and hip hop, she posits that, "Puerto Ricans who have taken part in New York's hip hop culture have constructed their identities, participated and created art through a process of negotiation with the dominant notions of Blackness and *latinidad*."[20] The term *latinidad* represents "Latino-ness" in the same way that *blackness* functions in African American public culture. It is meant to represent the core essence of what it is to be a Latino. Rivera writes that "caught between *latinidad* and Blackness, Puerto Ricans may fit in both categories and yet also in neither," an explicit acknowledgment that the struggle to define oneself is difficult in the face of dueling politics of identity that force people to choose between identities rather than finding a syncretic middle ground.[21] Rivera's basic argument is that this tension between the two identity poles—blackness and latinidad—has dominated the ways in which Puerto Ricans have to negotiate their position within hip hop. Neither completely black or brown—in the simplified discourse of hip hop's racial politics—Puerto Ricans have had to fight against a racial binary that rarely offers a middle ground. In her words, "Puerto Ricans who participate in hip hop culture have sought to acknowledge their Afro-diasporic Caribbeanness without wholly submerging themselves under the reigning Hispanocentric definition of *latinidad* as nonblack, or under a Blackness that takes only African Americans into account."[22] In other words, forced to choose between worlds, some Puerto Ricans have instead sought to reject the binary logic of declaring one's allegiance to either blackness or *latinidad* at the expense of the other.

In *New York Ricans from the Hip Hop Zone*, Rivera traces the complex paths this tension has followed. She convincingly documents, for example, how Puerto Ricans were assimilated into the pan-*latinidad* category of "Latin rap" that was in vogue in the early 1990s—an attempt at creating a subcategory of hip hop that was meant to acknowledge Latino contributions but also had the effect of erasing differences.[23] Under this pan-*latinidad* rubric, Puerto Ricans were lumped in with Dominican, Cuban, and especially Chicano rappers, despite the significant social differences that exist between these ethnic communities. Most important, Rivera notes that pan-*latinidad*'s "Hispanocentric bent" distanced Latinos from the African diaspora even though many Latinos, especially those from the West Indies (including Puerto Ricans and Dominicans) trace their roots directly back to the slave trade, which brought African slaves to both North America and the Caribbean. Rivera argues that the pan-*latinidad* label, quickly seized on in the media, flourished through people's popular imaginations and as a result effectively remarginalized Puerto Rican identities by denying a unique social history that could embrace both blackness and *latinidad* without contradiction.[24]

Rivera's analysis offers much to this essay's engagement with how Asian American rappers have had to deal with the question of race and identity in their own careers. In her work, Rivera traces the fluid ethnic identities that Puerto Ricans have had to negotiate over time, contextualizing how these change with shifting understandings of race, ethnicity, sexuality, and so on. In similar ways, Asian American rappers have changed their subject positions in relation to race over the last fifteen years.

Of course, this does not suggest that an analysis of Asian Americans in hip hop will reveal similar issues and challenges facing the Puerto Rican community. To begin with, there is no equivalent to *latinidad*, let alone blackness, within Asian American cultural discourse. While the very ideas of blackness, *latinidad*, and Asianness are reflective of imagined communities, with Asianness in particular the ties that bind different Asian communities together are far more tenuous.

As many scholars have expressed, most notably the sociologist Yen Le Espiritu in *Asian American Panethnicity*,[25] the possibility of forging a uniform Asian American identity is rent by any number of contrasting, sometimes hostile differences in history, language, culture, class, and so on. While all panethnic identities involve a certain amount of glossing over of difference — this is one of Rivera's key points of criticism as well in the case of pan-*latinidad*—Asian American panethnicity especially is held together by a very fragile thread of political necessity rather than cultural, historical, or social similarity. To put it another way, the concept of blackness is being increasingly problematized,[26] but the concept of Asianness has been problematic from its inception.

However, Asianness is real enough insofar as Asian Americans have to contend with a racialized identity placed on them by external forces. Groups as diverse as Taiwanese, Hmong, and Filipinos have effectively been lumped together and fixed as unchanging others—positioning them in opposition to, or at least separate from, the rest of American society, including both whiteness and blackness. The historian Gary Okihiro rhetorically poses the question, "Is Yellow Black or White?" to acknowledge that Asian Americans are expected to cast their allegiance with one of the two dominant American racial poles while erasing their own subjectivity as Asian Americans.[27] Yet the contradiction is that Asian Americans are always already othered; even if they are racialized in white or black tones, the presumption of their Asianness / otherness makes it difficult for them to be accepted as either.

As such, one of the fundamental tensions with which Asian American rappers have to contend is the distance between Asianness and blackness. Within hip hop, as Rivera notes, there is considerable distance between blackness and *latinidad*, and it goes without saying that whiteness and blackness have had a long, complex, and convoluted history.[28] The perception of difference between Asianness and blackness is no less pronounced, if not greater, especially given the historical forces dividing the two communities, to say nothing of highly publicized, contemporary tensions.[29] Moreover, if contemporary Black masculinity is associated with stereotypes of hypermasculinity and sexuality, physical aggression, and the underclasses, these stand in almost diametric opposition to so-called model-minority stereotypes of Asian masculinity: effete or asexual, passive, and middle class.[30] In other words, one could argue that what largely defines Asian masculinity is the absence of traits associated with black masculinity. These cultural stereotypes only serve to further polarize blackness and Asianness. Thus, Asian American rappers walk into hip hop with an authenticity crisis on their hands before they even open their mouths to rhyme. The remainder of this essay explores how Asian American rappers have dealt with their racial distance through shifting strategies of self-representation.

Rap, Race, and Asian Representation in the Early 1990s

In June of 1992, *SF Weekly*, an alternative paper, put a public face on Asian American rappers. The cover story that week featured Davis Yee, also known as D-Yee and Nunchuck C, sporting a bald head, a throwback baseball jersey and a medallion with Chinese lettering on it. Behind him stood his partner, Rich Francisco, wearing a heavy jacket and beanie hat. Both men wore sunglasses. In the bottom left corner of the cover, a blurb explains who these two were and what they were about: "Breaking It Down: The Asiatic Apostles Are Attacking Stereotypes and Encouraging Dialogue with Their Own Style of Hip Hop—Darow Han Talks to Bay Area Asian American Rappers about the Street Credibility of the 'Model Minority'."[31]

The Asiatic Apostles, who hailed from Davis, California, were far from the only Asian American rappers of the time.[32] While there has yet to be a full accounting of early Asian American rap artists, anecdotally there are stories of Asian Americans, both men and women, rapping at parties and in battles (i.e., competitions) dating back to the late 1970s and throughout the 1980s.[33] What set the Asiatic Apostles apart from their predecessors were their perspectives on art, politics, and hip hop. In the *SF Weekly* article, Yee and Francisco expounded on their mission as rappers: "We need to be very vocal, because Asian Americans are still an 'invisible' minority. Rap is becoming more and more popular among Asians. . . . I want our group to stir up controversy and talk about important issues."[34] Yee saw a connection between his work and that of the popular African American rap group Public Enemy, later recalling that he and his partner "thought it was pretty cool what Public Enemy [was] doing, using music as a medium to educate and elevate consciousness. So conveying what we learned in the classes through hip hop was nothing new. But we didn't know too many Asian Americans doing the Public Enemy thing."[35] Public Enemy's front man, Chuck D., was known for calling rap music the "Black CNN," linking the music with access to mass media for African Americans. In similar fashion, Yee recalls that the Apostles wanted to use hip hop as a way to reach a larger Asian American audience and create a dialogue about social issues such as interracial tensions and anti-Asian discrimination.

These were familiar sentiments being expounded by other Asian American rappers at the time. Darow Han, the author of the *SF Weekly* article, was in a rap duo himself, San Francisco's Fists of Fury. In Seattle, there were the Seoul Brothers, in Los Angeles there was Art Hirahara, and in New Jersey there was Yellow Peril.[36] While these groups formed independently, together they established a cohort of early 1990s Asian American rappers who shared many key similarities in their political and artistic approaches to hip hop.

It is important to note that all of these artists came up with the idea to become rappers while in college. The Apostles were attending the University of California, Davis; Fists of Fury's members originally met at Columbia University; the Seoul Brothers (who are brothers in real life) attended the University of Washington; Art Hirahara was at Oberlin College, then UCLA; and the members of Yellow Peril were students at Rutgers University. The collegiate experience weighs heavily here because all of these artists convey social and political knowledge gained through university classes, especially Asian American studies courses. Moreover, in the late 1980s and early 1990s, when these artists were attending school, hip hop had just begun to cross into the mainstream, finding a welcome audience among politically charged college students, just as folk music had among collegians in the 1960s.

Practically every one of these groups was inspired by Public Enemy, a Long Island group that by 1990 had captured the imaginations of listeners worldwide through their assaulting, forceful soundplay, outspoken politicized lyricism, and controversy-plagued celebrity.[37] In various interviews and publications, members of Yellow Peril, Fists of Fury, and the Seoul Brothers all mentioned the importance of Public Enemy to the formation of their groups.[38] For example, Darow Han's rap partner in Fists of Fury, Han-na Che (now known as Hana Choi and formerly known as MC R.A.W., Radical Asian Woman) echoed Davis Yee in her desire to use hip hop as a tool for political agitation: "I was influenced by Public Enemy and it was a perfect form for expressing anger. I wanted to stir shit up."[39]

In its press biography, Fists of Fury is described as "an innovative political rap group . . . [whose members] rap about their experience of being Asian Americans"[40] and seek through their music to engage a range of political issues deemed pertinent to Asian Americans. Their output included songs that dealt with interracial dating ("Sleeping with the Enemy"), black-Korean tensions in the inner city ("Black Korea II"), and misogyny and sexism ("Dissed by a Femme"). For one song, "After School," recorded for a three-song demo tape, Han, also known as C.Y.A.T. (Cute Young Asian Terrorist), wrote the following lyrics and chorus.

First grade to college
You're pushed to work hard,
Get all A's on every report card;
Your teachers will say,
"Isn't he a bright child,
Not like the Blacks,
Who always act wild."
Everyone expects you to be a genius,
Valedictorian when you're a senior
But, hey, brother, sister, haven't you heard?
Behind your back, they're calling you a nerd!

(Chorus)
American schools create whitewashed fools
Cause the man from the caves wants mental slaves[41]
American schools create whitewashed fools
Cause the man from the caves wants mental slaves[42]

"After School" offers two threads of social critique. First, the chorus attacks the American educational system, suggesting that schools only serve to indoctrinate youth into accepting hegemonic racial hierarchies that privilege whites. However, the song is directed not at whites but at Asian Americans in an attempt to deconstruct the myth of the overachieving Asian American student[43] and show how it is used to drive a wedge between Asian Americans and African Americans. Han's intent was to challenge the idea *within* the Asian American community that educational achievement should be emphasized at all costs, arguing that by buying into this mentality Asian Americans are "enslaving" themselves to a white supremacy. It is a provocative argument but one in line with Choi's desire to "stir shit up" and agitate as a way to educate.

This kind of approach was popular throughout the cohort of early 1990s Asian American rappers. Yellow Peril's Bert Wang, also known as Shaolin, expressed many of the same sentiments as the Apostles and Fists of Fury, explaining that "Rap, to us, is really about political expression. It's about rebellion. We see it as a medium for disseminating information."[44] In 1995, Yellow Peril released its own sampler tape with a song called "Asian for the Man," which critiqued Asian stereotypes in the mass media.

> House Asian, happy slave, sell out, Hop Sing
> They say it's just movies, just TV, just acting
> But it serves a higher purpose in American society
> Administering self-hate for a racist ideology
> Hop Sings and impostors, ya get the back of my hand
> You sold out our culture, Asian for the Man![45]

Like Fists of Fury's "After School," "Asian for the Man" is a dual critique. Yellow Peril attacked the "racist ideology" of American society and media, but it also took Asian American actors to task for accepting roles that the group deemed demeaning to the image of Asian American men. In effect, Yellow Peril was dialoguing with the larger American society but also calling on members of the Asian American community to take responsibility for their potentially detrimental actions.

What we can see in these examples is that groups such as Fists of Fury, Yellow Peril, and others explicitly expounded racial and ethnic identities through the hip hop they made. In an adaptation of W. E. B. Du Bois's famous perspective on African American culture, this was music made *for*, *by*, and *about* Asian Americans. While all of these groups also expressed the desire to reach audiences beyond Asian Americans,[46] their foremost commitment was to consciously write songs that dealt with Asian American social issues they deemed important, whether that meant racism in the media, anti-Asian violence, or interracial dating.

These examples show how Asian American rap groups of the early 1990s took a deliberate stand to make their racial identity the foremost part of their image and artistic message. What is also strikingly similar about these groups is how they perceived hip hop as a vehicle for political expression. Bert Wong called it "a medium for disseminating information," Davis Yee saw it as a way to "stir up controversy and talk about important issues," and the members of Fists of Fury wanted to "rap about their experience of being Asian American." Hip hop's perceived power to reach a youthful audience with political or politicized messages was a common thread in the formation and mission of all these groups. As stated by Darow Han in a personal interview, "We just felt that [rap] had a lot of strengths as far as being a cutting-edge medium. Probably politically, it had the most potential. It was the music that most young people who were politically attuned would be listening to."[47]

What is conspicuously absent, in both comments by members of the group and their songs, is an engagement with hip hop as a form of cultural activity or an artistic mode of expression. These artists may be quick to list inspiring artists such as Public Enemy, Boogie Down Productions, and Queen Latifah—the so-called conscious artists of the late 1980s and early 1990s known for their outspoken social agenda. However, very few of them talk about being inspired by the music of hip hop or by the aesthetics of its language and delivery. In other words, this cadre of artists tended to treat hip hop as a means to tap media access. In the process, they often favored the rhetoric of the medium over its aesthetics. As will be seen later, this stood in marked contrast to later Asian American rappers, who pursued hip hop as an end unto itself.

This prioritization of hip hop's politics over its aesthetics came at a cost. With time, all these groups could have balanced the power of their message with an equal competence in their production, but much of their material, both recorded or played live, reflected their limited experience with hip hop's musical craft. For example, for Fists of Fury's "After School," the group recycled a track made popular by New York's Stetsasonic a few years earlier on their hit "Talkin' All That Jazz." Moreover, with the group's limited access to studio equipment, "After School" sounds thin and tinny, lacking the sonic impact that characterized other hip hop productions of that era. The same limitations can be found in many of the songs by the Fists' cohort of peers, a reflection of these groups' desire to focus on the message over the music.

I suggest that this, in no small way, explains why none of these early 1990s groups were able to sustain a viable musical career.[48] In most cases, one or more of the group members lost interest. The Apostles' Davis Yee observed, "The industry is really difficult to break into. I can't speak for the other group members, but I wanted a little more financial stability, which I could not get doing hip hop as a career."[49] Likewise, Choi admitted in her 1998 interview with Judy Tseng, "We were more interested in spreading our political message. We produced our own music and sold our tapes. We knew that our material was not commercially viable."[50]

It is also worth noting that, according to the Fists of Fury's press biography, the group toured almost exclusively at Asian American student and community events rather than playing for more diverse audiences, a trend shared with other Asian American rappers at the time.[51] For example, Davis Yee tellingly recalled that "April was often hectic because it was Asian American month"[52] while Bert Wong noted that "our audiences were predominantly Asian American."[53] While there is some practical logic to this—often rappers will try to establish a core audience before branching out to others—given the topical specificity of their music, it seems more likely that their audience was always intended to be select. Although hip hop has subgenres that appeal to more discerning listeners, as a whole, the music has always been geared toward a populist agenda. Ever since "Rapper's Delight" became a worldwide hit, most aspiring hip hop artists have sought to tap into as wide an audience as they can. The fact that these early 1990s Asian American rappers sought to dialogue specifically (though not necessarily solely) with Asian American listeners limited their appeal and potential to succeed in a competitive industry and environment.

The next generation of Asian American rappers would take a notably different route.[54] While they recognized the importance of maintaining ties to Asian American listeners, they also wanted to fashion viable careers that courted larger, more diverse audiences, and this influenced how they identified themselves to that public. It is not that they lacked an Asian American consciousness but that they saw touting an explicit racialized identity as detrimental to their prospects as recording artists. Instead, they sought to appeal to an idealized hip hop community in which race and ethnicity are downplayed in favor of more seemingly race-neutral values such as "talent," "skills," and "personal expression." While these values are an important part of hip hop's heritage and belief system, they are also the ones most easily deracinated and therefore an attractive alternative for artists seeking to avoid the authenticity dilemma based on race or ethnicity.

"Where You're At": Abilities versus Origins in the Mid–1990s

The Mountain Brothers has the odd distinction of being one of Asian America's most prominent rap groups commercially speaking. Literally, it does commercials. In 1996, it won a national contest to record an ad for Sprite soda. In 1999, the voices of the group's three rappers, Scott Jung (known as Chops), Steve Wei (Styles) and Chris Wong (Peril), were used in a television commercial for Nike sneakers. In both cases, though, the Mountain Brothers cameoed as disembodied voices—the Sprite ad ran on radio only, and in the Nike commercial they provided the voices for three cartoon basketball players: Tim Duncan, Kevin Garnett, and Jason Williams. Until their video "Galaxies" debuted on MTV in 1999, the Mountain Brothers was the most famous Asian American rap group no one had ever seen.

Early in their career, these three Chinese American rappers composed a song entitled "Invisible Man," which speaks to how they, as Asian Americans, do not exist within a black-white racial spectrum. Chops offers the following observations:[55]

> I sit in the aisle in the back of class silent
> 'cause I can't relate
> debate is about race, today that makes me out of place
> only a two-sided coin so me I'm thru tryin to join . . .
> I'm disagreein with steven believin even the blind could see
> that ebony and ivory could never be applied to me[56]

In these six lines, Chops lays out a succinct summary of American racial awareness and how it marginalizes those who fall out of the black-white binary. In a play on Stevie Wonder's "Ebony and Ivory," Chops argues that Wonder's ode to racial harmony still offers no space for himself, as an Asian American, since he is neither ebony (African American) nor ivory (white). One of the first songs the group recorded, in the mid-1990s, "Invisible Man," would be one of the last times the Mountain Brothers tackled identity politics in its songs. By the time of its first album release, in 1999, the group, like other Asian American rappers from the mid-1990s onward, had turned away from making explicit statements on race and ethnicity and instead focused on a different kind of identity allegiance: as hip hop artists.

Joined by rappers from the mid-1990s onward, such as Los Angeles's Kikou Nishi (Key Kool), Chicago's duo Pacifics, and Orlando's Southstar (real name unknown), the Mountain Brothers has been markedly different from the previous generation. These are artists with ambitions to succeed in the record industry, which necessitates a wider, multiethnic audience than their predecessors, with their focus on Asian American audiences, could attract. Groups such as Yellow Peril, the Asiatic Apostles, and Fists of Fury wanted to make their identities as Asian Americans explicit as a way of directly targeting Asian American listeners. For the Mountain Brothers, Key Kool, and others that followed, the quest for a more diverse audience has meant that many try to downplay their ethnic identities. Although they do not reject their identities as Asian Americans, they choose not to highlight it. Put succinctly by one of hip hop's more lauded lyricists, Rakim, in the song, "I Know You Got Soul": "It ain't where you're from, it's where you're at," which could very well be the mantra for this generation of Asian American rappers.[57]

This difference in attitude is reflected in Chris Wang's comment about who the members of the Mountain Brothers were trying to appeal to: "Our core audience is basically hip hop heads. People who truly appreciate the essence of hip hop music—fat rhymes and fat beats period. People who can understand, comprehend, and enjoy the level of complexity and creativity involved in our lyrics and music."[58] In this short response, Wang introduces a series of shorthand terms and ideas and then explains them succinctly. His group is trying to appeal to "heads," who are "people who truly appreciate the essence of hip hop music," defined by "fat rhymes and fat beats," that is, quality lyrics and music.

Wang does not mention ethnicity or race at all—to him, his core audience has little to do with ethnic heritage. Instead, he wants his music to appeal to the listeners he feels are best able to appreciate the kind of aesthetic that he and his group members work in, that is, "hip hop heads." Jung elaborates further, saying, "Hopefully we have a sound and feel that can appeal to more than just straight heads because that's not too many, and we're hoping to move some units."[59] While Jung concurs with Wang that heads are part of their core audience, he also expresses the hope that more mainstream audiences can appreciate their work since he wants the group to be able to sell more records ("move some units"), and he realizes that straight (meaning dedicated) hip hop heads are not numerous enough to provide the group with the success he desires.

This stands in contrast to the attitudes of older artists, such as the members of the Fists of Fury, who admitted that they knew their "material was not commercially viable." Contemporary Asian American rappers intent on establishing careers in the recording industry need to strategize their commercial viability. Out of this ambition has come the belief that promoting themselves on the basis of race or ethnicity hinders them in the marketplace. For example, Nishi, a Japanese American rapper who released an album, *Kozmonautz* (1995), with a partner, DJ Rhettmatic (who is Filipino American), says, "In hip hop, it's a whole different culture . . . and you have to have a certain tact about things. Sometimes if you're too out there, then you lose people."[60] Although he does not use the words *race* or *ethnicity*, Nishi addresses the concern that being too prominent as an "Asian American artist" runs the risk of losing listeners who may not identify with the artist simply on this basis.[61]

Early in his career, Jung made the same observation, noting that, with audiences, "If they don't know what race we are, usually people just dig us because they just listen to the music. And that's what we're mainly about, the music. If they know we're Asian beforehand, there's . . . a certain amount of bias and they actually like the music less."[62] Jung's point suggests that the issue of racial authenticity in hip hop has the power to influence how listeners actually *hear* the music. When the group is deracinated, people are more open to the Mountain Brothers' material, but when the group's ethnicity is made explicit, those same listeners become more skeptical. Operating under this logic, Jung talks about the Mountain Brothers being mainly about the music, which, by extension, means that the group is not about its race and ethnicity.[63]

This is a key commonality shared by many Asian American rappers who emerged during or after the mid-1990s. Very few of them make explicit overtures to ethnic-specific audiences, preferring instead to appeal to larger audiences whose presumed interest in the music is based on the quality of their work rather than their ethnicity.[64] Nishi recalls how in the early 1990s he paired up with a rapper of Latino heritage but had to deal with a record label seeking to pigeonhole the two of them: "They were saying 'we want to market you as a Latino group more' and I said 'I'm Asian, why can't we just focus on all realms and be universal?'"[65] Nishi's employment of the term *universal* has less to do with him seeking unanimous approval than with the fact that he does not want to be pigeonholed as solely an Asian American artist.

In contrast, hip hop has a long history of outspoken expressions of racial pride made by African American artists. Yet even the most nationalistic rappers, such as X-Clan, Paris, and (most telling) Public Enemy, have been popular with multiracial audiences. Few are critiqued for being too focused on the black community. This reflects hip hop's racial history and politics; it is nearly impossible to be "too black" in a musical culture so intimately tied to African American cultural history, modes of expression, and personal affirmation. Compounding this is the enduring legacy of blackface and minstrelsy in shaping popular American culture. Much of contemporary popular culture is derived from representations of blackness, however accurate or perverse, and hip hop's syncretic melding of multiple cultural traditions only accentuates the enduring power of blackness within contemporary culture.[66]

These forces emerged from a racialized authenticity that Asian Americans cannot claim. Instead, in an effort to deracinate both themselves and their ideal of hip hop culture, they apply the utopian concept of the "universal," ostensibly a community freed of racial or other social boundaries. It is important to note, however, that the idea of the universal does not stand for the inclusion of *all* colors but instead is meant to represent the absence of color altogether. This desire to appeal to a universal hip hop audience, to target "hip hop heads," is a coded way of acknowledging that being seen as too Asian (versus too black) is a liability. Appealing to the universal is an attempt to alter the terms of authenticity—making it less about race and more about skills and talent.

Related to the ideal of the universal, Asian American rappers have also expressed the belief that hip hop should not be about race or color but about personal expression. This is not a sentiment held just by Asian Americans. Especially in a time when hip hop's appeal is undeniably multiracial and transnational, many have acknowledged that the music and culture have fostered the ability of many kinds of people to express themselves in meaningful and powerful ways. Focusing on personal expression however, also has the same effect as valorizing the universal: it becomes a coded way to avoid the issue of race.

For example, the following exchange between an interviewer, Futuredood, and Southstar, a Chinese Filipino American (real names both unknown), demonstrates some of the contradictions involved in trying to negotiate racial difference as an Asian American rapper.

> Q: (*Futuredood*) How does it feel to be working in an industry where you're looked upon as "different" because of your skin color?
> A: (*Southstar*) I don't even notice it most of the time because it's all hip hop. I just do what I do and not worry about what anyone else has to say.
> Q: Growing up rapping, have you ever had any criticism because of your race? If so, how did you deal with this?

A: Being Asian, it definitely meant I had a lot more to prove. I didn't get respect until I earned it. That's how I approached it. The most important thing was that I believed in myself and never gave up.

Q: After listening to your album, you didn't mention once your nationality. Is this a personal reason, or were you advised not to by your management?

A: I just write music. Whether you're white, black, Asian, or whatever, I feel hip hop is for all, so it never really crossed my mind to blatantly say I'm Chinese and Filipino in a song. My management definitely supports everything I do, and they allow me to say what I want.

Q: Didn't you once mention that you were the "rap Ichiro"?

A: I did mention I'm the rap Ichiro, because I do want to make an impact on hip hop as an Asian MC as Ichiro did in baseball as an Asian player. First Asian to win MVP [most valuable player]. I just feel no matter what nationality you are, if you make good music, it doesn't matter.[67]

These sets of responses reveal a complex, contrasting set of views. On the one hand, Southstar posits that he does not pay attention to how his race is perceived as different in the hip hop industry, but in the very next answer he admits that being Asian is also a liability. Likewise, while he shares that he once called himself the "rap Ichiro" as a way of expressing his ambition to become the "first Asian to win MVP" honors in hip hop, he also says, "I just write music. Whether you're black, Asian, or whatever, I feel hip hop is for all," and "I just feel no matter what nationality you are, if you make good music, it doesn't matter." While not entirely contradictory, Southstar's comments display an awareness of how his ethnicity plays out in complex ways.[68] He strives to maintain a standard based on the ideal that "it's all hip hop" and "hip hop is for all," both of which are alternative ways expressing the desire to be universal.

In these cases, rappers argue that hip hop should ultimately be more concerned with the quality of personal expression than the politics of racial group identity. Nishi explains, "Our whole concept is that we're not trying to exploit the fact that we're Asian. What hip hop culture is all about is it's a way for any person to express themselves. . . . What's most important is that you have to have your own flavor."[69] By "we're not trying to exploit the fact that we're Asian" Nishi means they are not attempting to sell his music to audiences solely on the basis of ethnicity. Likewise, the Filipino American Marwin Taba ("KP" of the Pacifics) says, "Our ethnicity really doesn't have to do with skills. You either got 'em or you don't. . . . Having skills and perfecting your craft goes beyond one's race."[70] The sentiments expressed by both Taba and Nishi are hardly unique in hip hop. Nishi's statement about personal expression reflects hip hop's validation of the individual's right to self-expression while Taba's valorization of skills relates to hip hop's competitive environment and the rappers' constant drive to distinguish themselves from their peers.

However, Taba's emphasis that his Filipino heritage "really doesn't have to do with skills" means he recognizes that his ethnicity could be treated as a liability and seeks to refocus people's attention on his abilities instead. In a sense, his point is correct—his talents as a rapper have little or nothing to do with his ethnicity. Yet how he is perceived as a rapper is very much subject to racialized scrutiny. The focus on skills is one way for Taba to avoid that problem.

In contrast, African Americans do not face the same standard. For a black artist to express sentiments about his or her blackness is a form of "personal expression" that, more than being accepted, is firmly validated and encouraged within the hip hop community. Especially as rappers of the late 1980s began to revisit the politics of the Black Power movement of the 1960s and 1970s, there emerged a series of overt appeals to blackness. Examples include Run DMC's "Proud to Be Black" (1986), Public Enemy's "Fight the Power" (1989), and X-Clan's "Raise the Flag" (1990), which were commercially successful as well as critically lauded.[71] However, as Nishi pointed out, if Asian American rappers speak out about their experiences as racialized (but not black) beings, this form of "personal expression" runs the risk of casting the artist as "too out there." The irony is that if expressing yourself is one way to gain audience favor, Asian American artists have to be conscious of not expressing those parts of themselves, such as their ethnic or racial identity, that could cause audience alienation. As noted in the beginning of this essay, the canonical narrative of hip hop's roots in African American history and culture dominates the popular imagination of hip hop worldwide. Anything that runs counter to that perception runs the risk of being dismissed as inauthentic or at least held in less regard. In this sense, Nishi's comment about not wanting to exploit his ethnicity is moot since drawing attention to their racial difference would be considered a liability for many of these artists in their own estimation.

On the rare occasions when race or ethnicity is spoken about, it is often made incidental rather than central. One illuminating example comes from the Mountain Brothers' debut album (1999) and their song, "Days of Being Dumb." Jung (Chops) opens the track with these verses:

flippin' the page / back in the days

when this little, fat Asian kid would sit makin' beats in the basement

on a basic roll and drum box / stolen from Scott's

sneakin' and listenin' to Dr. Rock-N'-Dallas in the PM on weekends[72]

In this example, ethnic identity is mentioned but only as one of many signifiers Chops lays out. Chops not only identifies himself as a "little, fat Asian kid," but he also crafts a narrative of his own hip hop upbringing, inclusive of retail stores where he stole his production equipment and radio stations where he listened to music—dimensions that helped shape who he is an artist. Ethnicity is part of it, but it is not necessarily the most important part. Chops clearly did not write these lines as a way to connect only with other Asian Americans. His appeals are far more than ethnic; they are also geographic and genera- tional. Even musically speaking the lush, organic production of "Days of Being Dumb" recalls the so-called Philadelphia sound pioneered by soul artists such as Gamble and Huff, Dexter Wanzel, the O'Jays, and MSFB. In this way, as an artist Chops identifies himself more with Philadelphia than with his Asian descent.

Elsewhere, in the video for the Mountain Brothers' song "Galaxies," direc- tors Richard Kim and Chris Chan Lee surround the group with a variety of images—some ethnic, many not.[73] For example, members of the group are shown playing mah-jong and eating ramen noodles, ostensibly signifiers of Asianness, but this is staged against a larger backdrop that includes scenes of Styles brushing his teeth, Chops's production equipment, and an extended dance sequence shot in downtown Philadelphia in which the Mountain Broth- ers is surrounded by a conspicuously multiracial crowd of friends and fans. As Chops puts it in the song itself, the rappers are "Illadelphy Asiatic / repre- sentin' from the West End section," a complicated mix of signifiers that says as much about where they're from (West Philadelphia) as about who / what they are (Asiatic / Asian).

Another telling example is the 1999 hip hop compilation *Elephant Tracks* assembled by San Francisco's Asian American music label, Asian Improv Rec- ords.[74] Two-thirds of the album's featured artists are of Asian American de- scent, including the Mountain Brothers, the Filipino American rap group KNT (Knuckle Neck Tribe), and the multiethnic, Los Angeles group The Vision- aries, whose members include Filipino, Japanese, and Chinese Americans. Despite this diverse collection—and the album includes many non-Asian art- ists as well—the compilation conspicuously avoids billing itself as an Asian

American hip hop anthology. There is no explicit mention of ethnicity in any of the liner notes, and save for the pictures of the groups inside the CD packaging there is little to indicate the race or ethnicity of the artists. Ethnicity is clearly a common thread that ties these artists together in concept, but in execution the need to express or reflect on ethnicity is anything but required (that said, it is worth noting that the Mountain Brothers' cut on this anthology is "Community," a song with an explicit antidiscrimination, pro-Asian American solidarity bent).

Elephant Tracks is less concerned with the need to proclaim that Asian American rappers exist than it is with showing what those artists are capable of. This compilation, like the song "Days of Being Dumb" or the video "Galaxies," suggests that contemporary Asian American rappers seek to define their community beyond ethnic or racial ties; instead they try to appeal to larger ties of alliance, allegiance, and experience. They offer the possibility that hip hop, not just as music but as a source of cultural identity, is a potential point of affiliation that can be shared across racial and ethnic lines. This is not to say that hip hop supersedes such powerfully resonant social categories as race, gender, and class, but it acknowledges that hip hop has become a prominent cultural force that many youth, Asian American and otherwise, have experienced over the last two decades. In the words of performance artist and cultural theorist Coco Fusco, "Rap music . . . is perhaps today's most resonant cross-cultural American language for defiant self-affirmation."[75] The scenes of the Mountain Brothers in downtown Philadelphia surrounded by a multiethnic crowd of well-wishers are just one example of how Asian American rappers have tried to express Fusco's argument in their own way.

In this social world, hip hop becomes the common thread that ties people together across race, geography, and age. Asian Americans have strategic reasons to champion a more utopian, inclusive ideal of hip hop since it helps deflect attention away from their own racial difference. Yet it also conforms to the philosophy about hip hop's egalitarian embrace of performers of all backgrounds. By seeking to form relationships with other artists and audience members from across the social spectrum, Asian American rappers are putting into practice their own ideas about hip hop's politics of inclusion while simultaneously crafting a space where they can fit into that matrix. By focusing on individual abilities rather than origins, contemporary Asian American rappers have found one way to cope with the expectations of the hip hop audience. But this is not the only strategy they have pursued.

Jin and Juice: Wielding Racial Consciousness at the Millennium

For his stage name, Jin Au-Yeung simply uses his own name: Jin. After spending most of his childhood in Miami, his family relocated to Queens, New York, and on a chance opportunity Jin appeared on the cable network BET's *106 and Park*, a daily television show highlighting rap videos and artists. Every week, *106 and Park* hosts a freestyle battle between opposing rappers, and Jin entered the rotation. Seven weeks later, he emerged undefeated, one of only two rappers to have entered the show's Hall of Fame at the time. With a national television audience viewing his exploits during this two-month run, Jin became what one magazine described as "the Golden Child."[76] With the release of his debut album in the fall of 2004, *The Rest Is History*, a long string of articles followed, many of them drawing attention to the fact that Jin was the first Asian American rapper with a legitimate chance to find mainstream success.[77]

What set Jin apart from his predecessors is that he was invited to join the Ruff Ryders "family," which at the time included top-selling rappers such Eve, Styles P, DMX, and Jadakiss. Whether Jin was more or less skilled than other Asian American rappers was a matter of subjective speculation, but objectively speaking he had far more resources than were available to previous rappers of Asian descent. However, in gaining the attention of the mainstream media and rap pundits, Jin's racial difference became all the more obvious. Yet, rather than downplaying these differences as previous rappers had, Jin strategically embraced them, drawing attention to his race in an attempt to minimize it.

For example, when Jin was on *106 and Park* almost all of his opponents were African American and many of them tried to attack him by ridiculing his racial difference. Examples of their race-baiting rhymes include: "I'm a star / you're just a rookie / leave rap alone / and go back to making fortune cookies" (week 2 versus Sterling);[78] "C'mon man / you ain't tough as me / what you wanna do? / battle me / or sell me dollar batteries" (week 3 versus Skitzoe);[79] and "Who you supposed to be? / Bruce Lee with your pants all sagging / I'll murder you dog / there'll be no return of the dragon" (week 7 versus Sean Nicholas).[80] Whenever he was baited—and sometimes when he was not—Jin would often flip the race card back on his opponents by embracing his racial difference and then using it to ridicule his rivals. For example, against Sterling, he responded, "You want to say I'm Chinese / son, here's a reminder / check your Timberlands / they probably say 'made in China.' "[81] Against Sean Nicholas, Jin pursued a similar strategy, rhyming "My pants are new / my sweater is new / don't be mad a Chinese kid / dress better than you."[82] Especially in the latter example, Jin drew attention to his perceived outsider status by ridiculing Nicholas for having worse clothes than "a Chinese kid," as if this was something to be doubly ashamed of.

However, when it came time for Jin to release his album, he willingly racialized himself without being prompted. The first single from *The Rest Is History*, "Learn Chinese," opens with a simple statement by Jin: "Yeah, I'm Chinese . . . and what?"[83] This was both an affirmation and a challenge. Jin recognized that his audience could not ignore his racial difference, and he was effectively daring potential critics to make an issue of it.

Although Jin prodded listeners to confront the specter of race, the topic was addressed on his terms. He issued a critique against stereotypes in the song, rapping, "This ain't Bruce Lee / ya'll watch too much TV," and proclaimed at the beginning that "The days of the pork fried rice coming to your door are over," symbolically "killing" the archetype of the Chinese delivery boy in favor of a hypermasculine Chinatown gangsta.[84] It must be said that while Jin problematized some stereotypes, he left others in his wake. For example, both the video imagery and the song lyrics for "Learn Chinese" portrayed Chinatown as a dangerous, violent neighborhood—an ironic gesture given how long Chinatown residents have tried to rid themselves of that stigma. In this respect, Jin failed to create an alternative to the problematic constructions of black masculinity; he was merely changing the face of it.

Elsewhere Jin displayed a keener awareness of race. In an early song that did not end up on his album, "I Don't Know," he responded to critics who compared him to the white rapper Eminem.

> I'm no Eminem / but I'm not wack either /
> The only reason you compare me to him /
> Is because I'm not black either[85]

These lines demonstrated how Jin was intimately aware of how race played into perceptions of him. He responded to accusations that he was attempting to ape Eminem's success and countered that the only reason people compared the two artists was because neither was African American and therefore both disrupted racial expectations. However, despite his claims otherwise, Jin and Eminem did share a similarity—both played *up* their racial difference as a way to disarm potential critics. On a song from his 2002 album, *The Eminem Show*, the rapper featured a song, "White America," that included the following lines.

Look at these eyes
baby blue, baby just like yourself
If they were brown Shady lose
Shady sits on the shelf[86]

By drawing attention to it and acknowledging that his race had helped him gain wider appeal, Eminem not only robbed his attackers of their main line of critique; he also earned broad acclaim in many critical circles. Eminem has been seen as more authentic because of his willingness to wear his race on his sleeve, so to speak. Compare this to the example of Vanilla Ice, the multi-platinum white rapper of the early 1990s who claimed to have grown up in the inner city when he was really from the middle-class suburbs. Vanilla Ice was rejected as inauthentic, not because he was white but because he lied about his background. In being up front about his whiteness, Eminem has been seen as more "real" by his audience.

Jin followed a similar strategy by tackling his racial difference head on. In doing so, he attempted to get his potential audience to look past his race and focus on his talent. It was a slightly more sophisticated version of a schoolyard taunt: "Yeah, I'm Asian. . . . You want to fight about it?" Jin and Eminem prodded listeners to confront the specter of race, forcing skeptics to confront their own biases. The main difference was that Eminem, in "White America," could afford to rub critics' noses in his record-breaking album sales. It has cost him nothing to admit that his whiteness is a selling point, and he displays that awareness in the song's unmistakably mocking tone. Jin, on the other hand, could not use his ethnicity as a marketing tool, but his explicit discussion of race demonstrated a willingness to talk about the issue openly, gambling that audiences would respect him for that frankness.

Jin pursued this strategy in different ways on *The Rest Is History*. For "Love Song," he penned a narrative about a teenage interracial couple—a "Chinese dude" and his black girlfriend—and detailed the challenges they face.

They found true love, living in a fantasy.
Then reality attacks, his pops couldn't see past the fact
His son was asian, but his girlfriend was black.
Imagine having to choose between the one that you love or your fam[ily],
That's like cutting off your right or left hand, damn.[87]

At the end of the song, Jin revealed that the "Chinese dude," was himself a few years back. "Love Story" was designed to appeal to people across racial lines, addressing the illogic of anti-miscegenation paranoia and prejudices. Jin deliberately drew attention to race again, strategically pushing his listeners to understand that people of different heritages can suffer the same forms of discrimination. Making this point within a personal story from his romantic past helped to humanize the issue further by creating a sympathetic set of star-crossed lovers with whom listeners could identify.

Elsewhere on *The Rest Is History*, Jin deployed a similar tactic of cross-racial identification in the song "Same Cry."

> Stuck between the rock and a hard place,
> Thinking about the refugees that went to see God's face.
> Sixteen thousand miles across the ocean tides,
> Some died, some got lucky and survived.
> I wouldn't call it luck—they reached the destination;
> Modern day slavery without the plantation.
> Them sneakers on your feet cost a hundred a pop,
> He's making fifty cent a day working in sweat shops.[88]

This was Jin's most politicized attempt to forge cross-cultural recognition between Asian and African Americans, appealing to a shared sense of struggle and oppression. Although comparing sweatshop labor with plantation slavery was a stretch, Jin suggested that Asian immigrants endured exploitation and suffering just as African Americans did. The chorus of the song repeats that same idea.

> We may look different,
> But we see the same sky.
> We may see different,
> But we cry the same cry.

The emphasis on *cry* proposed that both Asian and African Americans have endured their share of suffering and this mutual experience can lead the two communities to overcome their differences. Compared to "Learn Chinese," this is a different way of accentuating race as a way of defusing it. With "Same Cry," Jin drew attention to racial difference—we look different, we see different—but his point was that both communities suffered from similar histories and challenges, which ideally would help form points of commonality and coalition. In a sense, Jin brought Asian American hip hop full circle but with a twist. Like Fists of Fury, he discussed Asian American social issues—including sweatshop labor, refugee experiences, and oppressive conditions in Asia—but rather than broadcasting these issues just to Asian American audiences he sought to educate and entertain a broad, implicitly multiracial audience. Drawing attention to his racial difference was a way to push his listeners to look past it and instead find points of commonality.

Jin's emergence came at a time when there were other visible Asian American artists within hip hop, including the Neptunes' Chad Hugo (Filipino), Linkin Park's Mike Shinoda (Japanese), and the Black Eyed Peas' Allan Pineda, also known as Apl.de.ap (Filipino). Nonetheless, Jin recognized that he still had to convince people of his talents. In his own words, "I think all it comes down to is the quality of the music. . . . I'm not going to say that the race thing isn't a big issue, but when the music comes out, if it's good music, it will be good, if it's bad, it will be bad."[89] This echoes similar comments by the Mountain Brothers and other rappers, positing that ultimately they believe that talent speaks the loudest. However, until an Asian American rapper enjoys the kind of mainstream success and sales that other rappers have attained, the importance of race versus talent will remain an open question.

As an epilogue, in May of 2005, Jin announced his "retirement," though his reasons for doing so were unclear.[90] He dispelled the notion that it was due to poor album sales—*The Rest Is History* sold a modest hundred thousand units— but failed to articulate a specific motivation for leaving his rap career behind. Jin's announcement was surprising for numerous reasons, not the least of which is that it is unusual for a young rapper to announce his or her retirement (most simply disappear from the charts quietly). Moreover, considering how much press Jin had enjoyed just half a year earlier, to see that kind of media bubble burst so quickly and suddenly surely took many observers by surprise.

Jin's retirement also means that as of the completion of this essay there once again is no Asian American rapper signed to a major label contract. As seen with Jin's meteoric rise (and fall), such circumstances can change suddenly, but the experience also shows how tenuous a hold Asian American rappers have within the music industry.

Leaders of the New School: Conclusions

Despite the diversifying audience that hip hop enjoys, race continues to play a central role in people's expectations of the music and culture. Although some hip hop audiences have historically been more accepting of rappers of all backgrounds, in the more commercial, mainstream world, racial authenticity is still an entrenched part of audience expectations. In reviewing the different strategies and identity politics that Asian American rappers have engaged in over the last fifteen years, I have demonstrated the ways in which Asian Americans tried to position themselves and their racial difference vis-à-vis hip hop audiences.

What emerges, however, is not just the different ways in which Asian American rappers perceive themselves in relation to hip hop but also their very perceptions of hip hop to begin with. Rappers from the early 1990s, influenced by the example of Public Enemy and other politicized artists, sought to make their race and ethnicity explicit as a means of inspiring their peers to listen and take notice. For them, hip hop was a mouthpiece for political awareness and education. Rappers from the mid-1990s such as the Mountain Brothers and Key Kool saw hip hop as an artistic outlet for personal expression that could include, but did not have to be beholden to, issues of race or ethnicity. They sought to connect with like-minded audiences that similarly believed in an identity centered around hip hop itself as a culture and art. New rappers such as Jin may think of hip hop as a culture worth their allegiance, but they are also savvy in recognizing the business realities that come with public performance.

The remaining question is whether or not Asian American rappers will face a more welcoming situation within the recording industry over the next few years. The conventional wisdom is that one Asian American rap superstar would help convince record labels to consider signing other Asian American acts. However, the success of the white rapper Eminem suggests another, less optimistic scenario. The overwhelming popularity that Eminem has enjoyed could be interpreted as a sign that racial authenticity no longer matters. However, while Eminem has been legitimated by hip hop's multiracial audience, his success has not represented—as of yet—a fundamental shift in the acceptance of white rappers writ large. It is telling that the white rappers who emerged after Eminem's rise, such as Haystack and Bubba Sparxxx, were inevitably compared to Eminem even when their styles and content had little in common with his. Despite Eminem's success, white rappers are still treated as a novelty within hip hop, suggesting that Eminem, far from breaking down racial barriers in hip hop, has instead been fixed into a niche as *"the* white rapper" against which all future aspirants will be judged, at least for the time being. In this sense, he is a privileged token, benefiting from his status as the lone white rapper able to garner support from the hip hop community but a token nonetheless given the paucity of other white rappers. Likewise, even if Jin's career had taken off, this would not necessarily have been an indication that rap audiences are willing to support other mainstream Asian American artists. I would argue that until the current authenticity paradigm moves away from its sole association with blackness non-black artists are likely to face considerable challenges in finding mainstream support.

Moreover, it is not at all clear that such a paradigm shift is desirable, especially if it means that hip hop will be detached from Afro-diasporic traditions or the black community. As I have argued, the exclusion of nonblack rappers is less the product of conscious design and more an expected outcome given the deep ties that continue to connect hip hop with the black community. There is certainly a danger that the relationship will become overly essentialized, but the alternative risks treating cultural forms as strictly commodities with no sense of history or how culture moves within flows of power. As George Lipsitz warns, treating cultural forms as "infinitely open does violence to the historical and social constraints imposed on us by structures of exploitation and privilege."[91]

However, regardless of the current state of hip hop's racial authenticity paradigm, there is every indication that it will continue to play a major role in the cultural lives of Asian Americans. For the past twenty years, hip hop has been a dominant cultural and musical force for Asian American youth. Even in other areas of Asian American cultural expression, from car racing to spoken-word poetry and filmmaking, the aesthetics of hip hop have become a common influence and theme. It also needs to be reiterated that, although the profession of rapping is still dominated by this racial authenticity, in most other sectors of the hip hop community Asian Americans are prevalent, even dominant, as in the case of Filipino American DJs.[92] The marginality that Asian American rappers contend with is largely the exception rather than the rule in terms of how Asian Americans have taken to hip hop and been accepted by like-minded peers.

As noted earlier, hip hop has its own power as a locus of cultural identity, one that may not trump ethnic or racial allegiances but at least provides an alternative. For generations of youths coming of age in America, and truly around the world, hip hop has become a powerful source of identity and culture. In hip hop's social matrix, race and ethnicity will not disappear permanently, but their enduring primacy may yet wane with the ever-diversifying audience the music attracts, compels, and inspires.

This is not to suggest that race has faded in importance within American society; there are myriad examples of how it continues to enforce abhorrent social divisions. However, it is worth noting how hip hop's massive, multiethnic popularity, which began in the 1980s, parallels the development of the rhetoric of multiculturalism in American society. Caution needs to be displayed here, for liberal multiculturalism has been rightly criticized for deflecting attention away from the damage done by continuing institutional racism.[93] However, as examples of two powerful social movements of the post–civil rights era, hip hop and multiculturalism have become entwined to the extent that there is a rhetoric of inclusion within hip hop—expounded through lyrics and personal testimonials—that embraces diversity as a key force within the culture. This in turn has impacted society at large as hip hop has saturated a mass media network with a global reach. Newcomers to hip hop are continually being inundated with the ideology of inclusion, no doubt partially espoused by the very beneficiaries of such a politics (i.e., nonblacks wishing to challenge black-oriented racial authenticity). Likewise, commercially savvy artists have no reason to refute this embrace of diversity since it aids their attempts to reach larger audiences.

The collision of all these forces has helped to make hip hop a leading, if not *the* leading, cultural force in American society today, one that pushes a politics of inclusion against the traditional divisions created by racial and ethnic difference. Hip hop is far from a utopia of course, with many divisive ideologies still rampant, especially around issues of gender. As well, it must be said that championing diversity has many economic benefits that have nothing to do with social altruism—such as building larger audiences. However, the experience of Asian American rappers over the last decade suggests that the currents of culture, race, and politics are never stagnant. Asian American rappers may not have reached a point where their racial difference is no longer a liability (let alone an asset), but their ongoing attempts to negotiate these issues reveal the continual transformations that hip hop itself undergoes. In the midst of those changes, the presence and perseverance of Asian American rappers can influence the directions in which hip hop will move, hinting at (though not promising) a more viable space of acceptance and success for themselves and their peers.

Notes

1 Heller, "Streetology."

2 Chung, "Hip Hop Asian America." The main difference is that rappers are the most visible of hip hop's various actors within the mass media. As will be explored shortly, racial characteristics are an instant signifier of authenticity for rappers. Other, less visible artists such as DJs and graffiti writers do not have to contend with this.

3 "Major labels" refers to the five multinational corporations that control the bulk of the record industry in the United States. Labels not affiliated with the majors are known as "independents."

4 Smith, "Ain't a Damn Thing Changed," 125–28.

5 McLeod, "Authenticity within Hip Hop and Other Cultures Threatened with Assimilation."

6 One of the most famous cases was that of the white rapper Vanilla Ice, who was found to have invented his hard-luck childhood in an effort to seem more credible "in the streets." Despite having one of the best-selling debut rap albums of all time, Vanilla Ice's authenticity problems plagued him and, along with other factors, led to a second album that sold dismally, after which the artist quickly faded from public view.

7 Perry, *Prophets of the Hood*, 10.

8 Ibid. Perry bases this claim on four primary characteristics of hip hop, including its use of African American vernacular, its origins in African American oral and musical cultures, and its political location within black society and traditions.

9 Rose, *Black Noise*; Forman, *The 'Hood Comes First*; Rivera, *New York Ricans from the Hip Hop Zone*.

10 Mitchell, *Global Noise*.

11 In using the term *myth*, I am not contesting the veracity of hip hop's origin narratives. I only mean to suggest that the story of hip hop's roots has been told and retold so many times—in songs, magazines, books, and so on—that its narrative wields a power analogous to mythology.

12 For an argument that favors erasure, see Flores, *From Bomba to Hip Hop*.

13 Kelly, "Hip Hop Chicano"; Del Barco, "Rap's Latino Sabor," 63–84; Flores, "Puerto Rocks," 85–116; Flores, *From Bomba to Hip Hop*; Rivera, *New York Ricans from the Hip Hop Zone*.

14 Mitchell, *Global Noise*.

15 It should be noted that most of these attempts to diversify hip hop's scope in academic discourse continue to marginalize Asian Americans. In Tony Mitchell's critique of American centrism in hip hop scholarship, he reviews works written on Latino and Native American rappers but ignores any mention of Asian Americans, instead jumping directly to rappers in Asia (ibid., 5). Likewise, William Eric Perkins is one of the only scholars to acknowledge the presence of Asian Americans in hip hop, but his anecdotal review of Bay Area hip hop is rife with errors that suggest a lack of research. For example, Perkins claims that Lani Luv was "the first Asian American female rapper" to begin rhyming in the Philippines, neither of which is correct. He also misspells DJ (disc jockey) Q-Bert as D-Bert and erroneously claims that he is Filipino-Hawaiian. See Perkins, "Youth's Global Village," 262.

16 I distinguish mainstream rap consumers as part of a more general public versus the so-called underground, which is a smaller, subcultural community. As will be explored later, underground audiences tend to be more open-minded with regard to their racial preferences in artists, and as a result many nonblack artists have found a welcome in the underground, Asian Americans included.

17 Smith, "Ain't a Damn Thing Changed," 126.

18 The success of the white rapper Eminem remains a complicated exception, and his impact on hip hop's racial politics will be briefly discussed in the conclusion.

19 One key element that I am leaving out of this analysis is the *music* of these artists. Other Asian American hip hop artists have used music as a form of signification, most notably South Asians and the Indian *bhangra* remix culture in New York and elsewhere (Maira, "Desis Reprazent"; "Identity Dub: The Paradoxes of an Indian American Subculture"; *Desis in the House*). There is also the example of Jamez, a Korean American rapper from New York who in the late 1990s incorporated traditional Korean musical aesthetics into his beats (Ling, "Jamez Chang)." For the artists I cover from this same period, however, music was not the primary location of any kind of ethnic or racial signification, even among those who explicitly rapped about identity politics in their rhymes. Those artists, wanting to firmly establish and identify themselves as Asian *Americans*, would have derived little benefit from music that incorporates traditional Asian elements since they would have run the risk of painting themselves as alien or foreign. Therefore, their music tended to fall in line with dominant hip hop aesthetics in the 1990s that favored 1970s American soul and jazz influences. Ironically, by the early 2000s, mainstream producers such as Timbaland and Dr. Dre were drawing inspiration from Asian musical sources, most notably Indian movie soundtracks.

20 Rivera, *New York Ricans from the Hip Hop Zone*, 8. The title of this section, "The Afro-centric Asian," is taken from a song by the rap artist Nas, who on his 1994 single "It Ain't Hard Tell" rhymed, "Nas is like the Afrocentric Asian / Half Man / Half Amazin." Nas's self-description of himself as Asian led some to erroneously report that he was actually half Asian, half African American, which is untrue. His use of the term *Asian* is equivalent to *Asiatic*, which is explained in note 32.

21 Ibid., 9.

22 Ibid., 187.

23 Ibid., 94.

24 Ibid., 96.

25 Espiritu, *Asian American Panethnicity*.

26 Hall, "New Ethnicities," 441–49.

27 Okihiro, *Margins and Mainstreams*, 33.

28 Aaron, "What the White Boy Means When He Says Yo"; Wimsatt, "We Use Words Like Mackadocious," 22–41.

29 Koshy, "Morphing Race into Ethnicity"; Chang, "Race, Class, Conflict, and Empowerment"; Zia, "To Market, to Market, New York Style"; Prashad, *Everybody Was Kung Fu Fighting*.

30 Mercer, "Black Masculinity and the Sexual Politics of Race"; Espiritu, *Asian American Women and Men*, 86–107. (Thanks to Shannon Steen for reminding me of this dichotomy).

31 Han, "Asian American Nation."

32 The use of the term *Asiatic* by Asian American rappers represents the term's unusual journey through hip hop culture. Traditionally, *Asiatic* has been deployed

by African American artists (e.g., Big Daddy Kane's surname stands for "King Asiatic, Nobody's Equal") as a derivation drawn from the teachings of the Nation of Islam, an American offshoot of Islam. In Nation of Islam ideology, African Americans are referred to as Asiatic because their roots can be traced back to a mythical "black nation of Asia," the Tribe of Shabazz, which was the cradle of human civilization. Thus, calling oneself Asiatic, for African Americans, was a marker of pride for being descended from the original rulers of humanity. See Nathaniel Deutsch, " 'The Asiatic Black Man': An African American Orientalism?" Asian American rappers are not co-opting the term *Asiatic* so much as returning the term to its original scope, which was always meant to include people of "traditional" Asian descent such as Chinese, Japanese, and South Asians.

33 Han, "Asian American Nation"; Daphnie Anies, interview with the author, February 20, 2003; Eduardo Restauro, interview with the author, March 3, 2002. While there were Asian Americans rapping at the time, what is notable is that no official *recordings* were left behind by these artists. I am not privileging records over live performances, but it does reflect the extent to which Asian Americans did not exist within the urban music industry throughout the 1980s.

34 Han, "Asian American Nation."

35 Davis Yee, interview with the author, February 22, 1999.

36 The Seoul Brothers, Michael and Raphael Park, figure prominently in Renee Tajima-Peña's 1996 documentary, *My America . . . or Honk if You Love Buddha.*

37 Rose, *Black Noise.* While many of Public Enemy's songs attracted the attention of conservative critics, it was accusations of anti-Semitism leveled against a side member of the group, Professor Griff, that gave it the most negative publicity.

38 Public Enemy's influence was felt throughout the larger hip hop community. In an article on Latino rappers, Mandalit Del Barco quotes respondents who admitted that Public Enemy had inspired them too ("Rap's Latino Sabor," 77).

39 Tseng, "Asian American Rap."

40 Fists of Fury, press material, 1993.

41 The reference to the "man from the caves" is an allusion to the teachings of the Nation of Islam, which holds that white Europeans were uncivilized, savage, and lived in caves until Moses came to liberate them from their ignorance. The idea of whites as cave dwellers appears elsewhere in hip hop, most notably in a song by the Los Angeles rapper Ice Cube, "Cave Bitch" (1993), a critique of white women. Pement, "Louis Farrakhan and the Nation of Islam," 32–36, 38.

42 Fists of Fury, "After School," unreleased demo, 1993.

43 Brand, "The New Whiz Kids," *Time*, August 31, 1987.

44 Wong, "Asian for the Man!"

45 Yellow Peril, "Asian for the Man," song from an unreleased demo, 1995.

46 Wong, "Asian for the Man!"; Wong, "The Invisible Man Syndrome"; Wong, "We Define Ourselves!"; Tseng, "Asian American Rap."

47 Darow Han, telephone interview with the author, San Francisco, 1992.

48 While none of these groups survived, individual members have gone on to pursue musical careers. Han-na Che, now Hana Choi, is an aspiring singer. Bert Wang

now leads a rock-rap group called SuperChink in New York. Art Hirahara is a recorded jazz pianist now living in New York.

49 Yee, interview.

50 Tseng, "Asian American Rap."

51 Fists of Fury, press material.

52 Yee, interview.

53 Bertrand Wong, interview with the author, February 17, 1999.

54 Besides politically inspired artists, in the early 1990s there were other Asian American rappers, including Miami's Fresh Kid Ice (a Chinese Trinidadian), a member of 2 Live Crew, who recorded a solo album in 1992 entitled *The Chinaman*. There was also the Bay Area's Japanese American rapper, Rhythm X, also known as "the mental Oriental," who released his *Long Over Due* album in 1994. While both Ice and X drew attention to their ethnicity through titling (*The Chinaman*) and naming (the mental Oriental), none of their songs exhibited the same kind of political or issue-oriented fervor that groups such as Yellow Peril and the Asiatic Apostles invested in their music. Nor do they comfortably fit into the generation of artists I am about to discuss. Nonetheless, their presence is noteworthy.

55 When individuals are being interviewed or quoted from interviews, they are identified by their legal names. When rappers are being quoted from lyrics, their artist names will be used.

56 Mountain Brothers, "Invisible Man," song from an unreleased demo tape, 1996.

57 Eric B. and Rakim, "I Know You Got Soul," on *Paid In Full*, compact disc, 4th and Broadway, 1987.

58 Chris (Peril-L) Wang, interview with the author, December 5, 1996.

59 Scott (Chops) Jung, interview with the author, December 5, 1996.

60 Wong, "The Invisible Man Syndrome."

61 It is worth noting that Nishi included a song on *Kozmonautz* entitled "Reconcentrated" that both castigates the internment of his Japanese American grandfather during World War II and links it to current anti-Asian sentiment.

62 Jung, interview.

63 Ibid. Ironically, the group had to contend with racial stereotypes emanating not from audience members but from the recording industry. Jung recalls an occasion when a record executive approached the group about appearing onstage wearing Buddhist monks' robes, chanting, and hitting gongs.

64 The main exception to this was by so-called "azn" rappers who began to emerge in the late 1990s. While more research is needed to fully flush out the cultural moment in which Asian American youths begin to identify themselves as azn on Internet sites and in forums, this corruption in spelling bears similarities to other forms of linguistic alteration involved in black vernacular English, also commonly referred to as Ebonics. One particular musical product that emerged from these youths was rap songs with Asian themes using popular, preexisting instrumentals. For example, one widely circulated song, "Got Rice Bitch?" performed by a rapper only identified as azn (and sometimes azn Pride), features rhymes covering everything from Asian American import car culture to ethnic food but is set to the

instrumental from Tupac's "Changes." Many of these songs feature groups with such names as the Khmer Boys, the Chink Boys, and Slant Eyed Descendents boasting about ethnic pride (i.e., Filipino pride, Vietnamese pride, Korean pride, etc.). In some ways, they bear similarities to the Asian American rappers of the early 1990s insofar as their raps are for, by, and about Asian Americans, but the various AZN rap songs lack the political context and intent that motivated such groups as the Asiatic Apostles and Fists of Fury. It is also important to note that these various AZN rap songs exist solely on the Internet rather than on CDS or cassettes. Such particular distribution suggests that these artists are community focused rather than aspiring to larger popularity in the music market.

65 Yokota, "Key Kool."

66 Lhamon, *Raising Cain*.

67 Futuredood, "Interview with Southstar," September 2, 2002, http://www.azn raps.com/public_site/artist/interviews/southstar_only/south_only.htm.

68 Even more complicated is the fact that, as someone of mixed ethnic heritage, Southstar is racially ambiguous. In the course of my research, I discovered comments that described him as "Caucasian"; others were not sure if he was of African American or Latino heritage. The point is that Southstar is able to "pass" in complex ways that have the potential to help (if he is read as black or Latino) or hinder him (if he is read as white or Asian). For example, besides the interview already noted, very few interviewers have asked Southstar or his partner, Smilez, about how audiences receive this pairing between an African American and a Chinese Filipino American. It is possible that because Smilez is black, audiences and critics do not perceive the duo as racially different in the same way as the Chinese American Mountain Brothers. In other words, because of their partnership Southstar attains another kind of "passing" privilege. This is similar to Taboo, a Filipino American member of the rap group Black Eyed Peas. Because the other two members of the group are African American, the Black Eyed Peas rarely gets the same kind of questions about its ethnic makeup as would an all Asian American group or Asian American solo artist.

69 Yokota, "Key Kool."

70 Dan Emmiere, "Pacifics Interview 2001."

71 It is important to note that by the mid-1990s overtly *politicized* overtures to black identity had fallen out of favor with most fans and the recording industry. While blackness is still a vital part of contemporary hip hop discourse, it is now a blackness dominated by masculine ideals such as sexual prowess, criminal acumen, and violent temperaments rather than political affirmations of blackness that hark back to the 1970s Black Power movement. Regardless of what value judgments one makes over this change in attitude, it is worth noting that far from being a unitary, fixed ideal, blackness takes myriad forms.

72 Mountain Brothers, "Days of Being Dumb," on *Self Volume 1*, compact disc, Pimp-strut, 1998.

73 Mountain Brothers, "Galaxies," music video, dir. Richard Kim and Chris Chan Lee, 1999.

74 *Elephant Tracks*, compact disc, compilation by Asian Improv Records, 1999.

75 Fusco, *English Is Broken Here*, 32.

76 Parker, "Golden Child."

77 Coates, "Just Another Quick-Witted, Egg-Roll-Joke-Making, Insult-Hurling Chinese-American Rapper," 55; Kevin Kim, "Repping Chinatown."

78 Jin, *106 and Park*, BET, week 2, 2002, http://www.holla-front.com/media.html (accessed August 2003).

79 Jin, *106 and Park*, BET, week 3, 2002, http://www.holla-front.com/media.html (accessed August 2003).

80 Jin, *106 and Park*, BET, week 7, 2002, http://www.holla-front.com/media.html (accessed August 2003).

81 Jin, *106 and Park*, BET, week 2, 2002, http://www.holla-front.com/media.html (accessed August 2003).

82 Jin, *106 and Park*, BET, week 7, 2002, http://www.holla-front.com/media.html (accessed August 2003).

83 Jin, "Learn Chinese." On *The Rest Is History*, compact disc, Ruff Ryders, 2004.

84 Ironically, Jin was involved in a well-publicized Chinatown shout out with Chinese gangs in 2003. Christina Tam, "Jin and Juice."

85 Jin, "I Don't Know." (2003), http://www.ighetto.com/daveslyrics/JinThaMC/IDontKnow.html (accessed August 2002).

86 Eminem, "White America," on *The Eminem Show*, compact disc, Aftermath/Interscope, 2002.

87 Jin, "Love Story." On *The Rest Is History*, compact disc, Ruff Ryders, 2004.

88 Jin, "Same Cry." On *The Rest Is History*, compact disc, Ruff Ryders, 2004.

89 Jin, interview with the author, May 2002.

90 Strong, "Jin Says Rap Career Is Over, Records 'I Quit.' "

91 Lipsitz, *Dangerous Crossroads*, 62.

92 *Beats, Rhymes, Resistance: Pilipinos and Hip Hop in L.A.*, video, Lakandiwa DeLeon, Dawn Mabalon, and Jonathan Ramos (USA, 1997, revised 1999).

93 Lowe, *Immigrant Acts*, 84–96.

two

Silenced but Not Silent: Asian Americans and Jazz

Kevin Fellezs

In the early 1960s, a Japanese jazz pianist, composer, and big band leader, Toshiko Akiyoshi, dressed in a traditional kimono, made an appearance on the television game show *What's My Line?* The studio audience's laughter when she signed her name on the guest board in Japanese kanji script, as well as the host's stammering attempt to pronounce her name, revealed how unfamiliar mainstream American audiences were with Asians and Asian culture. Moreover, when she revealed her professional "line" as a jazz pianist to the studio and home viewing audience, the studio audience's audible reactions indicated the discrepancy between "American jazz" and "Japanese woman."[1] This distance has not been erased in the roughly forty years since Akiyoshi's appearance on the television show.[2] In a *JazzTimes* article in 2003, author Bill Shoemaker asks a central question about the continued marginality of Asian American jazz musicians "even within enlightened jazz circles," namely, "How [can one] change the American mindset about race and culture through the most American of art forms?"[3] His question answers itself, in part, by glossing over what the phrase "the most American of art forms" articulates. A reworking of the question might get at the central predicament Asian American jazz musicians face in the cultural marketplace: how are Asian Americans "not" American and thus foreclosed from participation in this form?

I would like to spend a few moments with Shoemaker's article as it succinctly displays the problematic positionality of Asian American jazz artists in normative terms. While his article is extremely thoughtful and gives voice to a number of significant Asian American musicians (all of whom receive some attention in this essay[4]), this predicament remains. Shoemaker is forced to admit that while "hybridity and multiple identities are increasingly central to jazz's discussions about race," it is still true that "if jazz is any barometer, the issue of race in the U.S. is still largely two dimensional: black and white."[5] Interestingly, he concludes his article by noting, "[The fact that] Hispanics have become the U.S.'s largest minority more than a decade ahead of consensus projections is just the latest indicator of the need to reassess the issue of diversity in jazz."[6] The inability to articulate an exclusively Asian American space in an article about Asian American musicians, even by a writer sympathetic to Asian American jazz musicians' marginality, indicates the difficulties they face in their attempts to be heard on their own terms, however unsettling that is to dominant perceptions of Asian Americans—perceptions fed by popular mythologies surrounding Asia and Asians in general that render Asians and Asian Americans "unfit" as "all-American" subjects.

Furthermore, Shoemaker argues that there are two underlying reasons for the exclusion of Asian American jazz musicians from jazz critics' historiographical project. One is the ability of "many Asian-Americans [to] assimilate into the American mainstream with considerable ease, sometimes, like ice-skating diva Michelle Kwan, rising to pop-culture-icon status with little or anything made of their ethnicity." Second, the "uncompromising [leftist] politics of the Asian-American jazz movement's early years" may also impact any inclusivist agenda Asian American jazz artists might hope to promote. While later I will deal at more length with how this version of the "model minority" negatively impacts Asian American jazz musicians' production of aesthetic works, I want to make the observation here that what Shoemaker perceives as an absence of ethnicity is actually a subsuming of ethnicity—a move that is not as innocent as the one he suggests. Finally, progressive leftist politics may indeed play some part in the critical reception of Asian American jazz, if it is perceived at all, by downplaying aesthetics and attention to actual performances in favor of promoting various political agendas, but this observation, as Shoemaker notes, does not speak to the contemporary moment.

I want to resituate the problematic predicament Shoemaker evokes by posing a question—"Is there such a thing as Asian American jazz?"—as central to my investigation of Asian American jazz artists, their relationship to jazz discourse, and the marginal position they occupy in the jazz world. Because my position is that there are many Asian American jazzes inflected in idiosyncratic ways by individual musicians, I attempt no definitive answer, tracing instead a broad outline around this question in order to contextualize the silencing of Asian American jazz musicians by critics, writers, and scholars. My primary interest is in how Asian American musicians negotiate the tensions brought to bear by a mute chorus of indifferent critics and a legacy of Asian American racialization that supports their disenfranchisement from dominant American culture.

Before I discuss specific musicians' strategies for dealing with this predicament, I want to briefly contemplate two formations: the discursive construction of a jazz canon and how certain stereotypes exclude Asian American musicians from participating as equals with other "jazz subjects."[7] My tracing highlights three important issues: recognition of Asian American jazz as protean and marked in different ways by different musicians; the fact that the heterogeneity of the Asian American jazz scene mirrors the diversity of the Asian American community itself; and the way in which the linking of culture, politics, community awareness, and individual creativity provides a rich and complex backdrop to Asian American jazz musicking.[8]

Black, White, and Beyond

Normative jazz discourse, both popular and scholarly, represents jazz as an indigenous American expressive musical form that emerged from the confluence of vernacular African American and Creole musicking and other social practices, as well as furtive traverses by black and white musicians across the color line.[9] This narrative emerged in early jazz writings such as those of the European conductor Ernst-Alexandre Ansermet, who in a 1919 review of early jazz clarinetist Sidney Bechet described "an ensemble of authentic musicians of [the] Negro race" whose jazz musicking had finally reached Europe "in its living reality."[10] One of the ways in which later writers such as Hugues Panassié, André Hodeir, and Gunther Schuller attenuated some of the racialized essentialist notions implicit in Ansermet's review was to declare that although jazz was "the music of the American Negro, its universality has long since been established."[11] Scott DeVeaux, writing more recently, resituates one of jazz's definitional boundaries within ethnicity, stating,

> Jazz is strongly identified with African-American culture, both in the narrow
> sense that it is expressive of, and uniquely rooted in, the experience of black

Americans. On the whole, [African American] ethnicity provides a core, a center of gravity for the narrative of jazz, and is one element that unites the several different kinds of narratives in use today.[12]

Accordingly, jazz evolved into an embodiment of a color-blind democracy in action cast in reductive, masculinist, black-white racial binarisms occluding, however, the lingering inequalities between racialized, gendered, and classed difference off the bandstand. As Gene Lees, a former *Down Beat* editor and jazz writer, wrote in the conclusion to his book *Cats of Any Color: Jazz, Black and White* (a title that underlines my assertion),

> One of two things is true. Either jazz has evolved into a major art form, and an international one, capable of exploring and inspiring the full range of human experience and emotion. Or it is a small, shriveled, crippled art useful only for the expression of the angers and resentments of an American minority. If the former is true, it is the greatest artistic gift of blacks to America, and America's greatest aesthetic gift to the world.[13]

Explicit in Lees's comment is the idea that jazz has moved from the African American community into other American communities and on to the rest of the world. He is explicitly not resigned to leaving jazz to "an American minority," a minority, moreover, that is clearly not Asian American. While there are notable exceptions (DeVeaux among them), dominant jazz discourse often assumes this particular shape whether a critic is arguing for a broader inclusion of white male musicians in various canonical projects or explicitly discussing race in jazz.[14] However, even as thoughtful a jazz scholar as DeVeaux is caught in this binary bind, writing that jazz "has been justly celebrated as an exemplar of racial harmony—a rare and privileged arena in which black and white compete and cooperate in an atmosphere of mutual respect, supported by a multiracial audience."[15] Asian Americans, positioned outside of this construction of "real jazz musicians"—as neither black nor white—remain silenced, and unheard, within jazz discourse.

In addition, the construction of Asian Americans as exoticized aliens, desired in certain constructions and moments but just as often vilified for their responses to the exclusionary practices of the dominant American culture, further reduces the chance that they will be heard as "real Americans," particularly when they are involved with a music that has been constructed within a racialized binary that excludes them.[16] Part of the "alienization" of Asian Americans has been the feminization or emasculation of Asian American males, who, stereotyped as either asexual eunuchs or passive males, are hardly the robust masculine figures jazz discourse produces in its valorization of the "kings" of jazz.[17] Jazz tropes such as the "cutting contest," "blowing hard," and the "battle of the bands" betray a masculinist slant that forecloses Asian American male participation.[18]

Asian American jazz musicians of both genders are further disallowed from being heard as "real" jazz artists due to the model minority stereotype, which positions Asian Americans as noncreative "nerdy" types, liminally caught between black and white America, serving as a racial "buffer zone" for whites while viewed suspiciously by other disenfranchised communities of color due to the false belief in the upward social and economic mobility of all Asian Americans.[19] The still active arguments in jazz scholarship concerned with the authenticity and ownership of jazz—even by those such as DeVeaux, who seek to disassemble the black-white binarism inherent in jazz historiography—cannot escape the inability to hear Asian American musicians as jazz musicians due in large part to the distance between stereotypes about black primitive genius, the white bohemian fascination with black emotional freedom, and Asian American exoticist stereotypes, foreign both to American cultural norms and the extroverted emotional display or passionate abandon required of "authentic" jazz musicianship. This remains true, as we have seen, even when scholars attempt to critique essentialist and outdated stereotypes within jazz. Jazz scholars have escaped explicit exclusionary gestures but implicitly support Asian American silencing through a distinct lack of interest in Asian American jazz musicians, due in part to the maintenance of a critical viewpoint I have been describing.[20]

There are a number of rhetorical strategies that Asian American jazz musicians have used to respond to this fundamental problem, but I am presently interested in mapping how the ideological frameworks for mainstream jazz discourse and the specific racialization of Asian Americans have worked in tandem to reduce Asian American jazz musicians' visibility as both "real Americans" and "real jazz musicians." Deborah Wong describes this perception:

> The long history of Other colors in jazz—that is, Asians and Latinos—is consistently refigured as absence. If the very idea of an Asian American jazz is new or strange, this demonstrates—successfully—the American hermeneutics of race as binary: either/or, Black/White. Any other kind of jazz simply isn't [authentic jazz].[21]

Needless to say, this conflation of "real American" and "real jazz musician" ignores the global reach of jazz musicking that produces, for example, South African, Filipino, and Norwegian jazz artists.[22] While critics and scholars may be quick to respond affirmatively to both the global appeal of jazz and the rise of non-American jazz artists, the bulk of jazz studies focuses on American artists (again, largely African American or European American males). To support this emphasis, the argument is made that American jazz musicians provided the primary innovations and creative energies to the music. While I am not arguing, for example, that Cantonese opera had more to do with jazz's "swing" rhythm than African American musical practices, the historical and social context for jazz musicking has long since reached beyond the New Orleans brothel, Chicago's "black and tan" clubs, or New York's Harlem district.[23] Nor am I arguing for the erasure of African American musicians or their importance to the creation and development of jazz; nor am I advocating that jazz now "belongs to everyone," having been sufficiently dislocated from the histories of oppression and creative contestation that African American musicking articulates. Rather, my point is that the long exclusion of Asian American histories in other areas is mirrored in the historiographical silence regarding Asian American jazz musicians, particularly in the present moment.[24]

"We've Been Here, Too"

The tenor saxophonist Francis Wong emphasizes the long historical trajectory of Asians and their involvement with "Western" popular musicking both within the United States and in Asia and the "Brown Pacific."[25] Pointing to historical and ethnographical work such as George Yoshida's *Reminiscing in Swingtime: Japanese Americans in American Popular Music*, Wong reminds us that Asians have been producing "Western" popular music since at least the beginning of the twentieth century. In an interview, Wong asked, rhetorically but provocatively, "What is the history of popular song?" In answering his own question, he revealed much that has been hidden in popular music discourse.

> [Let's suppose] that [the] American popular form was [not] limited to only music that was made in the continental United States. Let's say you included music that was made in Hawai'i, in those forms, and made, if not recorded, in places like Shanghai, Hong Kong, Japan. Because the great thing about Japan—a few years ago there was this Sony retrospective on swing music recorded in Japan but a lot of the musicians on those recordings were Japanese Americans. So what do you say about that? Is that American music? Should it be on the radar at all?[26]

Wong's answer provides a way of understanding the historical currents beneath contemporary Asian American jazz and a possible rationale for their discursive silencing. Because of racialized hiring practices in musicians' unions in the United States during the first half of the twentieth century, many Asian American musicians were forced to perform on Asia-bound cruise ships, and many of them found lucrative careers in Japan and China. Like black entertainers in America who found the life of an itinerant musician or dancer preferable to the miserable existence found at the bottom of the industrial labor force, many of these expatriate Japanese American musicians found the difficult life of an entertainer preferable to the manual labor jobs in agriculture, for instance, in which they would otherwise have been employed.[27] Doubtless, the promise of fame and fortune, though rarely achieved, also held out a greater incentive than an anonymous life of drudgery and hard labor that held scant opportunity for any real material gain. For these reasons, and because their careers occurred largely outside the United States, Asian American musicians (i.e., U.S. citizens) from this period have been effaced in jazz histories.[28]

In a similar fashion, Filipino musicians, because of their long contact with Spanish and American culture, were able to produce Western-style popular music and dance, becoming known as "the entertainers of the Far East" or, as Wong put it, "As part of the United States' territories, [Filipino bands] were the real territory bands!" Normative jazz discourse, however, has continually registered real jazz as an "indigenous" American cultural form.[29] Again, this "Americanization" of authentic jazz silences Asian jazz musicians. Wong elaborates on this theme.

> Sure, these records sold and had their influence in the world. [But] there's another way to look at it. Tatsu Aoki, my friend, the bass player from Chicago, he's the same age as I am. So he gets this question sometimes: "How come you play the blues or jazz? You're from Japan!" [His answer is] because it was forced down our throats during the occupation.[30]

Wong's anecdote about Aoki indicates the role of U.S. military power in the dissemination of American popular culture. Military and political leaders have long realized that the ideological underpinnings of cultural expression, particularly popular culture, serve to inculcate subordinated populations in dominant institutions and structures of feeling. Unfortunately, this is another topic that I can only point toward in this essay, but I cannot emphasize too strongly the value-laden labor popular culture is able to do as an adjunct to military strength and diplomatic pressure, a "forcing down the throats" of non-American populations of U.S. ideology or, at the very least, a show of American cultural domination.

More important to this essay, Aoki's response locates jazz musicking in Asia in a specific way. American popular music, of which jazz is but a part, is "forced down the throats" of occupied populations. The colonialist resonance is unavoidable, and yet, like the South Asian cricket player or the French-speaking Algerian, these coerced practices become "indigenized" or "made local" and begin to transform the once-foreign practice and the foreign introducer as well as the indigenous practitioner.[31] Aoki, instead of rejecting jazz, gains a cultural practice that he, in turn, makes "his own," transforming both the terms (jazz, Japanese musician) and the terms of engagement (occupation, cultural dominance). This admittedly disproportionate cultural reciprocity, then, becomes a new cultural expression, reflecting the histories on both sides of the exchange. I want to be careful here about raising the idea of hybridity with, as Paul Gilroy asserts, its presupposition of "two anterior purities," because I agree with him that "there isn't any anterior purity. . . . Cultural production is not like mixing cocktails."[32] As Gilroy indicates, cross- and transcultural contact and transformation happen in "already mixed" peoples, spaces, ideas, and dreams. The responsible task for the critic, then, is to follow the lines of contact, while acknowledging the futility of unraveling the fused object "back" into two single strands, to find the complex interweavings of histories, including power relations, cultural expressions (both as individual and collective expressions), and other social relationships without also reifying the moment of mixture (thus allowing the process to continue and enact other mixtures).

Again, in calling jazz an American music I do not want to elide the centrality of African American musical practice in forming jazz but to emphasize how jazz has been discursively shaped into a "multicultural" musicking that expressively renders American assimilation and integration. Jazz discourse allows for the transformative articulation of South American, Cuban, and European jazz musicians who are able to "indigenize" jazz musicking into legitimate jazz forms. "Latin jazz," "European jazz," and even "Gypsy jazz," while arguably problematic categories, are still considered legitimate forms of jazz, if somewhat subsidiary to a North American "mainstream." Yet a corresponding "Asian (or Asian American) jazz" has yet to emerge. As we will see, there are Asian American jazz musicians who are ambivalent or even antagonistic toward such a project. However, one only has to consider how differently Gonzalo Rubalcaba or Django Reinhardt is positioned in relation to Jon Jang or Mark Izu to comprehend this situation.[33] My point, however, is not to indicate how a musician becomes known or unknown, acclaimed or disparaged, as an *individual* but to point out how it is impossible for a musician to claim an Asian jazz background. An Asian jazz musician is always seen as "coming into" a jazz tradition from an external space.

Yet what is evident is that Asian Americans, even when they were displaced from the United States and normative jazz discourse, were nonetheless involved in jazz musicking as early as the 1920s.[34] In terms of indigenizing jazz in Asia, it is worthwhile to note that, because of expatriate Asian Americans' involvement in the popular music scenes of Shanghai and Tokyo, an inevitable blending of Chinese, Japanese, and African American music cultures occurred. The "jazzing" of Chinese and Japanese folk songs is one way to measure this cross-cultural traffic.[35] Francis Wong references recorded documentation of this movement (in fact, he has recorded "jazzed" versions of Chinese and Japanese folk songs).

> There is a record of that period [1910–46]; there were several record companies. Because, at least for Chinese [audiences], there were at least three record companies doing a variety of music—Chinese or Cantonese opera, dance music. You can find recordings of Chinese folk songs set to swing or Latin music. So it wasn't just covers of swing tunes, although I think there was some of that. But I think the most interesting stuff is Chinese folk songs or Chinese pop songs in popular dance rhythms, which is essentially [the] jazz of that period.[36]

This early historical record of the movement between jazz and Asian musical idioms has been sadly ignored by jazz historians and has implications that continue to resonate today.[37] If jazz musicking in its commodity form is partially invested in its marketability, then jazzed versions of Chinese folk songs may, in fact, be too marginal for large corporations to promote and distribute. Does the failure to promote jazz versions of Chinese folk songs further their marginality or would more active promotion actually induce greater sales? The issue I would like to raise here, though, is not whether such recordings would sell but whether there has been a predetermination made by the culture industry about the marketability of jazzed Chinese folk songs that underscores the critical silencing of Asian American jazz artists.[38]

The history of Asian American jazz musicking, as Francis Wong suggests, is the foregrounding of a series of "re-cognitions."

The idea [is] to recognize that the art form [jazz] is practiced in our communities and it has a relationship to the social historical development of our communities. . . . Fact: this art form was practiced in these communities. [The] fact is that it was practiced in these communities in the form that it was practiced in other communities—whether it's the drum and bugle corps or the swing band, the avant-garde free jazz, whatever. . . . It's just like saying, "We've been here, too." And recognizing that we've been here too actually strengthens the idea about how important this art form is.[39]

Wong testifies to the fact that Asians not only have a long trajectory of producing Western popular music but have done so in ways that resemble the methods of other producers of Western popular music. Asian Americans, in other words, produce music that would have the ability to move beyond the Little Tokyos, Saigons, and Seouls were it not for the cultural politics of the culture industry and the "perpetual foreigner" image that disbars Asians and Asian Americans from participating in "non-Asian" cultural endeavors and prevents audiences and critics from viewing Asian American artists and audiences as possessing the same acumen, talents, and taste formations as do members of other communities.[40] The representational legacy of "exotic" Asian Americans results in a widely held perspective that does not allow for Asian American participation in contemporary mainstream cultural production—in which jazz musicking has taken its "proper" place.[41]

Opening Chords

The time of the burgeoning Asian American jazz scene had much to do with the links between Asian American jazz, a nascent pan-Asian identity in progressive Asian American politics, and collaboration with, as well as inspiration from, African American models.[42] Asian American jazz came to its first maturation during the late 1970s and early 1980s when leftist political activism, pan-Asian American identity formation, and a growing sense of a specific Asian American aesthetic and musicking intersected in provocative ways. Similar to the ways in which some African American free jazz musicians connected black nationalist politics with their musicking, these young Asian Americans began to formulate a similar connection, explicitly drawing on black mentors and models. As the pianist Jon Jang relates in an interview with Nic Paget-Clarke,

Part of what Francis [Wong's] and my music is about is the collaboration of Asian Americans and African Americans. As musicians who work in the world of jazz, who speak the language of jazz, we honor that tradition. We respect African Americans. Our race relationships have been strong because as artists we've developed that respect and understanding.[43]

Jang's second recording, *Are You Chinese or Charlie Chan?* was released in 1984, and on the day of its release he performed with his ensemble at the Asian Pacific Student Union conference. As he related later, "We sold about sixty records at the conference. Students were asking me to autograph the record. There was a tremendous response."[44] Francis Wong expands on this theme.

I think it's the politics. The period in which we emerged, '84, '85, '86, and '87—when we finally formed Asian Improv [a record label owned by Wong and Jang], those were the years of Jesse Jackson's first run for president. It was the years of the Vincent Chin campaign. It was the years of the fight against the Simpson-Mazzoli bill. '82 through '88 were high-water marks for the Asian American consciousness movement. I think that was the context for the formation of an Asian American music label.[45]

Though Jang and Wong both designate 1988 as a pivotal transformative moment in their association with an explicitly political Asian American stance, the early years of their creative endeavors were also informed and shaped by an Asian American political agenda. I will deal with how this position changed for them shortly, but for the moment I would like to remain situated in the first years of the creation of what is now known as Asian American jazz.

Another band, United Front, included both Asian American and African American members, reflecting the trans- and cross-cultural perspective within Asian American jazz. Founded in 1980 by two African Americans, the alto saxophonist Lewis Jordan and trumpeter George Sams, the band soon added Japanese American bassist Mark Izu and, somewhat later, African American, Choctaw, and Japanese drummer Anthony Brown. Their political activism led them to perform at political rallies as well as jazz clubs. Another connection to progressive political struggles was their use of texts written by such African American thinkers as Frederick Douglass and Malcolm X in conjunction with their music. As Brown explained to Brian Auerbach in *Down Beat* magazine,

It wasn't a conscious choice to select political works, but it fits right in with the music. It just happened that poetry that is really strong and to the point is oft-times political. It makes sense considering the times we are in. Words go right to the heart of the matter, which is what we try to do with the music. So it fits right in.[46]

The debt to African American artists and activists can also be seen in the strategies these Asian American jazz artists utilized in order to distribute their creative musicking. Francis Wong states,

> RPM was the label for the band, United Front. It was the label they had created to be a vehicle for their recordings. The self-produced approach has a long tradition in creative music, in jazz—from Strata East that was run by African American musicians; to Debut Records, Max Roach and Charles Mingus's label; to Sun Ra who had his own label. . . . The idea is creating the work, producing it yourself, and trying to have some independence. We didn't really have a choice because we were excluded and disenfranchised. We needed to have something. It's not like Jon [Jang] could make a recording and then automatically have an outlet for his work. He had to create that vehicle for himself so we collaborated together to form [the record label] Asian Improv.[47]

This turn to self-determination in the face of disenfranchisement is not only found in African American models. But while African Americans have a long history of political and social struggle they can draw from in their continuing fight for social equity, in the existing national mythology Asian Americans, particularly after World War II, had quietly assimilated in the limited ways allowed them. There was little public consciousness about Asians who challenged racist stereotypes such as the labor organizers on Hawai'ian plantations and Californian agricultural concerns in the early 1900s, writers such as Carlos Bulosan and Sui Sin Far, and World War II era activists such as Fred Korematsu and Frank Emi.[48]

The Asian American political movement of the period heightened awareness of these earlier struggles, and Asian American jazz musicians began to weld their aesthetics (largely based in a free jazz idiom) to progressive leftist politics. Jang, in an article for *East Wind*, wrote about how acquiring a politicized aesthetic began to inform his musicking.

> Feeling the thrust of the [Asian American] Movement helped reshape "East Wind" and "Are You Chinese or Charlie Chan?" on a higher political and artistic level. The "Charlie Chan" piece was no longer a "light" sarcastic blues rap, but also expressed "heavier" elements revealed in the anti-Asian violence theme of Vincent Chin.[49]

He also notes the coalitional possibilities for the music as he recounts different moments at concerts where he felt it opened "people's vision and feelings for revolution more broadly," stating unequivocally that "these experiences have shown me how music can play an important role in building unity, not only for

Asians, but for all oppressed nationalities and working class people."[50] The late 1970s and early 1980s saw the political awakening of a sizable minority of Asian American youths, who were largely college educated and politicized during their college tenure. Asian American jazz musicians, taking a page from African American jazz artists, began to link their musicking to their political beliefs. While they began to generate small but dedicated followings, organizing jazz concerts (eventually establishing the Asian American Jazz Festival), forming distribution networks, applying successfully for arts grants and musical commissions, and pursuing other funding opportunities, their music, which was indebted to the free jazz aesthetic as performed and conceptualized by Archie Shepp and the Association for the Advancement of Creative Music (AACM), was not readily accessible to mainstream audiences.

They were also blending Asian instrumentation and, for some such as Mark Izu and Jon Jang, exploring traditional Asian musicking, including pedagogical methodologies and performance practices. This attention to traditional Asian musicking marked their seriousness and designated their music as more than merely an additive "exoticism," as was often the case in earlier attempts to blend Asian musicking with jazz.[51] It is this aesthetic and cultural turn that begins to signify the shift of Asian American jazz, away from the political awakening of its early formation for some artists.

Asian American Jazz Changes

The drummer Anthony Brown defines *Asian American jazz* as "jazz produced with an Asian American sensibility."[52] The questions begged, of course, are what is an Asian American sensibility and what differentiates it from other musical sensibilities? Brown, who holds a doctorate in ethnomusicology, elucidates what he means by listing the five criteria he uses to define *Asian American jazz*. Asian American jazz is "played by Asian Americans, reflecting the Asian American experience [and] involving traditional Asian instruments [as well as] traditional approaches to those instruments." Moreover, the use of traditional instruments and approaches must be "malleable or open enough to really start to incorporate and start to take on other influences—in this case, jazz."[53] He explains,

> I think that in the Asian American community we wanted to express our experience, not only through African American jazz—and it's primarily African American sensibilities because of the examples set by Charles Mingus, Rahsaan Roland

Kirk, Archie Shepp, the Art Ensemble of Chicago, these people who also had invested such a great deal of social justice, social activism, and spirituality in their music. And so they served as our original models. [But] when we started to create our own music . . . [it started] to take on another shape because of the inclusion of Asian instruments and sensibilities.

Asian American jazz, for Brown, is rooted in the struggles for Asian American empowerment and identity. Brown continues, highlighting the self-determined identification that the signifier "Asian American jazz" provides: "I don't like labels but I think it's a necessary evil. [And] if [the label Asian American jazz] is going to be used, then I want to be able to define it. I want to have something to say about its definition."

The saxophonist Fred Ho also sees his musicking and political beliefs as part of a unified aesthetic, merging creative work and political activity. Here is his summation of his artistic and political activities.

I have been a professional baritone saxophonist, composer / arranger, band leader, writer, activist and (more recently) producer in New York City for almost two decades. Some regard me as "successful" because I am able to make a living solely from my music. . . . I consider my "success" not in mainstream bourgeois terms of "fame and fortune" but in the fact that I have been able to unite my career, my art and my revolutionary politics.[54]

Ho has managed this in spite of—not because of—current jazz discourse and contemporary cultural industry practices. Moreover, it is his intention "to continue mixing African and Chinese influences in the musical score to be performed not by a standard Western European-style orchestra, but by my Afro Asian Music Ensemble."[55] Ho sees the importance of the label Asian American jazz, as it

may very well be cross-cultural, we in the "Asian American jazz" movement saw as the focus of our music / cultural work to help catalyze Asian American consciousness about our oppression and need to struggle for liberation. The very identity and term "Asian American" in our sobriquet "Asian American jazz or music" is a political signifier.[56]

Ho states in his article that the decision by Asian Improv Records (AIR) to produce more "accessible" works meant for him "tailing the familiar and conventional," which caused him to leave AIR.[57]

Ho's and Brown's insistence on a highly visible political stance, as well as the resilience of the label Asian American jazz, may be increasingly anachronistic, however. In response to the political and social contexts in which Asian American jazz often enunciates itself, Francis Wong declares,

> The problem with this whole political thing—which I don't like—is that somehow it's like we're choosing [that] the primary aspect [of our music] is to express our political [views]. But it's not. I'm really into the music. . . . Now I'm also a political person. I've been through the 1960s, so I'm a serious person. . . . I care about what happens in the world. So a lot of it is like truth comes from the music and I express my truth.[58]

Wong's reluctance to place his musicking in an explicitly politicized space may militate against a visible social impact for it. On the other hand, he may be simply attempting to foreclose a "ghettoization" of his musicking, that is, if his recordings are labeled Asian American jazz the potential to reach a wider jazz audience remains minimal given the situation I have been describing. I also believe Wong wants his musicking to represent more than his political views and his creative work to speak in the broadly expressive ways other musicians are afforded. In fact, perhaps due to an interest in widening the appeal of his musicking, Wong emphasized how diverse the "Asian American experience" can be, declaring,

> A lot of times, interviewers want to know the stylistic thing, how to put the music in a bag so that people will buy it. But how we want to express ourselves in our own context in our own vehicle is more about how we want to bring our culture to people in our music. We want to bring a sense of the complexities and subtleties and contradictions of that culture. By saying our culture is not Chinese culture, it's the culture that we've come up with. It's a very specific set of experiences.[59]

In fact, Wong finds this specificity of expression to be aligned with an African American jazz tradition.

> How can I make the saxophone play in my image? Part of it is getting [knowledge] from the masters—certain traditions and sounds. But also, with that sense of control or mastery of the instrument, be able to have come out what's inside of me. Relating that to some sense of self-empowerment with the instrument.
>
> This is one of the basic messages of the African American masters. Be yourself. Looking at that whole tradition, every player that has come along to develop his individual sound has had to change the instrument or the way the instrument is played in order to be "themself" with it.[60]

Wong's stance addresses the stereotyping of Asian Americans as noncreative types with a "natural" affinity for technological and / or scientific occupations—a view that, as I have mentioned, forecloses the possibility of recognizable cultural production from Asian Americans. Wong addressed this, admitting,

> Another thing that I'm aware of is that not too many people have seen a Chinese American play the saxophone, or play anything besides classical music. . . . I've gone on in situations where people don't think Asian Americans can play this music, or any music. . . . Still, in this society today, when I walk out into a room of white people, or whoever, they haven't heard very much from us as Asian Americans. They haven't seen us do very many things.[61]

This "blindness" to—or what I am calling "silencing" of—Asian Americans in the cultural sphere maintained by scholarly elision and critical reiteration of a line of "great men of jazz" produces public interest in Asian American culture that remains voyeuristically orientalist, a scopophilia that reproduces exoticist fantasy. Being positioned as an exotic object is always the danger of being among the first of a marginalized group to break new ground in mainstream arenas, and Wong and his peers have been willing to traverse uncomfortable new spaces for Asian American artists. However, as I have been arguing, if normalizing Asian American artistic involvement in jazz musicking is to have any value beyond an insipid color-blind democracy in action, not only do ideas about real jazz musicians need to change but ideas about Asian Americans need to undergo a radical rethinking. This is not just a cultural claim but also a political one that registers in the ways Asian American jazz musicians have continued to make claims for artistic legitimacy.

Moreover, there is a linkage between spirituality and politics that Francis Wong, for one, perceives as missing in contemporary political movements. He asserts,

> I think that part of the trend of the twentieth century has been the separation of politics and spirituality. Hence you could have political music that lacks spiritual development. You've had politics in the twentieth century—not just in the twentieth century—but certainly in our time there's plenty of politics from the left and the right that lacks spiritual depth.[62]

The lack of spiritual depth in political movements Wong cites is indicative of a chasm between various progressive political and social agendas. Jon Jang is currently a Baptist Christian and stands in stark contrast to the Leninist-Maoist orientation of Fred Ho, for instance, marking a break not just politically but philosophically. Additionally, Jang sees his more normative Christian practice as another correspondence with African American culture, noting the progressive political, as well as spiritual, role African American churches have performed throughout history.[63]

More important, Jang and Wong state that after the signing of H.R. 442 (the Civil Rights Act of 1988, which allowed for reparations for the internment of Japanese Americans during World War II), the Asian American movement

> went in one direction, and . . . we founded Asian Improv Arts, a non-profit arts organization in partnership with a non-profit experimental theater company Life on the Water. Life on the Water wasn't Asian but it was experimental and they were very open to working with us and providing resources.[64]

Jang's admission not only indicates his divergence from explicitly politicized work but also how collaboration with non-Asian organizations signaled a growing willingness to move outside strict definitions of what it means to be an Asian American jazz artist. While all Asian American jazz artists collaborate across various racial, ethnic, and national lines, these are usually creative collaborations. Financial "collaborations" engender a different set of concerns, further troubling the demarcation of a space for Asian American jazz.

Similarly, while many of these early Asian American jazz musicians emerged from an avant-garde background, performing and composing free jazz, the ways in which they utilized that background subsequent to the 1980s have seen some important divisions in their various aesthetic approaches. Wong continues to perform in a free jazz idiom, his ability to weld Asian folk songs in this context rooted in a consistent search for an expression of the self and his belief in music's ability to use spiritual means toward political ends. Anthony Brown, while making no public statements about his religious or spiritual beliefs, has continued to look to the now-canonical works of Duke Ellington, Thelonious Monk, and, in a current project for which he has received a Guggenheim award, George Gershwin, striking a middle ground between the highly politicized jazz musicking of Fred Ho and the emphasis on self-expression that Francis Wong and Jon Jang advocate.

Still, Wong has admitted elsewhere that Asian American jazz and politics were born in a complex relationship. He recalls,

> We were trying to be active with our music and trying to identify with the Asian American consciousness movement. It was a very positive period. If it

wasn't for that time we would not have been moved to create a lot of the work in the context that we did, with the content and substance that it had. We wouldn't have been moved to create an organization or vehicle if it wasn't for that political context.[65]

But the contemporary political landscape has changed, and so have his "tactics." He explains that he is now

trying to deal with Chinese American spirituality and how it relates to social action. That's the direction we've gone in the '90s. The revelations about the eastern bloc and the Tiananmen massacre did create a crisis of meaning among people who were trying to make changes in the world. A need to look at other ways of thinking about things. How do you relate as an individual, and how you relate to humanity, has a lot to do with the developments of the work we've been creating since 1992.[66]

Jon Jang concurs, positing that an increased awareness of the global nature of Asian communities, particularly the Chinese diaspora, attenuates some of the purpose of naming a political movement Asian American. He admits that he has shifted from a political focus to a cultural one, insisting that the link between politics and music has "always felt uncomfortable for me."[67]

As I hope is clear, there are definite clefts within this group of "first-wave" Asian American jazz musicians. Normative political activity continues as a focus for some artists while for others spiritual concerns have superseded more prosaic agendas. What, exactly, might these artists say about Asian American identity and the growing fragmentation within the community sensed by Asian American social activists? Is it, as Anthony Brown asserted to me, that while "Asian American cohesion is a myth," it continues to retain political value in the face of a dominant culture that continues, as it does within jazz discourse, to marginalize Asian Americans?

For some, aesthetics and politics have been delinked, as, for instance, when Francis Wong continues to perform free jazz yet offers to transcend political statements through an aesthetic agenda of personal expression or when Anthony Brown seeks to recontextualize canonical works in a political project of self-determination and self-definition. In a brief, and rare, interview in a 2003 *Down Beat* column, Anthony Brown was one of three artists asked who they would choose if they were able to schedule artists for the new Carnegie Hall facility, Zankel Hall.[68] His response addresses the syncretic approach he champions in his self-definition of Asian American jazz.

I'd like to see Carnegie Hall continue its legacy by programming classic music of all genres as well as presenting contemporary expressions of those traditions. . . . I received a Guggenheim Fellowship this year to recompose [George Gershwin's] *Rhapsody in Blue* for a 21-piece intercultural, intergenerational and intergender ensemble, combining Asian instruments and sensibilities with a jazz orchestra. I would love to present this new version reflecting 21st century realities in the U.S. in juxtaposition with a performance of the original version orchestrated by Ferde Grofe for its premier in 1924 by Paul Whiteman's orchestra.[69]

Brown, in his wish to reflect "21st century realities," seeks to root "contemporary expressions" within "classic traditions." No longer can one ascertain a given Asian American musician's political beliefs simply by determining which aesthetic camp his or her musicking embraces. In other words, free jazz no longer signifies explicit political activism, nor does the performance of canonical works reveal a reactionary position.[70] But what would Brown's juxtaposition mean for my question: "What is Asian American jazz?"

One way of mapping Brown's wished-for juxtaposition is by noting how critical discourse about jazz authenticity, particularly in its assumptive racialized binarism, is linked to the attempt to mark out a space for jazz's status as an art object rather than folk art, or, worse, a mass cultural commodity, by obscuring the relationship between museum ("autonomous" art) and market (commercial) cultures. As jazz writers began to emphasize jazz musicians' use of complex thematic and harmonic materials, older ideas about primitivist black creation receded before the perception of the jazz musicians as artists involved in projects with markedly modernist tendencies, particularly since the rise of bebop in the late 1940s.[71]

While Brown's juxtaposition seeks to mediate how the American cultural landscape has been transformed by "intercultural, intergenerational and intergender [music] ensembles," I mean to note again how normative jazz discourse impacts Asian American silencing by instantiating a high-low cultural divide—with jazz inhabiting a liminal status, mixing elements of the museum and the market—that reinforces racialized hierarchies of taste even while arguing for jazz as color-blind democracy in action. To highlight how this operates, I want to turn to the musicking of an Asian American fusion band, Hiroshima, as it further complicates notions of real jazz as well as Asian American jazz. As a telling critical aporia, Bill Shoemaker never mentions this most successful of Asian American jazz bands.[72]

Before I turn to Hiroshima, however, I want to note how this shift from the explicitly political to the spiritual and cultural for some of these now elder statesmen of Asian American jazz points to the growing fragmentation of an Asian American political project. With a number of immigrant populations unfamiliar with the Asian American struggles of the 1960s and 1970s, as well as a younger generation of Asian Americans that faces a different set of negotiations with the dominant culture, the cultural resonance of a free jazz aesthetic coupled with a highly politicized "identity politics" may no longer be as powerful (in many ways, hip hop artists have inherited much of the cultural capital and progressive political cachet once held by free jazz musicians). There is also a growing sense, as Jang notes, of the global nature of an Asian community and diaspora(s). Moreover, an emergent "hapa" (mixed race) consciousness is supplementing, or even replacing, older categories of ethnic identity internal to the broader Asian American community.

Hiroshima: Between Aesthetics and Politics

While the Asian American jazz artists I have profiled share a common political history (even if it is articulated in quite different ways today), the most successful Asian American musicians in terms of visibility and commercial success—though ignored by critics and scholars—are the members of the fusion group Hiroshima. I would like to take the time to consider Hiroshima at some length, as it is the most successful Asian American musical group, and I hope to broker its elision both in jazz studies and by Asian American scholars. Hiroshima's less trenchant appeal to Asian American issues does not mean its members are silent about political and cultural issues relevant to the Asian American community. Their albums have no less political resonance—their name speaks to the atomic bombing in World War II and the intertwined historical legacy shared by the United States and Japan—and one must consider the titles of their albums and compositions, the concerns they express in interviews regarding the political and social world around them, and their own reflexivity about their representative role, which is wider, perhaps, than that of any of the other artists in this essay.[73]

More important, it speaks volumes that Hiroshima is the only high-profile Asian American band built around a specifically Asian American aesthetic and yet it has never been the subject of serious and sustained critical investigation. For instance, Hiroshima's incorporation of Japanese koto, taiko, and shakuhachi as integral components of its "sound" is often ignored. Critics, when they mention the group at all, tend to focus on its status as a "fusion band" rather than taking seriously, for example, the virtuosity of kotoist June Kuramoto. Yet, while Hiroshima's commercial success overshadows the struggle for recognition and economic survival of countless other Asian American artists, it remains glaringly absent in discussions of Asian American aesthetics and cultural visibility.[74]

I believe there are reasons for this silence that reach beyond the marginalization experienced by other Asian American jazz artists. Chief among them is Hiroshima's designation as a fusion band or, worse, a "smooth jazz" or "world music" band. These genres all face critical devaluation, as they are seen as too compliant with bourgeois concerns to resonate with progressive political activity not only by critics and scholars (many of whom do not worry about a musician's political views) but by other jazz musicians, particularly those profiled above, who perform free or avant-garde jazz.[75] Jang admits that when he was studying at the Oberlin Conservatory, other Asian Americans "valorized Hiroshima, but the music didn't speak to me. It didn't have the power or spirituality [I was seeking]."[76] Is Hiroshima merely processing (multi)cultural eclecticism for non-Asian consumption? Or is there something behind the band's willingness to blend "contemporary root music, mystical Eastern exotica and melodically rich smooth jazz," as its Web site declares?[77] Is it musical exploration or cultural exploitation? As its Web site also affirms, Hiroshima has a "larger commitment to global unity on the cusp of the new millennium." Can Hiroshima, then, be more than an exoticized attempt to reach mass audiences with a self-conscious agenda that blends commercial interests, political awareness, and transcultural musicking?

Before discerning whether or not Hiroshima's aesthetics can be connected to a progressive social agenda, I would like to touch on how the devaluing of fusion bands and musicians has its roots in otherwise antithetical soils. Mainstream critical jazz discourse views any musicking that is performed without acoustic instrumentation, a "swing" rhythmic sense, and an obvious resonance with blues musicking as illegitimate, inauthentic, and simply "not jazz." While free jazz artists face some of these same critical barbs from mainstream critics (they neither swing nor proffer many blues riffs in their performances, to their detriment according to dominant jazz discourse), free jazz advocates' criticism of fusion bands rests on more subtle—and elitist—stratagems. The alignment of free or avant-garde jazz with progressive politics, as well as an aesthetic approach more closely mirroring the art music world (although much of what passes for "new" in free jazz even today positions it firmly in the avant-garde scenes of the 1950s and 1960s), allows free jazz apologists to decry fusion's willing, even eager, embrace of popular musicking's rhythms, electronic in-strumentation, and production techniques. For this reason, Hiroshima, for all the Asian sensibilities it brings to its musicking, fails to achieve the same critical assessment that Jon Jang received for his "Two Flowers on a Stem."

Might some of the criticisms stem from a perception of Dan Kuramoto's assertion—that Asian American culture is "between black and white" instead of a dynamic culture in its own right that can be envisioned as equal to African American and European American culture—as politically naive or even dan-gerously complaisant with the status quo? Seen in this light, Dan Kuramoto's conception of Asian Americans' positioning implies a passive acceptance that is highly problematic. Dan Kuramoto has publicly expressed how he sees Asian American culture as being "between black and white," the title of Hiroshima's 1999 Windham Hill recording.

> We create musically a cross-commentary about a multitude of cultures that comes from our backgrounds as Asian Americans growing up in a racially diverse Amer-ica. The album title grew from the idea that as people of Japanese heritage, we are ethnically in the middle of black and white, drawing from the traditions of both races yet also creating an identity that is unique to our heritage.[78]

But what does he mean when he accepts the "in the middle of black and white" racial paradigm? What can he mean by the assertion that Japanese Americans "are drawing from the traditions of both [black and white] races"? Is he speaking of Japan or the Asian and U.S. cultural mixture or is he position-ing black and white as subordinate and dominant cultural positions? His state-ment, then, would seem to position Hiroshima's music in a racialized liminal space, quietly celebratory but problematic.

Thought of in another way, however, this positioning allows Kuramoto to remain outside of partisan struggles over authenticity. As a hybrid subject, Kuramoto's claim about how Hiroshima's fusion is "bridging cultures and music . . . with our message of peace and multiculturalism"[79] acts as a way of destabilizing the black-white binarism of not only jazz criticism but also public discourse about American racial politics. In this light, Kuramoto's elaboration positions Asian American culture and identity as disturbing the crudely con-ceived racialized dialectic between black and white. He continues,

> *Between Black and White* is not only a natural reflection about being in the middle, it's also a perfect metaphor for the subtleties of grays in everyday life, moderation and balance summed up in the Yin and Yang ideas of Eastern philosophy.[80]

Hiroshima's ability to create music that appeals to mainstream audiences yet promotes values such as "peace and multiculturalism" may seem contradictory to the avant-gardists profiled earlier in this piece. Jang's comment about the group's music lacking "power and spirituality" speaks to this antagonism. Yet, as a counterexample of the easy conflation of commercial success and political acquiescence to dominant values, June Kuramoto insists that

> there were times when, in all honesty, you might think of quitting, when times get hard, the business gets hard, whatever the situation, and yet [well-known jazz artists such as the pianist Chick Corea] told us we can't quit. We owe it to our community, our people, our culture, ourselves and for everyone, to continue . . . which is pretty heavy.[81]

Hiroshima's sense of connection to its community also drives a strong social awareness, and Dan Kuramoto emphasized this in the same interview with Baldwin Smith.

> We did the Isley Brothers—we did "Caravan of Love" because those are the messages that people have forgotten. . . . It is a song about brotherhood. It's the kind of thing that June talked about growing up with, like Marvin Gaye and people like that, whose message was, we need to bring people together. With 9 / 11 and the madness of war that's going on, we thought it was really important to make that statement. And so that's why we went back and tried to find the songs that did it for us and that song of brotherhood to us is really key.[82]

Why is Francis Wong's desire to seek a spiritual connection to a progressive political agenda received so differently than Dan Kuramoto's similar ambitions? Does commercial success necessarily compromise artistic and political integrity? While I would be extremely wary of drawing a direct correlation between commercial success and the lack of a progressive social vision, it is almost a truism in the aesthetic discourses surrounding popular culture that to be too popular is to be politically or spiritually compromised. The "underground," as opposed to the "top of the charts," serves as a site of authenticity and / or radical political orientation for some, and to sell well is to sell out.[83] However, I think we should take seriously Dan Kuramoto's assertion that he is affected by social situations and seeks to address them in his musicking. As he told an interviewer, Paula Edelstein,

> I'm also very much influenced by the times and the people around me. On [Hiroshima's newest release] *The Bridge*, the song "Manzanar" (which I co-wrote

with June [Kuramoto]) was influenced by the whole epoch of World War II and all the Japanese-Americans being imprisoned for no reason. The direct inspiration was a story my mother told me about how strange it was to be an American one day, and then to be treated like an enemy the next. To be forcibly evacuated to a desolate place in the desert, to live behind barbed wire—and to hear the mournful wind at night. The song starts with me trying to replicate the sound of that wind on my shakuhachi, and then weaves the sound of the koto into those nights.[84]

Here he not only indicates a politicized aesthetic but addresses Brown's definitional criteria for "Asian American jazz," namely, Asian American musicians using Asian instrumentation in "traditional yet malleable" ways—clearly demonstrated by June Kuramoto's classical koto pedigree coupled with her willingness to perform in a modern fusion band—and the reflection of Asian American sensibilities as evidenced by Dan Kuramoto's statements. Moreover, Hiroshima's album, *LA* (Qwest, 1994), was released in the hopes of utilizing music to "heal the wounds and try to bridge peoples' differences" after the so-called Los Angeles riots.[85] The song "One World," uses a blend of genres (jazz, rhythm and blues, rock, Latin, and traditional Japanese music) in order to signify the unification of various ethnic groups, ironically positing the music industry's racialized genre schematic against itself. Hiroshima's positioning of traditional Asian musicking not as a static repertoire of gestures but as a dynamic source of soundings interacting with jazz and rhythm and blues (R&B) elements integrates seemingly disparate musical elements into a unifying vision. Dan Kuramoto affirms this aesthetic rationale, insisting,

> Some people say we're different, we're weird. Record labels have told us for 25 years we don't fit in anywhere, necessarily. There's no bin in the record store that makes sense for us. We're jazz, but we're not. We are world music, but we're not. We're rock, but we're not. We're R&B, but we're not. If you grow up on the Pacific coast, you get everything. If you grow up in Los Angeles, you're exposed to everything all the time. We took our background as Japanese Americans and we started to bring things together, and it's always a journey.[86]

Or, as he explains the choice of the photograph that graces the cover of the band's latest release, *The Bridge* (Heads Up, 2003),

> That's why the CD cover is a picture of the First Street Bridge in Los Angeles[; it] connects East Los Angeles, which is the main immigrant community, with downtown, where everybody goes to work. My dad used to drive that every day when he went to his gas station. I have all these cultures in me that created the music that we do.[87]

The recognition of Asian American social realities is the same for the members of Hiroshima as it is for the other jazz artists profiled here (Brown, Ho, Izu, Jang, and Wong), but their status as members of a fusion band and their enormous commercial success preclude them from a serious engagement by critics and scholars. This silencing is, in some significant ways, detrimental to the larger project of "making audible" the musicking of Asian American jazz artists. For instance, the high-profile engagements (e.g., the Playboy Jazz Festival) Hiroshima is able to acquire provide a much higher plateau from which to evaluate Asian American musicking in general, but the band's "exceptionalism," while speaking to Asian American cultural disenfranchisement writ large, is undermined by critical neglect or dismissal. Hiroshima, in many ways, can provide an entry point for subsequent Asian American artists to "become audible," yet the critical focus on Asian American jazz musicians whose aesthetic choices tend toward either the avant-garde or a somewhat exoticized "mainstream" places restrictions on the public perception of Asian American jazz musicking. Audiences that think of Asian American jazz and avant-garde as coeval and not simply one element in a large spectrum of jazz musicking by Asian Americans limit Asian American creativity (again note Bill Shoemaker's focus on free jazz musicians).

Finally, Hiroshima challenges racialized conceptions of music genres by utilizing a syncretic approach to its musicking. The band members' focus on synthesizing or fusing various types of music in order to present "another place" (the title of their 1985 Epic recording) articulates a fundamental shift in the racial politics at the heart of critical jazz discourse. As there is no space for Asian American jazz artists in normative terms, the search for another place takes on not a utopic sensibility but rather an acknowledgment of the need to move "beyond black and white," blurring the definitions that support and instantiate a black-white binarism inherent in such an articulation and "graying" the space between black and white. This graying—or blurring—recognizes the difference in terms of both power relationships, heard in the highlighting of the koto alongside the saxophone, as well as the fact that Hiroshima has "no bin of its own" in retail record stores.

Hiroshima ably sifts through a wide spectrum of musical traditions while pushing them toward new soundings. Insisting on performing multicultural fusion, Hiroshima opens the door to the possibilities such a cross- and transcultural movement has for sound artists today and in the future. It performs, through the use of a diverse array of Asian instrumentation, a syncretic blend of Asian, Latin, and African American musicking, and a willingness to risk artistic criticism and even critical alienation in the arguably more populist desire to reach a broad audience.

The band's success also points to the broad affective resonance its particular blend of Asian and "American" musicking evokes, which more explicitly political Asian American musicians choose to ignore or denigrate. Jon Jang's cross-cultural musicking, for all its high cultural cachet (as evidenced by arts council commissions and the like), fails to resonate with a broad public. This "failure" is read as an asset for Jang by many critics and scholars, who see Hiroshima's commercial success as a liability.[88] The public may be the better judge in terms of sensing the promise of a sounding out of another place beyond the black-white racial binary, as well as recognizing that difference and respect need not be mutually exclusive.

Conclusion: The Many Faces of Asian American Jazz

The encounter between Asian American jazz musicians and normative critical discourse (popular and scholarly) ranges, as we have seen, from Brown's pro-active engagements with self-definition to Wong's active efforts to position his cultural work within a broader framework than the label "Asian American jazz" might indicate in the present social and cultural atmosphere. Ho, on the other hand, actively embraces "an Afro Asian new American multicultural music,"[89] seeking not to privilege any racialized notion of musical aesthetics but formulating an egalitarian approach through a broad dialectic between each signifier in his self-described multicultural music. Hiroshima fuses contemporary rhythms with ancient instruments, respectful of tradition yet energizing them with modern production techniques and aesthetic sensibilities.

While I have been concentrating on the "first wave" of Asian American jazz artists, artists such as Toshiko Akiyoshi have been integrating Asian musicking with jazz for quite some time. Her first RCA releases in the early 1970s preceded those of Wong, Ho, and Brown in her use of the Japanese shakuhachi, Noh singing, and other Asian instrumentation and musical practices. Akiyoshi's 2001 BMG recording, *Monopoly Game*, featured Miya Masaoka on koto, linking the two generations of musicians.[90]

A number of young musicians, such as the pianist Vijay Iyer, who has produced avant-garde works that utilize South Asian musicking as well as "new music" aesthetics, and the Filipina drummer Susie Ibarra, who is actively involved in improvised "new music" groups, have also emerged, contesting, in some ways, the older generation's ideas about the relationship between Asian

Americans and jazz. On her album *Songbird Suite* (2002), Ibarra highlights the ways in which "tradition" and "modernity" merge in nonoppositional ways with her use of non-Western drums alongside Ikue Mori's computer manipulations. Iyer's recordings, particularly *Blood Sutra* (2003) and *In What Language?* (2003), display a sensitivity to both global routes and personal roots, questioning the displacement of either in any effort to locate a particular musician's aesthetic and political concerns. The pianist and keyboardist Hiromi Uehara, born in Japan but currently based in the United States, performs an eclectic program of self-penned compositions ranging from stride piano to fusion, straight ahead jazz, and experimental musicking. Her eclecticism is indicative of young artists whose musical visions correspond to new ways of representing and expressing contemporary Asian American positionalities.

The spectrum of attitudes toward Asian American jazz that these artists voice across generations, aesthetics, and political perspectives indicates the expansive range of ideas that reflect and express the wide differentiation within the space demarcated Asian America. As Fred Ho asserts, "The failure of the discussion of race in jazz stems from an ideological conservatism that only sees color and race, one that does not really understand that the very concept of America is one of hybridity and multiple identities."[91] Ho's assertion underlines my nondefinitive answer to the question, "Is there such a thing as Asian American jazz?" Obviously, the movement involved in Asian American jazz across cultural and ethnic lines is more complex and multivalent than either unalloyed celebration of ethnic fraternalism or pessimistic perspectives about the status of Asian Americans allow.

With the presentation of Anthony Brown's music in one of the concerts presented under the 2001 San Francisco Jazz Festival banner, the sensibilities of Asian American jazz musicians may be gaining wider acceptance. If the applause at the end of Brown's set is any indication, there is an audience ready to recognize the efforts of Asian American jazz artists, even if normal circuits of music production and distribution seem deaf to Asian American jazz.[92]

Asian American jazz enunciates the tenuous relationships both back in time and space toward former patterns of immigration and forward in time to as yet unrealized social and political equalities yet embedded in present relationships of unequal power and normative racialized conceptions of jazz musicking, Americanness, and Asianness. As the musicking—however named— performed by Anthony Brown, Francis Wong, the members of Hiroshima, and other Asian American jazz musicians attests (whether publicly identifying with the moniker or not), the movement toward acceptance of their art is not only the recognition of their aesthetic value but also an indication of a broader recognition of the unique qualities that the cultural work of Asian Americans possesses due to their distinctive position in American cultural and political life. Moreover, as their different views about the label Asian American jazz imply, the "Asian American experience" is a highly contested space that inhabits the politically salient efforts to formulate a pan-Asian identity. In other words, there is no single answer to the question "Is there such a thing as "Asian American jazz"? as Asian American jazz musicians will contradict any strict definitional guidelines, especially through racial or ethnically determined parameters.

As David Palumbo-Liu attests,

> Modern Asian America should be read within a context of multiple subjectivities whose multiplicity can be depathologized through a close and critical reading of Asian, American, and Asian / American history, and that the unity presumed to be enjoyed by "America" is in fact better read as a set of adjustments and reformations that disclose the fact that America is always in a process itself. And a large part of this process in the twentieth century has particularly involved Asian America.[93]

In looking at Asian American jazz, one encounters the same multiple subjectivities that Palumbo-Liu describes while also engaging the historical aporia that Asian American jazz inhabits. Asian American jazz has only operated as such since the 1970s, when Mark Izu, Francis Wong, Fred Ho, and Jon Jang, among others, began to coalesce around their interest in jazz—particularly free jazz—and their political awakenings regarding an Asian American cultural heritage. Asian American jazz, especially as it moves throughout the globe, anticipates as well as generates the tensions that lie between pan-Asian sensibilities and the heterogeneous makeup of Asian America by sounding out various grapplings within that tension. By positioning their musicking in a jazz context, Asian American artists not only transform jazz but also introduce a new way of musicking that addresses Asian American issues and perspectives. In doing so, Asian American jazz musicking "makes audible" the silencing that has attempted to keep Asian American jazz musicians mute.

Notes

1 A clip of her appearance can be seen in a film documentary about Akiyoshi entitled *Jazz Is My Native Language* (dir. Renée Cho, Counterpoint, 1983).

2 There have been brief mentions of Asian American jazz artists in mainstream popular jazz magazines. I will quote later from a *Down Beat* article about the jazz band United Front. There have also been a handful of recording and concert reviews, but there have been no feature articles, nor has there been a cover story on an Asian American musician or band in any major jazz publication.

   See, for instance, Adam Shatz's article, "New Seekers in Jazz Look to the East," where, after quoting a dour comment by the South Asian American pianist Vijay Iyer to the effect that the music industry "just doesn't know how to shop around black music played by someone like me," he optimistically predicts that as "the Asian-American jazz scene blossoms, it could well become as hard to ignore as today's Asian-American literary renaissance." Unfortunately, the events of the years since his prediction have not borne this out.

3 Shoemaker, "East Meets Left," 83.

4 Unfortunately, I am also leaving out a large number of Asian American jazz artists, including, but certainly not limited to, the drummer Akira Tana; bassist Steven Hashimoto; pianists Flip Nunez and Glenn Horiuchi; saxophonists Rudresh Mahanthappa, Melecio Magdaluyo, and Hafez Modirzadeh; trumpeter John Worley; and violinist Jason Hwang. This essay focuses on Asian American musicians located primarily on the West Coast of the United States. There is a vibrant Asian American jazz scene in Chicago, for instance, as well as Asian American jazz musicians throughout the United States, who I am unable to give more attention here.

5 Shoemaker, "East Meets Left," 83. Shoemaker also notes that in 2001 Asian American jazz musicians were absent from a three-day symposium sponsored by San Francisco Jazz entitled "Jazz and Race: Black, White, and Beyond." I attended on all three days and was also distressed to note the absence of any discussion of the "beyond" category. One participant, Angela Davis, attempted to address Latin and female jazz artists, but in each instance her comments received no response from the other participants.

6 Ibid., 87.

7 *Canon* in jazz discourse refers to a core repertoire reflecting as well as obscuring the critical positionality and biases of its builders, similar to other critical discourses. Jazz critics and scholars debate various inclusions and exclusions to this core repertoire, but it can be loosely defined here as the popular songs of Broadway shows and Tin Pan Alley (also known as "jazz standards"), as well as the compositions of central jazz figures such as Edward Kennedy "Duke" Ellington (notably a majority of these artists date from the swing era of jazz, ca. 1930–45). A sizable minority of critics would also include popular music composers who have

arguably continued the songwriting traditions of Tin Pan Alley in contemporary terms, such as Henry Mancini and Burt Bacharach. Still others might include non-U.S. songwriters such as the bossa nova artist Antonio Carlos Jobim. As one can readily see from this short list, the jazz canon, like its literary brethren, is an elusive creation.

8 *Musicking* is a term I borrow from Christopher Small, who defined his neologism as a way of indicating how music is an activity (composition, performance, and audience participation in terms of listening and critical analysis) as opposed to its reification, especially in terms of notation and recorded objects (compact discs, cassette tapes, etc.). See his *Musicking*.

9 Clive Davis, describing jazz's inclusion at Lincoln Center, pronounced it "an indigenous classical music" ("Classical Jazz," 60). See also Sales, *Jazz*; and Murray, *Stomping the Blues*, for similar assignations that support the idea that jazz is an "indigenous" American (and, for Murray, African American) music capable of sharing the "art space" of the European concert music tradition.

10 Ansermet, "Bechet and Jazz Visit Europe, 1919," 742. Pointedly, Ansermet made no mention of the fact that Bechet was a "Creole of color," a racialized position that also complicates a simple black and white binary.

11 Hodeir, *Jazz*, 241. André Hodeir's seminal text laid the foundation for normative jazz historiography, and many of his ideas (e.g., his analysis of jazz through "objective" musicological methodology) became the basis for "modern" jazz criticism. Hugues Panassié's *The Real Jazz*, as its title suggests, sought to demarcate "real jazz" and built its argument through a line of "great men of jazz." Gunther Schuller's *Early Jazz* and *The Swing Era* are both notable for bringing a stringent musicological analysis to argue for jazz's status as a music tradition on a par with European concert music. While laudable, Schuller's reliance on a series of great men (all African or European Americans) and his teleological bias toward jazz history, make his contributions problematic. Moreover, he has been criticized for wielding musicological tools forged in analyses of European concert music that are insufficient for appraising African American music.

12 DeVeaux, "Constructing the Jazz Tradition," 529, emphasis mine.

13 Lees, *Cats of Any Color*, 246.

14 See Richard Sudhalter's *Lost Chords* for an example of a writer arguing for white male inclusion in histories of early jazz formation. Sudhalter struggles to demarcate a space for early white jazz musicians, countering what he calls "the black canon" (xvii). His misguided attempts to carve out such a space reveal the contentious field called jazz history.

Race has been a major theme throughout the history of jazz with writers commenting on its racial dynamics from its early years. *Reading Jazz*, edited by Robert Gottlieb, provides a survey of early writings on jazz, as does Andrew Clark's *Riffs and Choruses*. See also, LeRoi Jones's *Blues People* and *Black Music*; Gene Lees's *Cats of Any Color*; and Jon Pannish's *The Color of Jazz*. There are numerous others, but my point is that jazz is often written about in black and white masculinist terms, excluding women and musicians who are neither "white" nor "black." I might add that Pannish's book is a nuanced counter to much of the racial politics found in jazz writings, though he, too, concentrates on a black and white jazz world.

See Sherrie Tucker's *Swing Shift* for an important investigation into how gender and sexuality operated in popular jazz discourse during the 1940s. Unfortunately, many of her insights can be used to illustrate the continued patriarchal bent of contemporary jazz discourse. Tucker also ruptures the black-white binary by introducing the saxophonist Willie Mae Wong and cogently describing the liminal space between black and white that she inhabited.

While I view with some amount of incredulity Sudhalter's discursive intervention into the "black canon" with his project of demarcating a space for white musicians, particularly in the early formation of jazz, I do not desire to enter into the polemics surrounding the black and white racialization of jazz discourse; rather, I hope to break the black and white binarism that has overshadowed much of jazz discourse by opening up a space for Asian American musicians and their contributions to jazz musicking. I do not wish to merely perform an "additive" history to the normative jazz historical project, either. This essay is not meant to provide a broad, revisionist history, although it may be aligned with such a project.

15 DeVeaux, "What Did We Do to Be So Black and Blue?" 415, emphasis mine.

16 An essay by Mia Tuan, "On Asian American Ice Queens and Multigeneration Asian Ethics," investigates the "forever alien" status of Asian Americans through the ways Michelle Kwan and Kristi Yamaguchi were publicly figured in contrast to their white counterparts. For instance, Tuan begins her article with this telling anecdote: "I was working at my computer . . . when I first heard the news. The internet headline read, 'American beats Kwan,' a reference to Tara Lipinski beating out Michelle Kwan for the 1998 Olympic gold medal in women's figure skating. . . . The faux pas on MSNBC's part (both skaters, after all, are American—Michelle is second generation) illustrated so well . . . how deep the foreigner stereotype runs— Americans look like Tara, while foreigners look like Michelle" (181).

17 I recognize that other Asian male representations may speak to more masculinist perspectives. There is the Fu Manchu stereotype of the power-obsessed Asian male, as well as the skillful martial artist whose physicality is embodied in highly masculinized ways. However, both of these representative tropes place these males in an Asian location that is farther away (in temporal as well as spatial terms) than, for example, the Charlie Chan image, whose marginalization requires other discursive tactics.

18 David Ake describes these tendencies as a sense of competitiveness among jazz musicians that privileges an ability to "play faster, higher and louder while incorporating more intricate lines and complex harmonic substitutions than their adversaries did," noting that "as far back as the early New Orleans innovators, jazz musicians remained highly conscious of displaying a hearty and unambiguous heterosexual masculinity" (*Jazz Cultures*, 67). Noted jazz scholar Krin Gabbard, discussing the signifyin(g) tropes surrounding the jazz trumpet player, writes,

Louis Armstrong was only the first of many African American jazz artists to attract international attention by establishing phallic authority with that most piercing of instruments, the trumpet. Dizzy Gillespie, a celebrated musical descendant of Armstrong who frequently spoke of the "virility" of black jazz, may have been Signifyin(g) on the phallic nature of his instrument when he bent the bell upward as if to simulate an erection. ("Signifyin(g) the Phallus," 105)

The feminization or emasculation of Asian American males is a subject that I can only briefly touch on here, but it is evidenced in media representations such as the nerdy geek whose social inhibitions provide comic bathos to many film narratives. Or think of the Chinese laundryman whose occupation, once gendered notions regarding domestic labor became naturalized, emasculated him, as Robert G. Lee points out in a short conclusion to the chapter "Third Sex" in his book *Orientals*.

My main point here is to establish how both musicians and scholars have normalized heterosexual masculinity in jazz musicking, foreclosing the possibility that musicians external to such a construct will be heard as real jazz musicians.

Asian American female musicians, moreover, confronting the submissive female stereotype that is antithetical to normative constructions of the jazz artist, also remain external to normative jazz discourse. I am thinking here of dominant cultural representations of Asian females, particularly in popular culture. Laura Hyun Yi Kang's "The Desiring of Asian Female Bodies," confronts this issue in a close reading of the film *Come See the Paradise*.

For instance, the cover photograph on *The Tokyo Blues* album by the pianist Horace Silver (1962) shows him sitting uncomfortably between two Japanese women in kimonos, suggesting once again the discursive opposition between American jazz musicians and exotic Asian women. Further, composition titles on the album such as "Sayonara Blues," "Cherry Blossom," and "Ah! So" contribute to dominant projections of Asian exoticism back into the popular imaginary, underlining my argument regarding the vast distance jazz discourse has created between "American" jazz and Asia(ns). The musicologist Ingrid Monson addresses this issue, writing,

> The symbolic intersection of masculinity, music, and race perhaps explains the persistence of jazz as a fraternity of predominantly male musicians. While many women have successfully crossed the gender barrier, many cite their technical musical prowess as having compensated for the symbolic liability of their gender. Mary Lou Williams, for example, has remarked, "You've got to play, that's all. They don't think of you as a woman if you can really play." ("The Problem with White Hipness," 405)

The overlapping strains of race and gender reveal a discursive project antithetical to the inclusion of nonblacks, nonwhites, and "nonmales" as real jazz musicians. Williams's willingness to erase her gender, subsumed under the sign of virtuosity, pointedly reveals the way in which she recognized the stakes at play in the jazz world.

19 For a closer examination of this issue, see Timothy P. Fong's *The Contemporary Asian American Experience*; and the anthology *A Look beyond the Model Minority Image*, edited by Grace Yun. See also Lee's *Orientals*, particularly the chapters "The Cold War Origins of the Model Minority" and "The Model Minority as Gook."

20 As noted elsewhere in this essay, other nonwhite and nonblack groups, such as Latin musicians, while clearly subordinate to black and white jazz musicians in dominant jazz discourse, can be heard as legitimate jazz musicians.

21 Wong, "The Asian American Body in Performance," 67–68.

22 As this essay is concentrating on Asian *American* musicians, I will not spend time on Asian jazz musicians such as the Japanese trumpeter Terumasa Hino, the Filipino alto saxophonist Tots Tolentino, the Korean tenor saxophonist Lee Jung Shik, or groups such as Shakti (whose members include the well-known South Asian Indian musician Zakir Hussain), the Japanese fusion band Casiopea, and the internationally known smooth jazz artist Keiko Matsui.

23 The sites I mention are "origin spaces" for different developments in normative jazz history, and I am using them here somewhat ironically. In formal musical terms, jazz has also managed to incorporate a broad range of nonjazz musicking, including atonality, the use of "extended techniques," and even elements of aleatorism, without completely becoming another type of musicking. Jazz musicians' expansive ability to retain "jazzness" in their musicking, however, is not always compatible with critical or scholarly discourse.

24 I understand the reasons why African American scholars and artists would support a historiographical project that valorizes the accomplishments of African American jazz musicians and their notable contributions to world culture, and I fully support the recognition of those artists and their creative work. I find the exclusion of Asian American jazz musicians problematic, however, for the reasons I outline in the text.

25 I use the term *Brown Pacific* in reference to Paul Gilroy's naming of Afro-diasporic musicking in his *Black Atlantic*. I used the term in an unpublished paper, "Chants for Change: The Music of Sudden Rush and Hawai'ian Sovereignty," as a way of describing the diasporic musicking of Hawai'ian rap artists in their engagements with Afro-diasporic musicking as expressed in hip hop and reggae. I also mean to draw attention to the diasporic nature of Asian American jazz.

26 Francis Wong, interview with the author, October 4, 2001.

27 As one of many examples in George Yoshida's *Reminiscing in Swing Time* to attest to this situation, tenor saxophonist Masao Manbo articulates the tension of occupying this position.

> After the day's show . . . a kid—a solitary schoolboy in a somber black uniform—approached me as I was leaving the theater, thrust out an autograph book and said in good English, "May I have your signature?" I signed with a flourish for my only fan, adding "Hollywood, Calif." after my name. I had lived in the movie capital before coming to Japan and was proud of it. But I didn't want to return there to my old occupation, which meant pushing a lawn mower. (108)

Clearly, the employment options in Japan were greater for Asian American musicians than in the United States—and the "glamour" attached to American citizenship granted these musicians some additional cultural capital in their new home.

28 For a compelling historical investigation of jazz in Japan, see E. Taylor Atkins's *Blue Nippon*. While concentrating on Japan, Atkins also reveals the impact of Japanese Americans on the formation of jazz musicking there. He also takes a look at the provocative maneuvers Japanese jazz artists have used in order to formulate "Japanese jazz." Even more central to this article, however, are the many instances of Japanese artists, especially before the 1970s, making claims for their own authenticity as jazz musicians in relation to their firsthand access to American jazz artists, particularly African Americans.

29 More work needs to be done in unveiling the ways in which Filipino musicians fashioned "western" musical idioms into expressive mediums of their own. One also sees this in other Asian countries, particularly with hip hop culture in the contemporary moment, but there is a long history of this activity that deserves recognition.

30 Interview with the author, 4 October 2001.

31 I realize I am using problematic categories here that deserve more scrutiny than I can provide in this essay, but I deploy them as shorthand descriptions, begging the reader's indulgence.

32 Quoted in Hutnyk, "Hybridity Saves?"

33 Gonzalo Rubalcaba is a Cuban pianist who has recorded for Blue Note, a prestigious jazz recording company, and received a substantial amount of critical praise. Django Reinhardt is an iconic figure in jazz. A Gypsy guitarist who eventually became a highly esteemed jazz guitarist, despite the mutilation of his left hand in a fire, Reinhardt formed a legendary quintet with violinist Stephane Grappelli in the 1930s in Paris. His status as a non-American jazz artist provided the origin story for Gypsy jazz. Jon Jang is a Chinese American pianist who has performed with the legendary African American drummer Max Roach, as well as many other well-known jazz musicians, yet remains relatively unknown to the general jazz public. Bassist Mark Izu is a Japanese American who was, as a member of United Front, one of the first explicitly Asian American jazz musicians. He continues to pursue cross-cultural musicking with Asian musicians such as the tabla master Zakir Hussain and gagaku (Japanese art music) master Togi Suenobu. Yet Izu remains even less well known than Jang to the average jazz aficionado.

34 There is documentation suggesting that Asian musicians engaged with American popular music prior to the 1920s. See Yoshida, *Reminiscing in Swingtime*, particularly the first chapter.

35 While there are many approaches one can take to "jazzing" an Asian folk song, there are generally two main ones. The first is to state the folk melody with jazz instrumentation in place of traditional instruments and / or reharmonizing the melodic theme with "jazz harmonies" (extended harmonies as well as "blue" so-

norities, for example). The second method uses traditional Asian instruments within harmonic and rhythmic movement idiomatically identified with jazz musicking. The primary approach, however, is most like the first, which consists of a jazz rhythm (swing or some sort of Western dance rhythm, i.e., foxtrot, waltz, etc.) attached to an Asian melody performed with Western instrumentation. The primary function for early fusions of this sort was the performance of dance music, while contemporary fusions tend to downplay this aspect of jazz musicking.

36 Interview with the author, October 4, 2001.

37 For a recent exception, see Jones, *Yellow Music*. Chinese music, Jones explains, was initially "denied the epistemological status of music" (19) by Western commentators. His concern to "trace the contours of the trajectory through which Chinese music entered into a relationship of commensurability with that of the West" (20) corresponds to my attempt in this essay to illuminate a similar relationship between Asian American jazz musicians and normative jazz discourse.

38 Andrew Jones, in *Yellow Music*, attests to substantial sales of jazzed Chinese songs, if only in Asia. Circuits of distribution and sales, however, also run along racialized sensibilities, and such recordings' marketability was thought to be constrained by language and other cultural concerns. Are audiences and culture industry perspectives different today? What, for instance, does the popularity of so-called J pop (Japanese popular music) with non-Japanese-speaking audiences indicate?

39 Interview with the author, October 4, 2001.

40 There is every reason to celebrate African American musicking and its consideration as one of the United States' primary contributions to world culture. Black culture's hard-won status as a culture is noteworthy for the overcoming of racism and racist laws, ideological constraints, and social disparagements. However, as I hope to make evident in the body of the text, if jazz's cultural position comes with its own set of exclusionary practices, particularly those aligned with a black-white binarism, it comes at too high a price. Moreover, Asian American inclusion does not dilute African American creativity, nor does it work to keep African American artists from their much-deserved compensation (similar arguments were used by capitalists to prevent cross-racial union organizing in industrial workplaces). Rather, Asian American exclusion demonstrates how the culture industry, in demarcating markets racially, notes, among other things, the small population of Asian Americans and targets their interests accordingly. The ideology of a culturally inferior race—at least when it comes to jazz musicking—works to support the economic development of markets away from such groups. Additionally, as a group marked "forever alien," Asian Americans are foreclosed from participating in "America's classical music." Again, this orientalist construct, created for entirely other purposes, has been shaped to accommodate the culture industry's unique requirements. Audience reception, while not entirely determined by the culture industry, feeds from the same ideological trough that the advertising and publicity juggernauts exploit. In Asian American terms, their exoticized positionality is re-

inforced by popular culture imagery, film depictions, and other narrative (mis)representations. Mainstream audience apathy toward Asian Americans who do not resemble these (mis)representations, then, should not be surprising.

41 Oliver Wang notes how popular music discourse is formulated in such a way that Asian Americans are silenced in his "Between the Notes." He describes exceptions, such as vocalist Pat Suzuki, in the popular music culture of the early 1960s while noting the difficulty in contextualizing her "exceptional" status. His article, in seeking to describe a historical genealogy for Asian American popular musicking, concentrates on music consumption rather than production. However, it is important to keep in mind his admonition that "Asian American music, like Asian America itself, comes about from the willful effort of people to imagine new spaces of being, new ways of living" (463).

42 For more on the formation of a pan-Asian identity, see Pei-Te Lien's *The Making of Asian America through Political Participation* and Yen Le Espiritu's *Asian American Panethnicity: Bridging Institutions and Identities*. There is also a sizable amount of reportage on the links between African American social movements and the ways they modeled protest and progressive politics in the 1960s and 1970s for Native Americans, Asian Americans, Latinos, and others. Those links are even recognized in popular culture, as evidenced in *A.* magazine's 1999 feature article "Common Ground" by Jungwon Kim.

43 Jon Jang and Francis Wong, interview with Nic Paget-Clarke, 1997.

44 Ibid.

45 Ibid.

46 Auerbach, "Profile," 46.

47 Interview with Nic Paget-Clarke, 1997.

48 See Takaki, *Strangers from a Different Shore*, for an overview of many of these struggles and individuals. For a look at the Asian American movement in the period under discussion at this point in the essay (1970s and 1980s), as well as examinations of current Asian American struggles, see Ho et al., *Legacy to Liberation*.

49 Jang, "88 Keys to Revolution," 35.

50 Ibid., 35. I would also like to note that political activity and musicking have a longer history in Asian American life than might be ascertained from this essay. Folksingers such as William David "Charlie" Chin and folk groups such as A Grain of Sand and Yokohama, California, predate the Asian American jazz movement by a decade or more.

51 The history of Western musicians finding inspiration in Asian musicking deserves its own book, but I will just mention briefly that in the art music world composers such as Henry Cowell and Lou Harrison were inspired by Indonesian gamelan and Japanese gagaku, as well as Native American musicking traditions. In the popular music world, musicians such as Martin Denny and Alfred Apaka drew on non-Western musicking—albeit problematic and crude notions of it—but were not taken seriously by critics or jazz musicians due, in large part, to the highly commercialized strain of their musicking.

52 All of the quotes attributed to Anthony Brown come from an interview with the author, conducted on December 19, 2001, unless otherwise noted.

53 I would like to remind the reader that John Coltrane's affinity and exploration of South Asian musicking predates the Asian American jazz movement. There are other Asian-jazz fusions such as Joe Harriott's 1966 Atlantic recordings *Indo-Jazz Suite* and *Indo Jazz Fusions*. The drummer Buddy Rich recorded an album with tabla master Alla Rakha, *Rich à la Rakha*, for Liberty Records in 1968. There are other examples, but my point is that jazz artists had been "looking East" for some time before Asian Americans began to think of themselves as Asian American jazz musicians rather than simply jazz musicians who happen to be Asian American.

54 Ho, "Beyond Asian American Jazz," 45.

55 Ibid., 49.

56 Ibid., 47.

57 Asian Improv Records was founded by Jon Jang and Francis Wong to produce Jang's early recordings. It later became a nonprofit organization devoted to promoting Asian American musicians in a wide range of genres.

58 Interview with the author, 4 October 2001.

59 Interview with Nic Paget-Clarke, 1997, n.p., emphasis added.

60 Ibid., emphasis added.

61 Ibid. One can also point to the orientalist (mis)representations in film and television that feature, for example, exoticized and hypersexualized female Asians and emasculated Asian males or, conversely, submissive females and / or hypermasculinized martial arts fighting machines. At any rate, none of these figures are able to provide images worthy of the title cultural worker or artist.

62 Ibid.

63 See Jang's and Wong's comments on this topic in ibid.

64 Ibid.

65 Ibid.

66 Ibid.

67 Ibid.

68 Ouellette, "The Question Is . . ." Notably, Brown was the only artist without a photograph accompanying his brief statement.

69 Ibid., 26.

70 Free jazz's discursive connections to black nationalist politics have linked it to activist political sensibilities and have often been counterposed to mainstream jazz musicking. This opposition is often framed within a progressive-reactionary binarism, but, as is noted with regard to Asian American jazz, it is an outdated connection that may have only tentative historical veracity. For a reading of free jazz's politics that complicates this simple conflation, see Anderson, "Jazz Outside the Marketplace." It should also be noted that a revisioning of a particular jazz composition is not necessarily going to reflect a progressive sensibility, for one of jazz's dominant aesthetic suppositions is the creative reworking of given materials

and jazz artists of every political stripe are compelled to "reinvent tradition" in some fashion.

71 See DeVeaux, *The Birth of Bebop*, for a complication of the notion that bebop musicians were simply seeking art status for their musicking. DeVeaux argues that beboppers were also savvy about placing their musicking in new market spaces for jazz, especially as jazz became less popular in mass audience terms than it had been during the immediately previous swing era.

72 There are jazz writers, critics, and scholars who ignore Hiroshima on the grounds that fusion is not real jazz, and I do not mean to tackle that debate here. I do not know what Shoemaker's reasons were for Hiroshima's exclusion—or if, indeed, it was an editorial decision in which he had little input—but it remains an interesting "moment of silence."

73 For instance, the cover of their eponymously titled debut recording features a photograph of a female Noh mask on a gray beach with the eyes and lips blackened, a sneer or growl beginning to form. The eyes have slit irises, like those of a cat, further adding to the ominous character of the mask. A bright red ribbon, like blood, spills from the mask onto the otherwise black- and gray-toned photograph. The photograph, with only the word *Hiroshima* in the upper-left-hand corner, evokes a postapocalyptic setting. Given the context—an Asian American band led by Japanese American musicians who chose the name Hiroshima—the resonance of a critical politic is unavoidable.

74 In response, I would like to quote Akira Tana, a mainstream drummer, at length, as he notes the overarching dilemma faced by artists such as the members of Hiroshima.

> What is [Asian American jazz]? What does it represent? Because when you hear the music, you pretty much see the same group . . . or the same people that are always presented and are always presented under this umbrella, under this name of "Asian-American jazz." Is it the people or is it the music? For example, there are a couple of musicians who are Asian or Asian-American, but they haven't really taken the initiative to become part of this scene, and I wonder why. Is it because they play a different kind of music that will not really let them become identified with the kind of music that is being presented by these kinds of groups? So it's an interesting question.
>
> For example, [pianist] Kei Akagi isn't really a part of that scene. And I'm not involved so much, maybe because we're geographically separated from the scene, but maybe it's because the music that we play and the projects we're involved in, isn't really part of that scene.
>
> [Say] you're involved in the community, the Asian community, the Asian-American community. Do you stay within that realm and become part of it, or do you venture out of it, and try to explore different possibilities with different, other kinds of groups or other kinds of people that may not have any connection with that core group, ethnically speaking? Or culturally speaking? (quoted in Feng, "Akira Tana")

75 The jazz writer Will Friedwald voices the opinions of many critics of fusion, and the equivalence given to "commercial success" and "lack of aesthetic integrity" in his remarks is clear. He states unequivocally,

> I accept the basic notion that jazz itself, even in its purest form (whatever that may be) is a fusion; jazz was already a mixture of a million other musics even by the time it had left New Orleans. . . . I think the reason jazz-rock is such a big deal . . . is economic. [The fusion band] Weather Report could easily be Financial Report. Jazz musicians added electrification to their bands [in order to] expand not just their musical horizons but their economic base. (Quoted in Taylor, *The Future of Jazz*, 63)

Jazz critic Stanley Crouch, writing of Miles Davis and his fusion turn, notes contemptuously, "Desperate to maintain his position at the forefront of modern music, to sustain his financial position, to be admired for the hipness of his purported innovations, Davis turned butt to the beautiful in order to genuflect before the commercial" ("On the Corner," 166).

Pointedly, regarding Hiroshima's self-description as a smooth jazz group, Mark Gridley writes in *Jazz Styles*, a much-used textbook on jazz, that smooth jazz "is background music with a beat," continuing with a discernibly critical tone, "Most styles of jazz have had their easy-listening variants, and this is fusion's" (357).

76 Interview with Nic Paget-Clarke, 1997.

77 Although I would argue that the conflation of smooth jazz and fusion is done in error, the Hiroshima Web site uses the now-accepted radio and marketing appellation *smooth jazz*, which stands in for a broad range of musicking that encompasses adult rhythm and blues, urban contemporary, and New Age, as well as what I call fusion. These genre nominations are loosely applied terms, but in my other work I am attempting to mark a finer distinction between fusion (or jazz rock or jazz funk) and later developments such as smooth jazz. I am also extremely wary of using radio and marketing terms to distinguish musicking forms.

78 Quoted on the Hiroshima Web site, http://www.hiroshimamusic.com (accessed October 10, 2006).

79 Edelstein, "An Inventive Fusion of Music and Culture Has Hiroshima Building the Bridge."

80 Quoted on the Hiroshima Web site.

81 June and Dan Kuramoto, interview with Baldwin Smith, 2003. http://www.the jazznation.com / Spotlight / hiroshima / hiroshima2.htm (accessed August 10, 2003).

82 Ibid.

83 This truism is not applied strictly. Although, for example, the hip hop group Public Enemy enjoyed commercial success, its political agenda was never questioned. This difference can be arguably attributed to Public Enemy's explicit expression of political ideals and positions on a variety of social issues.

84 Edelstein, "An Inventive Fusion of Music and Culture Has Hiroshima Building the Bridge."

85 Quoted on the Hiroshima Web site.

86 Breest, "Bridging Music."

87 Ibid.

88 At any rate, there is little antagonism between what can be seen as opposing camps, though I admit I have presented it in a way that would make such a conclusion reasonable. For example, the Hiroshima koto player June Kuramoto performed with Mark Izu and Anthony Brown for a production of *Kuan Yin: Our Lady of Compassion*, a recent performance work by Mark Izu and Brenda Wong Aoki. Again, the complex relationship between ethnic, political, and aesthetic affiliations in the Asian American jazz community complicates easy analysis.

89 Ho, "Beyond Asian American Jazz," 47.

90 Kotoist Miya Masaoka performs experimental works that incorporate jazz, art music, and the traditional koto repertoire in ways that blur generic designations. Her recordings with artists such as the African Americans Steve Coleman, George Lewis, Reggie Workman, and Andrew Cyrille testify to the linkage between Asian American and African American artists. The title and musicking on her album *Monk's Japanese Folk Song* (1997), created with the bassist Reggie Workman and the drummer Andrew Cyrille, are sly comments on this cross-cultural collaborative effort.

91 Quoted in Shoemaker, "East Meets Left," 84.

92 As Anthony Brown remarked to me in a conversation about his recording of Duke Ellington's *Far East Suite*, "Well, we got nominated [for a Grammy], so somebody's listening!"

93 Palumbo-Liu, *Asian/American*, 389.

2

Popular
Places

Homicidal Tendencies: Violence and the Global Economy in Asian American Pulp Fiction

Christopher A. Shinn

A recent wave of sci-fi, suspense, and detective novels marks the arrival of an emergent literary genre: Asian American pulp fiction.[1] Beginning in the mid-1990s, during a season of mainstream success by Asian American writers and a literary boom of the paperback novel,[2] Gus Lee, Lisa See, and Amitav Ghosh, all serious and widely acclaimed Asian diasporic writers of memoir, fiction, and autobiography, produced a series of works in popular fiction that represented a decisive departure from the canonical writings of Asian American literature.[3] While these authors have worked within the narrowly circumscribed world that generally concerns ethnic writers, having penned Chinese American family memoirs of exile and diaspora or, in the case of Ghosh, the Indian postcolonial novel, they have also experimented in the more popular, and more controversial and risky, realm of thrillers and the occult, where exotic racist stereotypes frequently abound. Unlike other genres in which Asian Americans have written, pulp fiction depends largely on a mass paperback industry (rather than a niche market), one that has built its empire on popular exotic fantasies and shifting moral sentiments, especially the all too familiar orientalist kind, which can be traced back to the pulp novelists in the 1920s and 1930s, including Earl Derr Biggers, Sax Rohmer, and John P. Marquand, or to their literary progeny, the paperback giants of the 1980s and 1990s, Michael Crichton, Tom Clancy, and Clive Cussler, authors of such works as *Rising Sun*, *Debt of Honor*, and *Dragon*, respectively.[4]

Certainly one can find in the popular novels of Gus Lee, Lisa See, and Amitav Ghosh the exotic content that mainstream publishers and consumers of pulp fiction have come to fetishize. Their works no doubt bear the imprint and signature of the legacy and evolution of the pulp genre. Gus Lee's *Tiger's Tail*, a military suspense thriller, has been said to resemble in plot the writings of John Le Carré and Tom Clancy,[5] while Lee's *No Physical Evidence* might recall—admittedly, in a more modest but no less dramatic courtroom thriller—the works of John Grisham, Scott Turow, and others. Lisa See's *Flower Net*, *The Interior*, and *Dragon Bones*—all international thrillers along the lines of Martin Cruz Smith's *Gorky Park*—introduce a contemporary Beijing that recalls Dashiell Hammett's 1920s San Francisco or Arthur Conan Doyle's turn of the century London.[6] The Pynchonesque conspiracy in Ghosh's *The Calcutta Chromosome*, as one critic has put it, has "all the page-turning suspense of a Crichton thriller."[7] One does not need to examine their works too closely, moreover, to find much evidence of pulp fiction's mythic tales of ancient civilizations, bloodbaths by fiendish Chinese killers, and Asian cult figures and shamans. According to the *Columbus Dispatch*, Lee's *Tiger's Tail* offers an "engaging journey into the mystical Far East," while, as Lisa See's official Web site notes, her *Dragon Bones* "unfurls like an ancient Chinese landscape scroll."[8] In praise of her honed skills as a practitioner of the thriller genre, one critic of the *New York Times* stated that See's writing gives readers the "social detail that reeks of freshly raked muck."[9] Indeed, See's Chinese villain in *Flower Net*, a serial killer, seems as vicious as Sweeney Todd (the Demon Barber) and as vengeful as Ian Fleming's Dr. No.

Yet, despite the fact that the mass paperback industry thrives on such highly stylized and marketable conventions of the pulp variety, these Asian American writers arguably accomplish much more in their popular works than just entertaining the masses with cheap and tawdry thrills and literary sensationalism.[10] Indeed, the "spectacle" has been too easily dismissed as mere surface, shell, and style when it can accomplish much more in its deceptively glossy and winding carnivalesque mirrors. As Ralph Ellison's *Invisible Man* memorably illustrates, social maneuvers can be openly paraded in the most familiar and ordinary styles and dress, where the public supposedly sees and knows the tribal markings of its own people, an assumption that proves to be overly reductive and ideologically blinding.[11] The standard plot schemes of pulp fiction, with their characteristic twists and turns, their far-fetched scenes, and above all their utter dependence on the repetition of violence, can likewise function more seriously as what Fredric Jameson calls "socially symbolic acts" that operate as economic and political allegories of late capitalism and the destructive forces of globalization.[12] Pulp fiction has thus traditionally employed "strategies of containment" through a distinct Manichean order, enabling symbolic resolution of the question of evil.[13] Much pulp fiction becomes not just a form of escapism but escape with a purpose, a symbolic resolution that speaks to deeper economic and political matters that surface dramatically in the text only to be ultimately "contained" or dispersed in the collective fantasy of the narrative. This critical understanding is deeply significant for Asian American cultural production, as the Asian American pulp novels of Lee, See, and Ghosh situate material production itself in a new globalized space and display the spectacular violence that reflects the conditions of struggle in the practices of everyday life.

Rather than shunning the violent and crass world of the exotic spectacle, Asian American pulp novelists Lee, See, and Ghosh have deliberately exploited a wide array of monstrous vulgarities in order to expose and critique the social order—an order that, as Michel Foucault reminds us, disciplines and renders invisible the punishment that it inflicts and normalizes.[14] To put it differently, Asian American pulp fiction uses elaborate plots, patently formulaic devices, and what we might call ethnic typologies to dramatize the scaffolding of ethnic subjects in pursuit of social equality, law, order, and economic rationality, rendering grotesque an invisible global network of discipline that enacts violence akin to the torturing of the body under the ancien régime.[15] The criminal deviance of ethnic others highlights not so much a concern for the social rehabilitation of individual characters as it does a range of broader critical issues, including Sino-American relations (See's *Flower Net, The Interior*, and *Dragon Bones*), the enforcement of global security (Lee's *Tiger's Tail*), the policing of new superhuman computer technology, and the privatizing of genetic research and the world health industry (Ghosh's *The Calcutta Chromosome*)—all emerging mechanisms of global social control. In so doing, Asian American pulp fiction, I argue, exposes the murderous excesses of globalization itself. The use of explicit violence also contributes to a radical geopolitical upheaval as a highly specialized and technical crew of world Asians move proleptically from the streets of Seoul, New York, Beijing, and Los Angeles to the borderless regions of the Asia-Pacific, the Pacific Rim, and the North Atlantic world. In the process, our assumptions about Asians and Asian Americans must subsequently be revised as we enter a "Cybernetic Asia," "New China," and "New Korean Demilitarized Zone" that determine the fate of the entire global system.

Lisa See's *The Interior* and the Murderous Mergings of China's New Market Socialism and Western Free Market Capitalism

Responding to the trade wars between the United States and Japan, Clive Cussler's *Dragon* (1991), Michael Crichton's *Rising Sun* (1993), and Tom Clancy's *Debt of Honor* (1994) illustrate the old adage "Business is war" by showing quite literally how nation and empire building and control of technology have led to repeated and escalating acts of corporate violence. In these narratives, the first strike is initiated by business-oriented Japan in a display of "yellow peril," which justifies American retaliation and inevitably ends in American dominance. Underlying the premise of these popular works of the early 1990s is the samurai code of revenge, implying that Japan never left its pre-Meiji dynastic roots, no matter how "modern" and "civilized" it appears to be, and has always possessed epic plans to avenge America's military victory during World War II. The mythic cycle of war, purging, and a return to dominance once again affirms Richard Slotkin's provocative thesis of the American frontier and the national belief in "regeneration through violence."[16] According to Slotkin, the narrative lore of "savage wars," which has appeared in early American captivity narratives, nineteenth-century dime novels (especially westerns), and a variety of twentieth-century pulp fiction venues, has attempted to justify national violence as a regenerative and noble act that instantiates the divine destiny of the people of the United States. Slotkin joins other Americanists, such as Seymour Martin Lipset and, most recently, George Lipsitz, David W. Noble, and Deborah Madsen, among others, who have traced the long-standing and often violent history of the doctrine of American exceptionalism.[17] While cautioning against the dangers of American exceptionalism as a "double-edged sword," Seymour Martin Lipset, for instance, extends this discussion by comparing America's national belief in its own Protestant-based, capitalist-informed ideals and the "economic miracle" of Japan, which reveals the country's own values of self-discipline and prosperity that exemplify Japan's "unique and exceptional character."[18] While noting their dominant structural affinities, Lipset claims that the relationship between the United States and Japan is an essentially competitive one marked by cultural difference, Japanese protectionism, and an insurmountable "Pacific Divide." The two nations "vary from each other *in much the same way as they did a century ago* . . . [and] are like ships that have sailed thousands of miles along parallel routes. They are far from where they started, but they are still separated."[19]

The call for U.S. protectionism in the 1990s also brought together American economists, conservative critics, and corporate leaders such as James Fallows, Clyde Prestowitz Jr., and Donald Spero, among others, and coincided with alarming incidences of "Japan bashing."[20] Some of those popular assumptions, however, contradicted emerging economic and political realities that would appear forcefully in the pulp novels of Gus Lee, Lisa See, and Amitav Ghosh, which call attention to a massive global network that could not easily be disentangled into two eth(n)ically clear sides. With the Asian financial collapse in 1997, it would soon become apparent that, economically speaking, it no longer benefited the United States simply to demonize the other or see the other as categorically "different," that is, as people who operate transgressively outside of the American exceptionalist model, for those global interconnections meant that the United States' own security and financial well-being were being put at risk. The United States could not afford to upset the delicate balance of a global system that increasingly "networked" those economic and political realities and threatened to undermine all developed and developing nations. In the years ahead, China would join the World Trade Organization, Japan and the Asian Tigers (the "newly industrialized countries") would recover just enough to lessen fears of a global financial collapse, and the Pacific Rim would encourage more oceanic cooperation.[21]

Lisa See's popular fiction opposes a pervasive Manichean perspective toward Asia that has been supported by Crichton, Clancy, and Cussler on the very grounds that the economics of globalization depend on stable financial markets in Asia. While See's fiction underscores this global interconnection, her work takes issue with the logic of capital itself as she reveals the dark and violent underside of modernity and globalization in the United States and Asia. Scenes of mutilation such as steamed body parts and intestines shaped in the form of Chinese words (*Flower Net*) express not merely gratuitous violence but a highly developed and calculated action of the advanced criminal mind that leads upward to the highest levels of the state (to the Chinese minister of public security in *Flower Net*) and to the symbolic heads of industry (a Chinese American CEO in *Dragon Bones*). The murderous actions of these and other serial killers ultimately suggest a refined criminality that reflects the broad social realities of the post–Deng Xiaopeng era, in which the Chinese people exist under a highly bureaucratic state system that is undergoing the contradictory merging of China's growing market socialism and Western free market capitalism. In a reversal of textual meanings, See suggests that "modernity" and "progress" lead not to freedom but to a worse kind of barbarism and global imprisonment.

The popular novels of Lisa See describe a New China amid this tumultuous and potentially cataclysmic global transition. Out of all of her popular works to date, however, *The Interior* most clearly represents these global changes at the ground level of production. The book centers on a U.S. toy factory in the remote region of Shanxi Province (the "interior") in the village of Da Shui (globalization having reached the "core" of China). Tartan Incorporated, a U.S. media and manufacturing giant, plans to buy the American megacorporation Knight International, which produces action figures based on a children's television show, *Sam and His Friends*. The planned buyout causes Knight's stock to soar seventeen points, and the proposed purchase causes enormous speculation. The acquisition is being handled by the legal firm of Phillips, MacKenzie and Stout, which must respond to preliminary allegations by the media of a federal inquiry into alleged violations of the U.S. Foreign Corrupt Practices Act. The Chinese protagonist, Liu Hulan, an investigator for the Ministry of Public Security in China, travels to Shanxi Province in order to investigate the mysterious death of a young village girl, Ling Miaoshan, which may be tied to the U.S. company and its plan for corporate expansion. In the process, Hulan discovers more than just who murdered Miaoshan; she uncovers barbaric labor practices in U.S. factories in China. She also exposes the betrayal of the villagers of Da Shui by one of their own: Tang Dan, who has always appeared to be a dutiful Chinese Communist but is actually a cruel and ambitious capitalist in disguise. He becomes a symbol of the evil Chinese murderer following in the footsteps of his American business counterparts, who bring suffering and death in the name of new jobs and prosperity.

While the world of financial capital continues to swirl, with heightened speculation in the global marketplace about the merger between Knight International and Tartan Incorporated, the Chinese workers in Shanxi Province have seen their minimum wages cut in half, their three-year contracts made entirely dependent on a system of enforced labor, and their monies pilfered by corrupt legal and corporate investors and owners. In fact, as one Chinese factory worker, Pearl, observes, some American factories in China were paying the sum of "six dollars a month *less* than what the Chinese laborers working on the transcontinental railroad were paid in the last century."[22] Hazardous working conditions, as well as the company's Foucauldian surveillance techniques, force them to live in unsanitary and unsafe accommodations and tightly controlled collectives that amount to incarceration. The peasant workers, for instance, are crowded into concrete warehouse dormitory rooms where the latrine smells "[hang] in the air."[23] The main factory floor, moreover, generates "oven temperatures" and produces deafening noises that are caused by the "thrashing maw" of the machines.[24] Liu Hulan, the investigator from the Ministry of Public Security, also notes that the factory "seemed to have so much security and the workers were so much under the control of the managers, and yet actual assignments could be as haphazard as who happened to be standing nearby at the time."[25] Indeed, Madame Leung, the party secretary of the Knight factory, repeatedly warns the workers, "We'll be watching you."[26]

The organization of their labor into segmented parts introduces multiple hidden and minute social transformations that become routine, shaping the workers into a faceless mass that the book, in naming them, refuses ultimately to accommodate. The assembly-line products manufactured by the Knight Corporation, toy action figures that actually talk and possess moving limbs, exchange places with the Chinese female workers, who become inanimate objects and suffer bizarre mortal injuries that leave their limbs with a "rag-doll quality."[27] Their daily labor certainly alienates and dehumanizes them, but the mechanical regularity of the appearance and disappearance of dead bodies most dramatically represents their permanent transition from subject to object relations. Many of the Chinese female workers in the factory in Shanxi Province are brutally murdered or mangled by the machines that produce the plastic toy appendages. Xiao Yang, for instance, one of the workers in the assembly area, has her fingers chopped off and her forearm sliced open in a fiber-shredding machine while the other women must return to work.[28] The others understand that Yang will mysteriously disappear and her body will be disposed of to prevent the discovery of work-related injuries and allow the sale of Knight International to move forward. A tragic fire, however, will eventually trap the Chinese workers in the Shanxi factory and cause the death of 176 women. The inferno will come to stand for the spreading crisis that, if left "uncontained," will effect capitalism's planetary destruction. It also provides a convenient marker for the ways in which the text manages the growing discontent of the Chinese workers under a system of globalization and employs key strategies of containment to prevent a peasant rebellion. The murderer of the Chinese workers and the perpetrator of the deadly fire, Doug Knight, turns out to be the disgruntled son of the CEO, Henry Knight, who, in trying to please his generous and well-intentioned father, makes the struggle against corporate labor practices into the private, or domestic, conflict of a single wayward son.[29]

The advanced capitalist system seems to emerge morally unscathed, and it even regroups and strengthens itself after the fire because Doug Knight and Tang Dan are the American and Chinese scapegoats, respectively—the chief evil elements that are removed and ultimately blamed for the ugly manifestations of greed and corruption. Doug Knight tries to skim profits off the wages of poor Chinese peasants as the main ringleader of a secret American managerial operation, betraying his own father and murdering the Chinese workers individually and en masse in the name of rational capitalism. Tang Dan similarly betrays his own villagers by masquerading as a Chinese Communist when he is actually a power-mongering capitalist. These two criminals are part and parcel of the same economy of power. Yet *The Interior* not only illustrates the fact that the power of globalization has indeed reached the interior, revealing China's complicity in the process of governmental deregulation, but also shows that the Chinese people themselves will betray each other in a new era of market socialism (a betrayal that divides family and communal members) just as China must contend with its own material desires in the growth and spread of Western free market capitalism.

The Disease of Globalization in Amitav Ghosh's *The Calcutta Chromosome*

In Ghosh's *The Calcutta Chromosome*, the forces of technology and globalization operate according to the emergence and growth of modern empires. Perhaps no better analogy serves to illustrate the corrosive effects of this convergence than the logic and spread of disease. The fear of contact with the other, of course, routinely accompanies the colonial encounter and establishes a correlation in colonial discourse between modern exploration and the control and extermination of the natives.[30] The native other becomes associated inextricably with disease and death (malaria, smallpox, etc.), while the colonizer imagines himself or herself as the emissary of truth and life. The field of modern science and medicine, then, provides Amitav Ghosh with a potent means of addressing the crossover and contamination of these categories in the era of late capitalism. The quest to build an empire (and the ideologies of enlightenment that sustain such a project) persists not only during the colonial era but also in the attempt to conquer the world of cyberspace and in the multinational corporation's desire to control the global health care industry. In so doing, it tries to efface colonial history and the natives through calculated assertions of Western beliefs about the power of progress, science, and reason, and in the process it normalizes what are in fact repeated and concerted attacks of epistemic violence. Nonetheless, in *The Calcutta Chromosome*, the native other has conspiratorial plans of her own and will use the master's tools and her own secret society to construct a counterhegemonic world.[31] She will follow the path of infectious disease into a global cybernetic body in order to realize the West's worst fears concerning postcolonial rebellion.

Ironically, an old and powerless Egyptian immigrant in the United States will rise to the status of the "Chosen One," bringing together ancient hermetic codes and postmodern conditions, scientific reason and mythic truths, experiments in alchemy and new developments and research in biology and cybernetics. The immigrant, Antar, works as a low-level programmer for the International Water Council, a megacorporation in the public health industry. The company sees itself as a global institution "making History." Its managers "wanted to record every minute detail of what they had done, what they would do. Instead of having a historian sift through their dirt, looking for meanings, they wanted to do it themselves: they wanted to load their dirt with their own meanings."[32] Relegated to his home office in New York in the last year of his employment, Antar works alone on his computer and conducts data entry while the company docks his pay for "declining productivity."[33] As he becomes increasingly irrelevant to the company's grand mission, he inserts himself, or rather is himself inserted, into the stream of history by a subaltern group of Indian mystics. While the International Water Council attends to its own archaeological water experiments, attempting to acquire the mythic power of water itself and control its life-giving properties, its own low-level employee, Antar, is about to participate in a major discovery that promises to challenge the limits of human mortality and enable the "ultimate transcendence of nature."[34]

Because the Western colonizing impulse has always been to profit from new discoveries, for which it routinely takes the credit, and to control public health, scientific knowledge, and history, the International Water Council fails to see the potential contributions of native peoples to the birth of new revolutionary ideas. Its own rules of legitimation hamper the speed and flow of scientific research and channel the meaning of new discoveries toward the collective demands of the larger scientific community. The Indian mystics, however, represented by the cult figure, Mangala, operate in their own experimental fashion without having to "write papers or construct proofs . . . [Mangala, for instance,] did not need to read a zoological study to see that there was a difference between culex and anopheles: she'd have seen it like you or I can see the difference between a dachshund and a Doberman. She didn't care about formal classifications."[35] As Jean-François Lyotard reminds us, the high stakes of establishing scientific truth, particularly in the postmodern era, precipitate a crisis of legitimation that can only be mediated by an unexpected and experimental "move" or "movement."[36] This premise leads the reader of Ghosh's novel on an epistemological chase in and out of official history that moves back in time to the late nineteenth century and the British scientist Ronald Ross's discovery of the malaria vector, which revealed how malaria is transferred to humans (and for which he won the Nobel Prize). Readers travel back and forth according to multiple and overlapping temporalities and geographies, going back to nineteenth-century British India and forward to Antar's Manhattan apartment and his computer (which is called "Ava"[37]) as we piece together the facts: a secret cabal of Indian mystics has been planning and using Western knowledge for some time in order to achieve power over the natural life processes of reincarnation.

As knowledge itself represents the most coveted possession, driving the trade of information commodities and speculation in general, the secret knowledge that we learn from the postcolonial discovery of the "Calcutta chromosome"—the futuristic process by which humans can transfer and mutate their genetic structure to other humans and move from body to body[38]—remains the grandest and most lucrative prize of them all. By suggesting that subaltern peoples have been largely excluded from the world of science and technology and the making of history, Ghosh implies that an antiprogressive, colonialist, and anticosmopolitan view has been ultimately detrimental and costly to the human race. In fact, it suggests that what drives the flow of information and scientific research is increasingly corporate interest, institutional bureaucracy, and the attempt by a few to control the destiny of the world. The U.S. multinational corporation has effectively alienated Middle Eastern and South Asian workers at a level of bureaucratic sophistication far worse and more violent than what existed under the British colonial administration in India.

Only at the interface of the computer image and the human body can we truly confront the violence of this ethnocentric and unilateralist perspective. Antar significantly enters into this truth by means of a virtual reality in which the screen image and the physical body merge. A mutilated and disfigured Indian, L. Murugan, a former employee of the International Water Council (then known as LifeWatch), who has since disappeared, returns to the present world in a holographic projection with maggots and floating limbs: "The head was startling like a vision that often recurred in his worst nightmares; an image from a medieval painting he had once seen in a European museum, a picture of a beheaded saint, holding his own dripping head nonchalantly under his arm."[39] He beckons the Egyptian immigrant to join him in the computer, and Antar decides to enter cyberspace to "join" or "merge" with Murugan. We become witnesses to a critical scene of techno-bio-crossover, public-private scaffolding, and violent decapitation that connect decaying body and living matter inside the cybernetic world. The appearance of such a distorted and unsettling figure comes to signify the material transition from one world to the next, from the ancient city of Calcutta to the postmodern world of cyberspace. We are in turn led into a computer-generated hybrid body that brings together East and West in an attempt to undermine the monologic systems of truth and rationality that have been inherited from colonial history and perpetuated by the neocolonial structures of the multinational corporation (represented by the International Water Council).

By returning to Western stereotypes of "Indian mystics," Ghosh purposely overturns them in violent acts of epistemic reversal and dissemination. The dismemberment once again signifies the breaking apart of those fixed associations, as the mutilation of the body exposes the violence that has been enacted on formerly colonized peoples in the name of science, truth, and human advancement. In so doing, Ghosh reverses the Western epistemic violence that undermines the notion of modern progress, East and West, and the theory of biological determinacy. Because private corporations and the strict rules of legitimation increasingly determine the flight of modern science and technology, the quest for knowledge and rationality in the West has not led to the advancement of human civilization, Ghosh suggests, but has actually thwarted scientific discoveries that perhaps would have extended human life itself. The malaria virus thus provides the key medical allegory that enables more quasi-religious experiments. Computer technology and ancient rituals combine to create a new body, or a series of bodies, which merge to form a new incarnation—a new "avatar"—that can be traced back to the merging of Antar and his computer, Ava, the latter of which contains all the world's digitized information. The disease that spreads across the globe is essentially globalization itself, filtered through its primary technological apparatus, but Ghosh's novel gives agency to the subaltern subject by noting how the power of this technology can alter the "chromosomal structure" of the globalizing process itself and create a counterhegemonic world that uses the colonizer's tools subversively for its own designs.

Global Prisons: Korea's Demilitarized Zone and the "Prosperous" and "Rehabilitated" Nation in Gus Lee's *Tiger's Tail*

Gus Lee's *Tiger's Tail* describes the Korean border region of the Demilitarized Zone (DMZ) essentially as a prison that operates according to the cold war logic of global rehabilitation and engages critically the national belief in regeneration through violence. Through the construction of the prison border, Lee builds on a number of textual ambivalences that complicate the meaning of American citizenship and render the enforcement of global security along the Korean border problematic. He suggests, for instance, that American citizenship can be bought on the black market. Sergeant Patrick McCrail, a decorated American hero and prisoner of war (POW), sells false papers to recruit Korean nationals into the U.S. Army in order to acquire funds to buy freedom for American POWs. Following the Panmunjom Cease-Fire Agreement in 1953, the War and State Departments, the White House, and the United Nations all refuse to assist Sergeant McCrail in his fight to secure the release of his fellow POWs, who are being held in a Manchurian prison. According to McCrail, "The War Department gave 'em up for 'confessing' [after being tortured]. It was Joe McCarthy time. They hosed POW patriots."[40] With few options remaining, he turns to the Hong Kong triads, which agree to free his compatriots for half a million U.S. dollars, and the military recruiting scandal is born. This purchase can be, and is, considered "heroic" and "American," yet only because the country has exceeded its own nationalist agenda in Asia and betrayed members of its own military, having abandoned them in enemy prisons.

Corporal Frederick C. LeBlanc, otherwise known as the Wizard, has copied Sergeant McCrail's black market scheme to finance his own diabolical plan to smuggle nuclear bombs into North Korea. As a staff judge advocate of the U.S. Army, he intends to start a world war to destroy the enemy and the world of communism in a patriotic act of national absolutism and sees himself as acting honorably as a true "American." If the Demilitarized Zone can be understood as a modern prison created for the express intent to promote global security,[41] then its techniques of surveillance, its military duties and legal apparatuses, and its growing technological sophistication actually refine the broad criminality of the terrorist-minded Wizard. His madness relates directly to the fact that he was placed in the Demilitarized Zone as a form of incarceration, having been sent "punitively to the Second Infantry, Camp Casey, DMZ, his military career effectively ended."[42] The novel brings Corporal LeBlanc and Sergeant McCrail together thematically as the "evil one" and the "ideal," and both are born of an interrelated sense of moral obligation and desperate criminal activity, having become deeply entangled in the American military legal system and the inner workings of market capitalism. The violent dual nature of the deaths of McCrail and the Wizard makes the evil one and the ideal part of the same ritual scapegoating that seeks to regenerate America through violence and cleanse the nation of its economic and political corruption.

Just as the military functions as a superconductor for industrial growth in the modern world, so also does Lee's military thriller describe a thriving international smuggling operation that represents the dark underside of the outer industrialized world of the "European-styled Seoul Railway Station," the "herd of smog-spitting vehicles," and the "city lights" of the global metropolis.[43] The frozen and barren "no-man's-land" of the Demilitarized Zone, then, represents a highly volatile geopolitical border—in essence, a prison—that divides the capitalist accumulation of wealth and abject economic and political stagnation. Indeed, the crises of the Watergate investigation, President Nixon's resignation, the beginning of stagflation, the end of Keynesian economics, and the "demilitarization" of the U.S. presence in Vietnam all testify to America's own cold war entrapment in a military-industrial complex that invites but cannot entirely contain these various economic and political extremes.

Lee further exposes some of the moral contradictions of America's war against communism and critiques its costly military and political strategies of containment. He suggests, for instance, that President Nixon himself put atomic bombs in Korea despite the fact that the government states unequivocally in various Washington press releases that "the United States has no tactical nuclear weapons in the Republic of Korea."[44] He also reminds his readers of the many victims of the wars in Asia that have left Amerasian children, refugees, prostitutes, and orphans without homes or families, while the U.S. government refuses to take any responsibility despite its principal role in these tragic human affairs.[45] The dead themselves stand as a moral indictment against the construction of the border prison in Korea. The protagonist, Jackson Kan, a Chinese American army prosecutor and U.S. district attorney, notes, "A hundred and thirty thousand Americans had paid the price for our thoughtlessly splitting Korea with the Soviet Union. We figured we were cutting a cake, but we had halved an interdependent society, separating northern industry from southern agriculture and dividing great clans with the DMZ, making both parts suffer and inviting poverty, terror, war and the threat of world war."[46] As was mentioned previously, Lee critiques the legal and political failures of the U.S. government by noting the grave injustices that pertain to the abandonment of American prisoners of war. These U.S. soldiers have been kept in prisons on an Asian continent that represent "old debt."[47] This is a sum that the American government does not want to pay back because it has decided to deny certain political realities in its ideological war against communism and is willing to ignore a few U.S. countrymen being held prisoner to project the favorable image of a prosperous and rehabilitated nation.

Gus Lee's return to the memory of Vietnam and the Korean War in *Tiger's Tail* extols the cost in human lives of the spread of globalism. The story takes place in 1974, during the Vietnam War, but returns to the initial 1950–53 conflict between North and South Korea, as well as earlier to the time of China's civil war, and inevitably moves forward to the present day in Asia and the United States. The writing of history here serves as a commentary on the present. Jackson Kan suffers from post–traumatic stress syndrome (a symptom of the limits of the rationality of war), and the story creates a number of overlapping histories and geographies, as well as political and military interdependencies, that relate specifically to a distinct pan-Asian vision that brings together China, Japan, North and South Korea, and Vietnam in the mind of a Chinese American legal prosecutor.

These global interconnections of "Asia" most visibly appear in the grotesque, steroid-induced, pan-Asian bodies of the members of an army military force, a group of "mesomorphs" that included Captain Christopher Sapolu of Honolulu, Private Second Class Paek Ok-kyu, and Private Second Class Kim Chae-yo (the latter two soldiers hailing from Los Angeles).[48] They belong to a twelve-man unit that plans to carry U.S. tactical nuclear weapons, known as Special Atomic Demolitions Munitions, from Camp Casey in South Korea across the Demilitarized Zone into North Korea, thus initiating a plan to start a world war. This special forces operation is significantly based in part on the model of an elite all-Asian Peregrine Unit—"an Asian-American strike team of paratroopers, Rangers and Special Forces, a rich Eastern blend of Chinese, Japanese, Filipino, Samoan, Tongan, Hawaiian, Vietnamese, Thai, Campuchean, Okinawan, Laotian, Nien, Fijian and Hmong killers."[49] It is not clear, however, if this unit can be ideally promoted for its pan-Asian military collectivity or if it serves as an index to a war that involves Asians fighting alongside and against one another.

Lee does suggest, however, that nuclear war can be best avoided by promoting a progressive, pan-Asian consciousness that upholds the mystical words of

Korean shamans. A Korean shaman, Song Sae, tells her Chinese American friend, Jackson Kan, that he is a "tiger man, round and full with Korean *Sanshin*, tiger spirit."[50] Having been born in the Chinese year of the tiger, Kan later brings peace to Korean orphans of the war by donating monies recovered from the black market scheme of the Wizard. Song Sae fuses Kan's Chinese tiger spirit and the Korean Sanshin, making the nations of the U.S., China, and Korea, coextensive and continuous in a spiritual act of benevolence. Lee's novel holds to a planetary moral obligation to fight against all forms of terrorism and ultranationalism and for the cause of human rights (by finding soldiers missing in action and protecting the innocent victims of war, for instance) while remaining suspicious of government institutions and the potential for political abuses of power. Lee sees extreme military nationalism and political abuse and corruption as the greatest dangers to global security, but he further implies that military and legal authority can bring stability when those entrusted with power uphold the offices of their service and calling (Lee himself is a former West Point cadet and army and deputy district attorney). That is, while he expresses a profound distrust of bureaucratic institutions, and political leaders especially, he ultimately affirms the role and function of law and government in establishing and maintaining civil authority both at home and abroad.[51] In the end the Korean shamans "give proof to things invisible," as they are frozen in a journalistic photo that Kan observes keenly in the novel's final scene. Here Song Sae is found "smiling . . . towards America."[52] The invisible world might indeed serve to recall the many prisoners of war and the dead, whose lifeless bodies have been violently sacrificed in the narrative's ghostly national imaginings—another sign of capitalism's ascendance and the rise of multiple competing postindustrial nationalisms.[53]

Conclusion

Perhaps instead of rejecting pulp fiction on aesthetic grounds as being merely crass and melodramatic, we might find within it the critical resources for an economic and political critique far more penetrating and substantive than has hitherto been credited. By following new Asian American pulp fiction into forbidden areas that are shocking and explicitly violent, we might be able to confront controversial matters anew. We might directly challenge the kinds of negative representations that have led to an almost categorical dismissal or suspicion of the "popular" in the study of Asian American literature and culture.

When confronted with such characters as See's Chinese sadistic killers,

Ghosh's mystic and insane Indian cult figures, and Lee's mystical shamans, we might actually find that these familiar exotic types are employed for complex and counterhegemonic purposes rather than mere literary sensationalism. New Asian American pulp fiction by Lee, See, and Ghosh provides a useful tableau for an alternative approach to understanding the fine subtleties and savage exhibitions of modern power. The so-called respectable and civilized forms of culture invariably cross into, and are inseparable from, a world of convention, stylization, and mass culture, where the inner workings of advanced capitalism can surface in a most visible and vulgar display. Asian American pulp fiction dramatizes the inner and outer workings of established bureaucratic authorities that determine the current economic and political order and critiques the material forces that attempt to give and take away life. See's *The Interior*, for instance, draws attention to a series of murders in Shanxi Province in order to implicate the United States and China together in the widespread exploitation of Chinese laborers and critiques the forms of global material production that alienate the Chinese people, divide an American father and son, and undermine the lives of thousands of Chinese villagers. Ghosh's *The Calcutta Chromosome* enlarges the effects of globalization on displaced natives and immigrants through a multinational corporation's attempt to control the global health industry. Lee's *Tiger's Tail* dramatizes the effects of globalism on the policing of national borders in U.S. foreign policy and suggests that the Korean prison border stands in for the economic and political divide that gives rise to, rather than contains, the threat of nuclear war. The inattention to economic injustice and peaceful coexistence between North and South Korea produces a massive underground economy that leads to a crisis in defining American citizenship itself and causes a series of human rights violations and escalations of violence. The violence that emerges in all of these works can be found not only in the multiple and graphic displays of power but also in the many techniques of deprivation, secrecy, and surveillance— everyday "homicidal tendencies"—that have been, and continue to be, used to control society and the future of everyday life.

Notes

No list of Asian American popular fiction would be complete without reference to the science fiction dystopia and popular romance of Cynthia Kadohata and Amy Tan, respectively. Besides studying the literary boom of Asian American popular fiction from 1989 to the mid- to late 1980s, I offer an extended critical investigation of the complex and heterogenous uses of the popular, scapegoating, and ethnic typologies in the writings, media, and visual productions of Frank Chin, Maxine Hong Kingston, Gish Jen, Naomi Hirahara, Jessica Hagedorn, Don Lee, John Yau, and Kaiji Kawaguchi, among others, in a forthcoming book, *Homicidal Tendencies: Graphic Violence and the Obscure Trace in Asian American Popular Fiction*.

1 My use of the world *pulp* to characterize today's popular fiction is based on two assumptions: (1) that popular novels can be traced historically to the pulp novel through the content and form of so-called paraliterature (romances, detective fiction, westerns, etc.), and (2) that popular novels generally follow a pulp form that depends on plot-driven narratives and highly stylized literary melodramas.

2 Garrett Hongo, for instance, has noted that a large number of Asian American writers had achieved popular success by the mid-1990s and rendered obsolete some of the earlier authenticity debates that surround the continual lament concerning the lack of Asian American self-representation in mainstream America. See Hongo, *Under Western Eyes*, 1.

3 One notable exception is the writing of the popular romance. Amy Tan's *The Joy Luck Club* follows the distinct plot structure and melodramatic conventions of the romance and was serialized in magazines before it was published as a book. As the most popular work of Asian American literature to date, having spent eight months on the *New York Times* best seller list, Tan's novel could be purchased readily at grocery stores and on paperback racks, opening the door for other Asian American writers to pursue other forms of popular writing. Gus Lee especially has expressed his indebtedness to Amy Tan (Lee's father was married to Amy Tan's mother at one time).

4 Crichton, *Rising Sun*; Clancy, *Debt of Honor*; Cussler, *Dragon*.

5 Review of *Tiger's Tail*, by Gus Lee, *Publisher's Weekly*, January 29, 1996, 83.

6 Review of *Flower Net*, by Lisa See, *Mostly Murder*; Corrigan, "Beijing Body Count."

7 Publisher's note in Ghosh, *The Calcutta Chromosome*, i.

8 Johnson-Wright, " 'Tale' Filled with 6 Days of Excitement, Intrigue," *Columbus Dispatch*, March 17, 1996; Lisa See's Web site, "Buy Dragon Bones," http://www.lisasee.com/dragonbones.htm.

9 Jon Garelick, "Toys 'R' Murder," *New York Times*, October 17, 1999.

10 If public interest and critical acclaim can denote more than just popularity in a "society of the spectacle," then perhaps the fact of wide audience appeal might indicate more than the notion that groups of readers can be easily hoodwinked and deceived by mass culture. Because their literary reputations often precede them, Gus Lee, Lisa See, and Amitav Ghosh maintain a following among a diverse spectrum of mainstream and specialized audiences and enjoy a liberal circulation among academic and nonacademic consumers of ethnic literature; Book-of-the-Month Club readers (Gus Lee's *No Physical Evidence* was a 1998 featured selection); fans of sci-fi, crime, and detective novels and legal and military thrillers; and followers of books that have been recommended by noted critics in such venues as the *New York Times Book Review* (Lisa See's *Flower Net* was a *New York Times* Notable Book in 1997) and awarded prizes by prestigious firms (Amitav Ghosh's

The Calcutta Chromosome won the Arthur C. Clarke Award). Being published by mainstream presses such as Random House (Ballantine), HarperCollins, and Avon no doubt helps to garner public attention, but it does not fully explain to us why these works have been—and deserve to be—read.

11 Ellison, *Invisible Man*.

12 Jameson, *The Political Unconscious*.

13 "Strategies of containment" refers to specific governmental policies that relate to the cold war. Fredric Jameson, however, uses the phrase to suggest ways in which texts "are able to project the illusion that their readings are somehow complete and self-sufficient" (ibid., 10). The text can propose imaginary resolutions of real contradictions in history, a "way of achieving coherence by shutting out the truth about History—at once a limitation imposed by an underlying economic reality— not simply false consciousness since those limitations are imposed by the economic itself that prevents the individuals from seeing the real cause of their present misery—and also a repression of the underlying contradictions that have their source in History and Necessity." See Dowling, *Jameson, Althusser, Marx*, 77.

14 Foucault, *Discipline and Punish*.

15 Ibid.

16 Slotkin, *Regeneration through Violence*; *Gunfighter Nation*, 1–21.

17 Lipsitz and Noble, *Death of a Nation*; Madsen, *American Exceptionalism*.

18 Lipset, *American Exceptionalism*, 261.

19 Ibid., my emphasis.

20 Fallows, *More Like Us*; Prestowitz, *Trading Places*; Spero, "Patent Protection or Piracy," 58–67.

21 Connery, "Pacific Rim Discourse," 36.

22 See, *The Interior*, 261.

23 Ibid., 181.

24 Ibid., 181, 190.

25 Ibid., 187.

26 Ibid.

27 Ibid., 198.

28 Ibid., 189–90.

29 Ibid., 460–65.

30 See, for instance, Arnold, *Imperial Medicine and Indigenous Societies*; Crosby, *Germs, Seeds, and Animals*; and MacLeod and Lewis, *Disease, Medicine, and Empire*.

31 The native other centers around a mystical cult led by an Indian woman named Mangala. Hence, the native other here is gendered feminine.

32 Ghosh, *The Calcutta Chromosome*, 7.

33 Ibid., 5.

34 Ibid., 106.

35 Ibid., 243.

36 Lyotard, *The Postmodern Condition*, 3–17.

37 Ghosh, *The Calcutta Chromosome*, 4.

38 Ibid., 107.

39 Ibid., 291.

40 Lee, *Tiger's Tail*, 149.

41 Ibid., 10, 99.

42 Ibid., 20.

43 Ibid., 38, 262.

44 Ibid., 365.

45 For references to the Korean Demilitarized Zone as a prison border, see ibid., 184, 188, 350.

46 Ibid., 188.

47 The term *old debt* also refers to the filial obligation of Jackson Kan to his father, who reminds him to observe the Buddhist ancestral traditions in honor of his deceased brothers in China.

48 Lee, *Tiger's Tail*, 366.

49 Ibid., 43.

50 Ibid., 354.

51 Gus Lee's distinct insider-outsider perspective represents a political position perhaps akin to Tom Clancy's views, in which the populist-minded, vigilante hero, Jack Ryan, has little patience for Washington bureaucracy in *The Hunt For Red October*, preferring to "think outside of the box." Yet Ryan never abandons his duty to his country, and ironically in a later book he becomes the president of the United States.

52 Lee, *Tiger's Tail*, 367.

53 Anderson, *Imagined Communities*.

four ···

Visual Reconnaissance

Joan Kee

The body of cultural production known as contemporary Asian American visual art has long included references from American popular culture. While such inclusion was partly indebted to post-modern discourses that attempted to reveal the artifice embedded in the boundaries separating "high" and "low" culture, it was mainly due to the implied function of Asian American art as a project of reactive critique. Images and references to American popular culture enabled many Asian American artists to resist the ways in which Asian American subjects were positioned in the mainstream American imaginary. As the artist Ken Chu once stated, "Asian Americans have been so defined by popular imagery that the only way to thoroughly discuss Asian American stereotypes is by using such imagery.[1] Reaching its greatest point of visibility in the early 1990s, references to popular culture within material works of art often made their way into the work of art as an object of critique.

More recently, however, other artists have refashioned popular culture's role within the material work of art. No longer the object of critique, it assumes renewed importance as an important means through which critique is enacted. Capitalizing on their immediate recognizability, images and images of practices taken from popular culture readily dominate the viewer's attention. One tends to view these images and practices in light of the contexts within which they came to be known on a widespread basis. What actually determines interpretation, however, are the formal principles determining the function of each work. Often these principles are themselves imported from the visual tropes of advertising and other channels of mass media.

The use of immediate recognizability of images and images of practices in popular culture, however, allows the form's agency to remain largely undetected. The recognizability of images and practices from popular culture provides the artist with an alibi, releasing him or her from having to directly enact such representation. More important, such recognizability extends the scope of the work's political utility by inducing the viewer to generate his or her own readings. In the case of artists such as the Filipino American Paul Pfeiffer and Nikki S. Lee, this utility might be described as visual reconnaissance, whereby the formal depiction of images and images of practices within popular culture effectively reveals attitudes, preconceptions, and other constructions that might otherwise remain out of sight.

Strategic Turns

This is not to imply that earlier works incorporating references to popular culture consistently used images or practices taken from popular culture as the object of critique; for instance, the works of Tseng Kwong Chi and Martin Wong readily incorporated images from popular culture without such images acting as a self-evident subject of critique. Consider also Ken Chu's 1988 mixed-media work *I need some more hair products*. Densely packed within a small physical area are brightly colored icons highly suggestive of various landmarks of American adolescence: a red convertible, a hot dog, a record player, a bowling pin, and of course the mirror. Although varied in hue, all the images possess a similar level of saturation, which causes the eye to read them as part of a continuum. Coupled with its central placement within the space of the work, the relative largeness of the image of the Asian male compels the viewer to assume the presence of a narrative. The eye weaves in and out of the center, absorbing different images and in turn causing the viewer to adjust his or her view of the image.

With the image of the convertible, the road, the bowling pin, the record player, and above all the blond-haired, white male in the cartoon bubble, one particular reading consistently rises to the forefront: the Asian male's internal feelings concerning the trappings of American adolescence, and in particular adolescent desire. Even without knowing any biographical information about the artist or his prior activism with regard to promoting Asian American art,

Ken Chu, *I need some more hair products*, 1988. 21 x 25 inches. Acrylic on foamcore.

the formal logic of the work strongly moves the viewer toward a particular interpretation. Chu's generous use of bright, primary colors, as well as his reduction of forms to their fundamental contours (a single undulating curve for the road, an oblong tip suggestive of a surfboard), injects the work with a levity and immediate visual appeal often lacking in politically minded works of the time. Nevertheless, the work is a first-order representation to the extent that the images, taken together, outweigh formal organization and relationships as the generators of meaning.

The concerted importance placed on the agency of the artist, as opposed to the viewer's response, melded well with the sociohistorical context in which works such as *I need some more hair products* were made. The early 1990s in particular were characterized by a number of large-scale shows that promoted works by Asian and Asian American artists. Notable examples included "Across the Pacific: Contemporary Korean and Korean American Art" at the Queens Museum in New York in 1993, the landmark survey "Asia / America: Identities in Contemporary Asian American Art" at the Asia Society in 1994, "An Ocean Apart: Contemporary Vietnamese Art from the United States and Vietnam" at the San Jose Museum of Art in 1996, and "At Home and Abroad:

20 Filipino Artists" at the Asian Art Museum in San Francisco in 1998. These exhibitions, as the curator Alice Yang has pointed out, emphasize the social context in which identity is situated. In this brief period, mainstream visual arts institutions began to be actively receptive to artists of color making works reflecting their experiences as nonwhite individuals.

There was, however, an intense awareness that this receptiveness was only temporary and that artists had to act quickly to claim a share of the art world for themselves. As Thelma Golden, the curator of "Black Male: Representations of Masculinity in Contemporary Art" at the Whitney Museum of American Art, one of the most controversial and prominent shows mounted during this period, observed, they knew they had to "work hard while the 'getting was good' because we understood that a moment might come when it would no longer be."[2] The curator of "Asia / America," Margo Machida, contended that Asian American artists deliberately magnified their visibility through self-representation, namely, by linking conspicuous images of their racial selves to "the social and physical fabric of the nation."[3] For her, such self-representation played a crucial role in contesting representations imposed by the supposed American "mainstream" and in responding to a specific and finite moment within art historical time.

From the mid-1990s to the present, the frequency and prominence of these exhibitions, contingent on common ethnic roots or ethnic-specific experiences, have decreased with the waning of the art establishment's appetite for multicultural novelty but also because of the increasing disinclination of artists to concede their claims to difference, especially material differences of form within their respective bodies of work, for the sake of contributing to the notion of a unified "Asian American." In a letter to Godzilla, the now defunct Asian American visual arts organization that was instrumental in kindling a politically effective notion of Asian American art during the 1990s, artist Simon Leung wrote, "What strikes me is the demand such a voice of identity places on the viewer during such instances when it is the organizing principle of an exhibition."[4]

Leung's comment indirectly pointed to the problems with the "identity" rubric: though useful politically for its ability to consolidate the efforts of many Asian American artists attempting to be heard as individuals, it ironically prevented any attempt to formulate a holistic interpretation of individual works. The heuristic value of the artwork lay less in its status as a material object than in its perceived capacity to illustrate a particular critic or curator's intent. Resulting assessments often crystallized images into iconographies of displacement and racial anxiety. This happened even when the material forms and formal relationships used as supporting evidence more convincingly pointed to other, sometimes contradictory readings. A work's images were immediately seen as direct indices to a particular experience external to the material work rather than being initially considered as part of a discrete, physical system contained within specific material boundaries such as the picture frame, the film loop, or the beginning and end of a performance.

Even with hindsight, it has proven immensely difficult to break away from this programmatic mode of interpretation. In her recent introduction to one of the most recent additions to Asian American art criticism, *Fresh Talk / Daring Gazes*, Elaine Kim refreshingly engages in a close analysis of the early San Francisco-based painter Yun Gee (1906–31). Her exploration of the work's formal operation is adequately sustained to reveal the indeterminacy of meaning; the viewer, she concludes, cannot ultimately know whether the figure in the painting is "committing suicide or trying to soar like the birds in the sky above him."[5] Her analysis, however, returns to the paradigms of coherent, often nation-based subjectivities; she expounds on the ability of "Asian American" art to engage with "American" art, even when, as in the case of Byron Kim's monochromatic canvases, it is clear that the engagement takes place on the level of visual conceptualization physically articulated through the manipulation of form and its affect rather than on the level of textual rhetoric espoused by the artist or the viewer.

Other cultural critics have actively sought interpretative alternatives, however. Many look to rhetorics of transnationalism, globalization, and the like, though not as a means of confirming the subjecthood of Asian American cultural production. The anthropologist Arjun Appadurai, for instance, perceived the abandonment of the nation form as it pertained to culture to be the "most exciting dividend of living in modernity at large."[6] More recent is Kandice Chuh's argument for the active incorporation of transnational modes of analysis as an important means of reframing Asian American studies as a potent method of critique rather than a futile pursuit of abstract definition.[7] Transnationalism, she contends, offers the possibility of undermining the assumptions upholding the myth of coherence, with regard to both the paradigms of the singular American nation and the consolidated Asian American experience.

Other critics, of course, have long understood the pitfalls of globalization and its rhetoric. Witness the early warnings of Sau-ling Cynthia Wong, who speculates that transnationalism may aggravate what she perceives as "liberal pluralism's already oppressive tendency to 'disembody' ";[8] Dorinne Kondo, who cautions that transnationalism is easily absorbed into the falsely benign guise of "universality," which often exists in tandem with the privileging of Euro-American norms;[9] or Dorothy Wang, who states that delinking race from signs of locality "run[s] the risk of reifying something phantasmatic called 'Asianness.' "[10]

Most artists are keenly aware of these pitfalls. Yet most also understand the dialectical nature of globalization's rhetoric. While not directly addressing Asian American cultural production, the art historian Miwon Kwon's rejection of both the psychic alienation of nomadism and the fetishization of the stable, suggested that locality has special resonance for Asian American artists, an increasing number of whom travel back and forth between the United States and their countries of ethnic origin. Kwon takes issue with the notion of the liberated artist "freed" from the shackles of locality, yet she also emphasizes the need for a studied distance from the antinomadic nostalgia for a settled place proposed by the art historian Lucy Lippard among others.[11] Citing theorist Henri Lefebvre's configuration of a dialectical, rather than oppositional, relationship between the abstractions and particularities of space, Kwon contends that "it is not a matter of choosing sides. . . . Rather, we need to be able to think the range of these seeming contradictions and our contradictory desires for them together, at once."[12]

Kwon's call for a dialectic approach reflects the predicament of artists stuck between a sincere desire to enact change through critique and the desire to partake in the products and methods of globalization. Particularly included in the latter are the images and practices of popular culture. As Paul Pfeiffer comments, "Globalization does not only have to be of the corporate kind, with the frightening erasure of political meaning and agency that it suggests. Globalization can also be an antidote to American provincialism and its crippling effect on our creativity."[13] His functionalist approach reflects the approach found in his and other artists' works, where practices and images found in popular culture function as points of provocation rather than the central objects of critique.

How the viewer extracts representation from the work, however, depends on the work's ecology of form. In this context, *ecology of form* refers to a work's fundamental material structure as it is defined by recursive principles that bind its parts together as a coherent visual function.[14] In the case of Pfeiffer and Lee, these principles are closely related to those employed in advertising: the contingent relationship between images visible on a defined material field, the size of the images vis-à-vis the defined field of the image, and the physical dimensions of that field. It is principles like these that help to reveal the presence of negative attitudes and systems, including those pertaining to globalization, that might otherwise remain obscure. When coupled with the alibi of popular culture's instant and overwhelming recognizability, principles of form appear to disappear; in the brief few seconds that, on average, constitute the entire encounter between the viewer and the material work of art, a work's formal ecology remains subordinate to the immediately visible—and above all familiar—image.

One can describe this symbiosis between form and popular culture as a strategy of visual reconnaissance. The military provenance of this term alludes to the strategic nature of many works that seek to covertly uncover various phenomena of power external to the work (e.g., the inevitable superiority of capitalism as an economic model or the rationalization of essentialist categories in the name of efficient information processing) by having the viewer reveal his or her allegiance to them. This kind of stealthy operation is necessary, for the oppressive elements of any powerful institution, system of belief, or regime are cunningly intertwined with its benefits, including easier access to mobility, expanded possibilities for creativity, and better opportunities for dialogue with multiple groups and individuals. In addition, the oppressive aspects of multiple forms of power are widely propagated through visual forms of communication or the modes through which images are organized into systems of visual depiction. Individual images have less importance than the overall ways in which they are put together. As a result, an imperative exists for producers and critics to address this issue directly.

Visual reconnaissance's greatest importance, though, stems from its ties to notions of the local, the immediate, and the specific. Based in large part on the definition of *visual reconnaissance* in military strategy as the intentional act of visual observation as a means of obtaining information about a defined, chosen geographical area, visual reconnaissance in relation to visual art serves as both a marker and a reminder of the importance of material form, its logic, and its structure as active agents in the project of critique. The heuristic value of tracing practices of visual reconnaissance, then, lies in the inevitable prioritization of material form as the foremost index to a work's meaning. It forces the critic to deduce his or her evaluation from a visible, confirmable body of evidence accessible to all viewers. In this way, the practice of visual reconnaissance offers a methodological escape from the kinds of disembodied, irrelevant, and speculative aspects of globalization's rhetoric resoundingly criticized—and so enthusiastically embraced—by numerous cultural critics, Asian American and otherwise.

Advertising as Critique: Paul Pfeiffer's Visual Tropes

As an illustration of the workings of visual reconnaissance, take the digital works of multimedia artist Paul Pfeiffer. Celebrated for works such as *The Pure Products Go Crazy* (1998), *The Long Count (I Shook Up the World)* (2000), and *John 3:16* (2000), Pfeiffer chooses digital media as his medium of choice for its implied supremacy over "the will of the creator."[15] His meticulously crafted digital remasterings of popular films and athletic events have frequently been seen as commentaries on the way in which advertising and mass media tend to reduce the individual self to variables that are easily consumed, digested, and discarded. By using strategic editing and looping techniques to effect the absence or repetition of key images—techniques that are immersed in the dissemination of popular culture—Pfeiffer does not depict so much as mimic the tactics used by large global behemoths to manipulate individual perceptions.[16]

Such appears to be the interpretative consensus. Yet the agency of Pfeiffer's work lies in the formal structure that compels the viewer to generate representation from his or her encounter with the material work. His work replicates key tropes found in the formal structures of advertising, three of which are especially pronounced. The first is centripetality: the field of the image has a definite center, whether or not it coincides with the actual physical center of the projector screen. In *The Long Count (I Shook Up the World)* (2000), a digital triptych showing a three-minute clip of boxer Muhammad Ali's most famous matches, including his 1964 match against Sonny Liston, the ring and the audience are left intact but all images of the boxers have been expunged. Yet the erasure only emphasizes the concentric organization of the images projected on the screen. The crowd is an amorphous, shifting entity surrounding the boxing ring. Conversely, the ring is a space segregated by parallel ropes, which serve as a barrier preventing the eye from perceiving real spatial depth. The eye inevitably returns to the physical center of the projection screen.

Other works feature competing claims to playing the role of the center. *The Pure Products Go Crazy* (1998) shows a well-known scene from the popular Tom Cruise film *Risky Business* (1983). Here Cruise plays an imaginary guitar (the famous "air guitar" scene) in a moment of postpubescent liberation, wearing

Paul Pfeiffer, *The Pure Products Go Crazy*, 1998. Dimension variable. CD-ROM, project, mounting arm, and bracket. Courtesy of Projectile, New York.

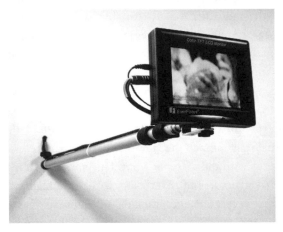

Paul Pfeiffer, *John 3:16*, 2000. 7 x 7 x 36 inches. LCD screen, mounting arm, and 2'7" video loop. Courtesy of Projectile, New York.

nothing but white underpants and Ray-Ban sunglasses. In the loop, Cruise is unceremoniously trapped within the suffocating confines of a small projector screen orgiastically and helplessly wriggling on a couch in repeated sequence. Only a scant two seconds in length, the loop arrests the image of Cruise within the field of the projector screen. The image never rises, never changes position; indeed, the image is almost completely parallel to the couch on the left-hand side.

Far more visible and recognizable than any other image on the screen, the image of Cruise appears to be at the center. Yet here the image is arrested, ossified, made into an object. The image's reduced status to that of a piece of furniture redirects the viewer's attention to the coffee table in the middle of

Kee

the screen as the real center of the image field. Still, Pfeiffer allows the viewer enough clues—namely, the underwear and socks—to recognize and contextualize the image. He or she may still perceive the image of Cruise to be the real center of the image field.

Two material readings thus exist: one is the image of Cruise as a long, tubular form within a larger system of geometric forms, and the other is the image of Cruise as an excerpted figure taken from, but necessarily tied to, a context external to the material work. The viewer accommodates both readings by locating commonalities between the possible interpretations that might result from either route. The first assumes the image to be ontologically identical with those around it—within the image field set up by Pfeiffer, the image is just a piece of furniture, albeit with the capacity for repetitive movement. The second reading summons the phenomena pertaining to the film— its establishment of Cruise as a major film star, the desires of heterosexual adolescent males, and the claims of the film industry to construct new myths and recycle old ones. The common subset between these two readings is an interpretation of Cruise as a product, on an ontological par with an inanimate object, manufactured and packaged in the same way as a couch in a suburban home or a multi-million-dollar film.

The trope of centripetality is enhanced by a second trope, a transformable kind of image magnification that consciously attempts to elevate the image to the status of an icon. Excessively used throughout advertising, it is a trope in which the camera zooms to magnify a particular image, imbuing it with a larger than life aura. The efficacy of this trope is based on the viewer's realization of the magnification process. He or she realizes this through two sets of contrasts. One is the proportional difference between the sizes of the projection or television screen and the subject when the viewer perceives both as objects in the physical, material world. A beverage commercial, for example, often features a sudden close-up of the product being marketed. Its actual size in the physical world may be six inches or so, but it comes to occupy more than half of an average-sized television screen. Its affect comes to have a disproportionately high impact on the stationary viewer.

The other contrast is the relational size of the image vis-à-vis the perceived surface area of the image field. An endless loop comprised of over five thousand images of basketballs collected from various NBA games, the primary image of *John 3:16* (2000), is that of a basketball whose physical size measures no more than seven inches. Yet it covers the entire surface area of the projection screen. The title resonates with the basketball image's domination, evoking the oft-quoted biblical verse heavily invoked by Christian missionaries ("For God so loved the world that He gave His one and only Son, that whoever believes in Him shall not perish but will have eternal life").

From this, the viewer easily derives multiple interpretations: that the ball is a virtual object of worship, granting life "eternal," as literally denoted by the players forever embedded in a perpetual loop on an LCD screen; that the use of the verse John 3:16 insinuates the blasphemy of those who manipulate globalization for their own purposes of accumulating capital; and, finally, that those who exploit the power of the deified ball and its aggregate promises of upward mobility, material affluence, and celebrity glamour are interested not in breathing life into professed believers but in capitalizing on those viewers who have disarmed their natural vigilance through the inertia of fascination. The viewer realizes certain antihumanistic tendencies at work behind the glowing facade of transnational kinds of popular culture, dovetailing with Pfeiffer's own words: "The diaspora is not about us; it's about Michael Jordan. To see him soar through the air, a sparkling shiny creature traveling at the speed of light, landing in every first, second and third world city all at once, is to understand you play a minor role in a very big game."[17]

All these secondary readings have much to do with the third trope, the elasticity of duration and its affective potential. The effects of Pfeiffer's works vary according to their length. As with *John 3:16*, the duration of the loop in *The Pure Products Go Crazy* is so brief as to make the image appear fixed in time. The viewer perceives the image as an object. In *The Long Count*, however, there is some trace of a narrative trajectory as the faces in the crowd change expression. A sense of expectancy greets the viewer as he or she anticipates the boxers about to emerge in the ring. Waiting and waiting, the viewer realizes that the expected event will never occur; the loop starts again. A few more minutes into the encounter, the repetition turns into tedium as expectations rise and fall. Yet another few minutes and the viewer becomes physically exhausted, his or her will to perceive sapped by repetition.

These three tropes greatly multiply the work's capacity for representation. However, the capacity of the work to act as a node within a larger visual system, including both advertising and visual art, also offers a ready excuse for ignoring, or obscuring, the artist's ethnicity. Following Pfeiffer's catapult into the New York art world limelight as a result of his participation in the Whitney Biennale in 2000 and his designation as the inaugural winner of the Bucksbaum Prize, the world's largest monetary prize given to a living artist, he was suddenly reinscribed into a universalizing rubric that had no space for his experiences as a nonwhite individual. During the awards ceremony for the Bucksbaum Prize at the Whitney Museum of American Art, Pfeiffer was presented "purely" as an artist working in multimedia with no mention of his ethnic heritage or sexual orientation, despite his previous involvement in and collaborations with Asian American arts groups such as Godzilla, as well as gay rights groups. In like manner, critical assessments of his work have consistently emphasized him as an "individual" artist, willfully or myopically ignoring how ethnicity contributes to the formation of real individuality.[18]

Granted, the mechanics of Pfeiffer's work, or the components of a given work and how they are put together to form a cohesive entity, support these attempts to deethnicize him. His emphasis on editing techniques such as splicing and looping catalyze almost all readings of his works. Yet, although a treatment of the mechanics through which a work is created is necessary, if only to circumvent the supposition that the primary merit of Asian American art is somehow embedded in the visualization of ethnic heritage, the glib erasure of his ethnicity is equally disturbing. It begs the question of whether the ascendancy of a nonwhite into the pantheon of the contemporary art establishment is dependent on that artist's surrender of his racial identity. As the writer Luis H. Francia rhetorically asks, "Are artists forced to check their ethnic baggage at the door?"[19] This example of the Bucksbaum awards ceremony points to an especially visible way in which identity is refashioned to suit the needs of those who control access to capital (in this example, the Selection Committee of the Bucksbaum award and the Whitney Museum) at the expense of revealing those parts of the self not in conformity with bright-line categories.

Hiding in Plain Sight: The *Projects* of Nikki S. Lee

How, then, to respond to this situation? Perhaps by the most overt means available. We turn now to Nikki S. Lee, whose series, *Projects*, demonstrates a remarkable experiment in remaking identity. Begun in 1997, the series consists of fourteen sets of multiple snapshots in which the artist posed as a member of various American cultures and subcultures, from a skateboarder in San Francisco to a hip hop groupie in New York. The sole exception is *The Schoolgirls Project* (2000), which is based on the artist's student days when uniforms in Korea were mandatory. Trained as a photographer, first as an undergraduate and later in graduate school in New York, to which she moved from Seoul in 1994, Lee is a keen connoisseur of styles, able to sort through and discern surface differences in costume, gesture, and environment. This is evident in the level of detail in her masquerades, such as the brand-loving yuppie banker in the blue shirt with the beefy white trader boyfriend in one scene from *The Yuppie Project* (1998) and the Jheri-curled neighborhood diva with a gold name-plate necklace in *The Hispanic Project* (1998). The artist avers that her preparation for the masquerade begins with "going to the places where people shop for clothes. More than anything you can tell what people are like by what sort of things they buy for themselves."[20] Yet she adds that "while style is important in my work I don't analyze the style. . . . That would be stereotyping. I become the style."[21]

Her premise of identity as an intrinsically malleable notion coheres well with one of the implicit premises found in curatorial and critical thinking pertaining to Asian American art: the struggle to assert and have others recognize the Asian American artist's capacity for autonomous decision making. As implied by the immense number of writings and exhibitions featuring some variation on the binary logic of "Asia" plus "America" (often dressed up in the rhetoric of hybridity), the enterprise of Asian American visual art thus far has been deeply invested in the notion that the Asian American artist can choose whether to be racialized or not. Lee's choices of attire, posture, and gesture certainly confirm the possibility of the autonomous artist; in *The Tourist Project* (1997), for example, she departs from the most likely model of the proverbial tourist from East Asia by donning tube socks, sneakers, and nylon fanny packs identical to those worn by the tourists that flood Times Square from the American Midwest. She borrows from the archive of popular idioms, but her cues are mixed, even erroneous, at times. This is not a reflection of her failure to assimilate but evidence of her agency manifested as the subjective choice.

What really enables Lee's hyperconsumption to exceed its presumed initial role as merely another form of self-representation are the visual tropes of exceptional centripetality and the dissembling capacity of magnification to eliminate the presumed boundary between the worlds of the viewer and that captured within the picture frame. Here the trope of centripetality becomes exceptional because it is an aggregate of formal relationships and tactics. Lee does not take the photographs herself but entrusts their shooting to a friend or even a bystander. Yet she implicitly chooses each photograph's formal organization by virtue of her relationship to other objects and subjects whose presence is expected within the photograph. Throughout the *Projects*, Lee is often at the physical center of the photograph, and the centrality of her image is reinforced by two primary modes of overall formal organization. One is a

Nikki S. Lee, *The Hip Hop Project (1)*, 2001. 21.5 x 28.5 or 30 x 40 inches. Fujiflex print.
Courtesy of Leslie Tonkonow Artworks and Projects and the artist.

Nikki S. Lee, *The Yuppie Project (4)*, 1998. 21.5 x 28.5 or 30 x 40 inches. Fujiflex print.
Courtesy of Leslie Tonkonow Artworks and Projects and the artist.

concentric model in which contextual props, or other members of a particular group, radiate from her. The second is the implicit frame, in which Lee may not occupy the physical center of the photograph but instead becomes the center by virtue of the other figures, which form an amorphous frame around the body of the artist as in scenes from *The Hip Hop Project* of 2001.

In both models, the artist often launches the trope of exceptional centripetality by means of her outward, frontal gaze. This leads to something of a paradox. Lee's gaze, positioned at the approximate eye level of the anticipated viewer, immediately draws the viewer's attention into the realm within the work—the specific context in which she finds her subjects, whether it be San Francisco (*The Skateboarders Project*) or various sightseeing locales around New York City (*The Tourist Project*). At the same time, however, the frontal gaze induces the eye to consider Lee as part of the material, physical world of the viewer. The barrier between the world of the viewer and that within the photograph gradually dissolves, causing the viewer to conflate the image of the artist with the artist in the flesh.

A scene from *The Yuppie Project* shows the artist outside the window of a boutique walking a small, well-groomed dog. In a sleek, fur-trimmed black coat, Lee appears to be overburdened with consumption—an expensive leather handbag and the telltale light blue of a Tiffany shopping bag. Slightly off center, Lee's black coat provides visual balance between the black suit of a doorman or passerby on the far left and the glossy finish on the doorframe of the boutique. Further consolidating black as a structural anchor for the photograph as a discrete visual unit are the clothes of a young white woman in the lower right-hand corner, who stops to pet Lee's dog. Her garments, too, are black, as is what appears to be the recognizable matte black of a Barneys New York shopping bag. At periodic intervals, patches of high-value color appear— the bright blue Tiffany shopping bag, the pale orange interior of the illuminated boutique, the light gray overcoat worn by the young white woman. The regularity with which this occurs suggests that the entire photograph is a world contained within the photographic frame. Yet the frontal gazes and smiles of the two women directly connect with the viewer, thus troubling the claims of the photograph to depict a world independent of that of the viewer.

Even more effective in compelling the viewer to disregard the presumed boundary between the world within the photograph and that of the viewer is the trope of magnification. An example is *The Hispanic Project*, which is set in New York City's Hispanic, particularly Puerto Rican, neighborhoods. Turned to the side, the artist looks out at a point that ostensibly lies outside the frame

Nikki S. Lee, *The Hispanic Project (25)*, 1998. 21.5 x 28.5 or 30 x 40 inches. Fujiflex print.
Courtesy of Leslie Tonkonow Artworks and Projects and the artist.

of the picture. This forces the viewer into a state of oscillation; on the one hand, Lee's clothes and the background scene position her within a specific world far removed from the gallery contexts in which her works are almost always viewed. On the other, the image of the artist is blown up to such an extent that she presumes to be a part of the viewer's immediate, physical world. The presumption is far less overt than it would have been if the image of Lee's face and torso had replicated the actual dimensions of the artist.

Yet the presumption is strengthened by the presence of acceleration compelled by the sudden magnification of the artist's image vis-à-vis the background. Part of her head is cut off by the photograph's frame, which implies that she belongs to a world outside the photograph. The unidentified man on the far right is also an excerpt, but this image clearly belongs to the world within the photograph on the basis of its inevitability of scale; that is, the image of the man coincides with the viewer's expectations concerning scale within the field of the photograph. Perceiving the interplay of foliage and sky in the far background, the viewer progresses to the bystanders milling about. Some appear to be bigger than others, but all coincide with the viewer's expectations of scale. The viewer next perceives the figure of the man, which,

Visual Reconnaissance

though somewhat of a jump from the tiny figures of the background, denotes a certain slowness in the pace of magnification. One expects a larger image in the foreground, but these expectations come to an abrupt halt as one perceives the image of Lee, front and center. Adorned with flashing gold jewelry, a bright green, low-cut dress, and a tiny rose tattoo, the image of Lee is not too far away from the colorful spectacles of David LaChapelle, for whom Lee once worked as an intern. The image immediately yanks the viewer into the world constructed by the images seen within the photograph.

It is this inseparability between the worlds of the viewer and the work that seems to make interpretation of *Projects* an almost absurdly facile task. Clearly one enters into the interpretation via the image of the artist. The apparent collapse of the viewer's world and that of the artist allows the viewer to read the work as a contemporaneous, mimetic part of his or her own world.

Or so the symbiosis of Lee's masquerade and the ecology of forms would have one believe. The exceptional centripetality of Lee's image and the connoisseurial eye for personal physical appearance make it the prime object of interpretation, yet it is remarkable how so many viewers structure their ensuing interpretations around the Asianness of Lee's physical features. Many perceive the figure of Lee as evidence of either the Asian immigrant body and its supposed capacity for unlimited malleability or the Asian body's inexorable foreignness. For some, the artist's appropriation of such cues triggers a definition of hybridity as physical and psychological malleability. As the curator Thomas Finkelpearl contends in an appropriately titled essay, "The Western Mirror," Lee enacts East-West self-portraits indicative of her integration into mainstream American society.[22] By blending into so many various fragmented social contexts, the artist, in Finkelpearl's view, implicitly conceives of the Asian body as a malleable object subsumed into the fabric of American society.

Others insist on the foreignness of the Asian body, itself betraying an inability to trouble one's own systems of ordering. Often the language used to describe the work is tinged with insinuations of deception, pathology, and even criminality, as words such as *undetected* and phrases such as "her Asian features almost always give her away" are constantly used to describe her work.[23] Even well-intentioned critics fall into this quagmire; in his otherwise thoughtful short essay on the claims of whiteness to invisibility and uniqueness, as dissected by Lee in *The Yuppie Project*, the critic Maurice Berger writes: "Though she masquerades in the fashions, make-up, and body language of white yuppies her Asianness and her visceral discomfort read as distinctly as their whiteness."[24] He categorically excludes other, more supportable readings

(Was Lee trying to fit into her own assumptions regarding the mental or emotional states of those in finance-related jobs? Was she trying to set herself apart from the other bankers and corporate law types despite a similar banality in dress?) of Lee's rigid posture and lack of facial expression in favor of one that positions her as a misfit.

The urge to describe Lee as a fugitive or deviant of sorts reveals the extent to which the perceivably non-Western artist in the Euro-American environment is constantly reconfigured into the binary of East versus West. This is arguably done so that the viewer can obtain psychological relief, for in uncovering Lee in her multiple performances he or she puts Lee back into her place, so to speak, and preserves the integrity of the system of ordering through which the viewer makes the external world personally legible. Intensified to the point where the only logical point of entry into the work is the body of Lee, the trope of exceptional centripetality deceives the viewer through the least evident means possible.

But the political utility of Lee's work is also based on another premise, one not so happily coincidental with the notion of the autonomous Asian American artist. Another look at the formal structure through which Lee deploys her masquerades reveals a vampiric kind of siphoning at work. Other participants exist almost as props in comparison with the artist, who, gazing directly at the viewer, almost always occupies the foreground and the center of every photograph's frame. Based on the compression of cultural difference into surface imagery, Lee's *Projects* suggest that tangible individuality can only be possible when the individual in question is juxtaposed against others. The artist states: "I always feel like I have a lot of different characters inside and I was curious to understand these things."[25] Or "I am interested in identity, but not identity politics. In dressing up as a Japanese living in the East Village or a yuppie, I become reacquainted with different parts of my own self."[26] But her most important statement is the question that recurs in each work of the *Projects* series: at what cost to other selves do I reaffirm my own?

Are Lee's *Projects*, then, too successful in inducing the viewer to reveal his or her preconceived notions? More than Pfeiffer's, Lee's brand of visual reconnaissance works exceptionally well as a strategy. It comes at a price, though. At its extreme, the practice of visual reconnaissance reifies a willful tendency within critical discourse on Asian American art to consider the material form of the work as a dependent variable of the artist's presumed intent to enact a specific representation. Such assessments have frequently led to an implicit assumption of the work of art as a strategy, shutting other agentive possibilities down for the sake of preserving the coherence of a particular message of critique.

To check this tendency, an evaluation of visual reconnaissance must be accompanied by a constant awareness of its basis in the relationships generated by the perceived material form of the work. To do so would offer three advantages. First, it directly challenges the mode of interpretation in which discussion of an artist's work turns on its alleged capacity to act as a direct metaphor for various allegories of racialized experience. Second, it reaffirms the validity of popular culture as a subject for serious critical inquiry on the basis of its visual forms. Looks matter. Third, it broadens the possibilities for critique, but, perhaps most urgently, it doubly serves as a reminder of critique's capacity for suppression when the viewer willingly surrenders his or her conceptual facilities to the enterprise of reactive critique. For visual reconnaissance to really work, it should be understood as a conditional heuristic. Hopefully it will be but one step en route to the moment when critics gladly relinquish programmatic modes of assessing the viewer's encounter with visual works of art or, more specifically, when programmatic modes of assessment are no longer necessary.

Notes

1 Interview with the author, November 23, 1996, New York City.
2 Golden, "Mama said . . . ," 73. "Black Male: Representations of Masculinity in Contemporary American Art" was organized by Golden at the Whitney Museum of American Art in 1994. It generated a staggering amount of publicity and criticism from progressive and conservative viewers alike, who objected to what was considered derogatory stereotypes of African Americans.
3 Machida, "Out of Asia," 59.
4 Quoted in Yang, "Asian American Exhibitions Reconsidered," 97. Godzilla was the name of a group of Asian American visual artists and arts professionals based in New York founded by artists Margo Machida, Ken Chu, and Bing Lee in 1990.
5 Kim, "Introduction," 6.
6 Appadurai, *Modernity at Large*, 23.
7 Chuh, *Imagine Otherwise*, 56–57.
8 Wong, "Denationalization Reconsidered," 18–19.
9 Kondo, *About Face*, 19–20. Kondo is speaking of theater, but the same concerns are highly applicable to visual art. Indeed, one might argue that the dangers of universalism loom even larger considering the persistent exclusion of contemporary non-Western art from school curriculums and mainstream discussions. This exclusion in the form of omission is at odds with the discrediting

of Enlightenment-style universalism in many academic circles, especially the humanities.

10 Wang, review of *Orientations: Mapping Studies in the Asian Diaspora*, 274.

11 Kwon, "The Wrong Place."

12 Ibid., 35–36.

13 Electronic mail communication with the author, March 25, 2001, New York City.

14 The notion of "formal ecology," I suggest here, is partly indebted to the seminal art historian Alois Riegl's idea of *strukturprincipien*, which assumes a work to be composed of certain fundamental principles that exist throughout. Riegl's notion, however, emerged from his most famous concept, *kunstwollen*, an ambiguous term for which the best English translation is probably "the will of the work" given Riegl's emphasis on dynamicism as a characteristic of the work of art. Hans Sedlmayr, a key intellectual descendant of Riegl, borrows Edgar Wind's phrase, "a real force," to interpret what Riegl meant by the notion of the kunstwollen. See Sedlmayr's preface to Riegl's *Gesammelte Aufsäzte* (Sedlmayr, "Preface," xvii–xviii). The preface was originally written in 1927.

15 Quoted in Carr, "Icon Remix," 65.

16 Paul Pfeiffer, interview with the author, March 16, 2001.

17 Pfeiffer, "Quod nomen mihi est?"

18 During his graduate school years in New York in the early 1990s, Pfeiffer was involved in Asian American arts groups such as Godzilla, as well as gay rights groups, but he maintained his ties to Filipino geospatiality through frequent travel and exhibitions.

19 Francia, "Memories of Overdevelopment," 25.

20 Nikki S. Lee, interview with the author, April 30, 2001, New York City.

21 Quoted in Hamilton, "Dressing the Part Is Part of Her Art."

22 Finkelpearl, "The Western Mirror," 164. Thomas Finkelpearl was the curator of the North American section of the Third Gwangju Biennale, entitled "Man + Space," in which Nikki S. Lee was a participant. Her selection caused some controversy among Korean critics and curators, who argued that Lee, a Korean citizen, should have been included in the "Asia" or "Korea" sections of the exhibition.

23 Paul Parcellin comments, "The idea that an Asian woman can blend and go undetected among Hispanics or white rednecks strains credulity" ("In Focus"). The tone assumed is one of *incredulity*, as if it would be an utterly preposterous idea for the "Asian woman" to cross what seems to be impermeable demographic categories. Less problematically, but still evocative of the prevalence of categorization as a conceptual tool, Merrily Kerr writes, "In gesture, makeup and clothing she plays her parts perfectly, but her Asian features give her away every time, resulting in an initially confused reading" ("Li'l Nikki 'N' Friends," 78).

24 Berger, "Picturing Whiteness," 55–56.

25 Vicario, "Conversation with Nikki S. Lee," 100.

26 Nikki S. Lee, interview with the author.

five

Chinese Restaurant Drive-Thru

Indigo Som

Chinese restaurants are so ubiquitous throughout the United States that they constitute an integral part of American life. They are the most pervasively visible manifestation of Chinese American presence in this country. For most Americans of non-Chinese descent, Chinese restaurants provide the main point of contact with Chinese culture and Chinese people.

Yet this potent influence remains generally unacknowledged, even invisible. Historical patterns of racism have stereotyped Asian Americans as perpetually foreign and intrinsically un-American, so that Chinese food, despite its position as a fixture in the American foodscape, remains an exoticized outsider to the usual considerations of "American" culture and identity.

The Chinese Restaurant Project aims to investigate and elucidate the complex relationships between Chinese restaurants and American culture. This long-term umbrella project encompasses several smaller projects, each focusing on a different aspect or interpretation of Chinese restaurants in the United States, and includes artwork in a variety of media, including photography, installation, and writing.

In May 2002 the Anderson Center in Red Wing, Minnesota, hosted me for a residency to work on the project. Afterward my friend and colleague Irene Chan joined me for a tour of Chinese restaurants in Wisconsin. The following is a brief account of our adventures.

Friday: Eau Claire

For $39.30 we get to stay a night in the Maple Manor Motel's Apple theme room. The top border of the wallpaper is all apples; there's an apple clock, apple lamp, a basket of plastic apples on an apple tray, apple pictures on the walls. Right by the door is a picture of a teddy bear with a flag and a basket of apples reading God Bless America.

This is the beginning of the six-day tour of Wisconsin's Chinese restaurants. Irene Chan is riding shotgun, playing translator, navigatrix, and moral support all rolled into some kind of superhero ubersidekick. We are on a mission to investigate Chinese restaurants in the heartland, one finger of my many-tentacled Chinese Restaurant Project.

We drove east out of the Twin Cities this afternoon, all stocked up with organic snacks from the co-op, maps and highlighters in hand. Among the malls of Hudson, we spotted Happy China Garden and pulled into the huge parking lot in front of a Christian bookstore called Heaven Bound.

Inside the restaurant I shot the fake ivy, the American flags, and the Vietnamese art, and then we interviewed Rich, the owner's son. He told us that everybody working in the restaurant is family or close family friends, and they are all Vietnamese except for one guy who is half Chinese. We asked if they serve any Vietnamese dishes. He said they had tried a few, but the customers

didn't go for them, so they gave up on it. We asked if he likes restaurant work; he answered, "I hate it with a passion!" Oh. But he is a good son doing his family duty; Irene and I were suitably impressed.

Across the highway at Kingdom Buffet, the woman at the front asked, "Are you Chinese? Do you speak Chinese?" I whipped out Irene, my secret Cantonese weapon; the woman spoke some of that, so they started talking. As I walked away toward the buffet, she gestured toward me and told Irene, "She looks like an artist." Reporting this to me later, Irene insisted that it's my new glasses; I think it has more to do with my unkempt hair and wrinkled cargo shorts.

Saturday: Wisconsin Dells

Breakfast at Maple Manor: poached eggs, too many hash browns, whole wheat toast, and grapefruit juice. Lilacs in a recycled mayonnaise jar on the counter.

At China Buffet, we talked to a young guy from Fujian; he said there have been lots of people from Fujian coming in the past three or four years. I have heard this as a general thing, too. He said he had been in Philadelphia before and liked this much better because he loves cold, cold weather. (Philly isn't cold enough?) Mystery revealed: China Buffet is a franchise operation! No wonder there's so many of 'em. Everyone is trying to become the Chinese

Taco Bell . . . except that it's mostly all Chinese, or at least Asian, and Taco Bell isn't. Mexican, I mean.

We worked our way east and south to the bizarre, tacky Americana that is the Wisconsin Dells. There's a car show this weekend, so the streets are roaring with hot-rodding testosterone. There's taffy and fudge, zillions of water slides, and every other possible kind of tourist trap you can imagine. For miles. Why are we here? Well, there's one Chinese restaurant, and it closed for the night right before we got to it. Can't win 'em all.

Sunday: Prairie du Chien, the Serbian-Run Holiday Motel Opposite the Train Tracks

With great relief, we left the Dells this morning, next encountering a bonus restaurant not in my database, and the guy there, Jeff, was friendly and talkative to boot. We were very impressed with him. He is completely aware of everything going on in his restaurant at all times, even while talking to us. He had noticed us taking photos out in the parking lot before we came in. Every single customer who came up to pay his or her tab, he asked if everything had been okay. Even just wiping off a table, he did it with great vigor and attention. He said that he had tried to do a drive-through restaurant before, but now he is older and doesn't have enough energy for that. We said, "You seem like you have plenty of energy!" He said, "No, when I was young I could party all night,

until three or four in the morning, and then get up and go to work at eight; I can't do that anymore." He talked about the other Chinese restaurant in town. He had had a neighborly relationship with the previous owner; they would borrow things from each other when they ran out. But he warned us that the people who are there now are not very friendly and said that he didn't understand that because Chinese people here should all help each other.

Sure enough, when we went to the other restaurant and asked if we could take pictures, the guy said bluntly, "NO. You cannot take pictures." And that was it. I gave him the award for Most Unfriendly Chinese Restaurant.

After lunch we hit another town with one restaurant, which seemed kind of uninspiring but probably just because we were tired. Leaving there we ate some chocolate, which revived us considerably for a nice drive on quiet two-lane roads through beautiful rolling farmland. We stopped at a yard sale run by a disheveled couple; their house was held together with Tyvek house wrap on one side and pretty much falling apart everywhere else, with many cats inside and a barking dog on a rope. They were selling total crap, nothing worth buying, including some very basic Christmas ornaments that the woman had made. They made small talk about L.A. freeways and road rage and then said, "If someone shot you out here or ran you off the road off a bluff nobody would ever find you for years." We didn't take that as a threat, can't say why exactly.

The next town really did feel like the middle of nowhere. The Chinese restaurant was all but lost in a very long strip mall with an enormous, almost

empty parking lot. The cashier there was obviously thrilled to see us. He showed us a picture of his wife back in China. She was beautiful, and we said so, Irene using one of her few Mandarin vocabulary words. He replied, "You are beautiful, too," and then sincerely added, "Any Chinese here is beautiful." He said he lives in a trailer with the other guys who work in the restaurant. I think there are four of them. He said there are only seven Chinese in the town (of approximately five thousand), and five of them are men. If it weren't for September 11, he said, his wife and child would probably be here with him now, but immigration has gotten really difficult.

Partway through our conversation he became occupied with a mild late-lunch rush, so we sat down and waited to talk to him again. While he worked, he kept beaming over at us. I said to Irene, "He's so happy to see Chinese people." She said, "Especially Chinese females!" He wasn't being lecherous or anything, just very enthusiastic. He offered to feed us: "I make banquet for you!" But we told him we had already eaten. He used to be a translator in China; his first translation was a book about Mike Tyson. Then he translated some other, more literary stuff. We talked about writing and telling the truth and how sometimes you may want to write the truth but you can't. He said, "This is what I am reading right now," and pulled a worn copy of Jane Eyre from behind the counter. He said, "I have nobody to talk to. I wish I had people to talk to here. . . . I talk all day, but 'broccoli with beef' is not really talking." When we left, he nearly followed us out the door.

As we drove away, I realized that the bachelor society is still the same 150 years later; we use the past tense and speak of it in the context of the Chinese Exclusion Act, but it's not a thing of the past.

In this melancholy mood, we arrived in Prairie du Chien around twilight. We stopped in at a restaurant run by a Korean family. The building was all decorated with Korean motifs, and everything about it was Korean except the food, which was the same old Wisconsin Chinese Buffet.

We checked into the motel and found dinner: fried catfish, the first fish I've had in these parts that was done properly instead of cooked to death. Maybe it has to do with freshness, being right next to the Mississippi. However, that was all there was to say about it, really, and we came back and drank some ginger ale anyway because of all the grease.

Monday: La Crosse

This morning we got up all dry-throated from the hot room and cut up fruit for breakfast. The weather was very foggy and gray out but still fairly warm. As we loaded up the car, it was raining lightly. I went through a whole roll of film trying to get the perfect shot of China House next to Dairy Queen, and then we left town, driving through more rolling farmland in the dreamy mist.

We crossed into the next county and stopped at the ubiquitous Frozen Custard ButterBurger franchise to ask for directions to the Chinese restaurant. Of course, they were very helpful in this latest installment of "Help the poor little lost Chinese girls find the Chinese restaurant," which is a board game concept we've developed. We followed their kindly directions up to the Great Wall, which, like some other Great Walls, involved a long, horizontal building necessitating Irene's wide-angle lens. These things always crack me up. We actually ate there. It was a modest-sized buffet with pretty high turnover; they kept coming out with a small saucepan and dumping more food in. I was kind of impressed that they were making it in such small quantities, like a regular serving amount instead of big vats. Irene decided to get one of everything, which was certainly her undoing because she didn't feel great all the rest of the day. I was more cautious but included crab rangoon and the eternal General Tso's chicken along with my decent broccoli, noodles, etc.

The crab rangoon was sweet! It reminded me more of a cheese Danish than anything else. So freakin weird. Or maybe a wannabe blintz. And then people dip it in that syrupy red sauce? Bleah! Anyway, after eating we talked to the manager, a sweet-faced young guy who had the most remarkable nose hairs I've ever seen. They were long, luxurious, thick, and black, and they stuck way out of his nose! Both Irene and I had a hard time trying not to look at his nose hairs while talking to him. He was very nice and told us about how his whole family all owns restaurants, about fifteen of them, including a few in Virginia and the rest all around here. He gave us a discount on our lunches for being Chinese. When I came out of the bathroom, Irene was talking to him again. In the car, she told me that he had asked what she does, and when she said she is a teacher he said he wished he could have a job like that. She said it was heartbreaking, how he said that with such sincerity and no malice or resentment or anything. We talked about how lucky we are and have no right to complain about anything in our lives.

In Onalaska we optimistically went into the Hong Kong Buffet all ready to speak Cantonese, only to find that, just like most places on this trip, nobody there speaks it. Irene was indignant: "Why do they name it Hong Kong then?!" Eventually someone who spoke some English translated for us, and they let us photograph. They had decorated the place with those old-school prefab bows that you stick on top of presents; they were stuck all along the borders of walls and things. They had sushi there, and we were mystified because we thought they must be getting it flown in or something. Irene saw the manager sitting down to eat with a plate from the buffet: half of it was watermelon, and the other half was plain white rice. That kinda says a lot.

Tuesday: Econolodge, Rochester, Minnesota

As we were walking up to the door of China Buffet, I had this feeling like, maybe they will speak Cantonese in here. Sure enough there was a guy from Fujian who had spent a year in Hong Kong, so he and Irene yakked away while I took photos and cased out the extensive buffet. He had worked at a restaurant in New Jersey before. He likes it better here because the customers are nicer, but there is not much to do. He mentioned fishing, and said he also goes to Minneapolis to visit friends. At length, he invited us to try the buffet, so we did. It was better than the last place. But we left the crab rangoons alone!

Then we went to Hunan Restaurant, where we interviewed a young white waitress who loves her job. She looked barely twenty, but she had been working there for four years. She talked about her regular customers, who always order the same thing, how they come in intending to try something new but

end up with their tried and true favorites. She is clearly more adventurous; she said the best food is what the cooks make for the restaurant staff to eat, including octopus and squid and stuff like that.

At Peking, we talked to Kaiti, who was from Taiwan, lived in Brazil from age nine to seventeen, and then came to La Crosse. She loves it here! Her customers are very devoted to her and she to them; she said that she loves to see families come in with their kids, and then the kids grow up and bring their own kids. When new Chinese restaurants open up in town, her customers go size up the competition and report back to her. She said that she relates to Brazilians and other South Americans more than Chinese people. There is a large company in town that apparently brings temporary workers in from South America, and Kaiti is like the unofficial welcoming committee and tour guide for them. She has her Chinese mama side too, though: when she wished us a safe trip, she cautioned us against driving at night.

Som

Wednesday

Driving another two-lane road through farmland, I said to Irene, have you ever been on a plane flying over farmland and looked down and wondered who was that one car driving on those tiny little roads in between the farms? Well I just realized that's us! We're down in that landscape! And this is what it looks like on the ground. Of course, then Irene made a crack about how the little cars driving on these roads are all looking for Chinese restaurants.

The plan was to bring my boxes to FedEx on our way to the airport. We exited the freeway and immediately ran smack into David Fong's, which made us both scream. First of all, it's massive. Then there's the big sign: David Fong's, in that classic, horrible, chinky font. Then there's the building! The building is a marvel, an early-sixties modernist abstraction of the tired old Chinese pagoda theme. Instead of bright red it is a more sedate orangey-rust color. Truly, I have never seen anything like it. There was no question of not stopping, airport schedules be damned. I veered into the lot, both of us screeching with delight, and we ran around the parking lot and the building spastically taking pictures.

Inside it was dark, enormous, and busy. They had matches! I was almost beside myself with the matches and then went around the corner to the takeout counter, where they had magnets! Barely able to contain myself, I eagerly asked, "Are those magnets?? Are you selling those or giving them

away??" Just then Irene came around the corner and I said, "LOOK! They have magnets!!!" and Irene exclaimed, "Wow, magnets!" and the solid Midwestern white woman behind the counter said, in the most flattened-out tone she could manage, "Yes, we have magnets," as she handed them over. Then we left, laughing hysterically at ourselves. It was definitely the exclamation point on the end of the trip. We could not believe how fabulous it was and regretted not having more time.

At the airport, Irene ran to get her flight, and I sat in the food court with a view of the Wok and Roll, sipping a soda—I mean a pop—while I waited for my flight and tallied up the restaurants: thirty-five in six days!

Note

Many thanks to www.stretcher.org, where this travelogue was first published.

six

The Guru and the Cultural Politics of Placelessness

Sukhdev Sandhu

After 9 / 11, life changed dramatically for many South Asians in New York. Accustomed, however much they might deny it, to thinking of themselves as a breed apart, the nation's most wanted model minority, they now found themselves being stared at and resented. Some were chased down streets and beaten up. Shocked that they were being conflated with Middle Eastern "towelheads," many gathered in restaurants and wine bars to discuss their newfound feelings of discontent and estrangement.

"How does it feel to be a solution?" asked Vijay Prashad in *The Karma of Brown Folk*.[1] His question was addressed to those professional South Asians who arrived in the United States in the wake of the 1965 Immigration and Nationality Acts. This new lot of immigrants were a tonier flotilla than most. They came as engineers, medics, and tech workers sought out by the acts' new provisions for skilled workers. They were only distantly related to the sojourners and agricultural workers who had fitfully made their way across the *kala pani* (black or dark water) since the opening decades of the twentieth century.

Ashakant Nimbark, in an essay entitled "Hinduism in New York City," evokes the social world they routinely inhabit.

The NRI [Non Resident Indian] media scene in the New York area is filled with a mixture of worldly entertainment, intrawordly mobility and other-worldly worship. The coexistence of insurance agency ads, travel agency ads, and religious ceremony ads implies that the first ensures physical well-being, the second ensures constant touch with their roots, and the third should ensure well-being in the hereafter of these economically enterprising but socially marginalized NRIS. They spend millions of dollars inviting, sponsoring, and glamorising religious discourses of jet-set orators such as Murari Babu, who offer elaborate Ramayana discourses laced with worldly wit, melodious music and how-to lessons.[2]

The tale of these NRIS is a one of globalization and its contents. These South Asians, who have been brought up with a sense of ease and entitlement and led to believe that they can travel anywhere they like because of their educations and expensive diction, practice a vernacular cosmopolitanism, one largely shorn of intellectual or bohemian aspirations. The relative wealth of many South Asians in America today means that they are not pegged to conveyor belts, sewing pools, or restaurant kitchens, the microzones of urban identity where immigrants have traditionally ground out a sense of what it is to be a person of color in the United States. They can afford, more than their agrarian forebears did, to girdle the globe, travel back to India and Pakistan, to Europe, to whichever leisure resort they might wish. They can *consume* places.

The affliction they have in common is "placelessness." This concept, itself motile and restlessly nonspecific, has been spreading across the social sciences for over a decade now. James Howard Kunstler, in *The Geography of Nowhere*, uses it as an umbrella term to describe the graceless, resonance-free flatlands of so much recent American architecture. It encompasses such phenomena as suburban sprawl, conurbanization, mall culture, and overdevelopment. The French theorist Marc Augé, meanwhile, coined the term *nonspaces* to describe those urban nodes, such as cash points and airports, that are stripped of historical or local memory and are utilized as anonymous terrains for the flow of financial traffic and its largest possible accumulation.

Placelessness, as I conceive it, is a phenomenon as well as a process, one that is itself in the process of becoming more visible. Its distinguishing feature is the privileging of movement, especially across countries and continents, and a corresponding lack of interest in the poetics and politics of individual loci. The buzz of traveling is greater than that of arriving or digging below the surface of the destination point. All that is solid melts into slipstream. As Pico Iyer, an NRI author and self-declared "global soul," put it: "We are the Tran-sit Loungers, forever heading to the Departure Gate, forever orbiting the world. . . . We pass through countries as through revolving doors; resident aliens of the world, impermanent residents of nowhere. Nothing is strange to us, and nowhere is foreign."[3]

Small wonder, then, that New York, its quotidian texture, and its fault lines are so invisible in South Asian films set in the city. In movies such as *American Desi* (2001) and *American Chai* (2001), the city is alluded to, a fitfully present backdrop to the pampered shenanigans and listless identity crises being undergone by the bourgie characters, but never a live or forceful presence. These films are sites of radical deterritorialization; far from putting onscreen the kind of ceaseless Sturm und Drang that Gilles Deleuze and Félix Guattari would have advocated, they have been stripped bare of any social and historical materiality. For sure, a few shots of the Brooklyn Bridge or the World Trade Center crop up here and there, but this is picture-postcard urbanism, far less penetrating than an average episode of *Friends*.

I want to consider in this essay how the themes and processes I have outlined are played out in *The Guru* (2002), a comedy about Asian immigrants in New York. Executive produced by an Indian but made by white Americans, it stars a cast of Asians, predominantly from England, and is both a product of and a product for exactly the kind of mobile, well-traveled, "global Asians" I have been discussing. That it's a big film, of the sort advertised in teen mags and on town-center billboards, shown at suburban multiplexes and on cable channels, and racked up next to haystack-sized Doritos at the local video store, is also of some consequence. *The Guru* isn't part of the academic canon; it doesn't pitch itself as a contribution to op-ed debates or counterhegemonic discourse. It operates, according to its makers, in a "neutral," commercial idiom.

And yet, as Karen Fang has argued, the movie is "a remarkable event in the media history of Asian America."[4] In large part, this is because of its up-front, unashamed treatment of Asian male sexuality, which, far from being dormant or nonexistent, is seen here as propulsive and covetable. It's also because this film, less auteurist and more conglomerated in genesis, ends up being more progressive than more community-oriented productions. It manages to overcome the logic of placelessness that haunts so many South Asian films and journeys, almost despite itself, in a nongeneric direction, closer to the kind of *placeful* movie that up until now has been so rare.

Released in the United Kingdom during summer 2002 and in the United States at the start of 2003, *The Guru* wrong-foots us from the very first scene. We are inside an Indian movie theater where a classic Hindi film is being screened. There are songs. There is dancing. Everyone in the packed auditorium is delighted except for one squirming young boy. He scowls while everyone else scoffs *pakoras* and sings along to the dizzying melodies. He sneaks out and goes to an adjacent screening room, where he becomes rapt watching another musical that is also full of color and song and exaggerated romance: *Grease*.

We flip forward a few years, and that boy—Ramu (played by Jimi Mistry)—is now a slim-hipped and handsome dance instructor at New Delhi's Shanti Dance School, in charge of getting old aunties to jiggle aerobically to the tune of "La Macarena." They'd all like to kiss him, but, alas, he's about to leave for America. "You are going to drive a cab?" they ask. No, he tells them, he's going to become a movie star: "Anything's possible in America." When they demur, he shrugs his shoulders: "You must move your feet to the beat of your heart." And that refrain—singsong, groovy, vapid, cod-philosophical—anticipates the register of much of the rest of the film.

Ramu, expecting to be put up at the luxurious penthouse apartment of his friend Vijay (Emil Marwa), is aghast to find himself sharing a cramped hovel in Queens. Chaos ensues whenever there's a knock on the front door as the flat-mates hide, one of them—an illegal immigrant—scampering out a window in case officials from the Immigration and Naturalization Service have found out about him. In search of his starring role, Ramu answers a call for audition and eventually finds himself in Midtown Manhattan at the headquarters of Ramrod Productions, a producer of porn movies, unbeknownst to him. A smarmy producer (Michael McKean) gets him to drop his trousers and act opposite Sharonna (Heather Graham), who plays Senator Snatch from Wisconsin, a big-haired beauty washed up on a desert island after a terrible accident at sea. It's so hot that she drops her briefcase and most of her clothes, too.

Ramu is shocked but soon finds himself drawn to Sharonna. She says things that seem wise—"Your naked body is just a costume" and "The most powerful sexual organ God gave us is our brain"—or at least wise enough for him to steal and use in his one-on-one sessions with the idle rich denizens of the Upper East Side, who believe he's a swami, the Guru of Sex. It's an image created for him in part by Lexi (Marisa Tomei), an idealistic space cadet who becomes his manager and partner. Through her he enters supernova, chat-show celebrity territory. But he also falls in love with Sharonna, despite her impending marriage to a lardy firefighter called Randy.

Finally, at the peak of his success, and newly freighted with expensive cars, jewelry, and a flash apartment overlooking Central Park, he outs himself as a fraud and, following the beat of his heart, races up to Harlem where he rescues Sharonna from what would have been a disastrous marriage (Randy turns out to be gay at the last moment). The final scenes, as florid and extravagant as any of the Bollywood movies whose dance sequences *The Guru* pastiches throughout its ninety-minute duration, see the entire cast dancing to the raga-rhythm divine and the two lovers being airlifted toward the clouds in a moment of agreeably silly magical realism.

The film's box-office returns were far from spectacular. Reviews were mixed, too. Apart from the one that appeared in the *Washington Post* ("*The Guru* is a joyous genre-blender guaranteed to crank up your karma . . . tangier than a plateful of vindaloo . . . reminds us all that love is never having to say you're sari"),[5] the most enthusiastic notice appeared in the online magazine *Salon*, where critic Charles Taylor saw it as "a mistaken identity comedy that takes off from the musical comedy convention of the dreamer who wants to make it big in the big city" and was excited to find in it the "ditzy moonbeam spirit of screwball comedy."[6]

For Stephen Holden of the *New York Times*, however, *The Guru* was "a grindingly conventional comedy . . . lurching between a loudmouthed sitcom and a crude social satire."[7] More severe was Anthony Lane in the *New Yorker*, who framed his discussion of the film by talking about the "grisly history" of the representation of Indians in Western movies: "Things improved only with the advent of M. Night Shymalan, who, from *The Sixth Sense* onward, has used Indian actors in ordinary parts and offered no comment on ethnic difference. By those civilizing standards, *The Guru* is a wretched step backwards, with its unthinking nods to the exotic."[8]

Whether or not they praised or dismissed the film for its feel-good, candy-floss lightness, and whether or not they liked the way in which it deployed the tropes of the Bollywood masala movie in the service of a rather conventional "coming to America" narrative, no one at all was curious about the provenance of the film or the extent to which its preoccupations might reflect notable shifts in Asian (American) cultural production. *The Guru* seemed to have nothing to declare. To freight it, though, is the intention of this essay. I want to treat it as an immigrant, probe into its history, track its movement, consider the context of its reception, and rifle through the baggage it brings.

The film wrapped on June 20, 2002, and was released in England, with almost unprecedented alacrity, a mere two months later on August 23. It came out in the middle of what was known in newspaper and broadcasting circles as the

"Bollywood summer." The upscale department store Selfridges turned itself into a giant movie set created by Bombay film designer Nitin Desai. *Bombay Dreams*, a West End musical, cost 4.5 million pounds and was produced by Andrew Lloyd Webber (*Jesus Christ Superstar, Cats*), scored by the leading soundtrack composer A. R. Rahman, and scripted by Meera Syal. It attracted huge press attention and impressive ticket sales. London's Victoria and Albert Museum mounted the first ever exhibition of Bollywood movie posters in the United Kingdom. The British Film Institute launched a major season of Bollywood and South Asian films that toured the nation until the end of the year. Major monographs were published on classic Indian films such as *Pather Panchali* (1955) and *Mother India* (1957), and exquisite prints of Ritwik Ghatak's *The Cloud-Capped Star* (1960) and *A River Called Titash* (1973) were issued for the first time on DVD. Television station idents were modeled on Bollywood routines. Actors and actresses trotted up red carpets to various premieres sporting Kama Sutra T-shirts and dresses.

This wasn't the first time the mainstream media had shown an interest in Asian culture. Thirty-five years earlier, in the wake of the Beatles' pilgrimages to Rishikesh, it had rhapsodized about tie-dye spirituality and swami wisdom in exactly the same way that is sent up in *The Guru*. In 1997 and 1998, it had used many column inches celebrating the "new Asian kool" of bands such as Cornershop and Fun-da-mental and dance artists Talvin Singh, State of Bengal, and Joi. But neither of those two historical moments had seen quite so intense a spotlight as that during the summer of 2002.

What was new this time was the prominence accorded to film. The silver screen became the prism through which Asian identity was seen and analyzed. Any discussion of Asian culture had the term *Bollywood* appended to it, leading a reader of the leading liberal paper, the *Guardian*, to send in the following letter: "Shane Richie [the well-known English soap star] looked really good in a shalwar kameez. Shame that your reporter called it 'Bollywood garb.' Are *Guardian* readers so dim that they can only comprehend Indian/Pakistani clothes through the medium of Indian film?"[9]

The hyperbolic, excitable register that Bollywood tends to induce in those who write about it meant that coverage of such unglamorous events as the rioting by young Muslims in the north of England during the summer of 2001 was subdued. That was old news, grim news. Few wanted to dwell on issues of social exclusion, racial divisions, or postindustrial ghettoization when they could reprint photographs of the former Miss World winner Aishwarya Rai, now a star of the heavily promoted Bollywood blockbuster *Devdas*, itself a glutinously glossy remake—thin on realism, high on lavish sets—of a classic Hindi film about the class chasm that separates a courtesan and her upper-caste lover. And, as the writer Neil Biswas added, "People want the bits of Asian culture that are hedonistic and gloriously celebratory. A bit of Hinduism is very attractive—the beautiful rituals, the incense. The West finds it harder to buy into the austerity of Islam."[10]

But what is this Bollywood invoked and quoted by so many ad agencies and newspaper headline writers and in such films as Terry Zwigoff's *Ghost World* (2001) and Baz Luhrmann's *Moulin Rouge!* (2001)? The term has entered common parlance only in the last two decades. Before that it was thought sufficient to talk of Hindi musicals. Unsurprisingly, the films that constitute Bollywood vary greatly and have changed a good deal since the glory days from the 1940s to the early 1960s. Growing urbanization and cynicism about politicians means that romantic heroes in current movies are no longer angry young men or avenging outsiders. The era of the "common man" is on the wane. Teachers and civil servants used to feature heavily in films; now, in an age when the middle-class population is 100 million strong, nonresident Indians are shown whooshing about in expensive cars and dancing in the verdant landscapes of Mauritius and New Zealand. The films are slicker and better edited, their actors buffed in private gyms and draped in leather T-shirts, the product placement for designer labels and cell phones just as pushy.[11]

The films themselves are being aggressively targeted at the estimated 20 million Non Resident Indians scattered across the world, including 1.6 million in the United Kingdom and 1.7 million in the United States. To combat the piracy that used to be—and still is—endemic in the Indian movie industry, individual titles are being released in these foreign territories much sooner than they used to be. Audiences in the Asian diaspora, happy to pay inflated ticket prices at modern multiplexes, are a boon for Indian producers. They have rescued films such as Mani Ratnam's *Dil Se* (1999), which flopped in India itself. The audiences there are as estranged from and jaded by Bollywood films as they have ever been, much to the consternation of Mumbai producers and studio executives, who know that barely 10 percent of their movies stand any chance of making a profit. In 2002, Bollywood's worst year ever, out of 132 films released 124 were flops.[12]

Given the drop in local consumption, small wonder that producers are eyeing the NRI market. The appetite of Indian audiences abroad for Bollywood products, however shoddy they may be (in 1999 Subhash Ghai's *Tala* became the first Indian film to hit the American Top 20), has encouraged Eros International, the world's biggest distributor of Bollywood movies, to campaign to get its titles stocked by Blockbuster. It has also led studios to green-light films that "speak" to Indians abroad. Hence the unedifying spectacle of Sanjay Gupta's *Kaante* (2002)—a heist flick, in the style of *Reservoir Dogs* and starring Amitabh Bachchan, that, although it is in Hindi, was shot in Los Angeles with an entirely American crew—being trumpeted as a bold new direction for Indian cinema.

For directors such as Shekhar Kapur, the creator of such award-winning films as *Bandit Queen* (1994), *Elizabeth* (1998), and *The Four Feathers* (2002), the future of cinema depends on the merging of Hollywood and Bollywood. Not only do Indian films need Western consumers, but "to survive," Kapur says, "the American entertainment business needs the overseas market." He notes:

> The demographics of Asia are much more in line with the demographics of the entertainment industry, which run roughly from 15 to 30; the market for Bollywood videos runs as far down as 14 to 30. . . .
>
> Why is it always Indians who win Miss World competitions? All the advertising comes from India: the competition would simply collapse without it. Indian cricketers are now the highest paid in the world: cricket survives because of Indian advertising. You have to get an Indian into Formula One racing now, to get the sponsorship from the tobacco companies. Where are the big tobacco markets? China and India. . . . Soon we will find that in order to make a hugely successful film, you have to match Tom Cruise with an Indian or a Chinese actor. What you're seeing now with films such as *The Guru* is just the tip of the iceberg.[13]

Of course, that cinema, right from its inception, has always been a syncretic, polycultural mishmash of styles and genres that borrows energetically from European and North American moviemaking. Now though, those forms are being deployed to represent a version of India—glossy, hi-tech, casually cosmopolitan, socially mobile—that, while it purports to be far more realistic than the homely, romantic fantasies of older Hindi cinema, is at least as partial. It offers up a fantasy of its own—one in which questions of caste, class, and social inequity have been pushed off the agenda. Indeed, even the idea of an agenda is increasingly unfashionable, as it apparently evokes notions of ideology, didacticism, and earnest clarion calls for social reform.

The ironies at play here are obvious. Bollywood is bigger than ever and is thought to have an indical relationship to past and present India. But those films, scarcely mimetic thirty years ago, are becoming attenuated from some of the less palatable social, economic, and religious realities of the nation. Now they're less popular than ever before with Indian audiences, a fact that, while it doesn't in itself illegitimize them, does suggest that they cannot be used to talk blithely about who or what contemporary Indians have become. Now more than ever before to use Bollywood as a device for dramatizing certain elements of Asian activity or presence in the East—and certainly in the West—is to buy into a crude and deterritorialized fantasy.

The Guru was born of these very dreams of deterritorialization. It was executive-produced by a Bollywood heavyweight, Shekhar Kapur, and made by Working Title, the production company behind *Notting Hill*, a film that featured only a single black character despite being set in an area of West London known as a hub of the capital's Caribbean community and as the site (in the summer of 1958) of one of the most famous race riots in British history. It was directed and written by Americans, Daisy von Scherler Mayer and Tracey Jackson (the latter "a self-proclaimed Indofile" who also wrote *Ashes to Ashes*, which was set in India, for Goldie Hawn).[14] The film's three main Asian roles—Rami, his pal Vijay, and another pal—were all played by Brits (Jimi Mistry, Emil Marwa, and Sanjeev Bhaskar).

A global production in every sense of the word, *The Guru* sought to be globally appealing. And whether or not one finds the film enjoyable, it's hard to see it as anything other than *entryist*. It wants desperately to be liked. And, while that desire would in itself normally preclude it from being lovable, *The Guru* has a charm and cheeky vivacity that raises it, aesthetically and politically, above other South Asian films set in New York. How?

To begin with, by luck or intuition, the film's creators happened on one of the most profitable tropes in Asian diasporic film and literature: that of the Indian as a faker. Novels such as V. S. Naipaul's *The Mystic Masseur* (1957) or Ved Mehta's *Delinquent Chacha* (1967), a TV series such as Hanif Kureishi's *The Buddha of Suburbia* (1993, originally a novel published in 1990), and a movie such as Shani Grewel's *Guru in Seven* (1998) all feature Asians who fashion themselves as spiritually blessed dispensers of transcendental truths. These characters are close relatives of Deepak Chopra, who, according to Vijay Prashad, "laughs along with the United States, as he dons the robes of the East to peddle a form of escapism that not only trivializes the conundrums of people in the United States but it also mocks the real crises of people in South Asia."[15]

Chopra's fatuous platitudes and Hollywood ego-massaging bloviations are, however, a little different from *The Guru*'s. Ramu is a con man, but he becomes one out of desperation. Most other career options are closed to him. He is a trickster, an Eastern hustler who ranges across Manhattan exploiting the parochialism and ignorance of its inhabitants to peddle pseudo-meaningful sententiae. In doing so, for all his occasional qualms about stealing his apothegms from Sharonna, he becomes more confident and dashing. And richer, too.

This kind of imposture and concealment is something that most migrants do: witness the Sylheti restaurant owner who calls his curry house the Taj Mahal because he knows India (palaces, pleasure) has more pleasing connotations to the Western diner than Bangladesh (floods, famine) or the nerdy student who concocts aristocratic relatives in order to seem grander than his small-town roots would normally allow him. Such fabrications and character formations are very much what artists themselves do, so it's no surprise that they are alive to the quotidian acts of automythopoeia engaged in by immigrants.

The Guru also scores in its wide, if rarely deep, use of the geography of New York. According to one of its producers, Tim Bevan: "You just can't replicate the atmosphere of NYC in a studio. It was that important to film on the streets of New York."[16] And so the movie features scenes set in Times Square, Chinatown, Midtown, the meat-packing district, Harlem, the Upper East Side, the Lower East Side, NoHo, Central Park, Hunts Point (155th Street), Queens, Brooklyn, and on George Washington Bridge. A Hindi-style dream-dance sequence and Ramu's Broadway were both filmed in Harlem at the United Palace Church on 175th and Broadway, also known as Reverend Ike's. The use of real locations lends the film much-needed crunch and verisimilitude. It counterbalances the creamy, woozy softness of its romantic elements and is a pleasing corrective to the vague and unlocatable cartographies of many South Asian films about New York. It serves to people the place and, especially in the wake of 9 / 11, when the pictures of the city broadcast around the country, and certainly to the rest of the world, were primarily close-ups of white-cheeked, blue-collared heroes, to offer audiences a wide-angled perspective on the extent to which, in a relatively short period of time, New York has become, along with Toronto and London, one of the hubs of South Asian settlement in the "Brown Atlantic."

This immersion in sidewalk solidarities means that the film has more in common with Asian films from Britain than it does with those from the United States. And it's this relationship—at the level of financing, casting, and sensibility—that makes *The Guru* more than simply Hollywood fluff. To list some of the most critically and commercially successful movies that have emerged from the United Kingdom during the last two decades is to be struck by how rooted they are in the poetics and social politics of specific geographies: skinhead-overrun South London in the mid-1980s (*My Beautiful Laundrette*, 1985), Blackpool (*Bhaji on the Beach*, 1993), Bradford (*My Son the Fanatic*, 1997), 1970s Salford (*East Is East*, 1999), 1970s rural Wolverhampton (*Anita and Me*, 2002), and contemporary Southall in West London (*Bend It Like Beckham*, 2002). All of these sidestep debates, most of them hackneyed, about whether their subjects are Asian or English; instead, they're keen to register the importance of class and locality in framing identity. With the exception of Gurinder Chadha's *Bend It Like Beckham*, they deal with dejection and dislocation (unsurprising, then, that it was this movie that performed best in the United States). They are feel-bad, or at least feel-fairly-bad, stories. Unsentimental and skeptical toward the idea of community, they also focus on the travails of a sector of the Asian population routinely ignored by American desi films—the working classes.

Amitava Kumar explains the difference in art produced by British and American South Asians.

> The violence of the National Front attacks on Asians in Britain forged a different, more resilient culture of resistance. The U.S. has not offered a similar challenge to Indian immigrants; the riots that had plagued the life of the earlier, working-class migrants to California or Oregon in the nineteenth and early twentieth centuries, have never been a part of the collective memory of recent, post-1965 migrants to this country.[17]

The National Front was never numerically or electorally significant, even during the 1970s, although it did contribute to the growth in anti-immigrant sentiment in that decade. Labor disputes such as the women's strike at Grunswick in 1977 were probably more inspirational. But Kumar is right to underline the centrality of dissent, couched in ironic or coruscatingly polemical terms, to British South Asian art. Kureishi started out working and writing for the famously left-wing Royal Court Theatre of the 1970s, and Chadha was a journalist and close to the Southall Black Sisters, a feminist Asian organization that did much to provide shelters to battered women. The 1980s saw the development of a critical and self-reflexive community of black and Asian filmmakers, often centered around the experimental Black Audio Film Collective, which gave rise to a number of heated but ultimately very useful debates (participated in by the likes of John Akomfrah, Stuart Hall, and Salman Rushdie) about the form and function of immigrant and second-generation cinema.

That dissent can also be heard in the records made during the 1990s by Cornershop, Fun-Da-Mental, Asian Dub Foundation, 2nd Gen, and Made in Britain. Traces of it are detectable in *The Guru*, particularly in its pointed raillery and badinage: "Do you know why they call it the American dream? Because it only happens when you're asleep." Rami's mates rag him that his dreams of Hollywood will come to naught, he'll play "man in turban working in gas station," and the only lines he'll deliver in his next role will be "Would you like chutney with your chupattis or popodums with your paneer?"

These British bands, and the films, too, especially those by Kureishi, are punk at heart. The likes of Aki Nawaz, the driving force behind Fun-Da-Mental, were punks in the late 1970s. An ideology as much as a musical style, it exalted mess, contagion, danger, not being cool. Dissent and permanent opposition were held to be good, once and always. The accompanying aesthetic was scratchy, samizdat, grimly black and white. This made it fiery and childishly and exhilaratingly apocalyptic. It also produced art that prized anarchy over amiability, passion over placation. To keep things local and do-it-yourself mattered more than national recognition. Exclusion, as can be seen from the ironic name of the pioneering late 1970s Asian band Alien Kulture, was embraced more than belonging. It's hardly surprising that punk and its ideology of abrasive resistance were pivotal to the concept of subculture so canonically formulated by Dick Hebdige.[18]

That kind of resistance is almost entirely absent from what Sunaina Maira calls the "remix youth culture" of New York's Indian and South Asian youth.[19] The scene she describes is based on college campuses and in clubs and restaurants: "They gather in cliques and couples, the women attired in slinky club wear (tight-fitting shirts and hip-hugger pants or miniskirts) and the men in hip-hop-inspired urban street fashion (the signature Tommy Hilfiger shirts and baggy pants), or in jackets and slacks if required."[20] This doesn't sound like the garb of rebellion. Nor does the music.

The mere segueing of records, or the cutting and pasting of disparate sounds for upscale desi youth to jiggle to, is not in itself an act of transgression. With lyrics subordinated to the hegemony of the beat, cross-genre modification, and the pick-and-mix sampladelia routine (a house track is tweaked into R&B, a hip hop number is technofied), there is less correlation than ever before between where musicians are situated and the sounds they produce. Now dance music, far from the automatically liberating and emancipatory free zone envisaged by theorists and journalists in the late 1980s, is in many ways just as rigid and straitjacketing as the guitar rock it was meant to supplant. It has become a polished and transnational musica franca that is at least as likely to limit the power and complexity of the "ethnic" voice as it is to provide it with a free and huge platform.

This glib, defanged lack of referentiality is a noticeable feature of much South Asian art, particularly in the United States, which lacks the long and complex ties to the subcontinent that colonialism gave the British. We see it in the hoopla and wonderment created by the commercial success of such hackneyed fare as *Bombay Dreams*, *Bend It Like Beckham*, and *Jism*. We see it in gutted, tasteful fare such as *American Chai*.

And this is the background from which *The Guru* emerges—and balks. The movie's odd charm and nagging memorability reside in the extent to which it chafes against the sappy impotence of most films about South Asians in New York and the way it clings to the tradition of South Asian British filmmaking. It does so by abjuring the maudlin rhetoric of confusion and identity crisis and homing in on that murky but fascinating terrain identified by Graham Huggan in *The Postcolonial Exotic* (2001) and explored famously in *The Buddha of Suburbia*, in which Asians are not only the victims of exploitation and commodification but very often the people who seek to stage and profit from it. *The Guru* may be, until its fairy-tale ending, bristling, vulgar, and insensitive—qualities that incidentally thrive in the urban sphere—but its attention to the fault lines created by class and filthy lucre is rare in recent NRI cinema. Its very subject matter reminds us of the pornography of many migrant lives and the venality of living in a city that prides itself on its lack of sentiment: screw or get screwed. Or, as the porn director tells Ramu, "Get hard or get going."

Hardness is a quality that young South Asian filmmakers would do well to project onscreen. Directors need to reacquaint themselves with New York, where they might find Asians increasingly in thrall to the lure of obnoxious communalist ideologies in India, the subject of tracking operations by the FBI and the Department of Homeland Security, and slowly undergoing a shift in cultural nomenclature—from "immigrant" to "alien." They might also find an increasing social and geographic polarization between South Asian haves and have-nots.

Plotting the shifting contours of South Asian standing in America today requires an active curiosity and a militant absorption in the crosscurrents of contemporary urban politics that entails going against the grain. All too often, NRI cultural productions have exhibited the same tendency "to glamorize a noncommittal political stance in one's land of principal residence" that Sau-ling Cynthia Wong has identified as being a danger in diaspora-focused theo-ries of Asian-American identity.[21] Or, as James Procter puts it in his account of the history of postwar black writing in Britain:

> Returning to the etymology of diaspora: "sowing" and "scattering" cannot be said to be uncontaminated by a "sedentary poetics." . . . A deconstruction of the concept "diaspora" provides a means of returning to the politics of place, location and territory within diaspora literature—a politics that too often gets endlessly deferred within its journeying metaphors.[22]

For all their racking up of air miles, their flip-flopping between time zones, their inhabitation—cyber and actual—of multiple geographies, it's not actu-ally clear that hypermobility creates in today's NRIS an apolitical sensibility; rather, it hinges on a willful avoidance of the local, a deliberate apathy. How strange, and what an indictment, that it takes a pulpy slice of genre cinema such as *The Guru* to highlight, almost inadvertently, the missing heart and soul, the missing landscapes, of South Asian American cinema.

Notes

1 Prashad, *The Karma of Brown Folk*, viii.
2 Nimbark, "Hinduism in New York City," 99.
3 Iyer, "I'm Anyone I Choose to Be," 21.
4 Fang, "Sex God," 8.
5 Kempley, *"The Guru."*
6 Taylor, *"The Guru."*
7 Holden, "Using Ditsy Maxims for Erotic Self-Help."
8 Lane, "Don of Creation," 98.
9 Ashraf, "Dear Weekend," 10.
10 Neil Biswas, interview with author, August 14, 2003.
11 Such transformations have not gone unnoticed in Hollywood. Columbia Tristar and Polygram have been involved in Bollywood ventures, while Disney is said to be looking for an Indian animation base. Aishwarya Rai was a jury member for the main competition at Cannes in May 2003. *GQ* has run a profile of heartthrob actor Hrithik Roshan, while *Vanity Fair* awarded *Bollywood* the accolade of "Pre-tentious Film-Snob Reference of the Month."
12 Vidhani, "Wake up Bollywood."
13 Kapur, "The Asians Are Coming."
14 *The Guru*, production notes, 18.
15 Prashad, *The Karma of Brown Folk*, 48.

16 *The Guru*, production notes, 8.
17 Kumar, *Bombay–London–New York*, 175.
18 Hebdige, *Subculture*.
19 Maira, *Desis in the House*, 12.
20 Ibid., 12.
21 Wong, "Denationalization Reconsidered," 17.
22 Procter, *Dwelling Places*, 34.

3

Consuming
Cultures

Cooking up the Senses: A Critical Embodied Approach to the Study of Food and Asian American Television Audiences

Martin F. Manalansan IV

Today cooking shows, cookbooks, and restaurants have become the new sites for articulating cosmopolitanism, modernity, and multiculturalism. Cooking and eating in contemporary urban America have become paradigmatic acts of possessing material and symbolic capital through facile travels across physical and ethnic borders. People in Chicago and other American heartland cities need not board a plane to eat Chinese or Middle Eastern food. At the same time, books, magazines, and journals have transformed the acts of cooking and eating into an academic field of study. Despite accusations of "scholarship lite,"[1] the emergent field of food studies, which spans the humanities and social sciences, has become a visible and compelling force in the study of contemporary popular culture.

Whether in the academic or entertainment realms, the allure of the exotic, as well as the popularity of the foreign and culturally distant, is dramatized in the ways Asian Americans are located in culinary discourses. This situation is made more troublesome by Asian Americans' complicated historical and symbolic relationship with food production, distribution, and preparation. Asian Americans came to the United States to fill the need for cheap labor, particularly in the agricultural industry in Hawaii and on the West Coast in the late nineteenth century and the early twentieth, and to work as meatpackers and take-out delivery men in the contemporary period. However, the long history of Asian American labor in the food production and service industries is rendered invisible by the mundane pleasures and banal presence of Asian, primarily Chinese, cuisine in American life. Chinese cuisine, heralded as the ultimate "ethnic" food, has become a ubiquitous "ethnic" presence in both American small and big cities. Meanwhile, Korean and South Asian Americans have been stereotyped as the convenience store owners and operators who enable the American public to access food and other products in their neighborhoods.

Recent novels by Asian American authors such as *The Book of Salt*, *Eating Chinese Food Naked*, *My Year of Meats*, *The Barbarians Are Coming*, *Dogeaters*, and *Hunger* feature food, cooking, and eating as integral to the fabulation of selves and identities in their various plots. In addition, literary criticism has long acknowledged the symbolic significance of food in Asian American fiction.[2] Overall, the alimentary construction of Asian Americanness can be read with and against the image of the "perpetual foreigner." In other words, Asian Americans' relationship with the material and symbolic aspects of food is part of their continuing marginal and abject status in the American cultural imaginary. While Latinos and African Americans have also been important sources of labor for the food production and service industries, Asian Americans have been symbolically and stereotypically linked to food. In recent memory, the popular clothing company Abercrombie and Fitch produced a series of racist T-shirts whose images primarily featured Oriental-looking faces linked with "humorous" ads about restaurants and food. Therefore, one could argue that Asian Americans are not only the conduits enabling American culinary consumption as delivery men and cooks but are also cultural products to be consumed.

Media consumption of Asian American culinary alterity need not be seen only in terms of contemporary orientalist fantasies and desires. There is a need to better understand how the so-called objects of these desires are actually active agents in reading and interpreting these mass media cultural productions. In other words, what happens when Asian American audiences engage with constructions of Asian and Asian American food on television? What roles do the senses play in enabling Asian American audiences to engage with these cultural forms?

Asian American, as I deploy the term in this essay, is not a universal panethnic identification describing my research participants but rather a product of the creation of and engagement with "official" categories. The people who participated in this project are from different ethnic and national groups even as they are constantly engaged with the discursive formation called Asian America.

Where's the Body? The Senses and a
Critical Approach to Audience Study

This essay has manifold aims. The first is methodological. One of the popular topics of both food cultural studies in particular and cultural studies in general is the audience—the spectators of theatrical, cinematic, and television productions. In keeping with this interest, I employ a qualitative ethnographic approach that grounds and privileges the voices of actual viewers or subjects.

The second aim is theoretical. I utilize a sensory-based, embodied ethnographic approach to the study of audiences. Unlike most audience studies, however, I go beyond examining the visual experiences of viewers and move toward other, less commonly explored senses such as smell and hearing. I explore the various ways in which such an embodied approach can be deployed in projects involving popular culture and typically marginalized audiences. This approach is founded on the idea that the senses are always culturally mediated. I argue that it is crucial to center the body and the visceral in the study of popular culture in understanding how people engage with mass media texts.

The third aim is conceptual. By utilizing a sensory and corporeally based approach to the study of an "ethnic" audience, I explore ways to engage with the politics of mass media consumption and racial and ethnic difference. In addition, I examine the very idea of the ethnic audience. By "ethnic," I mean audiences that have been rendered marginal from the mainstream, those that are not the usual target audience of prime-time "all-American" television and cinematic productions. How do cultural values, meanings, and practices influence an audience's interpretive behavior? How do people who are culturally and economically marginalized access these cultural arenas, and what do they provide by way of a critique of these new formations of the modern and multicultural? In other words, how do ethnic audiences and consumers apprehend, consume, and interpret these cultural forms?

While all audiences are composed of interpretive consumers whether or not they are the target audience for a mass media product, I would argue that different audience groups will have their own diverse interpretations. On this note, I do not want to argue that marginalized groups such as ethnic and racial minorities are more astute readers than other groups; rather, they have alternative readings that in most cases have either been devalued or rendered nonexistent. Part of the impetus for this work is to center an immigrant viewing public. Indeed, as Hamid Naficy has rightly suggested, exiles and immigrants bring to bear a different body of experiences to their viewing and interpretive habits.[3] As such, the Asian immigrant audiences I am concerned with bring to light the complicated intertwining of diasporic and immigrant histories and cultures with mass media reception.

At the heart of this work's analytical angle is the idea that race is an ideological construction produced, performed, and apprehended through corporeal means—through bodily processes that engage with visual, aural, olfactory, gustatory, and tactile stimuli. While race is established through numerous institutional, cultural, and quotidian practices, in all of these arenas the racialized subject's body filters, absorbs, and deflects various interpolating forces and practices. My project does not purport to uncover the secret, rich, sensuous lives of Asian Americans or to suggest that they possess highly developed sensory abilities or discourses. Rather, this essay disentangles a static notion of mass media consumption from a reliance on "optics" to a wider array of critically embodied experiences.

My approach is influenced by the intersection of several scholarly approaches. First and foremost is the feminist ethnography of the mass media. The works of Purnima Mankekar, Lila Abu-Lughod, and Jacqueline Bobo have emphasized the importance of power and the agentive dimension of marginalized people who are "cultural readers"[4] and members of interpretive communities, and not passive consumers of mass media products.[5] Asian American cultural critique and critical race theory, as demonstrated in the works of Lisa Lowe and Nayan Shah, have emphasized the ways in which racialization works with and through the body.[6] Shah, for example, emphasizes the embodied dimensions of health, labor, and cultural regulations among Chinese Americans from the nineteenth century to the mid–twentieth in San Francisco's Chinatown.

At the same time, works in the emergent field of an "anthropology of the senses" articulate issues of sensuous experiences in the world as crucial topics for research.[7] These works acknowledge that the senses are always culturally mediated and therefore subject to the forces of history, political power, and ideology. These anthropologists of the senses suggest that it is through an embodied subject that the world is apprehended and interpreted, and yet they are critical of the ocularcentric bias inherent in the study of the arts, cinema, theater, dance, television and other mass media. In other words, the "sensuous scholarship" of these anthropologists, to use a term coined by a practitioner, Paul Stoller, refuses the centrality of the visual and instead focuses on "bodily ways of knowing" as integral to an examination of how people understand, react to, and engage with the sensuous world.[8] This anthropology of the senses argues that cultures develop specific sensoria or sensory "arsenals." For example, some cultures refer to movement or kinesthesia as another sensory form and thereby apprehend the world using this sensory dimension. In addition, the anthropology of the senses unravels the monolithic conceptualization of "experience" in phenomenology-inspired works into highly specific and particular deployments of various sensory functions.

In particular, however, this work owes an intellectual debt to Laura Marks's landmark study of embodiment, the senses, and diasporic cinema. In *The Skin of Film*, Marks underscores the ways in which diasporic cinematic productions present spaces of sensory intersection. Utilizing what she calls "haptic visuality," she shifts the understanding of films as merely visual texts experienced by particular optics. Rather, the intersection of the haptic and the visual triggers viewers' physical reactions to the films, evoking the smell, taste, touch, and sound of other places and times.

In this essay, I bring together perspectives from the anthropology of the senses and Marks's theoretical framework. These two perspectives, I believe, are complimentary despite some methodological and theoretical disputes. Marks, for example, chides the anthropologists of the senses for committing the sin of "neo-orientalism," uncritically privileging a "soothing return to the senses" in turning their gaze from the deodorized West to the sensory paradise of the East.[9] She identifies a tendency among these anthropologists to overparticularize and fix a specific sensorium to one particular cultural location; in doing so, she emphasizes the importance of showcasing the fluid yet structured nature of the senses in relation to culture, history, and politics. However, I can imagine anthropologists scolding Marks for not empirically verifying and grounding her theoretical and conceptual frameworks. This work therefore attempts to address the concerns of both camps by not fixing and exoticizing the sensory experiences of Asian American participants and at the same time listening carefully to how these sensory experiences are products of the participants' social and cultural locations. Indeed, I do not intend to portray Asian American audiences as resembling the natives of ethnographies past, incarcerated by their physical location. I submit that they are part of a globalizing world that exists through intersections and conjunctions of cultural practices.

This essay is based on focus groups and ethnographic fieldwork conducted in January–August 2001 and June–August 2002 (see table 1).[10] All of the participants in these Asian American focus groups were adult immigrants residing in the New York City borough of Queens.[11] They were asked to watch two episodes of *East Meets West*, a cooking show hosted by a Chinese American chef

Table 1
FOCUS GROUP PARTICIPANTS

		SOUTH ASIAN	KOREAN	FILIPINO	CHINESE
GROUP 1:	Male	2	2		
	Female	2	1		
GROUP 2:	Male	2		1	
	Female	3		1	
GROUP 3:	Male		2		
	Female	3		1	2
GROUP 4:	Male			3	
	Female			4	
GROUP 5:	Male				3
	Female				4
TOTAL		9	8	10	9

named Ming Tsai. The show, which began airing in 1998, is a proponent of what is known as fusion cuisine, which began in high-end and elite restaurants. Using Ming Tsai's own words, *fusion cuisine* can be defined as follows.

> My food is based on ingredients and cooking techniques of both the East and West. Too often, however, so-called fusion cooking (con-fusion cooking, some of us call it) produces chaos on the plate and in the mouth. To avoid this, I have an enormous sense of respect for each culture's ingredients and traditional techniques. Successful East-West cooking harmoniously combines two distinct culinary approaches. Take my Savory Braised Oxtail with Preserved Lemon Polenta recipe: When a dish is not just new but better—when I can find superior way to celebrate oxtail's earthiness, say, or the deep sour tang of pickled lemons, and then join the two—that's real East-West cooking.[12]

East Meets West is a cooking show that combines Western and Asian cuisines and yet renders them as sensually separate. Fusion cuisine, then, is about the paradox of blending and separating, creating a space in which borders can coexist with the intermingling of flavors, colors, and odors. It thus reveals the boundaries of national cuisines at the same time that it reifies Asian images, practices, and ingredients. This paradox establishes an arena for contests of belonging and memory.

I chose this show because of its popularity and its focus on fusion cuisine and because Ming Tsai is the most visible Asian American chef on television. Instead of screening a cooking show that specifically targets an immigrant audience, I chose a show marketed to a wider, more educated, "foodie" population in celebrating the intersections of Asian and Western cuisine. Such intersections form the core of this cuisine, mimicking, if not metaphorically paralleling, the crossings and struggles of immigrant lives. Fusion cuisine therefore offers glimpses of homeland ingredients and dishes re-conceptualized and somewhat displaced by Western elements. My objective is to examine how immigrant audiences apprehend this particular cuisine in light of their own experiences of diasporic displacement.

Participants were encouraged to comment during the performance and after the screening they were given a series of open-ended questions to elicit their overall reactions and encourage conversations. These conversations were augmented and influenced by informal interviews and fieldwork observations during the research period. While the issue of sensory experiences was not the focal point of the questions, the comments and reactions revolved around not only the visual but also the auditory, olfactory, and haptic dimensions of the shows. What follows is not a faithful transcription of the conversations of all groups but rather includes highlights of what I construe to be themes and patterns arising out of the participants' words.

Where Is East? Where Is West?
Asian American Audiences Talk Back

The show *East Meets West* begins with the sounds of Asian musical instruments as the host, Ming Tsai, dressed in white with his hands clasped in a meditative pose, bows before the camera. The music then shifts from an "Eastern" style to a more jazzlike tune; still dressed in white, but in a tennis outfit, the next scene cuts to Tsai on the courts. The imagery of the show's opening credits thus heralds the culinary focus of the chef and the theme of the show, fusion cuisine.

The shifts in references to East and West, Asian and European (or American), punctuate the defining elements of the show. Ming Tsai habitually emphasizes how his dishes take an Eastern or Asian ingredient such as soy sauce or dashi and mix it with a European or American ingredient such as foie gras or maple syrup.

The topic of fusion cuisine became an important source of conversations about cultural inauthenticity. For example, most reactions were based on participants' insistence that certain ingredients should never be used for purposes other than those found in their native dishes. Another set of reactions to the cuisine and cooking techniques presented on the show spans issues of race, ethnicity, gender, assimilation, and economic survival.

An Indian man of forty-five commented not on the incongruities of the dishes but on the incongruities of the television personalities' (Ming Tsai and his various guest chefs) demeanor and bodies. For example, participants commented on the athletic body of the six-foot-tall chef. Born and raised in the Midwest, Tsai's speech and movements were read by one participant as an American "white jock" (sometimes cocky and too self-assured) demeanor.

> If you close your eyes and not think of these people [Ming Tsai and his guests] as you see them on the screen. You would think that you were hearing white people. No foreign accents. Why is that? He [Ming Tsai] reminds me of the big Irish men who work in Wall Street and come to the store [where I work]. Very loud. Very friendly . . . sometimes too friendly. I always feel little intimidated.

Other participants concurred but in different ways. The accent and the sound of the chef's voice elicited a wary reaction. Despite the Chineseness of Tsai's image and body, and the recipe ingredients, music, and other show accoutrements overtly marked as Asian, participants evaluated the chef and the show as being very American and Western. To them, Ming Tsai, a second-generation Chinese American, looked and acted like some of the participants' children, most of whom were born and raised in the United States. He seemed not only culturally but also temporally distant.

The midwestern lilt in Ming's voice emphasized what many participants felt immediately to be a dissonance between what they saw—ostensibly an Asian man about to cook what might be Asian dishes—and what they heard. The wariness many participants felt was not about Ming's lack of appeal or friendliness; rather, as one participant pointed out, it was the discrepancy between his skin color and physical features with the "whitening" of his voice and bodily comportment. Whiteness becomes less about skin color and more a series of aural and kinesthetic features. It is perhaps ironic that in Ming Tsai's body, voice, and movement participants in the focus groups found not a placid fusion of cultures but an uneasy conjunction of features and behavior.

One Filipina described the show as "very slick" and often confusing. She commented, "It is almost like, you know, too quick—the way he just shows this is a Chinese or Japanese thing and then he shows how he can make it more complicated. The mixing of ingredients is too *magulo* (chaotic)." As such, she was explaining how fusion cuisine was making everything culturally illegible.

A participant in another focus group affirmed this view. For this Korean woman, the attempt at cultural illegibility, and more specifically of cultural blurring, was an attempt to make the dishes appealing to a more Americanized palate. As she noted, "Really, this fusion thing is really about making things more exotic—you know, if you say something has something Asian, like a teriyaki burger—it will be more expensive than the ordinary burger." Many participants perceived fusion cuisine as exemplifying the dangers of assimilation, which are often equated with "becoming white." Fusion cuisine was and is, as most participants bluntly stated, "white food." While this may be seen as a symptom of immigrants exoticizing their own cultures and cuisines, I would contend that it is more about the inaccessible cosmopolitanism of "whiteness" that fusion cuisine represents, of fusion cuisine being yet another element or arena from which these immigrants are excluded. While this is not the space to discuss the travails of the immigrant participants, the Korean woman's statement is a way of saying that fusion cuisine is a food category for those who can afford it. Meanwhile, the kinds of cultural appropriation and accommodation that they negotiate in everyday life are never seen on television. For example, one Filipina said that when she cannot find tamarind she uses lemons for *sinigang*, a sour stew. Yet, she argued, no one would confuse her cooking with fusion cuisine.

However, some participants said that it is a good thing that Ming Tsai makes use not only of Chinese ingredients but of other Asian ingredients such as *nam pla* (Thai fish sauce) and Indian spices. A Pakistani woman approved of Tsai making these ingredients familiar to American households. She noted, "At least he is making other non-Asians aware of these things—you know, maybe one of these days somebody in Montana might want to do a curry—at least that person can at least try to get it right. Maybe some people will buy these ingredients and have them in their kitchens."

During one of the episodes, Ming Tsai fills a bowl with noodles and broth. While he was doing this, focus group participants cooed and marveled at the steam rising from the hot dish. Tsai next turns and mixes a vinaigrette dressing, which he pours into a bowl of salad greens. Then, to the consternation and uniformly disapproving groans of almost all members of the different focus groups, he mounds the salad on top of the bowl of noodles, broth, and fried eggplant. A Chinese American woman said, "He could have just added the greens to the broth. Why do you need a salad? Who eats a salad while eating soup and noodles? Oh yes, the Americans. Those white folks. Oh well, maybe this is something we might have to learn if we live here until we are old." On hearing this, another Chinese American woman exclaimed: "Oh no, they can force me speak English, but they cannot make my tongue like the taste of salad dressing and egg noodles . . . yuck!" For many of the participants, the limits of their culinary assimilation were clearly marked in terms of boundaries between specific ingredients and in tastes and temporality. For example, what tastes (e.g. bitter, sweet, or savory) are appropriate for particular times of the day and for which meals and what kinds of ingredients can go in one dish were for many participants markers of their ethnic identities.

With further prodding, some participants did admit to "cheating" or being more "flexible" than they first asserted. A Filipina and several Chinese women talked about the need to substitute ingredients, skip cooking steps, and "make do" when time, ingredients, and money are scarce. Donna Gabaccia, in her landmark book on ethnic food in America, especially noted the creative strategies of immigrant cooks, who devise ways to sidestep rules and create fusion-like culinary productions in order to survive.[13]

This reality was especially evident in the discussions around odors and other sensory experiences. Several discussions revolved around the okra and raw tuna featured in one episode. The okra was sliced and blanched. Then a mixture of soy sauce, herbs, and spices was poured over it. The tuna was diced raw and also treated to a soy bath. These ingredients sparked a discussion about the tactile and gustatory senses. Both okra and tuna were thought to be slippery in texture, and as such they were a cause for either concern or pleasure.

The okra dish was perceived by many participants as being too bland. However, many informants seemed to be transported to other times and places by the sight of and discussions about the dish. One Indian man remembered his mother's dish when he said:

I look at that [okra] dish and I think that had he made it by sautéing it with browned onions and some spices . . . oh . . . it would look and taste better. Look at it now [pointing to the screen]. The dish looks very simple with just the soy sauce covering it. It will just taste salty. But, you know, if you cook it like my mother, the okra's slippery texture will not be noticeable because you will have the onions and spices playing around in your mouth.

A Filipino said that soy sauce just made the okra dish salty without any kind of real flavor. He said that blanched or boiled okra should be dipped in shrimp paste. However, despite the conversations around flavor, the slipperiness of the okra was seen to be a constitutive element marking it as "ethnic" food. One Chinese woman suggested that perhaps "nonethnics" would be concerned that the texture might cause diners to make slurping sounds when eating. Although most people disagreed with her, they all said that slurping noises, particularly when eating slippery foods such as noodles, were especially important to note when one was not in an Asian restaurant. A Chinese woman related this story.

> I like the way noodles feel in my mouth. [It is] very comforting. But one time, I was in an Italian restaurant in Little Italy. The noodles were soft and I was having such a good time that I started slurping it. Then, I started to notice the white people looking at me. I stopped what I was doing and I ate quietly. [*Laughs*]

The pleasure of the texture of tuna, on the other hand, goes beyond the visual sight of the red rawness of the cubed fish to a more haptic dimension, affirming Laura Marks's contention that the synaesthetic intersection of touch and vision triggers sensory memories and biographic scenes. A Korean woman offered this lyrical description and haptic translation of the images.

> I can see the fish is raw. See it is bloody red. It is not sushi, but you know what I am thinking right now? How that fish will feel in my mouth. It would feel like fat—pork or beef fat. It slides from your teeth, to your tongue and gums. It can be a little weird at first, then you start to taste the sea—very slowly. Then it is delicious and it all dissolves and disappears.

The sensation of fish in the mouth was a topic for discussion and disagreement. Someone suggested that raw tuna felt slippery and moist, almost like an oiled piece of gelatin. While the texture and tactile nature of the fish elicited most of the discussion, there was also a series of conversations about odors, sounds, and other sensations having to do with seafood and frying food. One participant commented that serving raw fish would eliminate the danger of spreading food odors in their small New York City apartments.

In the second episode that participants watched, Ming Tsai battered and fried zucchini blossoms. The participants focused less on the ingredient than on the frying method. Many agreed that frying was not only smelly but also noisy. The crackling and exploding noises were interpreted in various ways. One Chinese woman said that the sounds of food frying in oil were soothing, reminding her of dinnertime as a child. An Indian man reported that the sounds of frying food made his stomach turn in anticipation; he asserted that fried food is tastier than boiled or baked foods. However, some people said that frying was too much of a hassle, especially in city apartments. The explosions from the hot oil made a mess of the kitchen and could be dangerous in small living spaces.

However, the conversation around smell was the most heated.[14] According to most participants, the smell of old cooking oil was what most people identified with immigrant households and in highly negative terms. While some people did not mind the smell, they were aware that it could permeate their clothing, becoming "mobile" and causing embarrassment. Afraid of being seen as ignorant immigrants "fresh off the boat," some participants' children were adamant that their mothers not fry at home. Some people have resorted to buying fried foods from ethnic restaurants and groceries in various neighborhoods. One said, "You save time but you also lose the taste and crispness of food fresh out of the hot oil." It was clear that while many participants embraced their immigrant status they did not want to appear to be "lower class" immigrants.

Gender is an important and looming issue that needs to be explored further in my larger project about food and Asian American immigrants in Queens. However, the issue of gender was the main topic of several conversations in three of the focus groups when someone noted that Ming Tsai was a man—who cooks. The women in the focus groups were the first to recognize that, while Ming Tsai may cook, he is a chef who cooks professionally in a restaurant and not a household.

For most of the female participants, the two episodes featuring male chefs as guests were not surprising. One Chinese woman said that cooking in public and for a salary was still the domain of men—both "back home" and in America. The men, on the other hand, argued for a more liberal and progressive view of men as cooks. Some contended that they had taken on tasks in the household that are traditionally seen as female work. However, in many Asian immigrant households the woman is still the bearer of tradition and source of domestic labor.[15] As one Indian woman aptly said, "It is the woman's body that smells of grease from the cooking and the chemicals from the cleaning products. The man goes out to work. He has a clean shirt and pants and he does not smell of the home."

Sensing the Alimentary Struggles of
Asian Immigrants: Toward a Conclusion

While this presentation of the focus group results can only give a very partial and abbreviated view of what is going on between Asian American audiences and food television shows, there are themes that can be gleaned to provide fodder for further study. While I have talked about Asian American audiences for food shows, I do not mean to construct them as one monolithic interpretive community. There were cultural particularities in their reactions and ideas. It must be remembered that their words do not form a unified voice but rather a collage of intersecting interests, habits, predispositions, longings, and desires that are mediated and regulated by culture, gender, class, and historical circumstances.

The value of what I have called a *critical embodied approach* relocates the body at the center of the discussion and challenges the hegemony of the visual in modern discourses. This move enables a reading of texts and behaviors that are often stereotypically seen as biologically determined. But, as we have seen, sensorial experiences can often be the basis for analyzing cultural, structural, and historical conditions.

The conversations among focus group participants, particularly in their reports of visceral reactions of fear, pleasure, shame, trepidation, elation, and other emotions, point to the complicated nature of audiences' interpretation and understanding of mass media. My analytical focus on other sensory processes breaks the rigid connection between the sense of vision and consumers' interpretations and reactions to mass media texts. I posit a more circuitous route between the senses, memory, social location, and history to emphasize the political and cultural dimensions of the sensuous and visceral. I believe this approach prevents the creation of monolithic and fixed narratives of and about race and ethnicity and allows for conflicting and crisscrossing interests and viewpoints. Indeed, it brings to light the rather messy contours of race and ethnicity.

I have also suggested that the body is a source of critical insight. Too often theories about race and ethnicity abbreviate their corporeal and sensual dimensions. Knowledge and attitudes about race and ethnic differences are more often than not seen as objective empirical "facts" and not behaviors and representations shaped by and apprehended through the racialized subject's body. From pain and discomfort to pleasure and titillation, the body, as it experiences an increasingly racialized and ethnicized world, needs to be foregrounded.

The Asian American participants' reactions to food textures, tastes, odors, and sounds have not yielded an orientalist fantasy of exotic difference. Rather, the participants' corporeal and visceral reactions, memories, and ideas are shown to be constitutive of marginal people's complex reactions to power and ethnic, racial, and cultural difference. The body and the senses therefore open up new vistas for experiencing, understanding, and intervening with difference and power.

Notes

Funding for my field research was provided by an Asian American Studies Program Faculty Research Grant, the Campus Research Board, and the Department of Anthropology, University of Illinois, Urbana-Champaign.

1 Ruark, "A Place at the Table."
2 For examples of critical works on food and Asian Americans, see Mannur, "Culinary Scapes"; and Wong, *Reading Asian American Literature*.
3 Naficy, *The Making of Exile Cultures*.
4 Bobo, "The Color Purple," 90–109.
5 Mankekar, *Screening Culture, Viewing Politics*; Abu-Lughod, "The Interpretation of Culture(s) after Television," 493–514; Bobo, "The Color Purple," 90–109.
6 Lowe, *Immigrant Acts*; Shah, *Contagious Divides*.
7 For notable examples of work in the anthropology of the senses, see Classen, *Worlds of Sense*; Geurts, *Culture and the Senses*; Howes, *The Varieties of Sensory Experience*, 3–21, 128–47, 167–91; Stoller, *The Taste of Ethnographic Things*; Stoller, *Sensuous Scholarship*; and Sutton, *Remembrance of Repasts*.
8 Geurts, *Culture and the Senses*.
9 Marks, *The Skin of Film*, 240.
10 For a recent methodological explanation of the use of focus groups in the study of mass media, see Gamson, *Freaks Talk Back*.
11 There were five focus groups. The first three were mixed, and the last two were composed of single ethnic groups—Filipino and Chinese. Overall, there were thirty-five participants, twenty females and fifteen males. The average age was thirty-four, and all were immigrants who came to the U.S. as adults (over eighteen years old). Most identified themselves as "middle class."
12 Tsai, *Blue Ginger*.
13 Gabaccia, *We Are What We Eat*.
14 For excellent discussions of the cultural dimension of odors and smell, see Clas-

sen, Howes, and Synnott, *Aroma*. See also Engen, *Odor Sensation and Memory*; Lake, *Scents and Sensuality*; Le Guerer, *Scent*; and Silverstein, Silverstein, and Silverstein, *Smell, the Subtle Sense*. For a specific example of the politics of aroma and the Jewish community, see Kaplan, *The Making of the Jewish Middle Class*. For spaces and aromas, see Rodaway, *Sensuous Geographies*.

15 Ray, "Meals, Migration, Modernity," 105–27.

eight

Performing Culture in Diaspora: Assimilation and Hybridity in *Paris by Night* Videos and Vietnamese American Niche Media

Nhi T. Lieu

The eyes of the Sphinx glimmer in a night filled with shining stars, as dancers dressed in "Egyptian" costumes move their hands in a serpentine fashion. A contemporary tune plays against this "ancient" backdrop as the Vietnamese American singing sensation Thien Kim enters the scene, reclining on a chaise carried by male servants. Made up to look like an Egyptian princess, Thien Kim is dressed in robes and adorned with gold jewelry. Her performance of a song entitled "Doi Em Nhu Cat Kho" (My Life is Like Dry Sand) commences as she alights from her chaise and walks across the backs of her slaves to her throne. Three white, male "little people" appear, playing the part of servants and jesters to the Egyptian princess, who is unsatisfied with the luxuries her life has to offer. As she finishes her song, the camera tracks out to reveal a colossal stage with a large TV screen and pans across a packed and appreciative audience. The little people then escort the "mistress of ceremonies" Nguyen Cao Ky Duyen, to the podium. Her cohost and "master of ceremonies," Nguyen Ngoc Ngan (no relation) makes a grand entrance riding a camel onto the stage. The two cohosts joke about Ngan's height, but the scripted dialogue quickly turns to the lyrics of the opening song. The performance allows the MCs to admonish viewers that wealth and material objects do not necessarily bring happiness. Dramatized by the figure of the lonely Egyptian princess, they point out that even her abundant surroundings bring misery. Although the musical show produces an image of excess—an elaborate set, lavish costumes, and a celestial ensemble of Vietnamese celebrities from all over the diaspora—such cautionary remarks are delivered in order to convey a simple moral lesson. Typical of the videos produced in the *Paris by Night* series, this opening scene trades in contradiction, exposing the complex and often paradoxical ways in which the Vietnamese experience in diaspora is mediated and showcased.

Paris by Night is a series of commercially produced videotapes of Vietnamese variety show performances consisting of elaborate musical and dance numbers, comedic skits, and fashion shows featuring Vietnamese women in traditional dress. Many Vietnamese, if they do not own the videos themselves, have seen them on television screens at Vietnamese business establishments or heard them being referenced in conversation. As postrefugee commodities, these videos are arguably the most popular cultural products circulating throughout the Vietnamese diaspora. They have entertained nearly 2.5 million overseas Vietnamese audience members worldwide and 72 million via a semi-legal "gray market" in Vietnam.[1] Designed to capture a wide niche of the Vietnamese diasporic audience, these colorful spectacles of song and dance are usually two hours long and are available on multiple VHS videocassettes for about twenty-five U.S. dollars. They may be purchased in Vietnamese-owned businesses throughout the diaspora and on the Internet. Over seventy video sets in the series have been produced since the early 1980s. A production unique to the Vietnamese diaspora, these musical variety shows are often staged at theaters and auditoriums located in tourist cities or areas where large populations of diasporic Vietnamese reside and are recorded for wider distribution and consumption. The success of the *Paris by Night* series has not only generated a mass audience base for touring concerts but also inspired the creation of several rival production companies and video series such as *Asia, Lang Van, Van Son,* and *Hollywood Nights.*[2]

This essay examines the cultural and representational work of niche media videotexts produced by and for the Vietnamese diaspora. Combining images and sounds, these music videos provide refugees and immigrants much more than pleasure and entertainment in a familiar language. These media technologies enable new ways of literally envisioning Vietnamese culture in exile, carving out spaces for the articulation and formation of postrefugee gender, ethnic, and cultural identities. As such, these inexpensive, accessible, and highly mobile technologies have become tools with which Vietnamese Americans can grapple with various issues, including gender, sexuality, acculturation, assimilation, and the "generation gap." These Vietnamese video and niche media productions use the variety show form to construct song and dance spectacles invoking an idealized, nationalist vision of an exile community advancing under capitalism. I argue that these cultural productions privilege a "new" diasporic Vietnamese subjectivity, shedding an "impoverished refugee" image for a new hybrid, bourgeois, ethnic identity.

A Musical Revival in America

Vietnamese refugees began rebuilding and creating elaborate alternative structures for Vietnamese-language media and entertainment almost immediately after resettling in the United States. The humble beginnings of this niche entertainment industry can be located with refugee musicians, who recorded and distributed audiocassettes of music that reflected their exile status. Although these singers and entertainers initially struggled with their professional adjustment to life in the United States, due in part to the lack of venues in which to perform, homemade audiocassette recordings of Vietnamese music allowed them to eventually regain their former audiences. Their music offered both scathing critiques of the Communist government and melodies that took listeners back to a time when peace existed in Vietnam. These sorts of productions garnered the most support from the exile community, enabling many former singers to revive and reclaim their celebrity. Free from the surveillance of the Communist regime, artists and musicians also experimented with other forms of music they had been exposed to before the fall of Saigon, including Western musical genres such as rock and roll and disco and Latin rhythms such as cha-cha, tango, and rumba.[3] In addition to incorporating music from previous eras, musicians and performers also fused aspects of American popular culture into their repertoire and made a conscious effort to become part of their new homes. Despite their low production values, homemade audiocassette tapes of Vietnamese music offered a medium enabling fans to voice political critiques against the Communist regime, express their sentiments on exile, and negotiate their new identities.

Enter the VCR

While music provided solace for the exile community, the audiovisual capabilities of the VCR changed people's relationships to these cultural forms. These machines revolutionized home entertainment, bringing commercial-free films and programs into domestic spaces and giving television viewers control over what they consumed. But especially for groups of recent immigrants, the VCR not only provided access to a world of entertainment and leisure in their native languages but also functioned as a tool to preserve ethnicity, strengthen nationalism, and forge ties with the home country. As the video scholar Dana Kolar-Panov argues in her study of Croatians in Australia, the VCR "allows for the production and reproduction of nostalgia and provides for the creation of personal [as well as collective] pastiche of images and sounds as no other medium has done before."[4] The VCR brought new meaning to home entertainment in non-English-speaking households while video, as a reproducible technology, became a portable global commodity connecting immigrants to their homelands.

Like other immigrants, Vietnamese exiles were eager to use video technology to document their lives through the practice of exchanging "video letters."[5] But, unlike other immigrants, who welcomed the potential for transnational exchanges between the diaspora and the homeland, Vietnamese exiles vehemently rejected cultural productions that originated in the Socialist Republic of Vietnam, believing that the work created there was tainted by Communist ideology. With few alternatives outside of mainstream American media and limited English-language comprehension, many Vietnamese newcomers turned toward imported kung fu films and dramatic epic serials from Hong Kong and Taiwan as their main source of entertainment. Chinese films dubbed in Vietnamese enjoyed much popularity among Vietnamese immigrants and refugees, especially romantic soap operas and kung fu dramas set in ancient China. Jesse Nash's study of this phenomenon argues that Vietnamese adoration of dubbed Chinese films stems from their reaffirmation of traditional Confucian values.[6] Unlike most American television shows and movies, which seem to glorify individualism, Nash suggests that Chinese films play an important role in helping parents educate their children by modeling Confucian ideals such as filial piety and family loyalty. Additionally, Stuart Cunningham and Tina Nguyen's research reveals that Vietnamese Australians preferred dubbed films from Hong Kong and Taiwan because they contain material and settings in which "Asian faces and values predominate."[7] Although ethnic and cultural differences between the Chinese and Vietnamese are at times contentious, racial identification minimized these differences, allowing many ethnic Vietnamese to enjoy media that centered on Chinese subjects.

The success of dubbed dramatic videos from Hong Kong and Taiwan paved the way for Vietnamese exiles to apply video technology in actively constructing new cultural forms and products for their own ethnic group. By the late 1980s, glamorous images of Vietnamese performers in music videos began to replace the politically overt voices of dissent recorded on cassette tapes. This is not to say that politics disappeared from the music industry with the introduction of video, but glamour and style diluted traditional notions of politics and gave them a different form. Out of residual nationalist sentiments and the desire to carve out a distinct cultural identity apart from not only communist Vietnam but also multiethnic America, there emerged a vibrant Vietnamese music video industry. This niche industry entertained exiles in the aftermath of resettlement and provided a link to others throughout the diaspora. Advances in stereo, audiovisual, and other electronic media technologies also aided in transforming the modest musical forms the refugees had brought with them into a multi-million-dollar niche media industry. Produced mainly in Southern California and available in multiple forms of mediated technology, including cassettes, CDs, videos, karaoke laser discs, DVDs, and video CDs, diasporic Vietnamese musical culture can now be found in Vietnamese homes all over the globe.

I first encountered these cultural products during my teenage years growing up in the mid-1980s in Southern California. My parents enjoyed watching these videos, waxing nostalgic over love songs they had heard in Vietnam and taking pride in the talent "our community" was able to nurture after migrating to the United States. On the other hand, my brother and I had no interest in the videos except when a Vietnamese performer would attempt to sing a familiar American pop tune. Growing up in the 1980s, we were loyal fans of popular American and British performers such as Michael Jackson, Madonna, and Duran Duran, and we laughed whenever a Vietnamese immigrant singer would perform in imitation of these stars in their heavily accented English. It was even more unnatural for us to see Vietnamese performers dancing and gyrating onstage as if they were the *Solid Gold* dancers. Though disgruntled by what they considered "inappropriate acts" that deviated from "proper" Vietnamese behavior, my parents used these startling images to instruct us how *not* to be. Meanwhile, they still wanted us to watch these videos because the next performance might teach us more about Vietnamese culture.

My parents' ambivalence toward these videos reveals a telling aspect about Vietnamese exilic cultural production and the relationships viewers form with these popular forms of culture. The experience of watching gave my parents and those in their generation a mode for reminiscing and preserving their memories, but their discomfort and reluctance to accept the videos' sexualized imagery illustrate not only disagreement but also uncertainty about the role cultural production would have in forming the identities of the next generation. Their hesitancy represented a larger fear and anxiety about our identities as Vietnamese growing up in the United States.

The low-budget productions of my childhood have since been transformed into arguably the most popular cultural form in the Vietnamese diaspora today. The proliferation of Vietnamese exilic cultural forms circulating on video, through the mail, via the Internet, and in marginal spaces of "ethnic" media has created a trend that Hamid Naficy calls "decentralized global narrowcasting."[8] Similar to the televisual productions of Iranians in Los Angeles profiled in Naficy's work, exilic Vietnamese media productions, coexisting with mainstream media, cater to ethnic Vietnamese in the diaspora. Placing Vietnamese bodies at the center and celebrating exilic talent with pride, the Vietnamese American entertainment industry has created a niche media system and a market that willingly consumes what it produces.

The successful progenitor of the contemporary Vietnamese music video industry is Thuy Nga, the corporate producer of the overwhelmingly popular *Paris by Night* video series. Inspired by former military USO shows, MTV, and other variety entertainment from Hong Kong, as well as American film and television, *Paris by Night* was born from the entrepreneurial and creative drive of To Van Lai, a former music professor from Saigon. To Van Lai owned a music recording company named after his wife, Thuy Nga, in Vietnam.[9] When the couple fled to Paris after the fall of Saigon, they rebuilt their company under the same name.[10] In 1983, with the assistance of the president of Euro Media Productions, Jean Pierre Barry, the first *Paris by Night* variety show and live recording took place in Paris.[11]

Paris by Night shows and videos made their debut in the United States while the Vietnamese American community was undergoing tremendous change. The increased use of multimedia technology, refugees' upward mobility, and the social, cultural, and commercial development of Little Saigon in Orange County, California, contributed to making *Paris by Night* videos a huge success. The creation of Little Saigon as an ethnic enclave not only brought new possibilities for imagining community, but it also resurrected the old capital in a new physical space, complete with cultural institutions to foster this imagined community. As I have argued elsewhere, the Little Saigon enclave enabled Vietnamese Americans to geographically anchor their niche media industry.

Emerging from this space as tools for constructing and authenticating Vietnamese cultural and political identity in the diaspora, these videos are cultural forms distinguished from those of other immigrants.[12]

For instance, exilic Vietnamese media offered an alternative to Hong Kong and Taiwanese films dubbed in Vietnamese, the preferred media choice of Vietnamese immigrants and refugees at the time. While dubbed Chinese films and serials maintain their presence in the entertainment appetite of Vietnamese immigrants, the increasing popularity of *Paris by Night* videos throughout the late 1980s and early 1990s presented stiff competition for the serial films to which Vietnamese immigrants were reportedly addicted.[13] The fan base for these videotaped shows grew by word of mouth, unifying Vietnamese audiences worldwide in order to celebrate ethnic pride and reimagine Vietnamese culture through elaborate song and dance numbers.

The first releases in the series earned a stable audience through their thematic focus on the exile experience. With titles such as *Gia Biet Saigon* (Farewell Saigon), *Giot Nuoc Mat Cho Vietnam* (A Teardrop for Vietnam), *Nuoc Non Ngan Dam Ra Di* (The Homeland We Left Behind), and *Mua Xuan Nao Ta Ve?* (Which Spring Season Shall I Return?), *Paris by Night* videos used popular memories and anticommunism as guiding principles for attracting potential viewers. With the refugee elites of the "first wave" as the primary target audience, the *Paris by Night* series produced propaganda-laden, glorified images of the former Republic of Vietnam. According to Stuart Cunningham and Tina Nguyen, members of the diasporic elites welcomed such representations because they not only addressed their "depth of loss and longing" but also the "still-strong politics of disavowal of the regime's complicity in its own downfall."[14] In reconstructing Vietnam's history of war and conflict, the leaders of the former republic emerged as heroic figures whose downfall could be wholly blamed on America's abandonment.[15] But, while such blame was placed on the United States, Cunningham and Nguyen note that these narratives also depict America as a "great and powerful friend" that saved the Vietnamese people.[16]

The efforts of the first-wave elites to adjust to American society were circumscribed by popular images of subsequent waves of "boat people" leaving Communist Vietnam. The mainstream media of the mid- to late 1980s depicted the influx of asylum seekers from Southeast Asia as a social problem draining the resources of the United States and often characterized these refugees as welfare dependents and gangsters.[17] In countering these images,

Vietnamese show producers veiled immigrant anxiety about refugee dependency. What shaped many representations of diasporic Vietnamese videos was not only an urge to cure homesickness but also a longing to become part of the American nation. Introduced to American consumer cultures in Vietnam, immigrants and refugees often associated assimilation with conspicuous consumption. Ronald Reagan's anticommunist and procapitalist politics of the 1980s particularly appealed to the elite refugees of the first wave, and his conservative politics seemed to promise access to the American Dream.[18] This Reagan era bourgeois indulgence and its celebration of consumer capitalism consequently shaped many of the images of glamour and opulence that *Paris by Night* would later produce and reproduce. In reconstructing Vietnamese cultural elements and selectively poaching from American popular culture, producers and entertainers used this hybrid cultural terrain to create and sustain a fantasy of "Vietnamese America," reinterpreting history and molding new cultural identities through the strategic marketing of commodity desire.

These projections not only altered musical tastes and preferences among Vietnamese immigrants, but these glamorous images began to replace the overt voices of political dissent. Sold as commodities of cultural preservation, as well as leisure and relaxation, these videos granted many Vietnamese people pleasure and forms of escapism, but they also functioned ideologically to promote a successful, middle-class, and assimilated image. As such, Thuy Nga's videos gave Vietnamese viewers variety entertainment updated and translated through the most recent trends in mainstream American culture, film, television, and fashion while assuring viewers that these translations were compatible with "authentic" Vietnamese culture.[19]

By the late 1990s, Thuy Nga Productions had established distribution centers in metropole cities in France, the United States, and Australia. With a focus on the contemporary Vietnamese diasporic experience, *Paris by Night* videos began to shift the themes of their titles away from the political. More frequently, producers began organizing musical arrangements around prosaic themes with titles such as *Tinh Ca* (Songs of Love), *Tien* (Money), *Anh Den Mau* (Stage Lighting), and *Vao Ha* (Holiday). Additionally, *Paris by Night* began incorporating *ao dai* fashion shows featuring Vietnamese designers into their productions and traveling all over the diaspora, to Las Vegas, Houston, Toronto, and the birthplace of the series, Paris, to perform for far-flung Vietnamese audiences. Releasing over four videos annually, each of which cost

nearly half a million dollars to produce, and selling an estimated thirty thousand copies of each video, Thuy Nga continues to dominate smaller, rival
productions in the exilic entertainment industry.[20]

Although *Paris by Night* videos have been in circulation throughout the
Vietnamese diaspora for nearly three decades, few scholars have seriously
considered them as subjects worthy of critical analysis. Neglecting cultural formations and transformations, scholars of Vietnamese migration have tended
to focus on the psychological aspects of refugee experiences, paying attention
only to cultural displacement and maladjustment. Scholarship on Vietnamese
refugees carries titles such as *Transition to Nowhere, Hearts of Sorrow*, and even,
more recently, *Songs of the Free, Songs of the Caged.*[21] Reasoning that Vietnamese
refugees would encounter difficulties because they were the "first sizable non-
European or European-culture refugees to come to the U.S. and no other large
refugee group has come from a land with so low a level of development,"
Barry Stein's sociological study explicitly states that most Americans believed
it was "too difficult for them [Vietnamese refugees] to ever integrate into
our society."[22] In her critique of such refugee studies, the anthropologist Liisa
Malkki observes that the "sedentarism reflected in language and in social
practice" in the scholarship not only functions to root cultures in geographic
spaces but also "actively territorializes our identities, whether cultural or national."[23] Because refugees no longer possess a national territory in which
to "root" their cultures, many refugee studies scholars pathologize their cultural displacement while ignoring cultural production in the aftermath of
migration.

When it is not represented as pathological, Vietnamese culture is oftentimes characterized as static, resilient, and unaffected, despite its multilayered
colonial past. The anthropologist James Rutledge, for example, observed that
"when the Vietnamese refugees left Vietnam they left their country of birth
but did not abandon their indigenous culture." Explaining the Vietnamese
worldview, he writes: "The Vietnamese view themselves historically, and presently, as harmony-oriented. To the maximum degree possible, Vietnamese
people desire to bring peace to other people and to respond to them in the way
that brings them the most joy."[24] Such orientalist constructions of the Vietnamese people mask the complicated politics of the U.S. military intervention.
Moreover, this uncritical description of Vietnamese "indigenous culture" un-
problematically idealizes the former world of the Vietnamese and ignores the
nation's history of colonial domination and cross-cultural fertilization.

Disrupting these beliefs through the staging of extravagant fantasy, Vietnamese variety shows offer a different glimpse of Vietnamese immigrant life, challenging the notion that the culture is composed of static tenets simply imported from Vietnam and applied in America. Undermining the notion of resiliency in Vietnamese culture, the cultural forms and objects created in exile exhibit an extraordinary process of relentless borrowing and appropriation to meet the perceived needs of the diasporic community. It is precisely because of this mixing and melding that exilic Vietnamese cultural production is often dismissed as trivial, frivolous, and made only for enjoyment.[25] Paying attention to undertheorized sites of the "popular" and the "inauthentic," my research examines cultural production and diasporic Vietnamese variety entertainment videos as serious subjects of study. Because these sites of the "popular" are repositories for generative forms of prevalent desires and fantasies, they appeal across gender and class lines to a mass Vietnamese diasporic audience.

Although cultural insiders have enjoyed *Paris by Night* videos for many years, these cultural forms caught the attention of a larger public with the controversy sparked by Thuy Nga's release of a special *Mother* video. In August 1997, hundreds of Vietnamese Americans in Orange County marched to the local Thuy Nga headquarters and protested the messages they perceived in the production company's latest release. *Mother* was supposed to be the most innovative and artistic *Paris by Night* video produced thus far. Deviating from the usual live variety format, the feature performances in *Mother* were presented with serious artistic intent, filled with images of Vietnam and filmed in the style of American music videos. Audiences waited with much anticipation for what Thuy Nga Productions promised would be a very special music video dedicated to Vietnamese motherhood. Filled with montages of rare scenery from Vietnam, as well as historical footage of war, the video was not only commemorative but also instructional and spiritual, highlighting filial connections between mothers and children.[26]

But controversy erupted when viewers saw footage of an American helicopter belonging to the South Vietnamese Army shooting at innocent civilians, interpreting its inclusion as a "procommunist" gesture. When angry fans marched in front of *Paris by Night* distribution stores and burned the videos, protesting what they argued were historical inaccuracies and demanding an apology, the scandal sparked public interest beyond the Vietnamese diasporic community, drawing the attention of some mainstream media.[27] *Paris by Night* sales momentarily suffered when fans looked to other production companies for entertainment. However, after Thuy Nga's contracted performers publicly defended the producers for what was explained away as the mistakes of an inexperienced young video editor, the *Paris by Night* series gradually regained its fan base. Nonetheless, the impassioned battle over representation attests to the critical relationship forged between the Vietnamese exile community and these media.

In one of the first published studies of diasporic Vietnamese media, the Australian cultural studies scholars Stuart Cunningham and Tina Nguyen provide a helpful analytical framework for interpreting the videos as cultural texts. Cunningham and Nguyen argue that the functions of these cultural texts can be classified through the categories of heritage maintenance, cultural negotiation, and assertive hybridity.[28] According to them, in assuming a stance against the Communist government, these cultural texts maintain a sense of heritage, and yet processes of cultural negotiation enable overseas Vietnamese to arbitrate aspects of the colonial past such as its French and Chinese influences, and the cultural assemblages of Vietnamese cultural and musical forms. At the same time, "assertive hybridity" highlights pastiche in its appropriations of American pop culture. Performers who represent this "new wave" of assertive hybridity play crucial roles in the formation of a diasporic youth culture, especially in its experiments with gender and sexuality.[29] For the remainder of this essay, I wish to expand on Cunningham's and Nguyen's observations and pose different possibilities for interpreting the *Paris by Night* video series as they pertain to diasporic identity formation and Vietnamese exilic self-representation.

Vietnamese Exile as Authentic Vietnamese

The majority of *Paris by Night* fans are between the ages of forty and sixty, but the videos are viewed by people of all ages and are considered "family entertainment." Older audience members who are fluent in the Vietnamese language tend to be attracted to two types of music, depending on taste and preference: traditional Vietnamese folk songs sung in an operatic style, called *vong co*; or more modern, European-influenced music with the familiar Latin rhythms of their youth. The elements that draw the younger generations are the dance beats and sounds of familiar American pop songs. As such, *Paris by Night* makes a concerted effort to feature and promote young singers who perform bilingual song and dance numbers "borrowed" from current American pop culture.[30] However, these videos seldom showcase works that are "new." Songs are often recycled and sung by multiple artists on different recordings to display the talents of the artists rather than the artistry of the songs themselves. Because copyrights are almost never enforced, these artistic borrowings and multiple covers of the same songs are common.[31] In his critique of the standardization of Western music, Theodor Adorno posits that pseudo-individuation numbs the minds of the masses, who seek leisure to escape from their everyday realities. For Vietnamese exiles, pseudo-individuation is familiar, as Vietnamese tunes provide an escape in nostalgia. Much more than a pastime, nostalgia-laden music requires the standardization of music to locate a sense of familiarity. This allows Vietnamese exiles to commiserate and share in the experience of listening. Although music preference and audience reception to specific songs are uneven, audiences of Vietnamese diaspora media draw on what is most familiar and enjoy entertainment that transports them to a nostalgic, prior moment untainted by the devastation of war, dislocation, and displacement.

Nonetheless, although much pleasure is derived from these videos, they should not be ignored simply because they afford pleasure. Instead, borrowing a phrase from Dorinne Kondo, Vietnamese variety show videos should be regarded as "contradictory sites of pleasure and contestation."[32] As I have shown, videos and their audiences also enforce an ideology of exile. This is most prevalent in the policing of Vietnamese American performers. Honored as celebrities in the diasporic community, entertainers are often invited to fund-raisers for charitable causes and even political rallies.[33] But when diasporic entertainers choose to perform in Vietnam they automatically become outcasts, losing their fan bases and popular standing.[34] (Conversely, when singers from Vietnam tour the United States, exiles organize protests and boycotts of their concerts, branding them communist spies.)[35] The business of entertainment for Vietnamese Americans is therefore fused with politics, and anticommunist politics dominate every aspect of the industry. While I agree with Cunningham and Nguyen that maintaining an anticommunist stance secures the ideological work of "heritage maintenance," I contend that anticommunist rhetoric also consolidates and strengthens Vietnamese exilic identities, as well as defining for them what is properly "Vietnamese." Because return is not a viable option for the exiles, the struggle to define what is authentically Vietnamese operates through nostalgia. In his study of Iranian nostalgia, Hamid Naficy notes that "for exiles who have emigrated from Third World countries, life in the United States . . . is doubly unreal, and it is because of this double loss—of origin and of reality—that nostalgia becomes a cultural and representational practice among the exiles."[36] A cultural project already thriving on fantasy, the historical past constructed by variety shows is sometimes imagined as untainted by war and devastation. Critical of the existing Communist regime, the Vietnamese exiles refuse to look to the nation-state as a place of "true" culture. For them, authentic Vietnamese culture only existed before the Communist takeover in 1975. In *Songs of the Caged, Songs of the Free*, the ethnomusicologist Adelaida Reyes argues that Vietnamese exiles hope to preserve "pre-1975 culture" and reinstate it when Vietnam is liberated from Communist rule.[37] It is through the fetishization of the pre-1975 homeland that, according to Naficy, "an electronic *communitas* that bestows a sense of stability and commonality to the exiles" is created.[38]

Constructing "High" Culture

While nostalgia for the homeland allows audiences to imagine a national community in exile, *colonial* nostalgia consolidates its class hierarchies. Consider the title of the video series. While Paris is the literal birthplace of Thuy Nga's entertainment empire, the name *Paris by Night* also evokes a colonial past, reminiscent of a time when the Vietnamese elite traveled to the metropole to experience the sophisticated glamour of the "city of lights." When referring to the video series, some fans pronounce *Paris* with a French accent, yet *Paris by Night* is not otherwise known as *Paris par Nuit*. This choice of a linguistically hybrid title implicitly invokes the historical relationships between former Vietnamese regimes and both the French and the American nations.

Colonial nostalgia is not only a longing Thuy Nga Productions promotes but also composes a set of ideological assumptions on which the company thrives. Drawing from Vietnam's colonial past, with its diverse cultural elements, enables producers and entertainers to invent an exilic culture that is disassociated from Communist Vietnam. Importantly, these colonial projects provide cultural forms loaded with signs of class distinction. For instance, almost every video produced after 1990 contains a fashion show modeled by young, attractive performers and showcasing the talents of young diasporic designers. Literally fashioning a particular bourgeois sensibility enables performers to project an idealized image of Vietnamese identity. Using colonial nostalgia and its images of cosmopolitanism, *Paris by Night* introduces its audiences to a world of fashion, plastic surgery, and commodity fetishism.

Unlike the diasporic music-recording industry of the late 1970s and early 1980s, *Paris by Night* videos grapple with immigrant alienation and displacement in a manner reflecting a newly forged bourgeois identity. In representing the experiences of Vietnamese immigrants in America, the Thuy Nga producers construct a trajectory of upward mobility. Staged and recorded at the famous Hollywood Shrine auditorium, the former location of the Oscar and Grammy awards ceremonies, a 1995 special edition commemorating twenty years of migration and exile began with a montage of documentary film footage of refugee flight. A reminder to the live and video audiences of their shared, collective past, these images of boat people flashed across a large movie screen, followed by a powerfully sorrowful performance about the exile experience. These stark images were replaced with an overwhelming celebration of the current success of Vietnamese Americans throughout the rest of the video.

Disruptions in Vietnameseness

Although a relatively conservative and traditional class of anticommunist elites holds sway over these representations of "Vietnameseness," what it means to be Vietnamese is constantly disrupted in the shows' performances. Musical acts by young artists often destabilize and refashion the categories "Vietnamese" and "Vietnamese America." Cunningham and Nguyen's third category, "assertive hybridity," celebrates these liberating aspects of diasporic performances. Encapsulated by the creative work of artists such as Lynda Trang Dai, known as "the Vietnamese Madonna," and others who transcend boundaries of tradition and culture, assertive hybridity enables Vietnamese youth to embrace aspects of Western as well as Vietnamese culture in an unfolding drama of assimilation.

No other feature of the *Paris by Night* series illustrates these ongoing struggles more poignantly than the banter between the master and mistress of ceremonies. Nearly every *Paris by Night* event is hosted by the prominent poet and political writer Nguyen Ngoc Ngan and his female sidekick Nguyen Cao Ky Duyen, a young lawyer turned performer, who is also the daughter of Nguyen Cao Ky, the former vice president and air force commander of South Vietnam. While the duties of the master and mistress of ceremonies generally consist of introducing performers and, when necessary, providing historical backgrounds for certain types of performances, the MCs also bear the responsibilities of setting the overall ambiance, offering moral instruction and comic relief, and staging debates about gender roles. As an eminent member of the exilic literati, Nguyen Ngoc Ngan presumes to represent the views of Vietnamese men and the "traditional values" upheld by the elders of the community. Nguyen Cao Ky Duyen, on the other hand, seeks to embody a vibrant youth culture and speak on behalf of Vietnamese women. Sometimes referred to as "the role model for Vietnamese women for the twenty-first century," Ky Duyen is respected by both young and old women.[39] At times, the playful dialogue and comedic exchanges between the two resemble the antics of morning-show hosts Regis Philbin and Kelly Ripa. Like the authoritative and cantankerous Regis and the cheerful and jovial Kelly, Ngan and Ky Duyen often contend with issues of power in gender and social relations. They even receive fan mail and requests from the audience to discuss such matters. For instance, in a debate about the transformation of gender roles in the immigration experience, Ngan often brings up the practice of gift giving as an example. Noting that women often complain about men not giving them gifts on holidays such as Valentine's Day and birthdays, Ngan explains that in times of war and economic hardship it was not common practice in Vietnam for husbands to buy gifts for their wives. Ky Duyen responds by asking, "Then, according to Vietnamese society in the past, what makes a good husband?" What follows blossoms into a debate about the qualities that define a good Vietnamese man.

> *Ngan:* In the olden days, most men were the heads of their households except for the few men who went astray and became addicted to gambling and alcohol or committed adultery. Thus, men who do not commit these vices are good husbands.
>
> *Ky Duyen:* You mean men do not have to help with the laundry, wash dishes, or help with the house chores?
>
> *Ngan:* You are asking for too much. That is, a husband who does not take in a concubine is good enough. If you ask him to do housework and vacuum, that's too much. We have migrated here, and we see that this society is different. Women here have noticed our American neighbors are so different from our own husbands. For example, an American man saw a Vietnamese man driving his wife home from the market and it is raining outside. The Vietnamese man gets out of the car and it is expected that he open the car door for his wife. But I don't know about you folks, but this is not a practice that Vietnamese men are accustomed to. . . . The American man was surprised to see that the Vietnamese man walks out of the car with umbrella in tote while his wife soaked in the rain.

The audience laughs, and Ngan pleads with the female members of the audience to understand the plight of men.

Ngan: In their transition from Vietnam to America, of course, there are certain old habits that are deep seated. We will change gradually, but we can't instantly become *gallant* like American men because it is not a practice that men of my generation are used to. Perhaps it will be possible for my children's generation to do this.

To which Ky Duyen quickly retorts:

Ky Duyen: This is the first time I have heard it explained to me in this manner. But I have a suggestion to make. We women will consider the situations of our men, and when there's a holiday or a special occasion you need not purchase any gifts for us. We just ask that you give us money so that we can buy gifts for ourselves.[40]

Turning to the audience for assent and applause, Ky Duyen smiles and adds, "This is because whenever men buy things for us we always have to exchange them, and if they buy diamonds they're always too small. So if you give us money, it's the only sure thing." Content with her final punch line, Ky Duyen turns from a potentially charged discussion that gestures toward feminism to one about female consumption.

After a musical performance by two young singing sisters, Ky Duyen picks up where the conversation ended with a monologue that revisits the discussion on gender roles.

Ky Duyen: The fact is, men do have faults, but the faults are minor. If a man forgets to buy a present for his wife or isn't gallant or meticulous, that's actually fine. However, I think there are certain things that men should never do. If men ever do these things, we should leave them. First, never hit a woman, and, second, do not ever drink excessively. Moderate social drinking is fine, but drinking too much is bad, right?

Ngan spontaneously replies, "Yes, I do agree. I dare not do any of those things. I am afraid to hit my wife, and I do not drink alcohol because I get these glances from her." Alcohol provides a segue for Ngan to tell a joke about three men at an Alcoholics Anonymous meeting, but Ky Duyen pushes the conversation back to the changing gender roles of men and women. She prompts, "What do you think is the main difference between Vietnamese husbands and wives now and then in Vietnam?" Ngan confidently explains, "I think the houses in Vietnam were too small. Husbands and wives shared one room with their children." Ngan then proceeds to tell another joke about lovemaking and the lack of privacy parents have when sleeping in crowded quarters and sharing a room with their children.

Rife with humorous exchanges ranging from intelligent to raunchy, the repartee between the MCs entertains, as well as enabling the audience to reflect on other, unresolved differences between Vietnamese American women and men. Through comedic rupture and recuperation, the master and mistress of ceremonies grapple with issues of gender differences, educating and provoking audience members to discuss on their own the complexities of the immigrant experience.

The debates about gender roles staged by the MCs reflect a larger concern over meanings of tradition and modernity, often writ large on the female body. The *Paris by Night* stage showcases an incredibly diverse range of Vietnamese femininities, but Nhu Quynh and Lynda Trang Dai exemplify the two extremes. A traditional female vocalist, Nhu Quynh represents an image of the virginal innocence of a young Vietnamese woman. Lynda Trang Dai, the Vietnamese Madonna, on the other hand, uses her sexuality (like the "original") as a way to express her art. Nhu Quynh has been described as "sweet," "pretty," "graceful," and "the girl that every man wants to marry." She always appears in the traditional *ao dai*, the long, flowing Vietnamese tunic that symbolizes not only Vietnamese ethnicity but it also essentialized, gendered, and classed forms of femininity. For *Paris by Night* audiences, it projects a particular image of beauty that evokes nostalgia for the beauty of the homeland. The symbolic meaning of the ao dai has also inspired the fashion shows featured in many *Paris by Night* videos. The person responsible for some of these ao dai designs is none other than Thuy Nga herself. Using fabrics from famous couture designers such as Yves Saint Laurent, Christian Dior, Paco Rabanne, and Nina Ricci, Thuy Nga uses Western high fashion to create a diasporic Vietnamese "high" culture.

In contrast to the female performers, who always wear ao dai in their acts, Lynda Trang Dai stands out as a symbol of the "Americanized" Vietnamese woman. Notorious for imitating Madonna's song and dance routines, she has been alternately criticized and praised by young and old generations alike for "lacking originality" and being both "too sexy" and "bold and daring." In the early 1980s, she became one of the first female exile entertainers to shed convention by styling herself as a seductress and "boy toy." Unlike the original Madonna, who embraces polymorphous perversity, however, Lynda denies any similarities between her stage persona and her "real life," insisting, "I don't smoke, I don't drink. I'm just your typical Vietnamese girl who wants to look different when she sings."[41] Nonetheless, many viewers refuse to see her sexualized performances as belonging to a typical Vietnamese girl. Many older Vietnamese people view her as a dangerous influence. Embodying a youthful style, her performances are believed to inspire young girls to transgress traditional notions of Vietnamese femininity.

The Pedagogy of *Paris by Night*

Gender may be a point of conflict in *Paris by Night* videos, but issues of cultural assimilation and acculturation also inform the performances. One reason Vietnamese variety show videos are immensely popular is because they actively poach from American popular culture. Offering their own interpretations and translations, young performers appropriate a wide range of stylistic elements from mainstream music, from contemporary love ballads to rock, hip hop, and rap. Young Vietnamese American singers often cover the music of pop artists famous in the 1950s and 1960s, such as Elvis Presley and the Beatles, more contemporary divas such as Madonna and Celine Dion, and trendsetters such as Ricky Martin, Britney Spears, and 'NSync. These performers introduce what they believe exemplifies American culture to Vietnamese audiences. Many bilingual pop songs serve to open parents' eyes to the interests of their Vietnamese American children.[42] By translating what is considered "foreign" culture for parents, *Paris by Night* videos can act as a generational bridge.

Poaching American culture also allows Thuy Nga Productions to familiarize their audiences with highbrow productions and other minority cultures. In *Paris by Night 46*, Henry Chuc and Dalena perform numbers from the Andrew Lloyd Webber's musical *Phantom of the Opera* for Vietnamese audiences, re-enacting scenes and translating lyrics from English to Vietnamese. Also known as the artist who brought rap and hip hop to *Paris by Night* fans, Henry Chuc demonstrated the range of his musical talent by performing the role of the Phantom. A blonde, Euro-American woman whose ability to mimic Vietnamese vocals made her famous in the world of Vietnamese niche entertainment, Dalena played Christine, the Phantom's love interest. This ethnic, off-Broadway version of a popular musical provides a glimpse of American culture to which audiences might not otherwise have access.

In another reinterpretation of a famous American musical, *Paris by Night* modified the lyrics of a popular song so that Vietnamese audiences might better relate to its sentiments. Performing scenes from *West Side Story*, Tommy Ngo and Bao Han change one line of Stephen Sondheim's lyrics to match the experiences of Vietnamese Americans. But this *Paris by Night* version remains true to the spirit of the original musical recording, complete with social commentary and a scathing critique of American society.

> I like to be in America, Okay by me in America
>
> Everything free in America, For a small fee in America
>
> Buying on credit is so nice, One look at you and they charge twice
>
> I have my own washing machine. What will you have though to keep clean?
>
> Skyscrapers loom in America, Cadillacs zoom in America
>
> Industries boom in America, Twelve in a room in America
>
> Lots of new housing with more space, Lots of doors slamming in our face
>
> I get a terrace apartment, Better get rid of your accent!
>
> Life can be great in America, If you can fight in America
>
> Life is all right in America, If you are white in America
>
> Here you are free and you have pride, Long as you stay on your own side
>
> You can have anything you choose, Free to wait tables and shine shoes
>
> Everywhere crime in America, Organized Crime in America, Terrible time in
>> America
>
> You forget I'm in America
>
> I think I'll go back to Saigon, I know a boat you can get on, bye-bye
>
> Everyone there will give big cheer, Every one there will have moved here.

Translated through a Vietnamese American lens, this performance of "America" was performed with the original choreography and sung with an "immigrant" accent. Dressed in clothing that resembled an amalgam of 1960s-era styles but with Asian accents, Tommy Ngo and his entourage wore kung fu tops with slacks, while Bao Han and her back-up performers wore cheongsam blouses with asymmetrical ruffled skirts and high-heeled tap shoes. Their rendition of "America," introduced by the MC as "Life Is Good in America," contains allusions to racial discrimination ("Buying on credit is so nice, One look at you and they charge twice. . . . Life is all right in America, If you are white in America. . . . Lots of doors slamming in our face. . . . Better get rid of your accent!"), the housing problems poor immigrants face ("Twelve in a room in America"), the lack of employment opportunities ("Free to wait tables and shine shoes"), and an overall disillusionment with the unattainable American Dream ("I think I'll go back to Saigon, I know a boat you can get on"). And, while the male perspective finds fault with American society, the presumably more Americanized women sing the praises of modernity and consumer capitalism ("Skyscrapers loom in America, Cadillacs zoom in

America / Industries boom in America") and other freedoms available there ("Here you are free and you have pride. . . . You can have anything you choose").

Film critics and theater reviewers have noted that the original lyrics of "America" were modified and toned down for the film version of *West Side Story* so that its critique of American society would not offend mainstream audiences.[43] Staying faithful to the original stage production allows immigrant men to momentarily find fault with American society, only to be countered by young, presumably more assimilated women singing the praises of consumer capitalism and material wealth. As in the original stage production, the immigrant experience is gendered. This critique of American society nonetheless creates ruptures in the normalizing representations of Vietnamese Americans, destabilizing the problematic elitism in many self-representations of Vietnamese Americans. However, certain consumerist desires still define the immigrant experience.

Carving Out Spaces for Creative Bodies

The alternative cultural public of the diasporic entertainment industry not only allows exiles to represent themselves, but it is also the only theater in which most Vietnamese immigrant and American-born performers can showcase their performing arts. Boasting of quality production values and the most prestigious venue in the industry, the *Paris by Night* stage gives diasporic Vietnamese performers a chance to attain fame and celebrity. In this setting, Vietnamese bodies are at the center while non-Vietnamese, such as some of the *Paris by Night* dancers, are on the periphery. These dynamics are even more pronounced in other productions, as in the shows staged by a rival production company, Asia Entertainment, in which the majority of the dancers are white.

The privileging of Vietnamese bodies in Vietnamese music video productions is, however, occasionally offset by non-Vietnamese performers who take on "yellowface."[44] One of the most beloved non-Vietnamese performers to ever join the diasporic music industry is Dalena, a blonde, blue-eyed, Euro-American woman who sings in accent-free Vietnamese. Dalena was discovered by an Asian restaurateur, who gave her a cassette tape of Vietnamese music after learning that she loved to sing in multiple languages.[45] Her ability to mimic and perform Vietnamese vocals catapulted her to the top of the industry, allowing her to play a large role in popularizing Vietnamese diasporic music in the early 1990s. Dalena does not understand the Vietnamese language, but her fascination with and willingness to embrace Vietnamese culture—donning the traditional ao dai and singing in a range of Vietnamese genres, including the traditional Vietnamese opera—has made her a huge star.

Dalena's success has not been matched by other non-Vietnamese performers, but her crossover appeal to Vietnamese diasporic audiences reveals their fascination with "exotic" non-Vietnamese others. Rick Murphy, an Irish American who sings Vietnamese opera; Frank Olivier, a French singer and songwriter; and Lynn, the Anglo-Australian wife of the famed performer Cong Thanh, have all made appearances in *Paris by Night* videos. Biracial performers such as Thanh Ha and Phi Nhung have also gained entry into the world of diasporic entertainment. Consistent with these attempts to thrill audiences with acts that are "out of the ordinary," Thuy Nga Productions has used "little people" as well as exotic animals as props in the variety shows. In recent videos, it has also created spectacular opening sequences that parody Hollywood blockbusters such as *Mission Impossible* and *The Matrix* and popular Western characters such as James Bond.[46] With an all-inclusive "family of entertainers" offering "something for everyone," the videos seek to bridge gender, generational, linguistic, regional, and to some extent class divisions in their representations of Vietnamese culture.[47]

Vietnamese diasporic engagements with questions of cultural assimilation are not unproblematic. Immigrant Vietnamese constructions of "American" identity are often reflected in the public figures featured in variety show videos. Like celebrities in Hollywood, Vietnamese entertainers are often looked on as icons of Vietnamese success and beauty. With the power of the diasporic entertainment industries behind them, these performers set the standard for how Vietnamese Americans might construct their own identities. Yet numerous performers, particularly female entertainers, have physically altered their faces and bodies (especially their eyes and noses) in order to achieve success. As proponents of plastic surgery and the cosmetics industry, performers project an idealized image of beauty that seems to inspire other Vietnamese to similarly transform their bodies to attain success. It is no coincidence that Vietnamese cosmetic surgeons often advertise their businesses in minutes-long "infomercials" in these videos.

Responses to an Internet survey I conducted regarding Vietnamese popular entertainment reveal that fans of Vietnamese videos are responding to this marketing of desire and hybridized beauty. Despite the option to fast forward through these ads, many viewers do take notice. A working mother and fan of *Paris by Night* videos, Lan observed that the ads are a "waste of her time," but she "can see how [they] can be effective in reaching all the Viet[namese] population."[48] One male respondent to the survey, Thuan, wrote: "I think it is overwhelmingly clear that Vietnamese people are really into this and that is strange." When asked, "Would you consider having plastic surgery to enhance your looks?" he answered, "Yes."[49] And a college student, Tricia, asserts, "It's amazing what technology can do for a person."[50] As an overwhelming number of respondents to my survey confirmed, fans believe that Vietnamese people, especially the performers, who are under constant public scrutiny, should have aesthetic surgery so that they will have "more confidence" onstage. Those who objected to plastic surgery cited only health and safety reasons for not going under the knife.

Cosmetic surgery has become a common operation among those who can afford it. Though men are only gradually adopting these practices, many upwardly mobile women have undergone major cosmetic surgery to shed their Vietnameseness in exchange for a new, hybrid identity constructed not only through Vietnamese but also mainstream American cultures. Popular Vietnamese diasporic videos have not only legitimated the social practice of plastic surgery but also encouraged it.

Conclusion

It is important to keep in mind that while *Paris by Night* videos present Vietnamese Americans as having transcended their refugee origins they do not abandon or disavow this history. But the image of the Vietnamese as frail, powerless boat people is found only in historical footage. According to the videotexts, these suffering bodies have been transformed into healthy ones, displaying not only middle-class respectability but even material excess. Playing with these ideas about poverty and progress, *Paris by Night 57*, a show entitled *Thoi Trang va Am Nhac* (Fashion and Music), features another debate about fashion, socioeconomic status, and the value people place on appearances between Ky Duyen and Ngan.

> *Ky Duyen*: My dress is designed by Calvin Hiep [a Vietnamese American fashion designer who designed many of the costumes worn by the *Paris by Night* cast]; Ngan's tuxedo was purchased from the swap meet.
> *Ngan*: You are mistaken, I rented it.
> *Ky Duyen*: Then we better not get it dirty.
> *Ngan*: In Vietnam, we learned that we simply "eat to satisfy hunger, wear clothes

to keep us warm," so that you do not die from hunger or freeze to death in the cold. But as we have progressed, the words have changed to "eat for gratification, dress to look good" now that we have all that life has to offer. But before, when we were poor, we adhered to the proverbs, fables, and folktales we learned about in grade school. We used to be humble about the food we eat, grateful for every grain of salt. But now when we are asked to go out for a meal we ask what kind of food are we eating. Is it lobster or steamed fish? When others give us gifts such as a tie or a suit, we now ask, what label or what designer made the clothes? Is it Calvin Klein or Donna Karan? We have now progressed to a higher level, so we no longer have to "eat to satisfy hunger, and wear clothes to keep us warm." We now eat well and dress to look good. We are now at a point were we can be fashion conscious.

Ky Duyen: Are you saying that you have to be wealthy in order to have fashion? Then countries that are poor do not have any sense of fashion?

Ngan: Yes, that's generally true. If you went to a poor country and gave its people a choice between diamonds and salt, they would take the salt instead of the diamonds.

Ky Duyen: Not me, I would want the diamonds. It doesn't matter how poor I am, I would still take the diamonds. [*Chuckles*] But you are correct. Society in general does value outward appearances more. But for the Vietnamese people, perhaps we may have been influenced by the West; therefore, we think that appearances are very important. But as you claim that we suffer in our wealth, I think that we have suffered through our poverty as well. What's worse is we suffer from the fear of others knowing that we are poor. And we may be poor, but when we are in public we have to dress nice and try to drive an expensive car, right?

Ngan: Yes, that is one of the problems Vietnamese culture suffers from.[51]

Both Ky Duyen and Ngan agree that the exile community has "progressed" to the point where relevant concerns are reduced to conspicuous consumption and the possession of material objects. Ky Duyen attributes these concerns not only to the immigrant experience but also Western influence. It is fear of the judgment of others from within and without the community that drives Vietnamese immigrants toward excess and materialism. As a popular cultural production, videos dramatize these urges and desires, presenting Vietnamese Americans as a successful immigrant group and replacing the image of the poor refugee with that of the new model minority. And through a cautious acceptance of the model minority label Vietnamese Americans insert themselves into a mainstream discourse on race in popular culture.

Variety show videos produced by Vietnamese Americans have transformed Vietnamese culture in the diaspora, producing both liberating and repressive possibilities. As a venue for the creative talents of people in the diasporic community, the variety show as a cultural form has contributed to the construction of an alternative public sphere that promotes a sense of ethnic pride. At the same time, however, the exilic media culture has also packaged representations that not only have problematic gender and class implications but also present an illusion of access. Diasporic videos have played a large role in the objectification of Vietnamese women's bodies, advertising plastic surgery and glamorizing high fashion. Aspiring to reproduce bourgeois tastes, these shows also project unattainable visions of assimilation for those immigrants and refugees who lack access to social, cultural, and economic capital. In their role as a popular cultural apparatus for linking diasporic Vietnamese, the *Paris by Night* videotexts have established hegemony over other forms and practices articulated by Vietnamese subjects who view themselves as peripheral to this particular vision. Their dominance in the diaspora continues to submerge other forms of independent art and culture expressing the Vietnamese American experience.

Notes

1 Ashley Carruthers, "National Identity, Diasporic Anxiety, and Music Video Culture in Vietnam." The attempts made by the Communist government to regulate and censor music in Vietnam have failed miserably. Hence, in Vietnam it is semilegal to buy and own music videos, CDs, and karaoke laser discs produced by Vietnamese in the diaspora. Moreover, because copyright laws are not enforced internationally, producers do not profit from the sale of these illegal copies. Gerry Hadden, "Vietnamese Singers Who Produce Western-Style Pop," *Morning Edition*, National Public Radio, January 18, 2000.
2 I have chosen to focus on *Paris by Night* videos because they have the largest fan base and have achieved brand recognition.
3 According to Adelaida Reyes Schramm, who did fieldwork in refugee camps in Bataan and Palawan, the Philippines, as soon as Vietnamese refugees regained their freedom of expression, they experimented with music that included "love songs, religious songs, and songs that express personal feelings that were not directed toward country, parents, Communism and Uncle Ho" ("From Refugee to Immigrant," 95).
4 Kolar-Panov, "Video and the Diasporic Imagination of Selfhood."
5 Ibid.; Schein, "Forged Transnationality and Oppositional Cosmopolitanism"; Koltyk, "Telling Narratives through Home Videos: Hmong Refugees and Self-Documentation of Life in the Old and New Country."

6 Nash, "Confucius and the VCR."

7 Cunningham and Nguyen, "Popular Media of the Vietnamese Diaspora."

8 Naficy, *The Making of Exile Cultures*.

9 Truong, "Paris by Night."

10 One of the strategies of Vietnamese business establishments throughout the diaspora is to continue to use the brand names of renowned companies and businesses so that they can play on the nostalgic sensibilities of customers who long for things associated with the days before the fall of Saigon.

11 Information gathered from *Paris by Night 24: 10th Anniversary*, video, Thuy Nga Productions, 1994.

12 Lieu, "Overlapping Diasporas."

13 Smith, "The Big Mix."

14 Cunningham and Nguyen, "Popular Media of the Vietnamese Diaspora."

15 *Paris by Night 10: Gia Biet Saigon* [Farewell Saigon], video, Thuy Nga Productions, 1986; *Paris by Night 24: 10th Anniversary*, video, Thuy Nga Productions, 1994; and *Paris by Night 32: 20 Nam Nhin Lai* [Twenty Years Looking Back], video, dir. Richard Valverde, Thuy Nga Productions, 1995. All of these videos contain actual footage of war and the violence of exile in clips that feature a strong American presence in Vietnam and the American withdrawal from the fallen capital of Saigon.

16 Cunningham and Nguyen, "Popular Media of the Vietnamese Diaspora," 119.

17 Colburn, "Terror in Saigontown, U.S.A."

18 Silverman, *Selling Culture*. The glamorous, self-indulgent politics of individualism undoubtedly influenced Vietnamese immigrants and refugees as it celebrated capitalism and the freedom to buy.

19 The word *recent* is relative here because there are delays in the translation and production processes.

20 Mui, "Culture on Rewind."

21 Liu, *Transition to Nowhere*; Freeman, *Hearts of Sorrow*; Reyes, *Songs of the Caged, Songs of the Free*.

22 Stein, "Occupational Adjustment of Refugees," 37.

23 Malkki, "National Geographic," 441–42.

24 Rutledge, *The Vietnamese Experience in America*.

25 What constitutes "authentic Vietnamese culture" is the subject of constant debate. I believe that an authentic Vietnamese culture does not exist. Rather, Vietnamese culture is constantly *authenticated* by the Vietnamese in different social and historical contexts for very specific political purposes. See Do, "A Space of Their Own.

26 *Paris by Night 40: Mother*, video, Thuy Nga Productions, 1997.

27 This controversy received uneven media attention in different parts of the diaspora. Because it coincided with the death of Princess Diana, one journalist claims that mainstream media channels may have overlooked it. See Ha, "Some Seeing Red over Videos."

28 Cunningham and Nguyen, "Popular Media of the Vietnamese Diaspora," 121–24.

29 Ibid.

30 The "younger generation" can be between the ages of five and thirty-five. These fans of *Paris by Night* tend to be foreign-born immigrants, but many American-born Vietnamese also enjoy the videos for their "cultural" value. According to one young Vietnamese American woman, one can learn the Vietnamese language by listening to the music (Chaffee Tran, interview with the author, October 16, 2001).

31 Tran, "Songwriters Return to Love." One of the problems this has created is that Vietnamese songwriters often do not receive the royalties they deserve. Some songwriters claim that it is difficult to make a living under such conditions, but others argue that their music will not live on if singers do not perform their songs.

32 Kondo, *About Face*, 16. Other scholars who have written about the politics of pleasure include Janice Radway (*Reading the Romance*) and Tania Modleski (*Loving with a Vengeance*).

33 In cities all over the United States, community-based nonprofit organizations that assist Vietnamese Americans often invite Vietnamese performers based in California to perform at fund-raisers. In California's Little Saigon, community leaders joined with Vietnamese singers for a campaign that would register Vietnamese citizens of Southern California to vote. The "Rock 'n' Vote" concert, which was modeled after MTV's "Rock the Vote," featured singers who performed for free.

34 This has happened to a number of performers, including seasoned professionals such as Huong Lan, who made the "mistake" of returning to Vietnam.

35 A show in Chicago suffered from low attendance because of protests against two popular *vong co* opera singers from Vietnam, causing the organizer a net loss of approximately thirty thousand dollars. Tam Van Nguyen (Community Economic Development Coordinator, Vietnamese Association of Illinois), interview with the author, August 2002.

36 Ibid.; Naficy, *The Making of Exile Cultures*.

37 Reyes, *Songs of the Caged, Songs of the Free*.

38 Ibid.; Naficy, *The Making of Exile Cultures*, 295.

39 Nguyen Cao Ky Duyen, telephone conversation with *Viet Horizons*, radio broadcast, April 14, 2001, http://www.viethorizons.com/audio/04142001_rec.rm (accessed April 2003).

40 Dialogues from *Paris by Night 46: 15th Anniversary Celebration*, video, dir. Michael Watt, Thuy Nga Productions, 1998, translation mine.

41 Do, "Dazzling a Crowd."

42 I would like to thank Son Lieu for his keen observations and numerous helpful suggestions in analyzing musical and cinematic imagery.

43 "Fun Facts for the Film Buff on West Side Story," http://www.alt.tcm.turner.com/essentials/2002/trivia-westside.html (accessed July 25, 2002); James Berardinelli, review of *West Side Story*, http://www.movie-reviews.colossus.net/movies/w/west_side.html (accessed July 25, 2002).

44 The use of this term borrows from the work on blackface minstrelsy and subsequent studies on yellowface performance. See Lott, *Love and Theft*; Rogin, *Blackface, White Noise*; and Won, "Yellowface Minstrelsy."

45 Dalena's Home Page, "Dalena's Biography," http://www.dalenanet.com/biog raphy. asp (accessed October 10, 2006).

46 *Paris by Night 57: Thoi Trang va Am Nhac* [Fashion and Music], video, dir. Kent Weed, Thuy Nga Productions, 2001.

47 The MCS and performers often refer to themselves as a "family of entertainers" or the "brotherhood and sisterhood of musicians and performers."

48 Respondent to Web survey, "Study of Overseas Vietnamese Culture Website," http://www-personal.umich.edu/nlieu, February 22, 2002.

49 Respondent of Web survey, February 14, 2002.

50 Respondent to Web survey, August 23, 2001.

51 Dialogue from *Paris by Night 57*, translation mine.

nine

Indo-Chic: Late Capitalist Orientalism and Imperial Culture

Sunaina Maira

At a historical moment in the United States when orientalist discourses about Islam and the Middle East have taken on ever more transparent connections to U.S. foreign policy, the cultural contradictions of U.S. orientalism are increasingly manifest in everyday practices of consumption and commodification. On the one hand, there is a public preoccupation, in the mainstream media as well as in the rhetoric of state officials, with "oppressed Muslim women" in Afghanistan, who need to be liberated by U.S. intervention, and with unruly "natives" in Iraq, who need to be governed by a civilizing foreign occupation. At the same time, there is a popular fascination with belly dancing, Arabic fusion music, and henna, not to mention other markers of the "East" that continue to ride the trend of orientalist cool. This ambivalent fear and desire about the oriental other has long pervaded European and U.S. cultures, as first argued by the Palestinian American scholar we recently lost. Orientalism, in Edward Said's words, is "a style of thought based upon an ontological and epistemological distinction made between 'the Orient' and (most of the time) 'the Occident,'" which is situated in histories of colonization, economic penetration, and academic voyeurism.[1]

Today, orientalist images circulate in new ways with the expansion of satellite television and the Internet and the globalization of the media, fashion, and music industries. This essay focuses on the emergence of "Indo-chic" in the mid- to late 1990s, a phenomenon that extends back in time to an earlier fascination with Indian cool in the 1960s counterculture, now packaged as mainstream retro style, and to the currently heightened neocolonialist rhetoric in the United States about the Middle East. The stakes of this analysis of popular orientalism at the heart of empire are high, but they have not been articulated clearly enough in Asian American studies at the present moment. While the research on which this article is based focuses on an earlier instance of U.S. orientalism, I am interested in raising questions about the link between popular culture and globalization, qua empire, its implications for Asian American youth, and our contributions to work on the cultures of U.S. empire in Asian American studies.

Indo-Chic 1990s Style, or
Late Capitalist Orientalism

The mass-marketed objects that most visibly exemplify the new Indo-chic in U.S. youth culture are style commodities, notably, *mehndi* (or henna), *bindis*, and saris. Henna is a practice generally done by and for women, particularly for wedding ceremonies, in South Asia but also in North Africa, the Middle East, and Southeast Asia. In the United States, this association with women has been a motif that has been used in various ways: in performances of an exoticized femininity by a certain segment of "New Age" movements and youth subcultures and in bolstering an imperialist feminist ideology about women in the "East" visible, for example, in Laura Bush's claims on behalf of oppressed Afghan women as justification for the 2001 U.S. invasion. The marketing of henna as "temporary tattoos" seems calculated to reconstruct mehndi as a painless, temporary alternative to tattoos while appealing to the current fascination with body art. Henna has thus been reinvented to fit within the parameters of popular American traditions, whether as New Age ritual, feminist beauty practice, bridal shower, or sex toy. Entrepreneurial body artists "perform" mehndi for a price in places as far-flung as Madison, Wisconsin, Tucson, Arizona, and Artesia, California, and companies such as Mehndi Mania, Temptu, and Body Art sell do-it-yourself henna "kits" as part of their line of tattoo products. The online Web site "The Henna Page" features letters from mehndi fans in Europe and Latin America sharing their excitement about this new, global, body art subculture.[2]

Bindis, the powder dots or adhesive felt and plastic designs worn by South Asian women between the eyebrows, have also been repackaged as body art or "body jewelry" that can be worn on the shoulder or navel ("belly buttons"), appealing to clubbers and ravers who seek styles that have an impact on the dance floor. The third major category in this catalog of South Asian orientalia includes various fabrics, from brocade sari borders and mirror work to five-hundred-dollar pashmina wool shawls, that have penetrated both teen fashions and designer clothing produced by the U.S. and European fashion industries.[3]

Indo-chic, and "Asian cool" more generally, exemplifies a particular set of historical conjunctures and social anxieties, a "late capitalist orientalism." Somini Sengupta, commenting on the flurry of interest in South Asian writers and musicians during the fiftieth anniversary celebrations of India's independence in New York, noted that "the new Indo chic" did not generally include artists who were Pakistani, Bangladeshi, or Sri Lankan, demonstrating the fascination with the notion of "India" in the U.S. public imagination and perhaps also the implicit colonialist fantasy of a pre-independence, undivided Indian subcontinent.[4] The image that most clearly exemplified the emergence of this late 1990s Indo-chic orientalism was superchameleon Madonna's 1998 MTV Awards appearance. Singing the single "Frozen," from her album *Ray of Light*, Madonna performed pseudo-Bharatanatyam moves with henna-painted hands, the work of an Indian American beauty salon owner, Sumita Batra. Batra later coauthored a lavishly illustrated book on mehndi with a testimonial from Madonna on the cover: "When Sumita [Batra] hennas my hands and feet, I am transported to another time and place. A world of magic, passion, and romance." The transparency of this manifestly orientalist rhetoric and performance was evident in numerous iterations by other celebrities, models, and actresses in subsequent years.[5] A 2001 issue of the *Mary-Kate and Ashley* magazine featured U.S. teen fashion and television icons wearing saris and seated in the lotus position on the cover for an "East Meets West" fashion spread. The caption read:

> Imagine a society . . . where you are constantly trying to . . . get closer to becoming a more enlightened and more complete person. That's India. The country's social and religious structure has remained pretty much unchanged for 4,000 years, so the connection between mind, body, and spirit in India is strong and healthy.

Indo-chic thus became an orientalist trope par excellence in the late 1990s, making visible an exoticized India while simultaneously repressing the social histories and material relations that connect India and the United States. In his analysis of the emergence of India in U.S. orientalism, Vijay Prashad notes that the construction of the "spiritual East" was required to atone for the material-ism of "the West"; in an era of global capitalism, this binary is complicated by the overt commodification of India's appearance in U.S. popular culture, but there is clearly still an excess of spirituality projected onto "the East."[6] Ameri-can orientalism is not only constitutive of "India" but also of the "American" cultural imaginary at a particular historical moment.[7] The United States has not been involved in a direct colonial relationship with South Asia or with the regions in the Middle East and North Africa that Said discusses in his excava-tion of British and French orientalisms, even though imperialism does not always entail direct colonial governance.[8] Yet images of the "Orient" have long provided Americans with "opportunities for creating selves and settings of aesthetic appeal and social charisma" and with a "foil for the 'progress' that many Americans so assiduously pursued as their birthright and destiny."[9] Robert Lee's astute historical analysis points to the multiple guises of "the Oriental" in U.S. popular culture in the first half of the twentieth century,[10] exemplifying more recent approaches to orientalism as "multivocalic," evolv-ing, conflicted,[11] and "overlapping with rhetorics of gender and class."[12] The production of orientalism in late-twentieth-century American youth culture is embedded in a mass culture that is internally diverse and fragmented into diverse subcultures and implicated in discourses of race, nationalism, and gender that are contradictory and contested.

Reina Lewis argues that analyses of gender and race suggest "points of resistance within the fantasized unity of Orientalist discourse," which in actu-ality is "relational and fragmented" but still hegemonic and long-lasting pre-cisely because it can incorporate these relations of difference.[13] Multivocality in orientalism, therefore, does not always lead to strategies of resistance but rather suggests the multiple iterations and citations of orientalism that rein-force its doxa even as they purport to deviate from it.[14] In this essay, the responses of young women and henna artists to Indo-chic shed light on the ways in which orientalism re-creates itself in and through difference. Critiques of orientalism, however, have often reduced women to "a metaphor for the negative characterization of the orientalized Other as 'feminine.' "[15] Decon-structions of orientalism need to go beyond the discursive, looking at the links between the representational, material, and historical contexts of orientalist images of femininity.[16]

My study also fills a glaring gap in the literature by looking at the workings of orientalism in youth popular culture, an obvious site for examining contem-porary instances of orientalist commodification that pervade mass media and global fashion. I am interested in the ways in which Asian American youths re-create or absorb the meanings of orientalism in their own lives, drawing on orientalist tropes to construct their own narratives of authenticity and differ-ence, thus demonstrating what Said has called "second-order Orientalism,"[17] or what Sadik Jalal Al-'Azm calls "Orientalism in reverse."[18] Moreover, by focusing on the experiences of South Asian and South Asian American youths this study offers not just a multivocalic but also a multisited approach to the meanings of this late orientalism. It allows young Asian American women to voice their understandings and critiques of orientalism from a place *within* the "West," yet the diasporic experiences of these youths also evoke the ways in which orientalism is understood in reference to *other* places outside the United States that these women have called home.

Selling Indo-Chic: Henna Entrepreneurs and Imperialist Feminism

The marketing of Indo-chic is replete with the imagery and rhetoric of the new orientalism and with an imperialist feminist discourse about Asian, Arab, and African women. Carine Fabius, a Haitian American who owns a mehndi gallery in Los Angeles, writes that "henna is a capricious, mysterious, and elusive substance."[19] The book *Mehndi: The Timeless Art of Body Painting*, by Loretta Roome, who helped popularize henna in New York in the mid-1990s, overflows with orientalizing pseudo-folkloric analyses of henna.[20] Roome writes that henna evokes "women, eroticism, mysticism, privacy, religion, sacred ritual and ceremony, matrimonial and romantic love, folklore and su-perstition."[21] She laments that henna is an endangered practice in South Asia due to modernization and urbanization.

> Sadly, much of the meaning behind the use of these symbols has been forgotten and lost. What I have learned in talking to many women from India and the Middle East is that mehndi is often looked down upon by women eager to become "modern" and successful. . . . It is associated with primitive beliefs and rituals. Equally distressing is the fact that many women still practicing the art help to contribute to the misunderstanding surrounding it. . . . It was very confusing for me when I first began my research.[22]

I quote Roome at length here because her statement encapsulates many of the dense, and highly problematic, associations of henna as metonymy for a mysti-cal East that in this case is being abandoned by those living in the third world in their misguided quest for modernity. Roome positions herself as a folklore expert recuperating lost traditions and safeguarding "culture" for non-Western women, setting up an imperial feminist relationship with subjects struggling to gain access to modernity. White American women thus become the enlightened saviors of Asian and Arab women who cannot understand their own traditions even as they practice them, and the discussion of privilege or class differentials is masked by the admission of "confusion." As John Hutynk points out, the orientalizing nostalgia of "Asian cool" in Britain insidiously denies that "India is subject to ongoing participation in capitalist production, structural adjustment programmes, tourist and service industry expansion, [or] satellite installation."[23] The "recovery" of henna by U.S. entrepreneurs is tied to their implicit critique of third world societies where women are both too modernized to know their own rituals and too repressed, or even oppressed, to fully enjoy their potential sensuality.[24] The marketing of henna as a women's ritual rests on an imperialist feminist rhetoric: "Women in the West . . . have none of the cultural restrictions of those who practice this art form traditionally. We don't have to veil our faces or cover our bodies from head to toe . . . [and] we [Americans? White Americans?] enjoy the privileged position of feeling free to learn from, adapt, and expand upon centuries of experience."[25]

For every unbridled expression of colonialist appropriation by the liberated "West," there are hints of anxiety about cultural borrowing by other American henna practitioners. The Henna Page features the confessions of mehndi users who express the need to get a stamp of approval from a "native," a tactic that also seems to alleviate the anxiety of appropriation for non–South Asian authors of mehndi manuals. Barb writes to the Henna Web site of her visit to an Indian store, where she learned about mehndi from the store owner, a "most gentle woman."

> I had been worried that mehndi might be a religious ceremony . . . and it seemed disrespectful for my wanting to partake in the beauty of the art. She immediately allayed my concerns by saying mehndi was a joyous act . . . and it would bring happiness to Indians (her word) everywhere to see others enjoying its beauty, too. I was *so* relieved.[26]

Importantly, this recasting of mehndi as a mystical practice or spiritual ritual available to all is an important way in which the presumed taboo of crossing cultural borders is mitigated against by the universalistic humanism of New Age worshippers or "tribal" ravers.[27]

The mass marketing of Indo-chic also raises questions about the intended viewers of advertisements featuring it at a time when the Asian American population is growing rapidly and consumers can no longer be assumed to be only white, middle-class Americans.[28] The flows of people, goods, and images between Asia and the United States in an age of late capitalism complicate this manifestation of orientalism in mass culture. What meanings do young Asian American women, grappling with gendered notions of nationalism and racialized understandings of citizenship, make of Indo-chic? What does it mean to consume Indo-chic in a town where South Asians are relatively invisible or in an academic setting where difference is defined through multiculturalism?

NoHo

Northampton is a town where white liberals, academics, affiliates of Smith and other area colleges, and a visible lesbian community (NoHo) collide with older New Englanders (Hamp) in a not so typical town and gown conflict over gentrification and "alternative lifestyles" in largely rural Western Massachusetts. Northampton has been remade over the last decade or so into "Paradise City," a hub of chic restaurants and stores that draws visitors from the Pioneer Valley area; the local resident community (the town population was 30,898 in 1998) remains predominantly white and middle class.[29]

Given the homogeneous population of Northampton, cultural and racial difference often enters as packaged, if not exoticized, difference, making this a site ripe for a study of commodified orientalism. World music, third-world handicrafts, and New Age enterprises seem to find a ready niche market in the "Happy Valley," where fliers for yoga classes crowd the walls of vegetarian restaurants.[30] Ten Thousand Villages, a store purporting to sell fair-price crafts from the developing world, is just down the street from another multiculti-goods store called, fittingly, the Mercantile. Henna and bindis began to appear in clothing stores and bookshops in 1996 or 1997, but at the time I conducted this research, in 1999–2000, they were not yet visible on the street on an everyday basis. Less a part of daily performance than commodities to be viewed and individually consumed, they seemed to circulate through the stores that sell them. A flier for a local henna artist and herbalist, Joni, stated: "Henna-Body art: Express yourself—ritual, healing, exotic, celebrate yourself, art, needle-less, natural, ancient." Joni was attracted to mehndi because, she explained, "It's a blending of cultures, and different cultures have so much to offer. . . . I wanted it to be a ritual, I wanted people to come in and do a ceremony to do with some kind of commitment, some change in their life. . . . But people weren't into the commitment." She became discouraged when a man came into the salon and asked her to do a mehndi design of Tweety Bird on his shoulder.

The consumption of Indo-chic in Northampton exemplifies the meanings of the new orientalism outside of large metropolitan centers in settings where the consumption of "other" ethnicities is equally pervasive and vexed, though in different ways. Much of the literature on commodification and style focuses on urban contexts, so it is important to extend this cultural geography of consumption to nonurban or small-town locations as well to understand how commodities such as Indo-chic are reinterpreted by "local taste communities."[31] The landscape of cultural consumption is heterotopic not just in large urban centers[32] and global cities but also in suburban or rural areas where people are aware that they are not living in the "centers" of cultural production. Indo-chic provides youths with access not just to "exotic" difference but to "urban" cool. In Northampton, young women can buy henna stickers at the clothing stores downtown, but when Indo-chic was at its peak in the area in 1999–2000, they could purchase a wider selection of boxed bindis and "henna amulets" at stores, such as the Express Too teen clothing chain, in the shopping mall in nearby Holyoke. Here the consumption of Indo-chic is linked to the spread of chain stores and the diffusion of global fashion culture to small towns and even rural areas; consuming orientalist style becomes a way not just of accessing ethnic difference but also of being drawn into the globalization of consumer culture.[33]

Northampton does not have a local Indian American community of any size to speak of, but it does have in its midst the presence of South Asian and South Asian American women who attend Smith College, an elite women's liberal arts institution, as well as the less steady appearance of desi (glossed as "women of South Asian origin") students attending the other four of the Five Colleges: Mount Holyoke, Hampshire, and Amherst Colleges and the University of Massachusetts, Amherst. South Asians are invisible and yet hypervisible in the town because of their small numbers and bifurcated class profile. There are a handful of Indian, Pakistani, Bangladeshi, and Tibetan immigrants working in stores and gas stations; those who are not part of this tiny working class are generally faculty or staff at one of the colleges or professionals who have moved to the area. The South Asian student community is, by definition, transient and thus not considered "truly" a part of the town.[34]

South Asian and South Asian American women attending Smith may seem to some an "anomalous" population (middle to upper middle class, college student, diasporic, and American born) but they offered very interesting insights into the commodification of orientalia.[35] The critiques these women offered extended beyond the issue of mainstream exoticization, focusing inward on questions of ethnic authenticity and extending outward to the contradictions of globalization. Perhaps their responses were shaped by their transient location in the town and their membership in immigrant communities, their experiences of material privilege but also of being considered partial outsiders to the local community, the ethnic "homeland," and the American national culture. As women who had grown up in the United States, South Asia, the Middle East, and Southeast Asia, they brought varying relationships with the "local" and "structures of local feeling" to their encounters with Indo-chic.[36] These translocal imaginaries are complex, as I will demonstrate, for they do not just construct the local as "authentic" but suggest the ways in which young people struggle with questions of nationalism, capitalism, and globalization. In their narratives about henna and other orientalized commodities, these youths participate in what Nestor Garcia Canclini calls "an interpretive community of consumers."[37] They are part of a diaspora of consumption, a collectivity linked by memories not (just) of "authentic" culture or "traditional" practices but also by relationships to the same commodities that have appeared to them in different guises in different places and which they have used to understand the workings of power and belonging. This notion builds on Daniel Miller's conceptualization of moral projects embedded in consumption practices. Miller emphasizes the mutually constitutive ways in which material culture actively influences social practice and illustrates the possibilities that commodities offer to reimagine cultural ideologies such as those of "self" and "other."[38] Miller observes that consumption is "a use of goods or services in which the object or activity become simultaneously a practice in the world and a form in which we construct our understandings of ourselves in the world."[39] Indo-chic, it seems to me, represents a traveling moral project, for I am interested in tying Miller's notion of consumption to questions of migration and globalization and to the ways in which traveling selves and others use commodities, which are themselves part of globalized flows, to negotiate issues of nationalism, authenticity, and belonging. Thinking about a diaspora of consumption as a community (re)created in relationship to objects, or constituted by practices of consumption of particular commodities, provides a framework for analyzing potent issues of appropriation in expressions of diasporic identity but whose rhetoric often conceals the material structures in which they are embedded.

Staging Indo-Chic: Multiculturalist and Polyculturalist Projects

Talking to desi women in Northampton revealed that they are engaged in cultural productions that reconstruct mehndi and Indo-chic, suggesting that they are not passive bystanders or consumers but active participants in a commodification process about which some still feel ambivalent. At Smith College, a visible instance of this kind of agency and its attendant contradictions is expressed in a Mehndi Night event organized by the South Asian (American) student organization, Ekta (Unity), which had a hundred members at the time. Three years earlier, before mehndi became popular in Northampton, students of South Asian origin had organized an annual mehndi party-cum-Indian dinner, which is now their biggest fund-raiser and draws over four hundred students. South Asian women students offer mehndi painting for two dollars, packing the ballroom with Smith undergraduates and even local high school students. Clearly, the success of this event is tied to the popularity of Indo-chic in Northampton and among young women. A part of the big draw is cheap Indian food and Indian dance performances, so participants at the event can consume "Indian culture" visually and orally.

Mehndi Night is a successful production because it fulfills several kinds of desire at the same time due to the strategic packaging (and perhaps even strategic self-orientalization) of its organizers, and it plays an important role in the multicultural economy of the liberal arts college. It fulfills the desire of South Asian American and South Asian women to enact representations of national culture or ethnic ancestry for a non–South Asian audience. Shamita, the "cultural chair" of Ekta, who helped organize the event, pointed to its performative dimension: "Now there are many more people for Mehndi Night than for the culture show because it's interactive." Without overstating the metaphor, Mehndi Night allows ethnic "outsiders" not only to consume the culture of the other but to have the other literally imprinted on their bodies. This marking has a particular significance at Smith, which is "gung ho about spreading diversity," according to Ameena. Mary, who is a white American student at Smith, said she felt "uncomfortable" about the popularity of mehndi but commented, "White girls go to Mehndi Night because they want to show they are prodiversity, and because they support their friends." The organizers are strategic about marketing the event to meet the institution's multicultural agenda, using it to fulfill the resident life policy on "diversity" programming requirements. Clearly, these women entrepreneurs understand that multiculturalism in higher education is about the negotiation of resources and the performance of a certain liberal politics of cultural difference,[40] and they have staged the reappropriation of Indo-chic to their own (material) benefit.

What the official performance of Mehndi Night does not address, but some of its producers and participants acknowledged in their private reflections, is the ways in which multicultural programming is used by the academy in its claim to be an institution to which all racial and ethnic minority groups have equal access, and in which all are represented, while masking the degree to which the larger institution still fails to address the needs of populations of color, "recuperat[ing] conflict and difference through inclusion."[41] While Ekta has cosponsored parties with the Black Students' Association on campus after Mehndi Night, the event itself has apparently not drawn as many African American students as it has white American women. It became clear that Indo-chic is often seen as primarily an interchange between South Asian and white Americans in the eyes of both South Asian and white youths, despite the growing adoption of Indo-chic by female hip hop stars in recent years. Representations of Indo-chic intensify the politics of cultural appropriation, for even if cultural exchange is seen as a two-way street it is rarely understood as a many-forked circuit affecting different groups, as a *relational orientalism*. More research is needed to explore what could be called a *peripheral orientalism*, the relations between the orientalizing practices of different groups of youths of color in the United States that are inflected by gender as well as race. Clearly, youths of color do not have the same access to power as colonial or capitalist producers of orientalism do, but they engage with orientalism in complex and largely understudied ways.[42]

The desi women I spoke to remained deeply ambivalent about the implications of mehndi's mainstreaming, viewing mainstream popular culture as white, middle-class public culture. Their uneasiness reflected the general responses to Indo-chic I heard from desi youths at workshops, conferences, and classroom discussions across the United States, where they expressed varying degrees of curiosity, pride, pleasure, guilt, and confusion. On the one hand, many desi youths resent what they see as the unfair appropriation of cultural markers and practices that embody national authenticity. Shamita, who grew up in Calcutta, felt that mehndi was a marker of cultural boundaries between "home" and "here."

> How we perceive mehndi is very different from how people see it here. For us it goes back many years, it's part of our culture. . . . Sometimes I feel annoyed because we're so used to seeing it in the proper context . . . at home, you wear a sari, you have the proper jewelry, the proper makeup. . . . I also don't know where it's from and the history, but we've just seen it around us or we know the context, where it stands, but people not from South Asia wouldn't know.

The argument that mehndi should only be worn by those who understand its cultural significance is a common one, but it is often contradicted by the kind of hesitation Shamita expressed in asserting knowledge of its "origins," reverting instead to an ambiguous, and essentialized, notion of cultural "context," that overlooks the many young women in South Asia who wear bindis with jeans or without traditional jewelry. Reflecting on the use of Indo-chic by second-generation South Asian women, Shamita commented, "I think South Asian American women from traditional families know about mehndi, but there are some others who say, 'I don't know where it comes from.' I may be confused, but they're more confused!" It is interesting that the use of Indo-chic has become a site for waging the contest of ethnic authenticity, where *tradition* is defined against hybridity, the disavowal of pure origins.[43]

While these young women were cognizant of the nuances of regional and religious differences in relationships to adornment practices in South Asia, these differences were less important to them than their overriding concern with cultural authenticity. Women who have grown up outside of South Asia confront questions of stylistic appropriation with different histories of nationalism, religious affiliation, and ethnic positioning. Some second-generation women participate in the contest of authenticity themselves. Surina is an undergraduate at the University of Massachusetts who has traveled to and from Bangladesh, where her family is from, while living in different countries outside of South Asia. In her view, the meaning of Indo-chic for South Asian youths is relative to the authenticity of their memories of "home": "Some South Asian Americans may not compare the bindi craze to what's going on at home because they've never seen home. They don't even know what bindis look like. It might be bad because then they'll think this *is* South Asian culture. But it depends on the individual, on their upbringing, and on their values." There seems to be an underlying fear that Indo-chic might muddy the category of "real" South Asian culture, depending on individual and collective "values." Consumption clearly becomes a moral project where selves can be imagined but where alternative selves may also need to be reined in or surveilled according to the need some feel to define the appropriate geographical spaces for consumption and generational categories of appropriate consumers. Consumption is thus embedded in this temporal and spatial web, spun to bring together a dispersed and highly diverse population through the fiction of "pure" culture.

This web begins to unravel with other stories suggesting the complexities of the ideologies and social contexts underlying the production of diasporic South Asian identities. Ameena, for example, has a very different narrative of remembering henna, having grown up in Oman, where henna is a local practice associated with Eid and weddings, much as it is in South Asian Muslim communities. Ameena is from an Indian Muslim family that is part of the wave of labor migration from the South Indian state of Kerala to the Middle East, where she attended an international school in Muscat. Ameena's first observation of mehndi being worn by a white person was at a school event a few years ago in Oman, where "desi aunties" applied henna for European students. She commented, "I didn't see it as 'white people being interested in mehndi'; it's a very Omani thing, so I saw it as something we do in Oman." Ameena vividly remembers getting henna done for the Muslim festival of Eid and seeing Gujarati immigrant women in the salons "fusing Indian and Omani designs."

Narratives such as Ameena's disrupt the binaries of pure versus inauthentic national cultures and memories. To wear mehndi, for Ameena, is to affiliate simultaneously with multiple communities: as an Indian, or South Asian, belonging to a larger diasporic community; as a Muslim; and as a member of the local Omani population. So for Ameena henna is hybridized from the very outset, or, as suggested by Robin Kelley, it is polycultural, a cultural practice that is always complicated by its affiliations with multiple communities rather than a product of two or more discrete, pure cultural strands.[44] Ameena's narrative is a critical one, for it shows the ways in which henna can be simultaneously told as a story of multicultural market appropriation, nationalist reappropriation, and polycultural experience; but, significantly, the story that is often told in mainstream contexts, or among South Asian American youths, is only the multiculturalist or nationalist narrative. Ameena is eloquent about the fluidity of cultural meaning and memory in her relationship to this polycultural practice: "I personally don't think there's a meaning to it [mehndi]; it's pretty, I have fond memories of it. If it's managed to cross oceans to reach this part of the world, they may not have the same attachments to it that I had because of my childhood, but they've made the effort to try it, that's a good thing. It's the commercialization I just feel uncomfortable about."

What Madonna Didn't Say: Regimes of Appropriation

The commodification of Indo-chic in public culture seems to provoke uneasiness, resistance, and opportunities for staging cultural memory for desi youths; for some women, it also evokes a certain national pride, the satisfaction of seeing what were previously hidden markers of ethnicity, or links to other homes, enter the public sphere in the United States and make their South Asianness visible. Surina, for example, experienced a surge of South Asian pride when Madonna made an appearance in Bombay dressed in "full sari and blouse; she was wearing it the right way, everything was perfect." As with British Asian women in the 1980s,[45] the emergence of Indo-chic provides for some an expression of a hybrid sensibility that they had long crafted for themselves or of a style that was associated only with private, invisible spaces. The paradox of Indo-chic is that in the United States henna marks non–South Asians as trendy while until very recently mehndi worn by South Asian women simply marked them as traditional, or at best exotic, and certainly always other; in becoming mainstream, Indo-chic has changed the meaning of the distinction it once lent to (at least young) South Asian American women. One of the most layered performances of henna as a reinvented ritual is evident in the film *Chutney Popcorn*, in which a lesbian Indian American woman who is a henna artist applies mehndi to her lover and her own belly when she becomes pregnant; henna is reappropriated as a queerly erotic ritual marked by the tensions and contradictions of living in the diaspora rather than an imperialist feminist or New Age practice.

Surina's reading of Indo-chic as a positive cultural recuperation of South Asian authenticity is built on a critique that contains within it an understanding of the political economy of "ethnic cool." She comments: "Now I'm really happy and proud to see South Asia represented. Of course, it's sold at a higher price. . . . And a lot of these things are not even made here." While living in Thailand, although she was part of an elite expatriate community, Surina had witnessed the inequities of global markets and incisively concluded, "If you are going to reproduce trends from another country, then you need to work with them. Why not have South Asian–owned stores? Why not sell South Asian products? . . . I don't think it's fair to go to a third world country and get their goods and then mark up prices." All the South Asian women I spoke to shared in this critique of the regime of flexible accumulation,[46] a regime in which South Asians have migrated to the United States to work at low-skill jobs even as the Indian market has been opened to the United States with structural adjustment and economic liberalization policies.[47] Shamita's response to the question "why Indo-chic now?" was succinct: "I think it's globalization." In late capitalist orientalism, India is the site of offshore (and often invisible) production, exoticism, and authenticity but apparently not of hybridity, which can only be produced in the West according to this international division of cultural labor. Surina raises an additional issue that is especially relevant in the case of a commodity trend that is targeted at the American youth market: "It's robbing money from young people. . . . I know my age group, and I know they can't really afford it." Young consumers are stratified by class and have varying amounts of disposable income, but it is clear that the women I spoke to responded to Indo-chic on many levels: as subjects belonging to the South Asian diaspora, as Asian women critical of the inequities of American capital, and as young consumers in the United States.

The question of the visibility of South Asia in mainstream popular culture is only one part of the equation in responses to appropriation by South Asian diasporic youth, and it is balanced by their structural critiques. The politics of representation is a limited framework for understanding the presence of South Asians in the public sphere, for it is important not only to focus on what is appropriated but also to ask "what is not appropriated or what is considered digestible by the cannibalizing appetite of consumer capitalism."[48] In the case of Indo-chic's commodification and construction as a series of moral projects, what does not lend itself to appropriation by multinational corporations and U.S. entrepreneurs and what is ignored or only implicit in these discussions as they are framed in terms of consumption and youth style? Why Indo-chic *now*?

The young desi women helped address this question by pointing out that the marketing of Indo-chic in the United States rests on the extraction of huge margins of profit by American corporations and entrepreneurs, yet this is an issue rarely brought to light. India occupies a somewhat different niche in the American cultural economy than it did in the 1960s and 1970s, and with the opening up of India's economic market in the wake of economic restructuring and neo-liberalization policies it has become part of the global sweatshop where American multinationals browse for cheap labor, cheap goods, and profitable market trend ideas.[49] In some instances, the sweatshop involves child labor as well, with Indian children painstakingly making by hand the glitter bindis that are resold in the United States at anywhere from twenty to forty times the price.[50] Henna kits and "bindi body art kits" manufactured by U.S. or British producers sell for 10 to 25 dollars, and "startup" packages for aspiring henna "professionals" range from 75 to 150 dollars. The exorbitant markup of goods that sell for nominal prices in South Asia is tied to the clever marketing concept of the "kit": a packet of henna becomes transformed into a do-it-yourself hobby and perhaps a part-time occupation.

American "henna artists" charge many times what women in India are paid for their services, and their self-packaging is also an effective marketing strategy. For example, the self-conscious highlighting of henna's "ritual" nature is made to appeal to the "alternative lifestyle" or New Age followers in a town such as Northampton. South Asian Americans are no less likely to try to benefit from this trend, yet some non–South Asian and Arab American henna entrepreneurs, including Fabius and Roome, dismiss as unreliable the products sold by South Asian or Middle Eastern stores—which of course were the only source of henna before it became a mainstream fashion trend. Henna entrepreneurs obviously have their own products to sell, and they effectively remain the cultural translators and product endorsers for the growing consumer market in the United States. South Asian immigrant businesses seem to have been cut off from the profits flowing from this trend; the concern among henna fans about violating some kind of cultural "taboo" in appropriating henna does not seem to extend to a concern that consumers should support South Asian American or Middle Eastern business entrepreneurs in making a living—which is probably more important to them than white women wearing henna on their bellies. The economics of Indo-chic and the vagaries of global capital are clearly one aspect of commodification that is not "digestible" by the discourse of packaged ethnicity and is left undiscussed in the mainstream media, although it is clearly articulated by youths of South Asian descent. The material production of Indo-chic is a key link between popular orientalism and the workings of globalization and one that should be understood in the present moment of orientalization in the Middle East as well.

A second major dimension of these suppressed material processes is the presence of South Asian immigrant workers in urban centers, where Indo-chic has been most apparent. The first wave of South Asian immigrants, which came to the United States after the Immigration Act of 1965, consisted mainly of professionals and graduate students who eventually moved into middle- and upper-middle-class suburban neighborhoods. What is different about the 1990s version of Indo-chic, in contrast to that of the 1960s and 1970s, is the influx of South Asian Americans who come primarily as labor migrants, on family reunification visas, or as undocumented immigrants that began in the 1980s.[51] Currently, in cities such as New York, it is taxi drivers, newsstand owners, and domestic workers who are the most visible South Asians in the public domain. (There has emerged a new category of Indo-kitsch, which includes comic books about taxi drivers, and Indo-pastiche, which expresses a somewhat different imagining of difference than mainstream Indo-chic.)[52] The indigestible fact of working- and lower-middle-class South Asian Americans, who are not considered bearers of Indian mysticism or avatars of Indo-chic, is precisely the unassimilable contradiction with which we must grapple.

Indo-chic does the political and symbolic work of domesticating difference, extracting not just profit but the very signs of difference from South Asian immigrant workers and South Asian Americans at large. This commodification of the threat of difference is even more apparent as the "war on immigrants" of the 1980s and 1990s has extended into the "war on terror," affecting Muslim, Arab, and South Asian immigrants, as well as undocumented immigrants more generally. The visual signs of ethnic difference, clothing and adornment, are re-created as signifiers not of South Asian bodies but of American "cool." The exotic becomes mainstream, and the superficial otherness of this growing Asian American group is incorporated into a repertoire of American subcultural practices reinvented as New Age or feminist ritual, as rave or body art style. There are certainly South Asian Americans who continue to wear ethnic markers, but this now happens in a context where whiteness, especially white femininity, can also bear the mark of the exotic. Ethnic difference, specifically difference coded as the essence of South Asian "culture," can be consumed and made safe, in a sense, its threatening foreignness now neutralized. Writing about the production and consumption of the "new exotica," Stuart Hall writes, "Globalization cannot proceed without learning to live and working through difference . . . [and] in order to maintain its global position, capital has had to negotiate, has had to incorporate and partly reflect the differences it was trying to overcome."[53] Indo-chic, then, is not just a symptom but also a *medium* of late-twentieth-century globalization; following Hall's analysis, globalization processes clearly live and work through late capitalist orientalism.

It is not coincidental that this manifestation of orientalism occurred just as the national debates and anti-immigrant hysteria of the mid-1990s, exemplified in legislative measures such as Proposition 187 in California, ostensibly died down in public discourse and reappeared as specific, localized attacks on Asian, African, and Latin American immigrants.[54] An incident from an earlier decade brings into sharp relief the connections between anti-Asian violence and the recuperation of ethnic difference. In 1987–88, a multiethnic group of youths, the Dotbusters, were responsible for a string of physical and verbal attacks on Indian Americans in Jersey City, New Jersey, leaving one man dead. Indian immigrants had begun to open successful small businesses in Jersey City and were perceived by local residents as economically threatening and culturally unassimilable "dotheads."[55] The violence of this incident is even more painfully ironic given the fetishization of the bindi ten years later, with all signs of brutality completely erased. Indo-chic is not only about contests of authenticity and cultural appropriation but also about discursive shifts and ideological strategies that accommodate difference in the face of changing patterns of immigration, labor, and citizenship.

Conclusion

The emergence of Indo-chic has to be tied to a structural analysis of global capitalist production, immigration trends, and the contradictions of cultural citizenship, even as it is largely understood within the framework of ethnic authenticity, nationality, and cultural ownership. Indo-chic is tied to both the political and economic dimensions that link nations to globalization and is embedded in the workings of late capitalist *imperial* culture. If imperial projects work through both domestic and foreign policies but obscure the links between these two faces of empire,[56] it becomes crucial to uncover the ways in which these two arenas are conjoined. Multiculturalism, as both a state and unofficial policy of managing racial and ethnic difference and securing consensus within the nation, is the domestic component of a larger international strategy of global economic and military dominance of U.S. empire.

Anne McClintock, writing about nineteenth-century British advertising, claims, "More than merely a symbol of imperial progress, the domestic commodity becomes the agent of history itself. The commodity, abstracted from social context and human labor, does the civilizing work of empire."[57] Henna and Indo-chic are not just commodities but also performances and so constitute imperial spectacles, and, as Michael Rogin argues, public spectacle is key political form for "postmodern American empire."[58] I argue that the mystique constructed with, and packaged into, Indo-chic as commodity and spectacle does the work of global capital by resolving the tension between national identity and consumer identity that arises due to the flow of people, goods, and media images across national borders. Indo-chic mediates the "important but unstable" opposition between citizenship and consumption[59] and alleviates the anxieties of U.S. consumers in the face of globalized capital; it erases traces of South Asian labor from Indo-chic and allows a celebratory, "one-world" consumer identity to deflect questions of economic inequity, racial difference, and nationalism. At the same time, the commodity works within a national frame to intervene in "domestic" debates about racialization, immigration, and citizenship.

However, the contradiction of Indo-chic is precisely that the consumer identity that it offers to Asian American women does not travel unchanged across national and racial borders but is locally produced as the meanings of commodities change in specific sites of consumption. Moreover, the universalization of a global Indo-chic consumer breaks down not only along lines of nation, race, and class but also along lines of gender. Gender is assumed to be the modality unifying Indo-chic—henna for women by women—but this incipient transnational feminist vision is riven by disjunctures of race, class, and citizenship that are produced by nationalist and capitalist formations.[60] The link between gender and nationalism is often obscured in putatively "international feminist" projects in the United States, thus supporting the neoliberal orthodoxies of globalization and empire.[61] Imperialist feminism is layered with orientalist imaginings of other women and enacted through consumption practices of objects but also of universal humanist discourses about saving "other" women from their cultures. As such, it is devoid of a political analysis of globalization or neocolonialism (witness Eve Ensler's classically imperial feminist-as-savior performance in the *Vagina Monologues* and in orchestrating a campaign *for* Afghan women). The ambivalence of South Asian diasporic women, as this preliminary study suggests, highlights the ways in which youths are savvy to the implications of global capital even as they wrestle with the contradictions of ethnic authenticity and national belonging.

After September 11, 2001, and the subsequent backlash against those who look "Middle Eastern, some South Asian American women in the New York and New Jersey areas stopped wearing bindis for fear of being attacked or harassed; many women wearing headscarves were victims of anti-Muslim sentiments and violence. Clearly, this study would elicit different responses if it were conducted now, but the questions raised here have an even deeper resonance today as it becomes apparent that late capitalist orientalism in the United States continues to permeate pressing questions about imperialism, feminism, citizenship, consumption, and racialization. Indo-chic is no longer simply a sign of ethnic authenticity or racial difference to be safely consumed as a commodity but has become a symbol of foreignness that has, at least temporarily, been transformed for some into a threat to the United States. Transnational economic and cultural ties are now viewed as potential conduits for supporting terrorism. As always, the "dark face" of globalization is discussed in terms of the transnational circuits of the targeted population or the "enemy within" but not in terms of the increasing global military and economic reach of empire. Popular culture is a site where anxieties about borders and difference have always been negotiated, but it is also a site where the tensions of empire are enacted and normalized. What does it mean for subjects living in an imperial regime to understand their relationships to the subjects of occupation or invasion as consumers of liberating commodities? What does it mean when these subjects at the heart of empire are Asian American, and how does it differ for Asian American women and men, immigrant or second-generation youths, small business owners, or migrant workers? On what terms, and whose terms, do we produce an analysis of these relationships? Commodities such as Indo-chic represent mixed impulses of contestation and complicity, desire and evasion, ambivalence and contempt. The notion of relations along the "periphery" takes on new meaning when difference is seen as a Trojan horse that might implode and when borders within and beyond the nation become militarized bulwarks meant to defend our imperial way of life and preserve the new world order.

Notes

An earlier version of this article appeared in *Meridians: Feminism, Race, Transnationalism* 3, no. 1 (Fall 2002). I wish to thank Thuy Linh for her editorial feedback and all the women in the "Happy Valley" who shared their thoughts with me.

1 Said, *Orientalism*, 2. Much existing work on the orientalizing of India has focused on European imperial projects. See, for example, Inden, "Orientalist Constructions of India"; King, "Orientalism, Hinduism, and Feminism"; and Pollock, "Indology, Power, and the Case of Germany." India, and South Asia more broadly, has generally not been a major topos in the American public imagination, as it has been for its former colonizer, Britain, but it certainly has provided a site of fantasy and redemption for U.S. intellectuals and philosophers at different historical moments.

2 Cartwright-Jones, "The Henna Page."

3 Rosen, "Wrap Artist."

4 Sengupta, "Beyond Yoga, Curry and Nehru Jackets Into Film, Publishing and Body Painting."

5 Batra, *The Art of Mehndi.*

6 Prashad, *The Karma of Brown Folk*, 18.

7 Macfie, *Orientalism*, 7.

8 Magdoff, *Imperialism without Colonies.*

9 Edwards, "Curator's Preface"; "A Million and One Nights," viii–x, 11–57. The exhibit "Noble Dreams, Wicked Pleasures: Orientalism in America, 1870–1930," held at the Clark Art Institute, Williamstown, Massachusetts (June–September 2000), focused on American artists who produced orientalist images primarily of the Middle East and North Africa. See Çelik, "Speaking Back to Orientalist Discourse at the World's Columbian Exposition," on Arab women at the World's Fair in Chicago in 1893; Shohat, "Gender and Culture of Empire," on "the sheik"; and Lee, *Orientals*, on the "New Woman."

10 Lee, *Orientals*, 12.

11 Edwards, "Curator's Preface," ix.

12 Lowe, "Turkish Embassy Letters," 325.

13 Lewis, *Gendering Orientalism*, 19–20.

14 Yegenoglu, *Colonial Fantasies.*

15 King, "Orientalism, Hinduism, and Feminism," 335–42; Lewis, *Gendering Orientalism*, 18.

16 Çelik, "Speaking Back to Orientalist Discourse at the World's Columbian Exposition"; Lewis, *Gendering Orientalism*; Lowe, "Turkish Embassy Letters"; Shohat, "Gender and Culture of Empire"; Yegenoglu, *Colonial Fantasies.*

17 Cited in Yu, *Thinking Orientals*, vii–viii.

18 Al-'Asm, "Orientalism and Orientalism in Reverse." A creative instance of Orientalism in reverse is Indian American artist Prema Murthy's Web site, "Bindigirl," http://www.thing.net/bindigrl (accessed April 2, 2004).

19 Fabius, *Mehndi*, 32.

20 Loretta Roome, who learned about mehndi from an Indian woman, launched the Mehndi Project in 1996 in Manhattan, featuring live demonstrations and photographs of henna. It is now an agency for "henna artists." I contacted Roome, but she was unfortunately not able to do an interview.

21 Roome, *Mehndi*, xi.

22 Ibid., 37.

23 Hutynk, "Magical Mystical Tourism," 104.

24 Roome, *Mehndi*, 37.

25 Ibid., 49, 64–65.

26 See "Index of /henna/discuss/messages," http://www.hennapage.com/henna/discuss/messages (accessed March 2000).

27 Maira, "Trance-Global-Nation."

28 Hing, "Reframing the Immigration Debate"; Jiobu, "Recent Asian Pacific Americans." Advertisements for Indo-chic seem to be prominent in mainstream, rather

than ethnic-specific, magazines and fashion catalogs. My thanks go to Toby Miller for raising this question.

29 U.S. Bureau of the Census, 2000 Annual City Census, Northampton Board of Registrars. In 2000, African Americans constituted 2 percent of the total population, Native Americans 0.3 percent, Asian Americans 3.1 percent, and Latinos 4.1 percent.

30 Yoga classes have exploded over the past few years and become integrated into health club repertoires to serve a growing population beyond the New Age clientele. See Rosenzweig, "Attack of the Killer Yogis."

31 Gilbert, "Urban Outfitting," 7–24.

32 Mort, "Boulevards for the Fashionable and Famous," 180–84.

33 Evans, Taylor, and Fraiser, "Shop 'Til You Drop," 158–62.

34 There is one Indian American community association in the Amherst area that seems to consist largely of middle-class immigrants and families, most of them associated with the area colleges.

35 I did this research over a period of six months in 1999–2000 and conducted open-ended interviews with one henna artist and four female college students, three of whom were attending Smith College and one of whom was at the University of Massachusetts, Amherst. One of the students had grown up in Bengal, India, one was from a South Indian family who lived in Oman, another had grown up in Bangladesh and Thailand, and the fourth was Pakistani American. Clearly, their diverse national and ethnic backgrounds make it difficult to come up with any generalizations about the responses of young South Asian women; the point of this study was to elicit responses from a small group of young people that would shed partial light on the meanings that desi youth are making of Indo-chic.

36 Evans, Taylor, and Fraiser, "Shop 'Til You Drop," 161.

37 Canclini, *Consumers and Citizens,* 43–44.

38 Miller, "Consumption and the Vanguard of History," 30.

39 Ibid.

40 Shohat and Stam, *Unthinking Eurocentrism,* 47.

41 Lowe, *Immigrant Acts,* 41–42.

42 See Wilson, "Orientalism"; and Shohat, "Gender and Culture of Empire," 47.

43 For more on the politics of authenticity in Indian American youth culture, see Maira, "Henna and Hip Hop."

44 Kelley, "People in Me." I'm indebted to Vijay Prashad for helping me think through the applications of polyculturalism. See also Shohat and Stam, *Unthinking Eurocentrism.*

45 Khan, "Asian Women's Dress," 61–74.

46 Harvey, *The Condition of Postmodernity,* 171.

47 Chomsky, "Free Trade and Free Practice"; Sklair, "Social Movements and Capitalism."

48 Kalra and Hutnyk, "Brimful of Agitation, Authenticity, and Appropriation," 340.

49 Ross, "Tribalism in Effect," 284–99.

50 Bachman, "Buy a Bindi—or Boycott?" 24–28.

51 Lessinger, *From the Ganges to the Hudson*.

52 A Thai artist, Navin Rawanchaikul, created an installation of a "taxi café," which was on view from June through September 2001 at the P.S. 1 Contemporary Art Center in Long Island City and Madison Square Park in Manhattan, and a comic book, *I Love Taxi*, featuring a Punjabi cab driver in New York. Mass-produced Indo-kitsch items include T-shirts and tin lunchboxes with images of Hindu deities taken from cheap calendars and reproductions of the picture charts used in Indian elementary schools, products familiar to working- and middle-class Indians that are packaged as "retro" or "cool."

53 Hall, "The Local and the Global," 91–92.

54 In 1998, a young Indo-Trinidadian American man, Rishi Maharaj, was beaten senseless by three white men in Queens, New York, who complained that Indians moving into the neighborhood were bringing it down. See Sengupta and Toy, "United Ethnically, and by an Assault."

55 Misir, "The Murder of Navroze Mody," 55–75.

56 Rogin, "Make My Day!" 499–534.

57 McClintock, "Soft-Soaping Empire," 141.

58 Rogin, "Make My Day!" 499.

59 Miller, "Culture and the Global Economy," 41.

60 Grewal and Kaplan, "Introduction."

61 Barlow, "International Feminism of the Future."

4

🌸 Troubled
Technologies

Asian American Auto/Biographies: The Gendered Limits of Consumer Citizenship in Import Subcultures

Robyn Magalit Rodriguez and
Vernadette Vicuña Gonzalez

The camera pans onto a nocturnal urban landscape pulsing with a hip hop soundtrack and revving engines, signaling an illicit yet irresistible spectacle. In a scene in the 2001 film *The Fast and the Furious*, an array of Japanese import cars line the streets of Los Angeles, where male racers and female fans mingle in the prerace, club atmosphere. This particular scene displays the tensions between racial groups, technological muscle, and automotive expertise and ingenuity, as well as the homosocial rituals of affirmation and competition and heterosexual courtship dramas, that characterize import car racing. Investigating a series of daring highway heists committed by a "gang" of import car racers, the protagonist, a white under-cover cop, must prove his technological prowess and racing know-how in order to break into the tight community of clandestine street racing. The criminal element is highlighted by the marked racialization of the scene—all the other racers (and potential perps) and a majority of the spectators are of color, and one of them is the key to the crime spree. Four men—one Latino, one white, one Asian, and one black (the Hollywood formula for cinematic multiculturalism)—rev their engines at the starting line, their cars glistening with decals and vibrating with heavy bass lines. A white woman walks over to the black racer, places his hand on her breasts and indicates that if he wins she (along with her girlfriend, who waves from the sidelines) will be his prize. Finally, the race is on.

The release of the film was met with widespread disgust among Asian American viewers—yet another Asian American scene had been co-opted by a Caucasian actor and Hollywood. The Asian American element, represented by the orientally ambiguous Johnny Tran, is a secondary plot, a distraction from the main action between Vin Diesel's Latino racer and the white undercover cop. Tran, reminiscent of Yakuza corporate criminality, is the initial suspect until the protagonist delves deeper into the other, alternative criminal profile—Diesel's tortured Latino patriarch.

Despite the marginality of Asian Americans in cinematic representations like those of *The Fast and the Furious*, Asian import culture is actually dominated by Asian Americans. Concentrated primarily on the West Coast, but also in significant East Coast pockets, the Sun Belt, and Hawai'i, import racing, also known derogatorily as "rice rocket" culture, is a public, visual performance of racial and cultural citizenship. The term *import* refers to the types of cars the racers modify, most of which are of Japanese manufacture. Honda Civics and CRXs. Mitsubishi Eclipses, Acura Integras, and other standard factory models are subjected to aesthetic transformations particular to the scene and are further customized by means of body kits, sound systems, and other individualizing accessories. The goal of such conversions is to make the car sleeker, sexier, louder, and faster than the "original." Import cars are tailored to stand out, and the cars in *The Fast and the Furious* represent a palette of possibilities of individual styles, as well as corporate adaptations to this trend.

In the highly publicized car show circuits, racing events, print media, and Internet networks that make up the import scene, we can see a young, middle-class Asian American brand of masculinity being forged. Rooted in an "American" tradition and vocabulary of muscle car masculinity and mobility, the rice rocket scene took its initial customizing cues, as well as its "ethnic statements," from the predominantly southern Californian and southwestern tradition of "lowrider" culture.[1] Unlike lowrider culture, however, import culture, which gathered speed in the 1980s and 1990s, rewrites the Japanese—as opposed to American—car through an updated, technology-heavy script of Asian masculinity. Today the prosthetic technologies required by import culture are produced and sold by the automobile manufacturers, requiring less improvisation but more capital. As such, the mutual production of rice rocket masculinity and technology invariably requires greater disposable income, and ultimately a different relationship with transnational capital and identification with ethnic politics, than lowrider culture did.

Faster, sleeker, lower, and louder, rice rocket culture is a site where competing ideologies and economies of identity and community formation, ethnic and racial pride, and diasporic nationalisms are being shaped. In the import scene, participants forge identifications with Asian capital, a nebulous and constructed Asian "heritage," and an American cultural citizenship and create a unique brand of economic and cultural politics. These engagements with the car, the icon of American mobility and freedom, as well as consumer citizenship, are at once a claim and a challenge to historically circumscribed Asian American mobility. Contrary to the image of the import scene as a frivolous or fringe practice, rice rocket culture structures the present and future consumer practices and politics of a large segment of Asian American youth. The insertion of an Asian American mode of consumerism and expression intervenes both in the autocentric American way of life and in the American economy.

But in staking out an Asian American space on American roadways, imaginaries, and economies import culture also makes claims to cultural citizenship using familiar vocabularies of nationalism and national belonging. "Rice boys" in their "rickies" deploy well-known codes of gender and sexuality to make themselves intelligible, even as they might alter the racial syntax of masculine prosthetic technologies.[2] How, then, should we understand the reclaiming of an Asian transnational and public space in this subculture? In what ways is the brand of Asian American masculinity forged in this culture constructed through and against—and at the expense of—reorientalized femininities? What are the politics of representation in these sites and why do they matter?

"The Car Is the Sacred Cow of America": Automobiles and American Autonomy

> What was special about Ford (and what ultimately separates Fordism from Taylorism), was his vision, his explicit recognition that mass production meant mass consumption, a new system of the reproduction of labor power, a new politics of labour control and management, a new aesthetics and psychology, in short, a new kind of rationalized, modernist, and populist democratic society.[3]

Cars have been central to the shaping of the American economic landscape and cultural imagination. As Paul J. Ling argues, not only did cars help to facilitate the extension of the market and capital accumulation, but they were also a palliative measure designed to incorporate the working class as consumer citizens in the face of potential class upheaval. He argues:

Given the continued unwillingness of capitalists to share the benefits of enhanced productivity equitably with their workers in the form of generally high wages, the key to mass participation in a therapeutic culture of consumption lay in the expansion of credit. This enabled workers to secure items that were advertised as having an enriching effect on individual or family life. . . . Thus, the consumer culture of which the automobile was such a conspicuous feature in the 1920s served both to facilitate the smooth acceleration of capital accumulation in a boom and to inhibit labour's desire to challenge the hegemony of capital.[4]

Soon after the end of World War II, the American automobile industry cashed in on the Great Depression highway projects that opened up the continental United States to further exploration by vacationing families. Because the war had halted the production of new cars, the postbellum automobile industry was inundated with increased consumer demand. In America, Fordist technologies and the Fordist organization of labor were definitive in the rise of early-twentieth-century capital, lending buoyancy to the postwar economy and the unique character of the industrial landscape. David Harvey argues that, "Postwar Fordism has to be seen, therefore, less as a mere system of mass production and more as a total way of life. Mass production meant standardization of product as well as mass consumption."[5] The Fordist revolution is thus credited with nothing less than a complete overhaul of not only the American economic scene but also its political and cultural terrain. Today the massive automobile market continues to drive American foreign policy as the United States reaches overseas to provide oil for the American way of life.

While cars play an important role in U.S. economics and trade, they have also carved out an important niche in the formation and imagination of American identity. The car is a sign of mobility and enfranchisement, a marker of the American Dream achieved. Its self-promotion of the modern, populist, and democratic is at once the fruit and fuel of Ford's vision. The car is also a significant American cultural icon that simultaneously re-members and shapes American national consciousness at different stages of U.S. history, functioning as a technology of periodization, from Henry Ford's triumphant Model T, the powerful and nostalgic Ford Mustang, and Daytona stock car races to the automobile manufacturing wars of the 1980s and Lee Iacocca's revision of Fordism. Cars also form critical aspects of American individual identities. Lifestyles and politics are signaled by the types of cars we drive or don't drive, whether they are suvs, minivans, convertibles, sedans, coupes, or trucks.[6]

The American cultural imaginary is thus populated by cars and car-related images. From the road trippin' Beat culture, the frontier mystique of Route 66, cars as teenage make-out spaces, and the seduction of chrome and Cadillacs to today's love affair with the ubiquitous sport utility vehicle, cars have dominated the ways in which American identity has been negotiated and contested. Hollywood films especially look to the automobile as the central tool in rites of passage for American manhood. The car culture of the 1950s and its investments in masculinity in particular illustrate the ways in which this cultural terrain has shaped race and gender in the United States. Young white men proving their masculine worth through car races (and thus getting the girl) was a popular image in post–World War II America. In the classic 1950s film *Rebel without a Cause*, a hot-rodding James Dean epitomized and brought into popular culture the romantic image of discontented American youth. When he died in a car crash soon after the film was released, Dean became an icon of toughness, and the American car, in its post–World War II, mass-produced incarnation, literally became the vehicle for a new brand of American heroism and masculinity. Even though female celebrities such as Jayne Mansfield and Grace Kelly were also killed in car crashes, the domain of cars remained masculine and in particular a proving ground for working-class men. With the gradual fading away of the Western cowboy lifestyle, the wide-open highways of America became the space where a new kind of cowboy could stake his claim to the American Dream with a new kind of Mustang. Indeed, the romance of the open road parallels that of the open range.

In the following decades, men and cars were paired in new, definitive partnerships in various television and film productions—from the *Dukes of Hazzard*'s "General Lee" to Michael and Kitt in *Knight Rider* and the A-Team's van.[7] Superheroes such as Gotham's Batman gained even more mystique with boy toys such as the stylized Batmobile of the film franchise.[8] Needless to say, the way cinematic America imagined itself through cars was exclusive. Protagonists were mobile (white) men, enacting their voyages of self-discovery on unpredictable highways. Thus, car ownership and the symbolic figure of the able-bodied American traveler go hand in hand with a certain kind of imagined America.[9]

When it comes to car racing, the stock car industry taps into a particularly concentrated keg of American masculinity, independence, and technological prowess. Following World War II, the stock car industry began to grow in earnest, answering the "crying need for entertainment violent and stimulating enough to get a rise out of the veterans returning to quiet towns after . . . four years of mayhem."[10] Stock car culture thus continued the enactment of American narratives of manliness, speed, and technological innovation that had played a critical part in the Allied victories against the Germans and Japanese. While later wars abroad demonstrated American military dominance, the growing theater of American domestic automobile technology capitalized on a growing pride in made-in-America steel and chrome. Peter de Jong mentions, in particular, a Charlotte Motor Speedway impresario whose prerace spectacle performs American military triumphs using Pentagon fighter jets in Hollywood *Top Gun* fashion.[11] The combination of the restaging of a U.S. military victory, the display of Pentagon muscle, and Hollywood drama is a heady mix—a convincing prelude to a "race" that recruits and shapes a certain brand of Americans. In the stock car industry, car ownership and racing signaled affiliation and identification with this national, military, racial, and masculine economy. To own, work on, and race an automobile was to be a particular kind of patriot.

But because the notion of private property underpins the culture and economy of the United States, as well as determines the hierarchies of its citizenry, working on cars evolved into a classed national masculine pastime that displays the means to purchase the car, the time and disposable income required to modify and improve it, and the individualism of mechanical ingenuity. As de Jong observes, while the spectacle accompanying stock car races is overwhelmingly consumerist, "a lot of time is spent simply watching men work on cars. It's American mechanical competence as theater."[12] Today's American "muscle cars"—epitomized by the Mustang—are the dominant sites of American auto/biographical performances of masculinity. Most visible in the multi-million-dollar NASCAR racing circuit, American stock cars are a masculine and patriotic ideal. Aided by an advertising machine eager to sell cars as accessories to American individuality, the Detroit automobile industry and the figure of the blue-collar American male have become central to the way America imagines itself. Paul J. Ling suggests that this motoring scene is an individualist antidote in an ordered, mechanized world of production. He argues that

> just as automotive transport provided the means by which American capitalism could gear up for a more rapid cycle of capital accumulation, so the same technology in its social and recreational use provided a therapeutic mechanism for individuals seeking to shift gears down to a slower more relaxed pace, even when that relaxation had as its preliminary the exhilaration of high speed."[13]

It seems that cars are emblematic of American individualism even as they are wrought through the circuits of industrialized production that puts individualism in crisis in the first place. As social texts of consumerism, individuality, and gender, it is as such that cars in the United States are sites where ideas about and claims to citizenry and culture are negotiated.

It is precisely because the car had become the "sacred cow" of America, especially as the stage of American masculinity, that Japan's emergence in the American and global automobile industry was such a slap in the face.[14] This new Japanese "invasion"—a threat reincarnated by the U.S. auto industry— was perceived as encroaching on this American territory in the 1970s and 1980s.[15] Lacking the space and natural resources to reproduce the Fordist manufacturing method, as well as the wide roads to accommodate American cars, Japanese automobile corporations instead designed smaller cars with greater fuel economy and sent them overseas to be assembled. This piecemeal assembly, carried out in developing countries where cheap labor, lower overhead, and loose environmental regulations abounded, produced an economically viable product at the same time that the oil crises and recession hit the United States. This post-Fordist moment not only signaled the emergence of Japanese technological and industrial innovation but also played itself out on American roadways. By 1973, Japanese cars such as Toyotas, Datsuns, Mazdas, and Hondas were cutting into a previously all-American industry both at home and abroad.[16] The ensuing "Buy America" campaign pitted the sentimental power of a heavy, Detroit-made car (and the beleaguered American autoworker) against the cheap, insidious new economic enemy.[17] In a hearing convened in 1980 by the Senate Committee on Banking, Housing and Urban Affairs on the effects of the expansion in Japanese imports on the U.S. economy, Sen. Donald Riegle of Michigan testified that "the administration seems to encourage the Japanese trade invasion" with the result that "America is hemorrhaging jobs and capital at an enormous cost to our Nation."[18] This "invasion" was Pearl Harbor all over again.

Today the everyday landscape of cars and drivers is much more diverse as a result of these car wars and much more overtly fraught with racial, gender, and class tensions. In turn, the ways in which cars function as social texts have become differently complex, illustrating the ways in which domestic practices of ethnic and racial expression are influenced by the larger global political economy. Mexican lowriders emerged in the post–World War II era as a result of the automobile industry's flooding of the market with new cars, creating a large, cheap, used car market from which the mechanically inclined culled the future lowriders.[19] Asian imports in turn became popular because they were the next set of used, cheap cars to enter the market.[20] The Asian import scene is thus a hybrid space, taking many of its masculine cues from Mexican American lowrider culture, patriarchal Japanese corporate culture, and African American hip hop culture.

Today's import scene traces some of its roots back to the 1980s, during which the crossover to Asian import cars often originated in Mexican American neighborhoods. Lowrider style arose out of the do-it-yourself mechanical expertise that poor people needed to develop in order to keep their cars in running order. Lowriders themselves are usually large American-made cars, such as Cadillac DeVilles and Chevrolet Monte Carlos and Impalas, that have been "chopped and dropped" (given a lowered roof and body), modified with hydraulics, and decorated in a style that challenges the rules of "good taste."[21] This customization became a way to claim a unique brand of Americanness that was distinctly Mexican—brash, different, and in your face. Drawing from the mechanical innovations of lowrider culture, the first customizer of import cars lowered the car body and added racing rims. Japanese cars, however, being small and reputedly badly made, demanded a different kind of customizing. Additional flourishes began to include thin tires and aerodynamic body kits, departing from the "low and slow" aesthetic and performance of traditional lowriders. Adding "souped-up" engines and taking advantage of lighter, more efficient technology, import customizing produced its own unique, hybrid vocabulary. Thus, Japanese cars, which had the reputation of being merely utilitarian and were often characterized as "roller-skates with engines," came into their own in the American car scene as alternative canvases for mechanical and aesthetic souping up.[22] Asian American youths, mostly young men, tapped into this scene in the late 1980s and early 1990s, building on the growing reputation of Japanese imports as reliable, fast, and high-quality automobiles. While lowriders presented an ethnic claim to American street life with their slow-cruising, bouncing automobiles decorated to offend middle-class Anglocentric tastes, the low, fast machines of import culture posed a different kind of challenge. Perhaps patterning themselves on the speed and ubiquity of transnational capital, import cars took to the streets with speed and sleek Japanese technology. Accompanied by a hip hop soundtrack that underlines an identification with the racialized and gendered criminality associated with African American rap culture, rice rockets stake out an Asian American masculinity that borrows from more established macho Latino and hypersexualized African American cultural cues.

Can You Feel My Bass?
Asian American Auto/Biographies

You can feel and hear a rice rocket coming before you see it. If the sound system is any good, it drowns out conversations in the immediate vicinity. Better yet, it sets off car alarms in nearby parking lots. Heralded by a thumping bass line blasting from custom speakers, the squeal of brakes, and the acrid smell of burning rubber, public space is put on notice. It becomes a mobile theater. Enter a young Asian male in the car, slouched, with left hand draped outside the window, cigarette burning, right hand at twelve o'clock. Attitude oozes from spiked coif, sunglasses, and the girl by his side. These are boys who do not know their place; these are model minorities who do not know their manners. You are not worthy. The light turns green, and you are eating their dust.

It is because the car is so central to a hegemonic brand of American identity that the sight of a young Asian American male in a souped-up, lowered, brightly colored (and loud) Honda Civic can be jarring. Claiming freedom and individuality, practicing mobility, displaying access to income and knowledge of the latest technology, and unashamedly buying and driving Japanese, these young Asian American men are not economically and politically dispossessed coolies. As they cruise (or race illegally) on American streets in their Japanese cars, drawing on a hybrid vocabulary of car customization and urban youth culture, they lay claim to America in distinctly spatial and visual ways. Import racers forge an imagined pan-Asian American community, though drawing primarily from Japanese aesthetics, mythology, and modernity. Yet this pan-Asian Americanness is contingent and highly local as specific ethnic Asian American groups mark their intraethnic difference within this subculture. Import racers thus perform a delicate balancing act, negotiating the tensions of the American muscle car industry and culture, the Latino working-class origins of the customization scene, urban hip hop masculinities, the Japanese corporate co-optation of import culture, and specific ethnic identifications.

While this is a predominantly Asian scene in terms of cars, technology, and aesthetics, and is Asian American in membership, it is also firmly situated in an American hot-rodding tradition. But, while stock cars refer to factory-built, out-of-the-showroom cars and muscle cars refer to large American cars such as the Mustang, import teams, which often form around more specific Asian ethnic identifications, are the Asian American answer to stock car racing teams. Though competing against each other in legal and illegal races, they also position themselves as challengers to the predominantly white stock car scene, whether on the street or on the track. Flipspeed, fashioned as a Filipino team, envisions the contested terrain as the "local quarter mile drag Track . . . [of] Bristol Motor Speedway's Thunder Valley," where "some of our cars are there pretty much every Friday night, showing the V-8 boys that we're not just little rice rockets with nitrous systems."[23] This exercise imagines the competition in terms of racialized car cultures. "Our" boys are set up against the "V-8" engines of the mainstream racing scene through which speed and mechanical brilliance are the measure of success (and thus masculinity). In this contest of technological mastery and masculinity, an Asian American male image is constructed that both affirms and resists a stereotype of Asians as the model minority. Import car racers' technological prowess under the hood signals engineering brilliance, while their expertise behind the wheel shifts the meanings of the "bad" Asian driver. As R. J. de Vera, the Filipino American scion of the import scene in California, explains, "A Mustang 5.0 would rev me at the light, and I would smoke 'em."[24] This improvised engineering know-how, produced by Asian and Asian American men, often beats mainstream hot-rodders at their own game, destabilizing the dominant narrative of masculinity and cars. The muscle car mantra of "there's no replacement for displacement" is proven wrong. That is, the size of the car's engine ceases to be an issue in matters of speed.

Derogatorily labeled "rice boys" by traditionalist muscle car enthusiasts, these young Asian American men occupy street spaces in hypervisible ways that grate against an American auto/biography. The rice rockets they purchase, modify, and race tend overwhelmingly to be Japanese import cars.[25] This emphasis on Japanese cars taps into a not so distant past, mentioned earlier, when the deterioration of the domestic auto industry was "cause" enough for racial violence against Asians, as the much-publicized murder of Vincent Chin in 1982 illustrated. At the time, buying and driving Japanese by everyday consumers became a political act "perceived as a disloyal act to American citizenship."[26] The struggling American car industry thus blamed its woes on Japan and, by extension, the disloyalty of those who failed to buy the more expensive, higher-maintenance American cars.

Import racers, however, did not necessarily make overt political linkages with their decision to modify and race foreign cars; initially, the decision to convert Japanese cars hinged on the fact that the price was right. As noted earlier, Japanese import cars were a cheap alternative to European and domestic models. In the 1990s, with phenomenal growth in their purchasing

Rodriguez and Gonzalez

power, Asian American youths became visible and dominant players in the import scene—shaping, promoting, and marketing it as a new space for young Asian Americans in the know and in the money. Today Asian Americans, particularly those with plenty of disposable income, largely dominate car shows, races, and media.

Even as racers and their teams organize themselves along the lines of distinct Asian ethnic groups, a corporate pan-Asianism structures the import scene around Japanese aesthetics and capital. The attraction to Japanese cars as the new medium for customization is tied to an identification with the clean lines of traditional Japanese aesthetics, as well as with Japan's global role as a technological powerhouse. Japanese cars are spare, with sleek curves and efficient lines. They are not meant for the baroque stylings predominant in lowrider culture. Thus, the cars, produced to be efficient, fast, and light, are modified to be even more so. This is Japanese efficiency and artistry linked and foundational to a modernity that combines both successfully in the global market.[27] As the moving canvases for the exhibition of Japanese-inspired technological and aesthetic innovation, import cars balance a samurai warrior mythos with futuristic fantasy technology. Inside, the latest car audio technology is showcased: gleaming amplifiers, vibrating subwoofers, arrays of speakers controlled by computers. Miniaturized television screens are inserted for no utilitarian purpose. There is barely room for a driver and passenger. This is a cockpit—perhaps where the "brain" of the robot warrior is housed. Outside, aesthetics reminiscent of Japanese space fantasy animé continue the stylization established in the interior. Customized car bodies recall animé images of high-technology robots and weaponry fighting in faraway space battles. These futurized, prosthetically assisted samurai want responsive, fast technology, but they also want it to look good. Low-slung bodies—a lowrider style—acquire a different kind of meaning; they are for show *and* efficiency. On import cars, low means sexy and fast. Exaggerated spoilers and oversized tailpipes are also markers of speed and efficiency. Bright colors—lime green, school bus yellow, and other unusual shades of orange, red, blue, and green are preferred over market colors. This is youth, this is future modern, and this is Japanese.

The "Asian" look in the case of the import scene is state-of-the-art Japanese, even as the import scene itself is a hybrid Asian American phenomenon. In the event that the hood is not up to display the engine, logos and stickers on the cars advertise its special features such as the presence of a nitrous oxide-injected engine or the brand name of a favored turbocharging system. These logos predominantly feature Japanese companies: Nissan, Mazda, Honda. For those whose identification with import culture fails to reach their pocketbook, orientalized stickers and graphics, some identifying them as members or fans of a car crew, are a more superficial kind of modification to their own rides.[28] But it is as such that, unlike the do-it-yourself ethos of lowrider culture,[29] early import customizing is increasingly marked by corporate infiltration of this emerging market.

In a 1997 *Los Angeles Times* article, D. James Romero commented on the "street monsters of choice," which are Acuras and Hondas: "The cars are much smaller, the engines have half the cylinders. But with high-tech modifications, high-speed freeway racing and high sticker shock, this new, modern version of ages-old hot rodding is still a high stakes game."[30] These high stakes thus come with a price; the import scene is not cheap. Serious racers tend to be middle class in order to afford the costly parts that have generated a domestic market for custom import parts worth more than one hundred million dollars annually. Many, like Marc Fata, a student, work years to afford the modifications to used cars. He has spent over thirty-five thousand dollars on his 1993 Acura Integra, a centerpiece for his crew.[31] The Asian American youths targeted by an import car industry worth twenty billion dollars annually are a very privileged group in many senses. Consumer citizenship in this car culture is extended to a market with an increasingly significant disposable income. While Japanese cars remain some of the more affordable today, import culture has been embraced by corporate sponsorship, minimizing the ways in which cars can truly be "individually" customized. Corporations that manufacture body kits, rims, and other custom paraphernalia used by racers increasingly circumscribe import aesthetics and values. Access to these modifications limits the citizenry of import car culture to the very ingenious with access to money and a lot of time on their hands or the very well to do. Corporate circumscribed customization, then, is also an advertisement for a particular kind of classed lifestyle. The extent of identification with the import scene also varies. While import showrooms sell lowered, customized cars ready to go for interested and moneyed customers, the do-it-yourself mantra still predominates and indeed is a rite of passage for many in the scene, whether racers or merely fans. But more and more often even knowledgeable car crews must have their performance car parts professionally installed at the import performance shops that have cropped up to cater to the burgeoning import scene.

The participation of a group traditionally excluded from the American mainstream as inassimilable aliens threatens the "law of genre," under which

American muscle cars and the tradition of hot-rodding constitute the tradi-tional American auto/biography.[32] Just as significant, a very specific kind of Asian aesthetic is applied to the way the import car scene members envision and stylize their vehicles, especially against the muscle car scene. The import subculture transforms existing codes and commodities—in this case, auto-mobiles as markers of American mobility and enfranchisement—in order to address the political and cultural exclusions of Asian American men.[33] Because commodities have social lives and social meanings,[34] the active reconstitution and rearticulation of these commodities create a "mechanism of semantic disorder, a kind of temporary blockage in the system of representation."[35] The appropriation of the car by Asian American youths to narrate their own processes of identity formation constitutes a "blockage" in established and understood codes of representation. That is, import car culture "adopt[s] and adapt[s]" the signs and symbols of mainstream car culture while infusing them with new styles and meanings.[36] The intrusion of "tinker toy" Japanese cars in the same arena as American muscle cars disturbs American narratives of masculinity and mechanical competence, which still characterizes these im-ports as "foreign" and thus badly manufactured, as well as feminized and infantilized.[37] An Asian American panethnicity is created with Japan as the mythic Asian reference. Here masculine power, already demonstrated by the mastery of heavy technology (and world domination of the automobile mar-ket), is tempered with Asian ingenuity and innovation.

In the new century, Detroit joined Japan in producing and marketing modi-fiable cars, testifying to the expanding influence of this constituency. *Asian Scene.com*, an online magazine addressed to the Asian American community, states that its "core clients include companies that would like to promote and market directly to the generation Y Asians of ages 15–25," especially as "Asians account for the highest income bracket in the United States, with a high percentage of disposable income to purchase online and offline goods."[38] The recognition of the particular demographic of Asian American youth as a ripe market for commerce gives it more economic clout even as it mainstreams its ostensibly "alternative" critique of American culture. Thus, the creation of a hegemonic Asian American imaginary empowers a recognized and valuable consumer citizen at the same time that it imposes a certain kind of undifferen-tiated, market-organizing principle (e.g., Asian American youth).

As such, the culture of the import scene is fraught with contradiction. It is at once a reaction to cultural exclusion (particularly regarding questions of masculine citizenship) and a claim to "America" through a reinscription of

Asian masculinity. The stylizations of Asian import cars indicate that import culture is much more than a mere reaction to the historical exclusion of Asian American men from this space; it is also about the active and creative construction of a transnational Asian American male identity. This "economy of cool" draws on the technologically superior Japanese car (and by implicit extension the globally central Japanese economy).[39] Identifying with a constructed Japanese modernity, as well as its mythic "heritage" of warrior masculinity, import racers thus construct their own claims to an American masculine belonging.

Like lowrider culture, customizing Japanese cars has become an ethnic statement and a practice in which ideologies of national culture, belonging, and masculinity are negotiated and transformed. Young Asian American men, in both their choice of commodity and their choice of stylization (a hybrid of lowrider ingenuity and imported Japanese corporate and popular aesthetics), create a particular kind of transnationalist subcultural space. "Rice racers" participate in this active process of cultural performance because it creates a space of belonging and competition. Many in the import scene, as Kwon claims, say they participate because of the overwhelming presence of Asians, which generates a feeling of inclusiveness. Additionally, for many of these Asian American males, the import scene provides images and realities of Asian Americans outside mainstream stereotypes. There is also cultural (and actual) capital to be gained within the import community with wins at races and shows and with exposure (for both racers and models) in print and virtual media. The more extreme and unique the customization, the faster the engine, and the more polished the expertise of the driver the greater the acclaim or notoriety. This is an arena where style and speed count for everything and attitude is the uniform.

This increasingly middle-class import scene is carried out in several venues. Customized cars are shown at sanctioned import car shows (such as Import Showoff, Battle of the Imports, Hot Import Nights, and Import Challenges), which rotate to different venues in Southern and Northern California. Sponsored by the import and modification industries, these shows display the latest in engine technology, car body art, and fashion. In any given month, at least one of these shows takes place nationwide. Import car shows are snapshots of illegal street and legal track racing, which provide opportunities to test the speed and technological expertise of car and driver. Drag racing, both legal and illegal (occurring on public streets), is another component of the import scene. Increasingly coming to the attention of law enforcement, Asian import culture's propensity to drag race in urban public spaces, with its high potential for injury and death, has resulted in a kind of racial profiling associated with Asian import cars (but not necessarily Asian drivers).

Along with the show and racing circuit, as well as the print media, that arose from import culture, a virtual import community is produced and maintained. Online magazines, team and personal Web sites, and published magazines (such as *Import Tuner*, *Super Street*, and *Sport Compact Car*) provide the informational backbone that holds the import community together. With thousands of online Web sites carrying out the "work of the imagination,"[40] community formation in the virtual national (and international) landscape is made possible. These Web sites are sponsored by racing teams, individual enthusiasts, and businesses, such as car parts companies, that have an interest in the import scene. Shaped and shaping the import community, the amalgamation of show, race, media, and virtual circuits is a powerful arbiter of cultural nationhood and citizenry.

Even as it challenges and alters the codes of American car culture, this transnational youth subculture is not straightforwardly transgressive. While dual adherence to social codes of American masculinity and Asian technological prowess might provoke and disturb established meanings of the social world and public space, racers and their cars are also easily co-opted by transnational circuits of capital. It is important here to note that they " 'negotiate,' not reject, dominant values."[41] After all, in order to participate in the field of American masculine formation, certain codes must still be followed.[42] Increasingly, as we have noted, rice rockets' style is constricted by corporate production; stylistic codes are not reworked or reassembled but appropriated intact from dominant commercial culture.[43] The investment in performative masculinity, in another instance, is one way in which the codes of mainstream car culture remain unaltered.

The Gendered Limits of Subcultural Transnationalisms

Lisa Lowe, in *Immigrant Acts*, identifies the immigrant as a figure that "challenges the global economies from the standpoint of the locality."[44] In this formulation, the Asian American immigrant is tangible evidence of a suppressed history and hegemony and thus, is an agent that can disrupt this hegemony. However, youth culture, diasporas, and diasporic imaginaries are not always subversive. They are highly circumscribed by the kinds of subjectivities made possible by the local and national contexts of race, class, and gender. As Inderpal Grewal cautions, diasporas provide "crucial locations where, under present political and economic conditions in the U.S. and world-wide, their cultural productions can be used both to challenge *and* to recuperate forms of nationalism, citizenship, and politics of the nation-state, as well as the disciplinary technologies of transnational capital."[45]

In the short story "Good Luck, Happiness, and Long Life," the Asian American writer Shawn Hsu Wong articulates a particular Asian American masculine desire for citizenship in the American imaginary. Prefiguring the controversial debate about the apparent emasculation of Asian American men against the hypervisibility and market attraction of Asian American women, Wong, a contemporary and cohort of Frank Chin, uses ownership of a trophy car and a "matching" trophy girl to stake his Asian American claims to the mobile narrative of American male entitlement.[46] Wong's short story is a critique of the social, sexual, and symbolic disenfranchisement of Asian American men in the arena of culture, desire, and representation. The narrator, a Chinese American male with a much younger girlfriend who is "the dream-girl, the Lolita of Chinese America, a patronizing blond-haired girl of fifteen," aims for shock value in his claims to Americanness.[47]

Along with a defiant claim to the fifteen-year-old Lolita, the narrator also tours the United States on a road trip, and road show, to prove his inclusion in America: "I have no place in America, after four generations there is nothing except what America tells me about the pride of being foreign, a visitor from China I've never seen, never been to, never dream about, and never care about."[48] Driven by this need to mark his ownership of and entrance into the American masculine ideal, the narrator lays claim to the symbols of American male popular culture: nubile women and fast cars. Wong's narrator thus enters the space of American male masculinity (and cultural citizenship) by claiming an objectifying eye vis-à-vis women and an expert mechanical eye vis-à-vis car technology.

> She is wearing a white T-shirt and white hot pants with no underwear, her blond hair shines in the desert sun. . . . Her perfect breasts bounce, making the T-shirt move in waves, her fifteen year-old ass peeks out underneath the cuff of the shorts; she has no shoes on. And as we walk through the casino in Elko looking for breakfast, the gamblers ignore her and stare at me like I'm crazy. . . . In the car she takes off her T-shirt because it is too hot, and I let her drive my snow-white Porsche in her snow-white hot pants across the desert at a hundred.[49]

In Idaho, the road show proceeds to showcase the "bare-asse[d]" blond bride, who is "polishing [his] car, bending, kneeling, stretching up on her toes," while the narrator gives a speech, and "some kids . . . [talk] in hushed tones about the Porsche engine."[50] Wong's short story is thus invested in the conventional symbols of American male citizenry: the car and the young woman. Both are recognized, and affirmed, as necessary accessories of American masculinity. A beleaguered Asian American male masculinity requires these props in order to participate in this version of the American Dream. Gender and race compete in this narrative of citizenship: Who is the most properly "American" subject (rather than object) in this story?

In this tale, women's bodies are the surplus value and currency through which a particular form of citizenship is negotiated. As Wong so clearly illustrates, Asian claims to Americanness require a parallel claim to women. For Asian American men, then, "trafficking" in women is a way to lay claim to a denied masculinity. Access to "Lolitas" of different races, particularly Asian, symbolizes a recuperation of a heteronormative masculinity already enhanced by prosthetic technologies. The display of both car and girl in public spaces is a performance of hypermasculinity that disturbs and yet is easily reabsorbed in the American landscape.

What Grewal identifies as the simultaneous challenge and recuperation of forms of nationalism and citizenship in import culture is contingent on the play of gender alongside Japanese transnational capital. The Japanese automobile industry's deployment of Asian American hypermasculinities is dependent on a particular yearning for citizenship in the masculine imaginary and fueled by a financial investment in the success of Japanese technology and capitalism. Capitalizing on a recognition of this fraught, gendered notion of citizenship as it applies to Asian American men, import culture offers a prosthetic masculinity through speed, mobility, technological savvy, and not a little danger. It offers masculinity through identification with distinctly Japanese homosocial corporate cultures, warrior mythologies, and sci-fi technological mastery. A majority of Asian American youths thus lay claim to an authentic (and problematic) Asian culture of masculinity, even as they simultaneously carve out an alternative scene on American soil. In this manner, import nationhood is built on layered and complex claims to different traditions of masculinity.

This discursive management of the category of Asian American masculinity in import culture blurs the ways in which Japanese capital has played a less than admirable role in Asian countries, particularly with reference to gender.

For many underdeveloped Asian countries, Japanese capital has brought employment, but at the price of exploitation. For instance, among others, Filipina entertainers are imported to Japan as underpaid laborers in its corporate, male-dominated scene. In this Asian American subculture, however, a kind of panethnic transnationalism is produced that does not fully take into account or willfully ignores a very gendered Japanese economic imperialism in Asia. In import culture, Asian American men enjoy the displayed bodies of cars and women alike, laying claim to mobility through their ownership of automobiles, as well as through their access to attractive young women.

Racers thus stage their masculinity in several ways, gendering the technological know-how of customizing and driving cars. In import shows, for example, a self-conscious masculinity attends working on and displaying cars. Showing a customized car is tied to other kinds of signs of masculinity such as blaring, hypermasculine hip hop or rap music and the inevitable female models that pose next to (but clearly do not drive) the car. These accessories are props in the performance of masculinities that are the rule in import shows.

The familiar vocabulary of Asian (read: Japanese, Chinese, or Korean) graphics—in the import fashion scene, the cars themselves—also plays on this highly gendered language. Borrowing from the mainstream vocabulary that renders both car and girl objects, import culture creates a specific Asian American repository of sexy models and hot-rods, a "cool" literacy that references a reclaimed, imagined (yet nonetheless real) Asian language. A pan-Asianness is produced by the sharing of Asian women, Asian cars, and Asian texts. Import culture, in creating a "nation," at once identifies with American hot-rodding cultures and challenges its singularity through the imagined legacy and invented tradition of Asian masculinity.

In this way, the logic of nationalism becomes highly sexualized, depending on a libidinal economics and a heterosexual matrix. The offspring of this logic, the hypermasculinity of both the mainstream and import car cultures, has consequences for who can attain membership in this particular subcultural nation. Import car culture is highly masculine and heteronormative. In an extremely homosocial arena where sweat, oil, rubber, and leather mix in intimate garage spaces, import concubines become a necessary badge of heterosexuality. This is especially significant in the case of Asian American men, who are still haunted by historical accusations of an ascribed, and despised, femininity or emasculation. Representationally restricted by legal and economic controls in early immigrant histories, and later by the model-minority stereotypes so prevalent in the 1980s and 1990s, Asian American men sometimes define their racialized masculinity and cultural belonging through the hypergendered and hypersexualized bodies of women. The investment in an erotics of heterosexuality becomes even more important in light of these anxieties about belonging, citizenship, and masculinity.

Import culture is thus glutted with the hypervisible figure of the sexualized Asian woman. Many of the ways in which car shows and Web sites are advertised rely on the seductiveness of "hot Asian babes." In one online import magazine, an Asian woman in a very small bikini dominates the page, with smaller graphics of other Asian women running across the top.[51] This is T and A territory. A caption reading "Asian Pleasures—The Scene's Finest Models" and a "Members Only" warning recall other Web sites and magazines that pander Asian pornography.[52] Photographs of female models of Asian origin are juxtaposed with images of import cars, participating in and reproducing an orientalist discourse on the exotic Asian woman. It is rare to see models of other ethnicities; the predominant look is Asian, slim, and scantily clad. Generating an orientalist narrative about Asian American women from within a hybrid import culture that deploys orientalist masculinities strategically is not unexpected. These are "their" women after all. Who better to control and display them? Asian American men, in this case, are up to the task, particularly since it redeems their masculinity, and it puts Asian American women in their place.

Poster graphics from import car shows such as Hot Import Nights sexualize the cars much as they sexualize the women used to advertise the show. The girls are sleekly styled, with state-of-the-art cosmetics, cosmetic surgery, and (minimal) clothing. In one of *AsianScene.com*'s photographs, their featured model, Justine, poses beside a sleek, red car with its hood up. Having the hood up is standard procedure at car shows—it displays the goods. Justine bares her belly in much the same way that the car bares its engine. She, too, is displaying her goods. Both woman and car are the ultimate accessories for the rice rocket racer. The women in this scene are virtually interchangeable, much like car parts. They are identically coifed and clothed modern-day geishas. Recent scandals regarding some underage models have led to stricter guidelines, but the majority of models have the same young and feminine look, coalescing and consolidating a certain technique for being (or becoming) an import girl in ways similar to the standardization of the import car aesthetic by the Japanese car industry.

Similar layouts of cars and women dominate the print media dedicated to the import scene. In the April 2000 issue of *Import Tuner*, for instance, the cover sports a barely clad Chinese Filipina model leaning against a lowered, souped-up Toyota MR2. The "Street Weapon MR2" caption captures both the meaning of the car as a dangerous, masculine space and the image of the girl wielding her sexuality as a particularly feminine weapon. Japanese characters underline the name of the magazine. Inside the feature article on the Toyota is "serious," engaging "man talk" about technologies and the newest innovations. The enticing female model is featured in her own interview (sans car) while the car merits its own six-page spread of text and detailed pictures (sans model). Captions containing import jargon about the hardware are slick and esoteric, necessitating knowledge of a certain vocabulary: "The rear end flexes Toyota Supra taillights with hyper-white turn signals and chrome housings along with a smoothed-in Veilside rear bumper sporting custom vents and a Greddy Power Extreme exhaust system."[53] The other articles and advertisements have similar overtones of technological masculinity, often using women's bodies as a foil. Interestingly, the interview with the model points out her "nice set of bolt-ons," likening the girl's enhanced body to the car's.

The import model's body as (sex) machine is an apt metaphor. Like the car, she is modified, improved, and disciplined. She is circulated as a marker of cultural capital. Heteronormative masculinities are vetted by her presence. The boys of the import scene are never compared to machines; they are always their masters.

Hyperfeminized and highly sexualized "girl on girl" action is staged for car shows and various media. But the queering potential of girl on girl action is disavowed, becoming instead a vehicle for male heterosexist fantasies. The Web sites containing photographs of girl on girl action by Asian models at car shows enforce a heteronormative gaze. This is clearly a man's harem, where women are interchangeable and their desires remain unknown. Membership in the import scene is consolidated in "booty contests" (at both shows and races) and other public displays of the female body. Women participate and (mostly) men watch. A particular gendered cultural consciousness is interpolated through the hailing call of wet T-shirt contests, thong fashion shows, and the aforementioned booty-shaking competitions. Masses of women are used for this process—their body parts assembled for the purpose of male bonding and for the consolidation of their cultural capital as straight, manly men. The potentially queer elements of the car scene (homosocial technologies and female-female desire) are elided through the heterosexual organization of women in this space. We "forget" that greasy, sweaty boys hang out with each other in close quarters to learn this trade. The masculine heterosexuality of the racer is contingent on the performance and mastery of both the technological prosthetic and its feminine counterpart.

Although the models and other young women who circulate in the import world have a measure of autonomy, even as their femininity is framed in such limited terms, women's participation in import culture leaves much to be desired. Lauding the recent emergence of "girl racers" in recent years avoids a critical reexamination of the complicities of the import industry in the first place. Including women in this scene as racers, not props, is analogous to the problematic politics of inclusion that created the import scene. Women who are included as racers are often safely marked as heterosexual. Mothers, such as the mother of the racer R. J. de Vera, Charlotte de Vera, act as team presidents and coordinators of their sons' racing teams. Young, tough, and tomboyish (but not "lesbian"), girl racers participate in these circuits but do not critique or alter them. Invariably, these girl racers continue to model acceptable forms of Asian femininity: sexy and photogenic, with just a touch of the Dragon Lady to make it interesting. While these women are not exactly sexualized props, they are easily absorbed into what remains a highly heterosexual, masculine Asian American domain.

Staking claims to citizenship within the dominant culture, subcultural nations, such as the import scene, too often employ hegemonic logics of heterosexuality and masculinity. On the road to a potentially subversive mixing of auto / biographical criticism and auto / biography, import culture is derailed by its own investments in heteronormative masculinity and capitalism's investment in the creation and maintenance of new markets. An uncritical pan–Asian American youth culture, as sustained by capital in the realms of import culture, is more about aesthetics than politics. The slick potency of American car culture and the current corporate sponsorship that capitalizes on its questionable libidinal economics are invested in reproducing a dubious, but standardized, myth of America. As import culture continues to foster a particular vision of Asian American aesthetics and mythology, it is important to remember that these gendered claims to citizenry are highly contingent on its use of women's bodies and its investments in a highly gendered Asian mythology and modernity.

Notes

The authors would like to thank Hertha Sweet Wong, Marguerite Nguyen, Evan Anderson, Mimi Thi Nguyen and Thuy Linh N. Tu for their valuable and critical comments on early drafts of this chapter.

1. Cowan, "Devils or Angels."
2. *Rickies* derives from a derogatory term used by traditional hot-rodders, *rickshaw*.
3. Harvey, *The Condition of Postmodernity*.
4. Ling, *America and the Automobile*, 10.
5. Harvey, *The Condition of Postmodernity*, 135.
6. The 2003 California recall election featured a Web site showing Ariana Huffington, one of the gubernatorial candidates, driving a hybrid vehicle versus Arnold Schwarzenegger's gas-guzzling Humvees. In an effort to placate California's environmentalist contingent, Schwarzenegger conceded that he would look into converting his four Humvees to electric vehicles.
7. Even James Bond's Aston Martin, which is British, has acquired a uniquely American Hollywood claim.
8. The Batmobile, according to Ben Chappell, arose out of the "kustom kar" movement of the 1950s, a young working-class mechanical aesthetic based in Southern California, one of the precursors of the lowrider aesthetic. See Chappell, "Take a Little Trip with Me," 100–20.
9. In *Thelma and Louise*, for instance, the quintessential girl road trip movie, the car provides the women with some degree of emancipation but also circumscribes the kind of liberation they attain in the end.
10. De Jong, "Fast Times in Stock Car Country."
11. Ibid., 70.
12. Ibid., 70–71.
13. Ling, *America and the Automobile*, 4–5.
14. "The car is the sacred cow of America" is the observation of Michael Angelo, an economics teacher at Columbia High School in New York in 1995–96.
15. Sassen, *Losing Control?*
16. Sobel, *Car Wars*, 220.
17. See the movie *Gung Ho* (dir. by Ron Howard, 1986), starring Michael Keaton, who plays an executive in a car company that is taken over by a Japanese corporation.
18. "Auto situation," hearing transcripts, 96th Cong., 1980, 2nd session, 3.
19. Cowan, "Devils or Angels," 8.
20. Kwon, "Autoexoticizing," 3. Also see Romero, "A Turbocharged Obsession."
21. Chappell, "Take a Little Trip with Me," 107.
22. Romero, "A Turbocharged Obsession."
23. Team Flipspeed Web site, http://www.flipspeed.com/about.htm (accessed May 7, 2000).
24. Romero, "A Turbocharged Obsession."

25 According to a recently published import scene ethnography by Soo Ah Kwon, the import scene is based in urban communities with large Asian American populations and is a predominantly West Coast phenomenon (Los Angeles being the hub). Kwon traces diverging perspectives on the actual origins of the import scene, one of which credits import origins to the Mexican American community's tradition of lowriding and another of which pinpoints Japanese Sansei (third-generation Japanese American) youths in Los Angeles, who took their stylistic and technological cues from Japanese car culture.

26 Kwon, "Keeping It Real," 17.

27 This linking of aesthetics, technology, and global economic power references the ways in which Japanese culture, capital, and products epitomize flexibility.

28 Shared aesthetics and spaces do not signal unified, homogeneous communities or politics. Other logos and stickers might also advertise the specific ethnicity of the driver or racing team, such as "Powered by Vietnam" or "Pinoy Pride." This insistence on ethnic-specific identifications suggests that there are tensions within the pan-Asian characterization of the import scene. Coming from traditionally more politically and economically marginalized groups within Asian America such as Filipino and Vietnamese Americans, these distinctions do not necessarily form a critique of their participation in these circuits of power and identity. However, they call attention to the tenuousness of this ostensibly collective space and make a statement about how space and communities are organized around a dominant pan-Asianism without taking into account different histories of oppression within Asian America. Ethnic hierarchies structured by class (i.e., with access to higher education, disposable income, cultural capital, etc.) produce moments of conflict.

29 Ben Chappell, in "Take a Little Trip with Me," notes that while early lowrider culture had a working-class background the lowrider show circuit demands a high level of disposable income.

30 Romero, "A Turbocharged Obsession."

31 Ibid.

32 Kaplan, "Resisting Autobiography," 208–16.

33 Clarke et al., "Subcultures, Cultures, and Class"; Hebdige, "Subculture," 130–42.

34 Clarke et al., "Subcultures, Cultures, and Class," 100–111.

35 Hebdige, "Subculture," 130.

36 Clarke et al., "Subcultures, Cultures, and Class," 103.

37 The "tinker toy" allusion is from Romero, "A Turbocharged Obsession."

38 *AsianScene.com* Web site, http://www.asianscene.com/mission.shtml (accessed May 7, 2000).

39 We are indebted to Mimi Thi Nguyen and Thuy Linh Tu for the term *economy of cool*, which they suggested in revising our initial draft.

40 Appadurai, *Modernity at Large*, 1.

41 Clarke et al., "Subcultures, Cultures, and Class," 103.

42 Bricolage is a "mode of adaptation" that transforms commodities from their original use and meaning. Bricolage, then, has a culturally syncretic feel that has

more to do with "refusal" of an originary meaning than "resistance" (Gelder, "Introduction to Part Two," 88). The ways in which import car culture deploys a narrative of bricolage calls to mind, however, not merely the ways in which Asian immigrants adapt to the United States but the ways in which they construct their linkages to Asia.

43 Cohen, "Symbols of Trouble," 156.

44 Lowe, *Immigrant Acts*, 35.

45 Grewal, "The Postcolonial, Ethnic Studies, and the Diaspora," our emphasis.

46 Chin is notorious for his vocal critiques of published Asian American women writers as emasculating and orientalizing Asian American men.

47 Wong, "Good Luck, Happiness, and Long Life," 464.

48 Ibid., 465.

49 Ibid.

50 Ibid.

51 GoFastr.com Web site, www.935draggers.com (accessed May 7, 2000).

52 See, for instance, Gonzalez and Rodriguez, "Filipina.com."

53 Funke and Mulroney, "Cover Car—Mister 2 Crazy," 14–22, 16.

eleven

Bruce Lee I Love You: Discourses of Race and Masculinity in the Queer Superstardom of JJ Chinois

Mimi Thi Nguyen

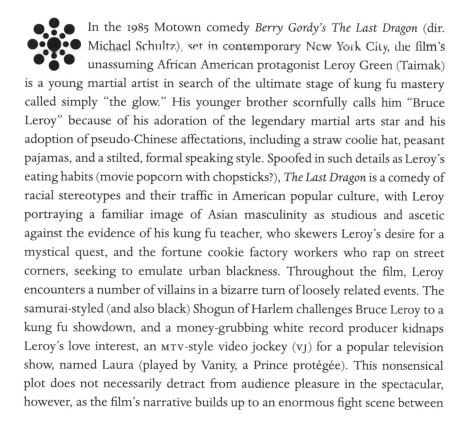 In the 1985 Motown comedy *Berry Gordy's The Last Dragon* (dir. Michael Schultz), set in contemporary New York City, the film's unassuming African American protagonist Leroy Green (Taimak) is a young martial artist in search of the ultimate stage of kung fu mastery called simply "the glow." His younger brother scornfully calls him "Bruce Leroy" because of his adoration of the legendary martial arts star and his adoption of pseudo-Chinese affectations, including a straw coolie hat, peasant pajamas, and a stilted, formal speaking style. Spoofed in such details as Leroy's eating habits (movie popcorn with chopsticks?), *The Last Dragon* is a comedy of racial stereotypes and their traffic in American popular culture, with Leroy portraying a familiar image of Asian masculinity as studious and ascetic against the evidence of his kung fu teacher, who skewers Leroy's desire for a mystical quest, and the fortune cookie factory workers who rap on street corners, seeking to emulate urban blackness. Throughout the film, Leroy encounters a number of villains in a bizarre turn of loosely related events. The samurai-styled (and also black) Shogun of Harlem challenges Bruce Leroy to a kung fu showdown, and a money-grubbing white record producer kidnaps Leroy's love interest, an MTV-style video jockey (VJ) for a popular television show, named Laura (played by Vanity, a Prince protégée). This nonsensical plot does not necessarily detract from audience pleasure in the spectacular, however, as the film's narrative builds up to an enormous fight scene between

Leroy's kung fu students and some colorful hired thugs, as well as Leroy's final success as an inheritor of Bruce Lee. In the climactic confrontation with the Shogun in a deserted warehouse, Bruce Leroy not only achieves the glow (visible as an electric-blue aura) but is shown in a cinematic conceit common in Bruce Lee films: the protagonist's bared fighting body is lovingly captured in slow motion and optical printing, tracking his sweeping arm movements across the screen.

Bruce Lee inhabits the film as a spectral mentoring presence. When the Shogun, also know as Sho' Nuff, delivers his challenge to Leroy in a rowdy theater showing *Enter the Dragon*, Leroy maintains the calm demeanor modeled by Bruce Lee onscreen; in the Harlem dojo where he trains a range of neighborhood children and teenagers, Leroy dons a yellow jumpsuit similar to the one worn by Lee in his final and unfinished film, *A Game of Death*; at a crucial moment in his quest to find the ultimate (bogus) kung fu master Sum Dom Goy, he is inspired to adopt a disguise after seeing clips of Lee in *The Chinese Connection*. However, the one dilemma for which Bruce Lee cannot offer aid is romantic. Patterning himself after his fan's perception of Bruce Lee—and I say "fan's perception" because it is not clear that his imitation matches the onscreen persona—Bruce Leroy is a sexually naive and repressed hero. His daunting physical skills as a fighter fail when it comes to love. Whereas his younger pubescent brother, a jive-talking, break-dancing wiseass, claims to know exactly what to do with a woman, Leroy's attraction to the sexy Laura confuses him in mind *and* body.

Bruce Lee's star power lingers as the first Chinese star to become a major celebrity in the West. Redefining both Hong Kong and American action cinemas in the 1970s, he continues to reign in absentia over the cinematic genre of the kung fu film in which Asian men are (finally) seen as hard, muscular, fighting bodies. As Nguyen Tan Hoang notes, this is all the more significant because the kung fu film is "the one 'positive' place Asian men occupy within the American popular imagination."[1] Immediately following his premature death, the Hong Kong and American action cinemas began to produce a series of mostly low-budget films meant to capitalize on Lee's legacy. These include a very loosely biographical entry from Hong Kong, *Dragon: A Bruce Lee Story* (dir. Wah Chan and Chang Chee, 1975), starring the self-proclaimed inheritor of the title, Bruce Li; the underground *Bruce Lee I Love You* (dir. John Lamar, 1975), a tabloid tale of his illicit affair and drug use starring his real-life mistress, Betty Ting Pei, of which more will be said later; a Hong Kong martial arts comedy called *Enter the Fat Dragon* (dir. Sammo Hung, 1978) about a young country bumpkin who idolizes Bruce Lee and travels to the city to earn a living (and practice his kung fu); a series of American B-movie spoofs on Bruce Lee's star image called *They Call Me Bruce?* (dir. Elliot Hong, 1982) and *They Still Call Me Bruce* (1986), in which a Korean comedian, Johnny Yune, portrays a fry cook mistaken for a martial artist by the mob; and an American biopic called *Dragon: The Bruce Lee Story* (dir. Rob Cohen, 1993), starring Jason Scott Lee (no relation) and based on the biography written by Linda Emery Lee, Bruce Lee's widow. A string of imitators also followed, with names such as Branson Lee, Bruce Lea, Bruce Li, and Bruce Lei, starring in a subgenre of films described by one fan as "Bruceploitation."[2]

This ever-growing wealth of impersonators and inheritors speaks to a certain tension between the discourse and practice of stardom.[3] Despite the popular notion that what distinguishes a star from "the rest of us" is unique and inimitable, Bruce Lee continues to offer a shape, a language, and an archive for how to be a star, even as this constellation maps the limits of a particular racially gendered embodiment. The visual representation of Asian masculinity in mainstream American popular culture continues to trade on the defining image of the karate master.[4] But, as the multiple reproductions of Bruce Lee demonstrate, the ideas, images, and themes associated with Lee's iconic presence can be inflected in radically different ways. What I find compelling is the fashion in which Lee's presence can be read as symptomatic of how Asian masculinity shapes a particular sort of erotic (or unerotic) physicality. The lack of sexual conquest or encounter is a striking feature of his cinematic oeuvre, through which the Lee character is inscribed with asexuality or quasi-Confucian asceticism. This "puritan sexual morality," as one critic describes it, is reproduced in the recent circulation of Asian male actors who have successfully crossed over into Hollywood but are never figured as sexually appealing or interested.

This is characteristic of the impersonations and homages to Bruce Lee and even becomes a source for comedic situations. In *The Last Dragon*, Leroy, having dedicated his life to perfecting his inner Bruce, is so sexually naive as to be unaware of the existence of "moves"; his younger brother, who anticipates his own mastery of sexual conquest at an early age, denounces Leroy as weird (e.g., dangerously close to queer) because "he won't mess with no babes." In an empty dance club, Laura attempts to seduce Leroy with a wall-high video montage of Bruce Lee's films, featuring multiple close-ups of Lee's face and body set to an energetic rapping soundtrack about the aforementioned glow.[5] That she resorts to another male's body as a sexualized spectacle in order to underscore her insistent flirting is played for laughs. Leroy's absorption in Lee's image is set against Laura's desire for Leroy's body, and he abruptly leaves her unfulfilled when an image of Lee's disguise inspires him to seek out yet another male master.[6] Pouting, the abandoned Laura glares at the ten-foot projected image of Lee and says, petulantly, "Thanks, Bruce!"[7] This is not the only instance of the failure of Bruce Lee's cinematic mentorship in matters of the heterosexual heart. A Malaysian film called *That's the Way I Like It* (dir. Glen Goei, 2000), participating in the millennial 1970s nostalgia, tells the story of a Bruce Lee fan who must find an alternate imaginary mentor in a disco-dancing, John Travolta look-alike in order to augment his physical skills for a dance contest and win the girl next door.

In this essay I address a queer iteration of the phantom presence of Bruce Lee. JJ Chinois is a wannabe styled after Lee (and apparently the former Journey front man Steve Perry) who aspires to be an international superstar. He is also the transgendered persona of a New York filmmaker and artist, Lynne Chan. Coming of age within contemporary queer subcultures, Chan's performance as JJ Chinois imagines a different order of access to stars' bodies while addressing her (and his) marginality under capital's conditions of uneven visibility. JJ Chinois first appeared as a live stage act on the New York City drag king circuit in clubs and bars introduced as a Southern California heartthrob "discovered" (so the story goes) by the drag king of comedy Murray Hill. Chan soon created a fan site and a music video (2002), both eponymously called *JJ Chinois* and featuring an archive not unlike the random clippings in a fan's scrapbook—personal trivia, favorite items of clothing, photographs with other stars (in this case, his "producer," Murray Hill), and luscious groupies. As an aspirant to celebrity, JJ Chinois critiques and appropriates the pleasures of pop stardom in global culture in the early twenty-first century and does so by sexing up Bruce Lee's star image in ways we haven't seen before. Some of these pleasures are obvious even as they are rendered queer. In a publicity photograph, the lean-bodied JJ Chinois slouches in a tight white T-shirt and mirrored sunglasses, his shaggy hair artfully bed-tousled. A pouting young Asian woman presses her barely clad breasts against his arm. But JJ Chinois is looking at the camera in *that* way, interpolating the viewer into the circuit of his bounteous desire. The photograph is a testimonial to his charms and also to an important motive for the fan to want to become the star—to be desired and envied, to be the object of longing, according to the devotions he or she knows so well. And so a star is born, or created.

JJ Chinois's star potential lies in his complicated interpellation of Asian masculinities, both as an individuated performance and as a reproducible commodity, and in the historical possibilities and limitations for stardom engendered by contemporary transnational circuits of culture and capital. JJ Chinois's key inspiration, martial arts superstar Bruce Lee, whose stylized racial masculinity and powerful physicality defined his star image, is immensely significant because Lee retains such a strong hold on the visual representation of Asian masculinity within the American popular imaginary. But JJ Chinois detours from the popular concentration on Lee's martial body to focus instead on extracinematic narratives of sex and scandal, in which the underground film *Bruce Lee I Love You*, featuring a Bruce Lee impersonator smoking pot and having simulated sex with Lee's alleged mistress, plays a significant part. In sampling from these multiple sources, JJ Chinois is positioned both as a fan consuming the spectacularization of Bruce Lee's body in films, albeit in a film that does not actually star Bruce Lee, and as the star being offered for consumption as a desirable commodity. Against the policing to which their bodies are subject—complexly bound through discourses of nation, race, class, and sexuality—both Lee and JJ Chinois (as Chan's alter ego) turn their bodies into spectacular bodies of pleasure through their labor. That is, both work their marginal bodies in different ways in the achievement of their star images. But JJ Chinois models himself after Lee as a lover rather than a fighter, transfiguring the iconic image of Lee's masculine physicality for its sensuality and eroticism. It is through the star text of JJ Chinois that I trace a recent history of how discourses of race and masculinity have been assembled for public personhood under particular configurations of political, social, and economic forces. JJ Chinois clearly spoofs the generic conventions for organizing the star as a reproducible performance of traits assumed to be "natural" and unique properties. But, as I argue in this essay, further deconstructing and contextualizing celebrity entails attending to discourses and affective manifestations of nation, race, class, and sexuality that activate celebrity's corporeal potency. As a fan's labor to organize a star's body, JJ Chinois is an act that pushes against multiple tensions—among them, between modes of dominant masculinities, drag or transgender masculinities, and Asian masculinities; between star production and fan consumption; between the discourse of an original and the instability of its commodity value; and between the promise of the star's body, the democratic appeal of public personhood, and the constraints put on achieving such star potential.

Fan Labors and Outlaw Bodies

Before I turn to JJ Chinois's packaging of his body as a star's, I outline the first of multiple forms of labor considered in this essay. I begin with fan labor, through which consumption and interpretation are conceived as highly constrained but nonetheless enabling sites of subject and discourse formation.[8] In accounting for his legacy it is clear that Bruce Lee is a significant figure authoring the identities and bodies of fans from across the world. His fans' devotion inspires intense debates about Lee as a heroic figure in his films and the Hong Kong and American film industries; it also takes the form of emulation and investment in his extracinematic image as a personification of strength and achievement against oppressive limitations. It is as such that Rosemary Coombes writes, "Part of the celebrity image's value might reside in its exemplifying a particular human embodiment of a connection to a social history that provokes its beholder to reflect upon his or her own relationship to the cultural tradition in which the star's popularity is embedded."[9] These social histories can become a sticking point for examining the conditions and circumstances for the star's publicity and for examining the stars themselves as constitutive of our cultural inheritance in ways that often exceed and even transfigure their original intentions. For example, there is a commemorative statue in Hong Kong, but also in the Bosnian town of Mostar, where Bruce Lee is bronzed in his familiar, spread-legged, defensive stance (muscles bared) and put to work as a symbol in the fight against ethnic conflict. It is a commonplace of cultural studies now that the fan's interpretative work complicates the notion that we consume popular culture simply or that the forms, meanings or structures of feeling attached to its reception are necessarily transparent or predetermined. For minoritized persons who have been historically refused access to the public sphere, authoring social identities through the use of popular culture and celebrity can be an important way to transfigure the politics of representation.[10] But this work is a complicated affair, for it implicates the fan in a script not entirely of his or her making. Fan labor negotiates with official and unofficial publicity apparatuses, including interviews, star profiles, biographies, promotions, celebrity magazines, tabloids, and more. All of these efforts are linked to the charismatic power of the commodity (including, but not exclusive to, the celebrity image) and the social order that assigns and regulates their value.[11]

The challenge to locate a "positive" image of Asian sexuality in popular representation is especially pronounced at the site of Hollywood cinema.

Scholars and activists note that in the cinematic archive Asian women are historically depicted as butterflies or dragon ladies and Asian men as delivery boys, nerds, or kung fu masters. Their sexualities are perverse (whether excessive or inappropriate), passive, or puritan. This dearth of "positive" representations is often greeted with the demand for more "realistic" images and fewer stereotypes of "ourselves." But a mimetic quality of resemblance is not necessarily an organic aspect of fan fascination or love. For instance, the hope of seeing public bodies that appear to be like our own is complicated when the bodies that *are* visible are often proscribed and marked through historically particular discourses of deviance and discipline. Furthermore, a recognizable hope for an altogether different body—the star's—complicates the call for images of our ordinariness. By engaging popular hopes for recognition and legitimacy, Stuart Ewen argues that "celebrity forms a symbolic pathway, connecting each aspiring individual to a universal image of fulfillment: to be someone, when 'being no one' is the norm."[12] Encompassing a promise of positive value and recognition, such fantasies of different embodiment represent the utopian wish to transcend our own shortcomings. It is through this symbolic pathway that the fan might express identification or desire for the star or, as I argue here, something else that might open up these categories to each other and alternate configurations. As Lauren Berlant writes in an essay on passing and publicity, this might be "a desire to occupy, to experience the privileges of [the star's] body, not to love or make love to her, but rather to wear her by way of wearing her body, like a prosthesis, or a fetish."[13] But this is complicated by the extent to which ideas and images of the celebrity's power—including its variable value—are intertwined with discourses of race, class, gender, sexuality, and nationality. What would it mean to want to wear the star's body when this body is not a salve or a source of relief from particularity or pain? Here I put aside Bruce Lee for a moment and turn to the actress Anna May Wong, who before Lee found greater fame in Hong Kong and Europe than in the America to which she was born, in order to highlight these questions and answer some of them in part.

Part of the fan labor on the commodity form of the cinema star resides in efforts to parse the star's image from the constraints of filmic narrative, its events, causation, and temporality. Which is to say that a rare photograph of Anna May Wong in a tuxedo once inspired me to contemplate a life in the cabaret.[14] Framed in close-up, she smolders from beneath the lowered brim of her top hat, her hair slicked back, a martini glass poised near her lips.[15] This publicity still seems to exemplify the beguiling promise and tragic neglect of her star image in classical Hollywood. Remembered at her death as "the screen's foremost Oriental villainess,"[16] her American and British roles are the embodiment of particular historical notions about Asian femininity, national belonging, and "oriental" morality in the early part of the twentieth century. In these films her characters are often punished (with death) for transgressing social boundaries. Nonetheless, her star image circulates in excess of those narratives that confine her to bit parts and Orientalist tropes. Withdrawn or rearticulated apart from a narrative of triumph over the inscrutable and sinister specter, her cinematic image is full (for some) of the delicious promise of moral corruption and sexual decadence. It is in the mise-en-scène that she lurks in the shadows beyond the purview of all that is good and pure, a sharp knife pointed at the back of an evil warlord, or she silences a room full of Victorians with her extravagant costume and commanding, alien presence.[17]

Wong's photographic turn in a top hat and tails seems to hint at other, subterranean possibilities for iconic status, not unlike the sort belonging to Marlene Dietrich, with whom Wong scandalously shared a traveling coach in *Shanghai Express* (dir. Josef von Sternberg, 1932), and who donned similar drag to kiss a woman on film. In her study of lesbian representations in Hollywood cinema, Andrea Weiss notes that rumors of Dietrich's sapphic liaisons fed public hunger for titillation; Paramount publicized *Morocco* (dir. Josef von Sternberg, 1930) as a star vehicle featuring "Dietrich—the woman all women want to see."[18] Such rumors (of sexual scandals in particular) became an integral part of the star's enduring legacy. In this instance, gossip and innuendo about Dietrich's possible liaisons with other women have long shaped queer aspirations in lesbian subcultures and film theory.[19] Such rumors played a starring role in *Shanghai Express*, in which Dietrich and Wong share a claustrophobic compartment aboard a train during the tumultuous Chinese civil war. Yet, despite the intimation of inappropriate intimacy between these two "fallen women," Dietrich's Shanghai Lily is recuperated into marital heteronormativity, leaving Anna May Wong's Hui Fei to her trespasses.[20] Dressed in Chinese gowns that "reveal her long, thin, boyish figure,"[21] Hui Fei is positioned as a rival to the white male love interest, glowering scornfully at his straightlaced back as he passes judgment on his former lover, Lily. However, her performance is not often remembered for its queer and outlaw potential. Without denying Marlene Dietrich her due, it must be said that her aristocratic (Germanic) whiteness, in conjunction with the historically specific material and social conditions of Hollywood stardom, certainly facilitated her iconic status. This comparison highlighting the relative obscurity of Wong's performance, and the queer iconicity of Dietrich's drag, must be situated within the historical conditions that have limited Asian American publicity. Some of these limits include popular racisms and anti-Chinese sentiments during the cold war; the Hays Hollywood Production Code (1932–62), which banned the representation of "sex perversion," a category encompassing both gay and lesbian images and interracial romance; and Wong's own unconventional lifestyle and critique of the Hollywood studio system. We might also speculate that her racial difference deflects both anxiety and anticipation about the revelation of her sexuality. Are her gender or sexual transgressions rendered less transgressive than Dietrich's drag because they are racially overdetermined or otherwise naturalized to her "oriental" body?

Surely the marginal status of Anna May Wong's star image in American popular (and by extension American queer) culture is a critical location for the interrogation of those conditions structuring what is public and visible and how these possibilities and constraints are informed by gender and sexual norms, as well as racial and national formations. But without sacrificing critical inquiry such an interrogation might also manifest pleasure in her performance. As Cynthia W. Liu traces in her essay "When Dragon Ladies Die, Do They Come Back as Butterflies?" Wong has long been a subject of fan fascination.[22] Resurrected in the work of Jessica Hagedorn and John Yau as a tragic but glamorous figure, Wong is situated in those historical conditions that give her image and these fan labors particular meaning and resonance, but not apart from their contradictions and complications. But it was the brief appearance of Anna May Wong in M. Butterfly (dir. David Cronenberg, 1993), adapted from David Henry Hwang's award-winning stage play of the same name satirizing the Puccini opera, that inspired this effort to think through the transfiguration of the star's performance of her body through the labor of a fan.[23] In a brief mise-en-scène, the transgendered singer and Chinese communist spy Song Liling enters her apartment, where, at her bedside, she picks up several film fan magazines. In the next shot, a close-up of a magazine cover features a publicity portrait of Anna May Wong. The accompanying blurb sells "Anna May Wong's Chinese Love Code," and Song teases, "I'm changing myself into a different person." It is a fascinating moment of reverence and homage. This trajectory between Wong and Song, the star and her fan, enacts linkages between the unacknowledged labor of their embodied performances and the historical and cultural contexts of enactment and exchange. Song's espionage depends on her display of a stereotypical Asian femininity in order to work against the machinations of neocolonial powers. That is, her seduction of the French diplomat

René Gallimard turns on her performance as a form of labor in which "being sexed" and "being oriental" coconstitute the body her labor purports to *merely express*. Linking her fan identification (however ephemeral) to the labor of maintaining a seamless cover as a clandestine agent, this brief moment brings into play a recognition of the also conditional status of the gendered and racialized performativity invested in Wong's star persona. So often interpolated as an obstacle to a "real" Asian feminine subjectivity,[24] the dragon lady–butterfly dichotomy as portrayed by Wong's cinematic body of work is made available here for other interpretations or appropriations that complicate concerns about representative realness. Fleetingly figured through her consumption of a fan magazine within the perverse intimacy of her boudoir (a "private" space that also operates as the "working" stage for her state-sponsored seductions), Song's ironic affinity with Anna May Wong permits a reevaluation of Wong's glamorous but repudiated image of sexual and racial danger circulated in the West. In recognizing the similarities between Song's and Wong's performative labor (enacting an orientalist image for an audience in an unequal exchange for her livelihood), this brief homage allows for a reading of Wong's performance of her star's body as a nuanced and complicated negotiation with the conditions and constraints set upon her labor.[25]

Like David Henry Hwang's Song Liling, the fan labor does not necessarily elide the contradictory components of assembling an icon and her publicity, but it can instead acknowledge and incorporate their force and influence. For Anna May Wong, whose most iconic performances were multiply ambiguous, her star persona was characterized by a blend of glamour and danger, and the range of her screen roles encompassed mystery and secret hidden selves. It is through such excesses of meaning, informed by historically and culturally specific practices of reception, that fans might use the resources available to them to generate utopian fantasies but also to counter and make visible social powers to radical interpretation. Hwang's fixation on, and recuperation of, the "oriental villainess" in the character of Song is the raw material for an exploration of the social forces, institutions, and material conditions that are particular to the production and consumption of an image—or its disappearance. Shaping a particular relationship of self to history, and of identity to difference, this brief homage is suggestive for what else it implies: that the star persona is not a stable consolidation of meanings, not an ontological identity, but a dynamic performance, an act of labor, that is scripted and rehearsed; that the fan often performs other related acts of labor in constructing a coherent identity or fantasy from these star images and star parts; and that multiple publics (e.g., the spy's bedroom or the queer stage play) expand the possible frames of reference for "seeing" the star.

But these insights are not the only interventions that this connection performs. Not only does Song Liling's espionage highlight the labor of her gendered and also racialized performance (because she displays an "oriental" persona), but she also reveals the futility of reading realness as a property on and of the body. Described by some Asian Americanists as a negative stereotype of sexual confusion and "disfigurement," the accusation that the transgendered Song is an affront to Asian masculinity (because she has a biological male body) posits that the only possible healthy or whole subject must meet specific masculine and heterosexual norms.[26] While the status of normative masculinity *has* historically been conferred on whiteness, against which Asian masculinity was rendered effeminate and emasculated,[27] the response on the part of some Asian Americanists merely reasserts a patriarchal and heteronormative ideal. The specific use of the term *disfigurement* suggests a damaged physicality, an unnatural maiming of the male body through its successful performance of a feminine demeanor (and thus an implied castration). It is an accusation that makes sense only when maleness and masculinity are understood through a metaphysics of substance in which the latter is the exclusive property of the former and both are defined by heteronormativity. This insidious implication does more than assume that both images and viewers are transparent placeholders for fixed and unmediated meanings. An interpretative strategy that shuttles images into categories of "positive" and "negative" or "real" and "fake" cannot avoid the dangers of becoming moralistic and prescriptive and of reproducing a conservative gendered and sexual moral economy. Such an approach reinscribes some social powers—heteronormativity and the privileges of masculinity—at the risk of obscuring outlaw performances such as Anna May Wong's "boyish" Hui Fei or the still photograph of her in top hat and tails.

Against such permeable performances of outlaw bodies, martial arts superstar Bruce Lee would appear to showcase a hard Asian masculinity. In the kung fu and action cinema, it is the disclosure of Lee's muscular fighting body that precipitates the resolution of conflict. Figured as a solitary hero, Bruce Lee's star image is constructed through a narrative of personal discipline and martial arts virtuosity. Eschewing firearms in his films and martial arts, the performance of Lee's muscles is his primary weapon and his signature style. It is true that the lack of conquest over *women* in his Western work might be indicative of a refusal to see Asian masculinity as "properly" erotic. But conquest over *men* is another matter. As Yvonne Tasker notes, the kung fu film allows "an identification with a male figure who other men will look at and who will enjoy being the object of that admiring gaze."[28] In his consideration of the Asian American porn star Brandon Lee, Nguyen Tan Hoang draws out at least one structural similarity between the kung fu film and the gay porn video, through which the much anticipated performance of an "erupting" male body (or several) triumphs over narrative complexity. And with the spectacular figure of her own wannabe, Lynne Chan launches an assault of a different order on the meanings of Lee's seemingly invincible masculinity and asexual cinematic character. She (or he if we're speaking of JJ Chinois) is a fan whose identity is constituted through an identification with the performance of the star's body. Furthermore, Chan reveals in her strategically transparent efforts to produce and promote JJ Chinois that the star persona is a laboring performance whose possible meanings both shape and are shaped by frames for "seeing" the star. Chan demonstrates the ways in which star bodies can be inflected with queer politics in order to reflect critically on the historical coconstitution of nation, race, class, gender, and sexuality as forms of embodiment. Rearticulating Bruce Lee's hardness, Chan theatricalizes racial masculinity and explores its erotic potential divorced from the perceived rights and privileges of hegemonic, but also cultural nationalist, heteronormativity. JJ Chinois's is a superstar Asian masculinity that is flexible, performative, glamorous, self-aware, exotic, and hard but also vulnerable and, importantly, queer.

Style and Drag in the Labor of Masculinity

Lynne Chan asks if that which is denied can be produced. That is, in her transfiguration of Bruce Lee (along with her incorporation of other masculine star qualities) she presses the commodity form of the cinema star into a new body that "corrects" an absence with a virile but also subversive presence, and also reveals a savvy knowledge about culture and capital's changeable and particularized attributions of value. It is as such that Eve Oishi counts Chan among a "new movement of Bad Asians—lesbian, gay, transgendered, and bisexual" in independent film and film production, "lay[ing] claim to a new store of images, attitudes, and technology, all of which come out of and respond to the specific cultural context of the late 1990s."[29] In her article by the same name, Oishi notes that these Bad Asians "find their voices through a 'perverse' identification and relationship with popular culture that uncovers, tweaks, and plays with the racialized fantasies, fears, and representations that make culture popular."[30] As described earlier, the publicity photograph in which the star poses with an adoring (and sexually available) fan stages this perverse identification in multiple senses of the term—perverse because popular culture does not often reciprocate, with few exceptions, and perverse because it is a glamorous image of transgendered or queer desire (and perverse because in this photograph JJ Chinois wears a sleeveless T-shirt featuring the Republican elephant, which is surely either hipster ironic or the height of kink).

As illustrated above in queer readings of those visible markings of Marlene Dietrich's or Anna May Wong's sexuality (signaled most often by an androgynous or cross-dressing display), the question of style occupies a central place in this discussion. Returning to and referencing a visual archive from Bruce Lee to boy bands, seventies retro to Williamsburg hipster, Chan assembles for JJ Chinois the recognizable body of an aspirant to super personhood and solicits the fans to prove he is worthy of being a star.[31] But style is hardly as ephemeral as its possessors (and certainly some of its fans) might argue; instead it is articulated through other discourses about the body and always conditioned and circumscribed by historical convention.[32] Gender is imagined as a "corporeal style";[33] race is tied to "practices of stylization";[34] and the promulgation of lifestyles in late capital is inextricably tied to the merging of identities, medias, and markets. It is as such that Judith Butler argues that "the body is not a 'being' but a variable boundary, a surface whose permeability is politically regulated."[35] Not coincidentally, both Anna May Wong and Bruce Lee are exemplary figurations of an intentionally styled but also politically regulated body; their star images are simultaneously enabled and confined by the performance of their gendered "oriental" corporeality.

Chan's performance as JJ Chinois as Bruce Lee throws into sharp relief the labor of certain sexualized and racialized bodies to conform to but also challenge the possibilities for superpersonhood. Most obvious is Chan's labor to produce masculinity on a (biologically) female body at the same time she reveals that masculinity as performative as well as political. "Discovered" by the drag king impresario Murray Hill and debuted on the drag king circuit in New York City, JJ Chinois is both a product of and a departure from this lesbian subculture.[36] JJ Chinois was first imagined as "a beautiful hairless man-boy that girls swooned over, like gay Hong Kong star Leslie Cheung." A Cantonese pop singer and actor who starred in such films as *Farewell My Concubine* (dir. Kaige Chen, 1993) and *Happy Together* (dir. Wong Kar-Wai, 1997), Cheung modeled an Asian masculinity that offered an alternative to the more popular drag king personas Chan observed on the local scene, which were comprised of "hyper-masculin[ity], bad mustaches, bad-fitting suits."[37] This initial persona then not only challenged the valuation of particular drag masculinities at the time of his emergence but also commented on the proliferation of Asian masculinities outside the purview of the American or Western circuit of culture and capital. Notably, the Asian imports to the Hollywood movie industry who have the most name recognition are those actors who starred in the action or martial arts cinema "at home" such as Chow Yun-Fat, Jet Li, and Jackie Chan. On the other hand, Leslie Cheung's popularity in Asian popular culture (especially among swooning girls) would seem to depend on qualities otherwise despised in the West in both dominant and cultural nationalist discourses of masculinity. Chan's early performance skewered the limited imaginary that offered only certain forms of martial masculinity as desirable. In this way, JJ Chinois, as a "beautiful hairless man-boy," potentially highlighted the acts of policing that non-gender-normative persons are subject to even with minoritized and queer cultures. This version of JJ Chinois is also evident in his next incarnation as a Bruce Lee wannabe. In transfiguring Lee through this echo of Leslie, Chan juxtaposes the obsession with Lee in the West as the reigning figure of a somewhat "positive" Asian masculinity with the possibilities unlooked for but found worthy elsewhere.[38] As such, her performance demonstrates how racialized bodies are eroticized or denied erotic presence and how such representations are constructed and circulated in multiple and differently connected public cultures. JJ Chinois both revels in Lee's physicality as hardness and lampoons the sexual anxieties that seem to haunt his cinematic persona (will he or won't he get the girl?), threatening to undo hardness as a necessity for an erotic Asian masculinity. This revelation is especially significant in relation to the action or martial arts cinema that so prominently features "men looking at men" in order to rearticulate that erotic purchase (or its seeming lack) in new ways.

Kath Weston usefully warns that understanding gender as a performance can focus too narrowly on the display of consumer goods—do clothes make the woman?—and not enough on gender as a discourse and practice of social and material production.[39] But I argue that in the case of JJ Chinois the clothes *do* make the celebrity as a sort of industrial commodity and that the performance of gender (and race, as I will note shortly) *does* operate here to elaborate on consumption as a critical component of social and material production. That is, performance is and can be a form of work through which the body is construed as variable capital; in the case of Anna May Wong or Bruce

Lee, their performances were constrained by oppressive limitations intertwined through discourses of nation, race, and sexuality. Furthermore, some of those tensions dramatized in the drag king show—between the interior and the exterior self, the privilege of public mobility and the violence of normalization, and the inspiring disruption and the fear of danger—can be made to push at other pressure points where social forces constrain the available possibilities for being in the world.[40]

Performances such as those of Song Liling and JJ Chinois (or performers such as Anna May Wong and Lynne Chan) demonstrate that race also operates and acts as both a dynamic and a dramatic mode.[41] In order to pass as viable spies or stars, they must adopt a highly constructed and coded, gendered *and* racialized demeanor. These diverse performances enable important observations about performance as an ideological embodiment of historically particular discourses. These possible insights include the star's body is an industrial set piece organized and functioning as a specific set of relations, practices, and gestures. The star persona is often celebrated as a body subjected to limits—social or physical—but capable of transgressing them; the fan can be constituted through an identification with this performance. Accordingly, JJ Chinois allows us to discern and acknowledge the preparations involved in Chan's transgendered performance of a racialized masculinity, as well as the (wannabe) star's labor of putting together a distinctive style. But, despite discourses of the star as a unique force of charisma, the limits of these individualizing discourses for racialized persons are tested here, as JJ Chinois must necessarily reference, and finally reconfigure, Bruce Lee in order to construct an intelligible but subversive Asian star masculinity for an *American* audience. As such, his queer iteration of Bruce Lee amplifies and underscores some of the structuring aspects of the performance that are not voluntary or discretionary—such as the relations of power that determine, among other things, which racial bodies are intelligible, sellable, and fuckable as star material.

Sex and the Superstar—and the Wannabe

Chan began with the dream of an all-Asian boy band.[42] The boy band embodies spectacular fantasies of desirable bodies and stylized gender performances; the sentimental expressive modes that characterize the appeal of the boy band, its intensely personal address, and its spectacle of erotic masculinity also contribute to its allure within drag king subcultures.[43] An all-Asian boy band might have offered a diverse range of Asian masculinities, but unfortunately none of the band members could sing. But there is a music video, despite the apparent lack of musical talent. As evidenced by the importance of MTV, VHI, and any number of public and cable programs and networks, music videos are a primary mode for the visual representation of stars and the circulation of their images in popular cultures. These videos offer millions of viewers narratives—or even the merest suggestion of a narrative—in which they might imagine themselves in proximity to their performers. The often direct and personal address of the pop song further individualizes the star's reception by the fan who might imagine himself or herself as the center of its emotional sincerity.[44] There is little doubt that JJ Chinois had no choice but to make a music video in order to become a star.

The video *JJ Chinois* features the minimalist Wire song "The 15th" hypnotically performed by Fischerspooner (a New York City electroclash group) and announces JJ Chinois's new project, called "Bigger and Bigger, but Keep More and More SLOWLY." (This name apes the tenor of a product pitch, although there is no indication what form this project takes—an album? a film? a reality television series? It might also describe a particular skill of JJ Chinois, one that is tantalizingly sexual.) JJ Chinois slouches around his apartment in a tight, sleeveless T-shirt and white cotton briefs in a series of claustrophobic interiors. At times, he stares into the camera lens, and at times he appears to be unaware of its scrutiny. These sequences are intercut with images of a scantily clad sexpot—at one point jumping rope and bouncing provocatively out of her top—and a melancholy glamour puss. The filmmaker and performance artist Patty Chang portrays both women, neither of whom appears in the same frame as JJ Chinois. These and other props for performing a charismatic star masculinity (including a keyboard and a slept-in bed) are augmented with scenes from an obscure Hong Kong film called *Bruce Lee I Love You* (1975), another fan's labor of love for the star. Also known as *Bruce Lee: His Last Days, His Last Nights*, and *Bruce Lee and I*, the film was written by Betty Ting Pei, Bruce Lee's real-life mistress, in whose apartment his body—dead of a cerebral edema from mysterious causes—was discovered. A postmortem love letter about their affair, the film features Pei, as "herself," and Bruce Lee's stand-in, an actor named Danny Li Hsiu-hsien, who went on to star in several low-budget Hong Kong martial arts films throughout the 1970s. This film appears in the music video through a montage of hazy images and, as an apparent third- or fourth-generation copy, is subtitled in Hungarian. In these reenactments, which are also staged as a series of tight interiors, Betty and "Bruce" lounge around an apartment boozing, smoking, drugging, and fucking. These debauched scenes are paired with slow motion shots of Betty and "Bruce" bouncing on the bed in their underwear and slugging it out with satin cushions, as if to testify to the innocence of their affair. Finally both the orgy and the pillow fight culminate in his death scene, in which a glamorous Betty emerges from the bathroom to find "Bruce" writhing on the shag-carpeted floor. In a shot featured in the video, she weeps inconsolably.

In order to understand the place of this film in *JJ Chinois*, I return once again to the spectacular star body of Bruce Lee. Pertinent to this particular discussion is a historical crisis of masculinity plagued by doubt, confusion, and ambivalence as enacted and subsequently "resolved" in the action and martial arts films of the 1970s. In a period characterized by social and political upheaval and economic shifts, the action hero in the tradition of American cinema defers (if only temporarily) calamity in his spectacular performance of a disciplined and masterful masculinity.[45] In an essay examining discourses of race and masculinity in action cinema, Yvonne Tasker outlines some of the generic conventions through which the action hero is organized: "While the hero is, by definition, an active figure, he is also frequently rendered passive, subject to a range of restraints and oppressive forces. The hero is also defined in part by his suffering, which both lends him a certain tragic status and demonstrates his remarkable ability to endure."[46] Bruce Lee, in particular, addressed multiple audiences through the trope of trial turned triumph. In his internationally successful Hong Kong martial arts films from the 1970s, he articulated a tough Chinese masculinity that proved popular with Asian audiences in Asia and the United States. His performance of underdog victory resonated also with American and European black and white working-class audiences.[47] But this heroism extends beyond these filmic narratives to encompass the "man himself." His obsessive commitment to transform himself from an unvalued Chinese man into an international star animates the star text of Lee. Sometimes portrayed as an indictment of the racism of the Hollywood film industry or the triumph of a disciplined Chinese masculinity, Bruce Lee became a protagonist separate from his contribution to action cinema.[48] Against a collective racialized history of being perceived as degenerate or devious, Bruce Lee's body circulated widely as a model of health and physical empowerment. This was no easy retrofit of American orientalism, however; as the "Little Dragon," Lee's star power in the West lay in part in the racialized spectacle of his corporeality.

Lee's body is a built body, a carefully constructed instrument. But his body is also a historical situation and a valued commodity, a technologized collection of words, sounds, and images that "stands for" the person who is the star. In his seminal work on stars, Richard Dyer identifies these markers of a star image as "continuities of iconography (e.g. how they are dressed, made-up and coiffed, performance mannerisms, the setting with which they are associated and so on), visual style (e.g. how they are lit, photographed, placed within the frame) and structure (e.g. their role in the plot, their function in the film's symbolic pattern)."[49] Some of these continuities are copied in *JJ Chinois*. The video splices clips of *Bruce Lee I Love You*, specifically clips of Danny Li Hsiu-hsien acting "like Bruce," with scenes of JJ Chinois cultivating his look in his apartment alone. The video enacts layered linkages between the star, the markers that stand for the star, and the fan who learns how to wear the star's body. But this identity formation is multiple. On the historical level, Danny Li necessarily transformed himself into Bruce Lee for this role but also for his own career as a Chinese martial artist in the immediate aftermath of Lee's success. In this video, the persona being constituted through an identification with the performance of the star's body occurs between JJ Chinois and this earlier imitator's embodiment of Bruce Lee. But neither Danny Li nor JJ Chinois engages in Lee-like displays of punishing physicality in this montage.[50] Instead these scenes evince a fascination for the star's glamorous and tragic lifestyle. Circulating also in magazines, television interviews, public appearances, studio stills, and other mediums for celebrity, other productions of "Bruce Lee" make possible a reading that forestalls the primacy of Lee's films as the site where the star text is completed.

Most other interpretations of Bruce Lee draw from the cinematic traces of his martial body. Animated instead by his personal scandals, JJ Chinois's star persona foregrounds his mojo rather than his muscles. That is not to say that Lee's films are devoid of sex or sensuality. While his relationships with women in his films are usually platonic or familial, Tasker notes, "If we reinstate the eroticized aspects of the graceful movement played out in these films, it also becomes apparent that the martial arts film has evolved as a cinematic form that allows men to look at men."[51] Still, despite the apparent sexual charge of Lee's powerful erupting body and "men watching men" in close physical contact, most narratives of his films limit the possibilities for provocation to a strictly martial nature, though for different reasons.[52] His final completed film, *Enter the Dragon* (dir. Robert Clouse, 1973), a coproduction between a Chinese film company and Warner Brothers, is often cited in this regard. The James Bondian plot begins with a British intelligence officer enlisting Lee in an undercover operation to infiltrate the drug- and human-trafficking organization of the evil Han. The crime lord holds a martial arts tournament at his island fortress to recruit new henchmen, at which Lee of course dominates. Offered an array of compliant women, his brothers in arms readily choose among them for a night of pleasure. Lee selects a woman he knows is a fellow spy for the British forces, and their nighttime exchanges are strategic rather than sexual.[53] This typical absence of sex scenes can be understood, however, through alternate interpretations of Lee's star image as an object of desire.[54] Because his cinematic sexuality is rarely directed at any particular body, Jachinson Chan reads Lee's apparent asexuality as "ambi-sexuality."[55] And JJ Chinois accesses Lee's sensual presence in the scandalous narrative of his personal life, as portrayed in the farewell film written by Lee's mistress. *Bruce Lee I Love You* thus provides (with the aid of an impersonator) the missing frames from Lee's films, figuring Lee as a lover and an ultimately vulnerable body. JJ Chinois refuses Lee's hard and infallible cinematic masculinity in borrowing from this alternative archive. Rather than being "forced" to construct Lee's sexuality from the interstices of his movie narratives, JJ Chinois *chooses* to locate his erotic purchase in precisely that indeterminacy.

Another point of likeness between the film (or what parts we see) and the video is the way they address the audience. Like *Bruce Lee I Love You*, JJ Chinois seems to provide an insider's glimpse of the "real" person behind the star's image. Both might be understood as meticulously staged "home movies," featuring scenes of intimacy to offer the appearance of unmediated interaction between the viewer and the star. But this level of access to the wannabe can also force a confrontation with audience expectations.[56] The brief glimpse of a shirtless JJ Chinois in his bathroom might arouse discomfort, or perhaps desire, in response to the contradictions revealed in his *particular* embodiment of Lee's iconic masculinity. Shaggy hair tickles the back of his neck above a broad, naked back before JJ Chinois turns around and the viewer catches sight of a nipple ring piercing one of his small breasts. (The voyeuristic effect is heightened by JJ Chinois's pretended ignorance of the hidden camera.) This brief interlude, which seems to reveal JJ Chinois as a female-bodied person, is perhaps not a revelation at all but a strategy meant to seduce and also confound. And it is not unlike a recurring audience tease of anticipation and revelation in Lee's films. The initial camouflage afforded by his small stature and affected meekness, reinforced at times through disguises that draw on the invisibility of the laboring classes (rickshaw driver, telephone repairman, or elderly street vendor), is forcefully stripped away as Lee removes his shirt and exposes his muscular body at an appropriately climactic moment.

In her essay on Lee's influence on kung fu cinema, Hsiung-ping Chiao addresses this repetitive revelation in Lee's films, writing that "his bare chest and muscles unremittingly demonstrate a pristine masculinity and immediately lend him an animal-like quality."[57] On the diegetic level, this revelation manifests a physical threat against his oppressors and opponents. At the same time, Lee's gaze and the posture of his fighting body are often directed at the camera, thus interpolating the viewer into the scene. Although the content of his body's secret is different from Lee's, JJ Chinois performs in much the same manner. Through these similar strategies, both demand viewers' confrontation with their respectively built masculinities. These cinematic tropes in Lee's films provide what Tasker calls the "remasculinization" of the Chinese body. The hardness of his body and his star image in the action cinema disrupts a history of softness impressed on Asian bodies and locates that disruption in the martial display. But JJ Chinois is not interested in resolving crises of masculinity through a performance of arrested meaning or the disclosure of an interior truth. Nor does he pursue the resolution of conflict through the eruption of violence, though it could be that his disclosure constitutes a radically different order of danger to the viewer. Instead, in the glimpse of what seems to be a female breast, JJ Chinois provokes these crises while eroticizing the porosity of masculinity through his performance of its deferral. Here the likeness to the star is accompanied by a difference (or distance) that does not seem to matter in the achievement of that likeness. Further, this difference does not detract from the desirability of his masculinity as a consumable object of pleasure. As such, this scene highlights the constructedness but also the naturalness (signaled by his sure grasp on the star's suave vernacular) of JJ Chinois's erotic purchase as a slippery and sensual masculine persona.

Not coincidentally, the soundtrack of *JJ Chinois* also reflects this counterstrategy. Unlike the signature grunts and screeches that punctuate Lee's films—sounds of masculine assertion and aggressive physicality—the video's music is wistful. The lyrics of the song suggest a search for something that the chorus sadly notes "was not there."[58] There are a few possible implications here. Despite the immediacy and intimacy implied in JJ Chinois's direct address to the camera, there are a number of unrequited searches and lost, or never realized, connections in the video. JJ Chinois does not interact with either the sexpot or the glamour puss. These women might be fans or ex-lovers; the nature of their longing is undecided. On another level, we might wonder if the thing that "was not there" is the presumption of gender stability. JJ Chinois's earlier self as a "beautiful hairless man-boy" might be relevant in asking what "remasculinization" requires. Can what Richard Fung calls "a striking absence down there" in his seminal essay "Looking for My Penis," on representations of gay male sexuality, be reconfigured as an erotic absence?[59] (And can we necessarily assume that JJ Chinois doesn't have a penis? It need not be a biological one, and his personal items do include a black leather cock ring.) In this sense, JJ Chinois ironizes all sides of the debate about masculinity, sexuality, and the Chinese body. Importantly, he does so without derision or definite resolution. The lack of both a clear object of desire and sexual union, mirroring Lee's cinematic ambi-sexuality, allows him to remain available to multiple erotic fantasies. *JJ Chinois* implicitly invokes the martial arts film as a "cinematic form that allows men to look at men" in the multiple copies of Bruce Lee, and yet it skewers this arrangement's anxious eroticism through its enactment of the martial arts star's intimate self. But, while *Bruce Lee I Love You* inserts a female-bodied, feminine persona into scenes with "Bruce" to affirm a heterosexual narrative, the lack of any such interactions between the video's designated femmes and JJ Chinois reiterates action cinema's homoerotic potential. At the same time, the bathroom revelation collapses the surety of desire's object. In this manner, JJ Chinois is a commodity body available to a variety of sexual desires and practices while also implying that all possible looks are necessarily queer.

This instability of address and reception is paralleled elsewhere. During the computer-animated sequences, which also feature personal trivia and rotating items particular to JJ Chinois's star biography (I address these later), a series of vague and often subjectless communications float across the screen. These include "It's like a dream being with you like this" and "Please make me clean." Reenacting the above uncertainty, who are the "you" and the "me" in these provocative addresses? What is this dream of being together? Is this wistful affirmation or plaintive request? The yearning is coy in its lack of specificity. It is again up to viewers to provide their own interpretations. We could apply these messages to any number of the visible and invisible participants in this multilayered, multitemporal production. It could be Betty Ting Pei, who, in making *Bruce Lee I Love You*, perhaps hoped to exorcise the pain of her secret affair—or capitalize on her associations—with Lee. It could be Danny Li, grateful for the opportunity to embody his role model. It could be JJ Chinois as a dissolute lover, contemplating his (failed?) relationships with the two video vixens; JJ Chinois as the fan in an address to Bruce Lee, acknowledging Lee's influence and his debt; or JJ Chinois as the star in an appeal to his fans, both playing the role of the star in fulfilling a fan's fantasy of reciprocal intimacy and the role of the star as a commodity selling himself to an audience. All of these interpretations are possible, the latter especially, since the orange sleeveless T-shirt he wears at one point features an ink drawing of himself. This reading of the music video's dreamy dispatches creates a sense of mutual recognition, enabling, as Lauren Berlant observes, "the commodity to appear to address, to recognize, and thereby to 'love' the consumer."[60] Full of the vague yet ardent longing that defines the pop quality of universal appeal, these various addresses can be understood as part of the utopian promise of commodities to consumers—fans who can be "made clean" or fulfill a dream in the encounter with the star.

As such, the video's addresses could be Lynne Chan as the fan paying homage to a childhood fascination or the drag persona that enables her to access the star's body or Lynne Chan as the artist, asking the audience to consider the complications of such relations between differentiated subjects—stars and fans, commodities and consumers—within the hierarchies of power and sexuality implicated at sites of encounter and exchange.

Chinois and Other Charismatic Commodities

What supposedly cannot be copied must nonetheless be duplicated. In order to amplify the consumption of the star, which includes the construction of both an inimitable personality and a physical body, the star is a product whose power depends on its mechanical, and in this age digital, reproducibility.[61] Here I turn to the critical labor JJ Chinois's celebrity Web site performs in its related, if distinct, ironic counterstrategies to achieve superpersonhood.[62] As an elaborate parody and an apt metaphor, the Web site holds together and satirizes the forces of commodity standardization and individualization required for the industrial production of the celebrity in the twenty-first century.

The Macro Media Flash animation that punctuates JJ Chinois's video, featuring his slim silhouette and shag haircut in a peek-a-boo of concealment and exposure, also introduces his digital incarnation. JJ Chinois strikes a series of slouching soft-butch poses behind peepholes that realign and reposition themselves across the screen in an audience tease—not unlike those cinematic tricks that prolong the revelation of the star's body. On entering, his biography tells us, "JJ Chinois is something special. His good looks and raw-throated vulnerability bring an immediate response from fans and critics." It would seem that he knows all the right moves. He possesses dubious though unnamed talents and an easily commodifiable sensibility; downtown sexy, he affects an attitude of careless sensuality and natural celebrity. His style references the recent fashion for seventies retro, which includes the popular fascination with Bruce Lee, as well as Jimmie "JJ" Walker from the sitcom *Good Times*. We are also given the visual cues for this periodization in the site design and the mirrored shades, shag haircut, and sleeveless muscle tees that so clearly identify JJ Chinois's inheritance. Brought together, this aesthetic assemblage assumes and addresses a savvy consumer familiar with these stylistic citations.

The site further stages personal access to JJ Chinois with biographical details about his turn-ons and pet peeves (a familiar fan formula)—"D.O.B.: April 25, 1975; Birthplace: Bakersfield, California; Sign: Taurus; Fave Book: The Bible; Collects: Hard Rock Café menus, knives." The itemized display of his favorite objects strategically includes a number of racy thongs and lacy panties donated by overcome female fans, a lighter featuring a portrait of Chairman Mao, and a black leather cock ring. We are told that JJ Chinois's favorite body part is his six-pack stomach, a hardness that once again is softened by the sensitive (but not overly so) admission that he *does* cry (admitted in a stoic "Yeah"). A generic staple of star profiles and interviews in magazines from *Teen Beat* and *People* to "edgier" publications such as *Fader* and *Nylon*, these personal notes function as differentiating mechanisms for a commodity culture saturated with competing star images. Much like the scenes of intimacy staged for the video, these details of a specific and embodied presence give the star depth and personality in an audience provocation of reciprocal connection. The "Ask JJ" feature on the site even offers a user interface field where the fan can enter a question for JJ Chinois, whose cartoon image mouths words as you type. Like a Magic Eight Ball or a mechanical fortuneteller, the virtual JJ Chinois generates a series of ambiguous answers such as "I'll have to get back to you on that" and "No, you're hotter." Of course, he might also say, "This is just more of the usual conservative Christian hysteria over teenagers swallowing miles of cock."[63] This feature not only lampoons the illusion of interactivity in digital space—an illusion first and foremost because it is preprogrammed—but also the hope for reciprocity between the fan in uneven relation to the commodity or celebrity image.

It is in keeping with this ironizing tactic that the site further implies that the dream of transcending one's corporeality through aspiring to the star's body is historically constrained. Here I return to those questions of labor and capital that JJ Chinois inhabits as a queer commodity. In particular, his is a queer commodity highlighting capital's gendered and racialized hierarchies of work and laboring bodies. These hierarchies are hinted at in his personal trajectory, trapped prefame in a semirural California town: "JJ's talent was prodigious, but squandered in the morning shift as a dim sum cart pusher at the local Chinese restaurant and at the evening shift at the local steak house, Steer and Stein. But it was there that JJ was discovered by a then young Murray Hill, the legendary producer." This biographical tidbit seems to mirror those tales of discovery that litter celebrity mythologies, tales of being seen at a malt shop or walking a dog. But the language of waste ("squandered") also points to the layers of visibility and invisibility that describe particular forms of work and disenfranchisement. There is, of course, the obvious structure of specialized and hierarchically organized relationships of stars to other categories of labor in the entertainment industry. These "labor power differences," as Danae Clark calls them, construct stars as an elite labor pool separate from ordinary performers. These labor power differences are also racialized, as Asian Americans actors are called on to provide "color" but not star power. But this story also calls attention to the often effaced presence of minoritized labor in forms of leisure, referencing the ways in which the United States is not only an economy dependent on immigrant and nonwhite labor but also one that regulates what kinds of racial bodies can enter the circuits of capital and where.[64]

This biographical note also obliquely references several Bruce Lee roles in which the invisibility of his labor, as an ice factory worker in *The Big Boss* or a disguised phone repairman in *The Chinese Connection*, propels the narratives of his films. Indeed, as Tasker argues, the prevalence of such working-class characters in Lee's Hong Kong films reiterates the merit of the hero's toil. Furthermore, these roles are often understood to mirror Lee's real-life struggles to break into the entertainment business as a young Chinese man in America. JJ Chinois as a dim sum cart pusher retraces Lee's personal triumph as a figure who achieved success both *despite* and *through* his physicality and who escaped the marginal spaces that denigrated his labor. Based on the biography written by his wife, Linda Emery Lee, the 1995 biopic *Dragon: The Bruce Lee Story*, starring Jason Scott Lee as Bruce, features a scene of Bruce Lee working in the dingy kitchen of a Seattle Chinatown restaurant while dreaming of "bigger and bigger" things. His labor as a dishwasher, normatively racialized as invisible and wasteful, is repudiated by the narrative, whose outcome is presented as fate, and audience foreknowledge of the controlled economy of power Lee eventually unleashes on his detractors. As such, Lee's gendered and racialized body is both the site of policing and the primary resource for his transformation. The hope that one might escape the oppressive limitations set on the body, through which one's body might instead become a spectacular site of pleasure through the proper exertion of labor, is one that JJ Chinois would especially appreciate.

Also found on the Web site are tour dates for JJ Chinois's upcoming appearances to promote not a film or an album release but the commodity that is himself.[65] This tour allows us to further explore the work of the star (or the wannabe) as a capitalist enterprise. With stops that included both actual and fictional locations such as Target, Payless Shoe Source, Chien's Buffet, OK Egg Roll, and the Jane Addams Book Shop, JJ Chinois's itinerary of strip malls and chain stores across the United States also defines the limits of his celebrity appeal.[66] In these commercial spaces of exchange, two readings of the retail scene are linked: the utopian promise of the mall (and even the stripmall) as a spectacular space where consumers create new erotic selves, circulating, augmenting, and exchanging bodies; and the specific conditions at independent establishments and discount retailers of cheap manufactured goods.

JJ Chinois's struggles in his bid for fame amplify the labor of organizing a commodity body in both American and transnational popular cultures. For JJ Chinois and other stars, their images are crucial properties (in the legal sense as well) to their commodity selves.[67] But the star is an investment in affect and discourse as well as capital. In this sense, JJ Chinois has an advantage that is also a disadvantage; his name prefigures his commodity body but also the exclusions and hierarchies it enacts. "Chinois," a truncated metonym for *chinoiserie,* references a history of the European incorporation of orientalism in arts and crafts and fashion design. In an interview with Karen Tongson, Chan reveals that she was inspired by Asian restaurants in Paris and Vietnamese restaurants in Southern California that evocatively summoned the legacy of French colonialism to provide a "touch of class."[68] As an allusion to these imperial projects, JJ Chinois is both a fabrication, weaving together the orientalisms implicated in his stage name, and a historied saleable commodity.

Locating JJ Chinois among the goods for sale at the mall and the discount retailer especially amplifies the commercial nature of art and celebrity, posing questions about the experience of commodity consumption and the measures of value—of quality and prestige, for example—assigned to him and similar commodity bodies. The mall is a suggestive space in which to consider fluctuating values in an unstable transnational, capitalist culture. Such questions must account for multiple economic transformations in the twenty-first century, as outlined by Marianne Conroy in an essay about the discount dream, in which she describes "crises in overproduction and restructuring; straitened business environments that find many major retailers in the United States operating under bankruptcy protection; pervasive consumer cynicism about the levels of service and price provided by retailers; and declines in real income and increases in consumer debt."[69] Bruce Lee's location as a Hong Kong and Hollywood superstar traversing the Pacific in the 1970s again provides a historical precedent for our understanding; the (momentary) blow to American hegemony in the later years of the war in Vietnam and the acceleration of deindustrialization and post-Fordist modes of production, for instance, are integral to the popularity of martial arts cinema (in both the West and the East, though for different reasons) and the crises of masculinity these films enact and attempt to defer. In situating the value of the star in these larger historical circumstances and political and economic conditions, with reference to mass production, consumer capitalism, and global communications, the body of JJ Chinois suggestively tempers capital's promise of abundance with the reminder that goods—including stars—are produced through uneven transnational movements.

Implicit at the site of purchase in the American mall is the manufacturing origin of many of these commodities—Asia generally, and often China specifically—as the rise in discount retailers has forced many manufacturers to transfer production facilities to "new economic zones" overseas. Asian stars' bodies are also imported from Hong Kong and "Asia"; Jackie Chan, Jet Li, and Chow Yun-Fat joined Bruce Lee on his tortuous route to global fame through uneven circuits of transnational culture and capital. The fact that Lee was born in California to Chinese immigrants and succeeded as a property in Hollywood only after he became a star in Hong Kong is especially provocative. At the simplest level, this suggests that "oriental" sells in the West as long as it can be located materially, but also imaginatively, as coming from elsewhere. Even in a historical moment marked by the neoliberal valorization of entrepreneurs, JJ Chinois's promotion of his "global brand" must account for these constraints on his bankable star potential. Can JJ Chinois only become a star in America if he leaves and "goes back" to Asia, even though he is from cosmopolitan New York City by way of semirural Coalingua, California? Do his references to the Western vogue for *chinoiserie* and the legendary Lee—whose degrees of belonging to Hong Kong or America are sites of contention—constitute a conscious self-orientalizing strategy even as JJ Chinois refuses his martial hardness? And does this refusal to reiterate the martial masculinity of the oriental other doom his efforts?

Encore: "Bigger and Bigger"

Even if JJ Chinois has not yet succeeded in his bid for transnational fame, he promises to persevere. The hero, after all, is defined in part by his suffering and remarkable ability to endure. We still can acknowledge the significance of JJ Chinois's parody of those discourses and practices that constrain the possible avenues for superpersonhood. He is an excessively laboring body inspired but also confined by Bruce Lee's iconic presence as the first major Chinese star in the West. In this light, Lynne Chan troubles Lee's legacy through the sexual indeterminacy of his cinematic oeuvre (including its homoerotic aspects) and in fantasies inspired by his personal scandal. Against his hardness and the glorification of the martial body, JJ Chinois's queer Asian masculinity is built on an admission of "raw-throated" vulnerability. However, vulnerability is evident in other, more problematic ways that are also uncovered in this act. Among the central focuses of this essay have been the labor of the body in constructing a racial masculinity as an intentional creation and the social and material conditions that structure the possibilities of work for those bodies in a global market, managing their meaning and economic purchase at specific historical moments. It is in this fashion that JJ Chinois highlights the vulnerability of a particularized body under such conditions at the same time that he models the seduction of superpersonhood. Clearly, he works hard, laboring in multiple modes to elaborate on the complicated routes discourses of race and masculinity take and to reframe theoretical debates that might otherwise remain stuck or stagnant. Finally, Lynne Chan's fan labor constitutes a strategic category for understanding popular cultural forms both as meaningful resources and prohibitive conditions for producing and organizing configurations of our selves.

I would like to end with a confession. I am a convert, a fan of JJ Chinois. In my fantasy, I imagine a world in which JJ Chinois has achieved the superstardom he so rightly deserves and all his fans can participate together in our adoration. This is an important part of the utopian impulse behind this and similar cultural productions—the desire to transform popular culture into a counterpublic for a radically different imaginary. Because popular culture is imagined as a shared cultural resource with access to an audience of millions, we might wonder whether desire for the star's body—especially one like JJ Chinois's—can deliver a ground on which to do politics. He could be our guide, bringing us together under the shade and shelter of his star power, as his own publicity suggests: "It soon became obvious that it's easier to skin an amoeba than to catalog the 'Typical JJ Chinois Fan.' The teens were there, but so were the 'dilettantes' and the 'squares,' the 'lesbians' and the screen starlets, the celebrities and those who make them celebrities." And so perhaps it is we who should be asking JJ Chinois—*please make us clean.*

Notes

An initial version of this chapter was presented at Ohio State University as part of a lecture series in April 2003. A later version was presented at the University of California, Berkeley, for the Art, Technology, and Culture lecture series in October 2004. My thanks to both series and their organizers for the opportunity to present this work. This version owes further thanks to the artist Lynne Chan for her vision, Vernadette Gonzalez, Kathleen S. Yep, Irene Nexica, Iraya Robles, and Thuy Linh Tu for their comments and Alana Kumbier for her librarian duties.

1 Nguyen Tan Hoang, "The Resurrection of Brandon Lee," 228.

2 See the Web site http://www.geocities.com/many_bruces/ (accessed January 2003). A three-part article by Dean Meadows on Bruceploitation films, from "action cinema to cult television," was published in the British magazine *Impact* in late 2002 and early 2003. These articles can be found on the Geocities Web site. They could also be found, as of December 2004, on the Web site http://www.kungfucinema.com.

3 Nguyen Tan Hoang's essay "The Resurrection of Brandon Lee," about the Asian American porn star Brandon Lee, explores another, more prurient aspect of Bruce Lee's legacy. It is worth noting that Bruce Lee's son, Brandon Lee (not the porn star), was tragically killed on the set of the film *The Crow* when a prop firearm misfired. His early death inspired many "like father, like son" comparisons.

4 When not extolling the karate master, it trades on his exact opposite, the physically weak and inept nerd.

5 The lyrics, written and sung by Willie Hutch, include such "mystical" nuggets as "To reach that upper level, your mind, body and soul must be one / Hah! / It's a sacrifice, it takes hard work / It's a way of life."

6 Interestingly, Bruce Lee does share a screen kiss with a female costar in this video compilation, but Bruce Leroy doesn't take the hint. Here, it appears that his fan's perception of the ascetic and asexual Lee persona notably fails match the actual archive of Lee's roles.

7 Certainly, a possible reading here might suggest that Bruce Leroy's fascination with Bruce Lee is "unnatural," with all the erotic dimensions this entails, especially when such a fascination detracts from the supposedly desirable, and all too willing, VJ Laura. Bruce Lee as a substitute for "the art of making love" might instead be the substitute for the object to whom the love is made!

8 For an extended study engaged with Marxist theories of capitalist production in looking to queer artists and intellectuals, see Tinkcom, *Working Like a Homosexual.*

9 Coombes, *The Cultural Life of Intellectual Properties,* 102.

10 These questions are compounded by the racial politics of representation and publicity through which often gendered and sexual metaphors of sight (invisibility, voyeurism, pornography, and possession) are used to describe the minoritized racial subject of U.S. popular culture. While not the focus of this study, I believe that psychoanalytic theory does not offer an adequate analysis of spectatorship. As Ellis Hanson asks in the introduction to *Outtakes,* "Does psychoanalysis valorize an illusion of interiority and urge us to privatize or individualize phenomena that are more radically social and political? . . . Is the erotic—as opposed to, say, the socioeconomic, the ethnic, the racial—always the constitutive or primary site of spectatorial pleasure and subject formation?" (15). In her study of British female fans of Hollywood cinema in the 1940s and 1950s, Jackie Stacey argues that dominant modes of film criticism (specifically, in her study, feminist film criticism) do not allow complex models of identification and desire because they consider "textual meaning as fixed and the sex subjectivities of cinema spectators are read across a binaristic determinism" (25).

11 These fictions can also involve those belonging to consumers who are not fans, fictions of immorality, infidelity, sexual pathology, and so on.

12 Ewen, *All-Consuming Images,* 95–96.

13 Berlant, "National Brands / National Body," 175.

14 Originally, I wanted to do what the photographer Zoe Leonard and filmmaker Cheryl Dunye had done in the independent film *The Watermelon Woman.* A semi-fictional docudrama about a filmmaker in search of the hidden history of a fictional black actress credited as the Watermelon Woman, for the film Leonard and Dunye staged a series of "found" photographs that became "The Fae Richards Archive," in which Fae Richards appears as an apparition from a historical past that is both visible and invisible. Imagined as a beautiful black actress in 1930s America, Richards performs the stock role of the "watermelon woman" in a series of Hollywood films documented in the archives and accompanying footage. As the housemaid or mammy to a white woman, she offers comfort and comedy in bit parts that are achingly familiar, while her affair with a prominent white woman director only complicates the relationship Richards has to Hollywood and its uneven erasures. Filmmaker Dunye plays a fictional version of herself as "Cheryl," a video store clerk and amateur filmmaker who documents the frustrations and the sorrows of her search for the scattered traces of this black lesbian actress. Despite reluctant interviewees, defensive (white) archivists, and friends who interrogate her obsession with this abject image of African American women, Cheryl scraps together a complicated portrait of a performer whose other roles included singing in lesbian clubs and acting in black-cast "race films." In the resulting archive, still images from such fictional films as *Plantation Memories* feature Richards in kerchiefs and exaggerated postures that signal (in the

racialized visual language of such films) primitivism, servility, and ignorance. But in other photographs Richards poses in the familiar fashion of 1930s Hollywood studio stars, elegantly coiffed and impeccably dressed. Whether lounging on an expanse of white satin or perched on the arm of her director's (and sometime lover's) chair, Richards radiates glamour and sophistication. Drawing on a series of technological effects to produce "real" and authentic period images, these photographs permit us to see what we have not been allowed to see: not just a glamorous image but also the labor and political economy of glamour. A (deliberately) incomplete collection of personal snapshots, film stills, and publicity photographs, the archive is a moving and poignant fiction that illuminates the complicated relationship of desire and denial minoritized persons have with popular culture as producers or consumers, as stars or their fans.

15　This photograph graces the cover of *Charlie Chan Is Dead 2: At Home in the World,* an anthology of contemporary Asian American fiction edited by Jessica Hagedorn.

16　Cited in Liu, "When Dragon Ladies Die, Do They Come Back as Butterflies?" 24.

17　Anna May Wong participated in the production of her own star image as an outsider; in interviews and profiles, she was articulate about her dissatisfaction with the U.S. film industry, her sometime defection to Europe, and her dedication to her craft. Once asked by a reporter about her unmarried status (she remained unmarried, legally speaking, all her life), she referred to herself as wedded to her art.

18　Weiss, *Vampires and Violets,* 32.

19　For instance, this image of Dietrich—recognizable even without her full face pictured—adorns the cover of Andrea Weiss's *Vampires and Violets.* Cherry Smyth writes that "part of the problem of inventing a queer dyke cinema is the difficulty for lesbians of what Tom Kalin refers to as the 'revisionist aesthetic,' which pillages and pastiches a vast store of images stretching back to Genet and Cocteau. In seeking past movies to parody, lost images to reclaim, icons to glorify, dykes have always had less booty to raid. Thank god for Marlene, Greta, and James Dean" ("Trash Femme Cocktail," 39).

20　Gina Marchetti, in *Romance and the "Yellow Peril,"* offers an extended analysis of Wong's character in *Shanghai Express.*

21　Ibid., 64.

22　Liu, "When Dragon Ladies Die, Do They Come Back as Butterflies?" 23–39.

23　However flawed the film version might be, this mise-en-scène is still interesting for what it suggests. See Dorinne Kondo's interview with David Henry Hwang in *About Face.*

24　In "When Dragon Ladies Die, Do They Come Back as Butterflies?" Cynthia Liu surveys Asian American scholarship on Anna May Wong and her career. She identifies an analytic body of work whose aim, "identifying and dismantling stereotypes," she argues, is theoretically limited by a binary of "positive" and "negative" images. In this school, these critics view Wong and her cinematic legacy as "damaging" and "distorting" false images that hide the "truth" of Asian American feminine subjectivity. Liu argues against the notion that these images are consumed easily or predictably, pointing to reinterpretations of Wong's star persona in works by Jessica Hagedorn, John Yau, and David Henry Hwang.

25 Of course, there are additional layers of reference (and reception), which depend on the contexts within which the play is performed and the film is screened.

26 See, for instance, Moy, *Marginal Sights*.

27 However, even this representational truism must be complicated. In the archive of the Western imaginary, there are numerous portrayals of Asian men as rapacious and lascivious, especially during times of martial conflict—World War II and Vietnam, for instance, and in the most recent U.S. "war on terror." The "homosexualization" of Asian men through the marked quality of effeminacy in popular representation must also be interrogated carefully and critically.

28 Tasker, "Fists of Fury," 320.

29 Oishi, "Bad Asians, the Sequel," 222.

30 Ibid., 223.

31 The slippage here between *celebrity* and *star* is deliberate since we are not quite sure what it is that JJ is a "star" at doing. The continuities and discontinuities between celebrity and stardom are not the focus of my argument; suffice it to say that stars are celebrities but celebrities are not always stars. For a more extended discussion of celebrity and stars, see Marshall, *Celebrity and Power*; and Dyer, *Heavenly Bodies*.

32 Butler, "Performative Acts and Gender Constitution," 270–82.

33 Butler, *Gender Trouble*, 139

34 Mercer, "Black Hair / Style Politics," 247–64.

35 Butler, *Gender Trouble*, 139.

36 Scholarship on drag kings is still quite sparse but growing. See Halberstam, *Female Masculinities*; and Troka, LeBesco, and Noble, *The Drag King Anthology*. There is also an increasing number of other cultural productions about drag kings, including videos, personal narratives, photography, and an annual conference called the International Drag King Extravaganza, held at Ohio State University, in Columbus, Ohio, which brings these elements together.

37 Lynne Chan, e-mail interview with the author, December 2003.

38 As a *Washington Post* feature on Leslie Cheung's death noted, "Cheung was at once a pretty boy cooed over by teeny-boppers, a pop star whose songs were sung by taxi drivers, and a serious actor admired around the world for his nuanced roles characterized by an ambiguous sexuality. He was part of a wave that helped Chinese film eclipse the old 'chop-socky' confines of the martial arts genre" (Goodman, "A Letter from Hong Kong"). Cheung committed suicide in April 2003 at the age of forty-six by jumping off the balcony of a Hong Kong hotel. See also the tribute Web site http://www.goodbyeleslie.com.

39 Weston, "Do Clothes Make the Woman?"

40 I am thinking here about such drag king troupes as Boy Bands against War, who appropriated the breakup song to launch a critique of the second Bush administration. See Nguyen, "Drag Kings and Democracy."

41 While the specific contexts for the transgendered espionage of Song Liling are

radically different from the lesbian bar stage, we can delineate the ways in which political tensions and social forces find expression in the labor of her disguise.

42 Although I am no expert on boy bands, I do believe that the popularity of the form is sporadic and their shelf lives short-lived. The early 1980s saw the bilingual Menudo skyrocket to the top of the charts featuring a revolving roster of Puerto Rican teenage boys. In the late 1980s and early 1990s, the New Kids on the Block became a pop cultural phenomenon of massive proportions until rock (in the form of "grunge") returned to the charts with a vengeance.

Manufactured in the United States but enjoying massive international success at end of the twentieth century, the stratospheric pop prominence of boy bands such as N'Sync, 98 Degrees, and the Backstreet Boys (along with a slew of similar aspirants) appeared to offer a range of (mostly white) masculinities (the bad boy, the sensitive crooner, etc.) for a consuming public to choose among and adore accordingly and for drag kings to re-create on stage. As a popular form, the boy band embodies spectacular fantasies of desirable bodies and stylized gender performances. In both their music videos and their live stage shows, these acts are highly theatrical; multiple costume changes and choreographed movements accompany the sentimental, expressive modes that characterize the pop appeal of the boy band. Chan's original conception of an all-Asian boy band is important because no corporate American boy bands currently feature an Asian American member, because the only all-Asian boy bands are located in Asia, and because the success they have enjoyed relative to their American counterparts has been limited. And as yet, conversations around race and performance are still tentative at best, and ignored at worst, in American drag king subcultures. The boy band, as a four- or five-"man" singing and dancing pop musical form, became a familiar convention for drag kings in the late 1990s, from specific acts such as the Backdoor Boys to N'Sexy; troupes such as the Disposable Boy Toys and the Transformers, which incorporate a boy band number into their repertoires; and Boy Bands against War, which was formed at the start of the U.S. invasion of Iraq. See Nguyen, "Drag Kings and Democracy."

43 For more on boy bands, see Wald, "I Want It That Way."

44 See McRobbie, *Feminism and Youth Culture.* The fact that music videos are largely consumed in private domestic spaces amplifies this illusion of intimacy and identification.

45 I recognize that this is a loose description of the historical moment—the specificities of these crises of masculinity are important to the local reception of action and martial arts cinema and Lee's films in particular—and I do not mean to blur either their similarities or distinctions. Nor do I mean to suggest that all such crises of masculinity are the same or equivalent. However, a detailed overview of the meanings of Lee's films for Hong Kong and American audiences (and specifically for urban black and multiracial audiences) is beyond the scope of this essay.

46 Tasker, "Fists of Fury," 316.

47 In *The Last Dragon,* this broad popularity is dramatized at a packed movie theater

in which a racially diverse, working-class audience rowdily interacts with the screening of a Bruce Lee film.

48 In this sense, the search for the "truth" behind the star's image is both repeatedly staged and endlessly deferred, and this final yet constantly shifting inaccessibility is an integral part of the power of the star and his appeal.

49 Dyer, *Heavenly Bodies*, 62.

50 In *Bruce Lee I Love You*, there *is* a plot that unfolds outside of Betty's apartment, and does involve some fight scenes, but these are not shown in the music video.

51 Tasker, "Fists of Fury," 320.

52 Ibid.; Nguyen Tan Hoang, "The Resurrection of Brandon Lee"; Chan, *Chinese American Masculinities*; and Chiao, "Bruce Lee," 30–42.

53 I would also suggest that reading this refusal to partake in the crime lord's harem (a crime lord who is involved in sexual slavery) as necessarily "bad" problematically reproduces certain masculinist and heterosexist discourses about how manliness is evidenced.

54 Both Tasker and Chan note that gay men in Lee's films are effeminate, mincing characters who are often traitors as well.

55 Chan, *Chinese American Masculinities*, 78.

56 One Internet commentator was disgusted with the "revelations" of *Bruce Lee I Love You*, writing, "The direction of the plot is laid out within the opening scenes as [Danny] Li Hsiu Hsien playing the part of Lee drives to Ting Pei's apartment. He takes a shower, whilst she prepares the bed. *The next scene leaves a real nasty taste in the mouth for all Lee fans.* Bruce and Betty have sex whilst the Little Dragon is depicted smoking cannabis, popping pills and washing the mix down with a glass or two of the hard stuff. Next up, Betty takes a shower, Bruce is dead and she feels responsible" (Kungfucinema.com, http://www.kungfucinema.com/articles/2003–05–25–01.htm [accessed December 2, 2004]).

57 Chiao, "Bruce Lee," 42.

58 Partial lyrics for "The 15th" are "Refuted seed as if someone was watching over it / Before it was as if response was based on fact / Providing, deciding it wasn't there / Swept to it, based to it, it was not there / Providing, deciding it wasn't there / Square [swept] to it, based to it, it was not there / Re-muted fault / As if it had a cause to live for / We might have learned / As if it should have been destroyed / It was not there / It was not there."

59 Fung, "Looking for My Penis," 148.

60 Berlant, "National Brands / National Body," 186.

61 The production of stardom trades on those tropes of "democracy" that American culture trumpets as its strength and inheritance. This egalitarian fantasy posits both that stars are found (or "discovered") in the everyday course of life and that stars are nonetheless unique and inimitable personalities. Digital technologies expand on and facilitate this fantasy and its constituent parts, through which even the wannabe might produce himself or herself as a *commodity self* to be looked at as star potential.

62 Through Internet "shrines" and Web sites, the authorship of star discourses is even more dispersed; freed of institutional control, rumor, speculation, and fantasy become integral aspects of these fan labors, though these "unauthorized" discourses do not fundamentally threaten the star system.

63 Another interesting response might be, "Hey, that was like the time four of my front teeth fell out. Great for blow jobs but a gift wasted on me," or the creepier, "Shhh, baby. Shhh. Don't ruin it, just let it happen."

64 Specifically, these biographical details recall histories of Chinese migration and itinerant labor both *to* and *within* the United States. Indigo Som's recent work touring midwestern Chinese restaurants is particularly relevant here. See her essay in this volume.

65 In 2003, JJ Chinois participated in a soapbox derby and taught a pole-dancing class that culminated in an amateur strip night while Chan was in an artist's residency. See Karen Tongson, "JJ Chinois's Oriental Express, or How a Suburban Heartthrob Seduced Red America," for a fascinating study of the spatial (and suburban) imaginary of JJ Chinois's tour and interactions with locals at the soapbox derby. Tongson argues for a reading of a "dykeaspora" in locating queer subjects in these nonmetropolitan spaces.

66 In this respect, JJ's tour is not unlike the one undertaken by an immigrant transsexual, the East German Hedwig, and her band, the Angry Inch, which performs in a series of local franchises of a restaurant chain called Bilgewater's in both the 1998 stage play and the 2001 film adaptation of *Hedwig and the Angry Inch*. In these productions, both of which were written and directed by James Cameron Mitchell, this "alternative" tour follows the corporate tour of a young male rock star who stole his hits from Hedwig after a protracted affair with her, which included musical tutelage. This situation, which drives the plot, allows a similarly multilayered commentary on "mainstream" and subcultural appropriation, notions of authenticity, and the hierarchically valued embodiment and performance of star power.

67 The complex articulation of the law and property with celebrity and image is the subject of many studies, including Coombes, *The Cultural Life of Intellectual Properties*; and Gaines, *Contested Culture*.

68 Tongson, "JJ Chinois's Oriental Express," 200.

69 Conroy, "Discount Dreams," 63–64.

twelve •••

Race and Software

Wendy Hui Kyong Chun

Race was, and still is, central to conceiving "cyberspace" as a utopian commercial space. To exaggerate slightly, without race there would be no cyberspace, either fictionally or factually, for through representations of raced others—through "high-tech orientalism" and "scenes of empowerment"—one of the most compromising forms of communication has been bought and sold as empowering.[1] Invisibly, the Internet turns every spectator into spectacle, and an enormous and unending amount of energy, money, and cultural and computer programming is needed to sustain the Internet as an agency-enhancing marketplace of ideas and commodities, as a cyberspace.

In this essay, I briefly outline high-tech orientalism and scenes of empowerment and examine the possibilities opened up by projects of the Asian American science fiction writer Ted Chiang, the filmmaker Greg Pak, and the collective known as Mongrel. These projects, to varying degrees, either make race visible and difficult to consume or resist the separation of mind from body that supports dreams of superempowered using. They erode the distance between spectator and spectacle sustained by the mainly televisual and literary separation between users and raced others by attacking narratives of "technological empowerment," and by refusing to celebrate "ethnic" self-representations as unmediated, "amateur" truths. Most important, they help keep open the promise of the Internet as a democratizing medium by exploring the ramifications of vulnerability and connectivity rather than erasing them in favor of superagent dreams.

Empowering Orientalism?

As I've argued in greater detail elsewhere, foundational cyberpunk previsions, from William Gibson's 1984 *Neuromancer* to Neal Stephenson's 1993 *Snow Crash,* use "Asian," "African," and "half-breed" characters to create seductively dystopian near futures. Gibson's fiction in particular perpetuates and relies on this high-tech orientalism, a "navigate by difference" tactic in which disembodied heroes and console data cowboys emerge through disembodied representations of "local" people of color, irrevocably fixed in the past, and cyberspace is made desirable and exotic through relentless comparisons between it and Ninsei.[2] Gibson's vision of cyberspace has little or nothing in common with the Internet—other than a common 1990s fan base.[3] Inspired by the early 1980s Vancouver arcade scene, Gibson sat at his typewriter and outlined a 3–D chessboard / consensual visual hallucination called the Matrix or cyberspace in which corporations exist as bright neon shapes and console cowboys steal and manipulate data. In *Neuromancer,* cyberspace is a "graphic representation of data abstracted from the banks of every computer in the human system."[4] Even though Gibson's cyberspace does not coincide with the Internet, its seductive vision of a consensually hallucinated network in which American cowboys thrive in an unfriendly, Asian-dominated corporate world made it an origin myth in the 1990s. Cyberpunk literature, which originated with the *desire for* cyberspace rather than cyberspace itself, seductively blinds users to their circulating representations through dreams of disembodiment (freedom from one's body) sustained by representations of others as disembodied information. Cyberpunk offers unnerving, disorienting, yet ultimately readable "savage" otherness in order to create the mythic user. Rather than brushing aside the fear of odd locations, strangers, and their dark secrets by insisting that we are all the same, these narratives, like the detective fiction on which they are often based, romanticize and make readable, trackable, and solvable the lawlessness and cultural differences that supposedly breed in crowds and cities. Racial and ethnic differences, emptied of any link to discrimination or exclusion, make these spaces readable yet cryptic. Difference as a simple database category grounds cyberspace as a "navigable space"; through racial difference we steer, and sometimes conquer.

High-tech orientalism offers the pleasure of exploring, the pleasure of being somewhat overwhelmed but ultimately "jacked-in." Importantly, this pleasure usually compensates for *lack* of mastery—*Neuromancer* was written at a time when the United States seemed to be losing its status as the number one financial power. The future in *Neuromancer* seemingly belongs to Japanese and other non-American corporations—the status of the United States as a nation-state is unclear—although U.S. console cowboys still ride high in cyberspace.⁵ High-tech orientalism is not colonialism but rather a paranoid reaction to global economic and data flows. It promises intimate knowledge, sexual concourse with the other, which it reduces to data. This "will to knowledge" structures the plot of many cyberpunk novels, as well as the reader's relation to the text; the reader is always "learning," always trying to understand these confusing narratives. The reader eventually emerges as a hero for having figured out the landscape, having navigated these fast-paced texts, since the many unrelated plots (almost) come together at the end and revelations abound. This readerly satisfaction generates desire for these vaguely dystopian futures. Thus, if online communications threaten to submerge users in representation —if they threaten to turn users into media spectacles—high-tech orientalism allows people to turn a blind eye to their own vulnerability and enjoy themselves while doing so. Silicon Valley readers are not simply "bad readers" for viewing these texts as utopian, for they do not necessarily desire the future described by these texts; rather, they long for the ultimately steerable and sexy cyberspace, which always seems within reach even as it slips from the future to the past. They also yearn for cyberspace as the space of "biz."

To be clear, I am not arguing that cyberspace is inherently an orientalist space, nor am I simply condemning Gibson—his elucidation of the dependence of dreams of disembodiment on others as data could be a sharp indictment of them. As well, given that Gibson wrote *Neuromancer* with almost no technical understanding of computers and networks, such a screening is not deliberate but rather is reflective of the hype generally surrounding technology—hype that we mistake for fact at our peril. Importantly, high-tech orientalism does not seal fiber optic networks. Cyberspace, rather than closing off meaningful contact, can inaugurate it. Used as a means to get people online, it opens up the possibility of the Internet as a form of (disruptive) communications, and the gap between cyberspace and the Internet can create dissatisfaction and a desire for something more.

The obverse of high-tech orientalism is scenes of empowerment, which use readable difference in order to sell decidedly sunnier futures. Advertisements such as MCI's 1997 "Anthem" and Cisco Systems' 1998–99 "Empowering the

Internet Generation" series feature variously "raced" humans extolling the benefits of global telecommunications networks, which they are portrayed as "ready for" or already using (until the 2001 dot-com meltdown, it seemed impossible to advertise an Internet-related business in the United States without displaying some raced or differently marked flesh). The aptly named "Anthem" commercial by MCI solidified the Internet as the "medium of minds" on U.S. television. "Anthem" features variously raced, gendered, aged, and physically challenged persons chanting, in succession and in concert: "People can communicate mind-to-mind. There is no race. There are no genders. There is no age, no age. There are no infirmities. There are only minds, only minds. Utopia? No. No. The Internet, where minds, doors and lives open up. Is this a great time, or what, what?"[6] A computer screen, on which these words and corporate messages such as "MCI has the fastest Internet network" are typed, punctuates the stream of bodies and body parts while an upbeat soundtrack provides continuity.

By picturing electronic text as enabling racial—and indeed gender and age—passing, telecommunications companies counter arguments that online communications are a poor cousin to face-to-face ones. Through this tactic, they take what could be considered drawbacks to "empowering" communications, namely, duplicity and unverifiability, and spin them into features that enable "free" and agency-enhancing communications. It is not that someone could be lying to you, or that you cannot be sure who someone is or what they are sending you, but that you can transcend the physical limitations of your body. This spin positions viewers and would-be users as speakers rather than listeners, which obfuscates the fact that most people "lurk" rather than "post" and that lurkers "speak" nonvolitionally. By featuring others who directly address the audience, these commercials also mimic and manipulate the empowerment that supposedly stems from speaking for oneself. So this commercial, along with Cisco Systems' "From the Mouths of Babes" series (in which young people of color from around the world offer statistics on the Internet's phenomenal growth) and Etrade.com's series (in which a twenty-something African American woman informs the audience that she is "not relying on the government"), makes pseudo subalterns speak corporate truths.

More significant, this rewriting of the Internet as emancipating also naturalizes racism. The logic framing MCI's commercial reduces to: what *they* can't see can't hurt *you*. Since race, gender, age, and infirmities are only skin deep (or so this logic goes), moving to a text-based medium makes them—and thus the discrimination that *stems from them*—disappear. Although "no race" rather than "no racism" leaves open the possibility of racism without race, this formulation effectively conceals individual and institutional responsibility for discrimination since it posits discrimination as a problem that the discriminated against must solve. The message is not even "do not discriminate." It is "get online if you want to avoid being discriminated against." For those who are already marked, the Internet supposedly relieves them of *their problem*, of *the flesh* that races, genders, ages, and handicaps them, of *the body* from which they usually cannot escape. Ineffaceable difference, rather than discrimination, engenders oppression, and the discriminated against, rather than the discriminators, must alleviate this oppression. Not accidentally, there is only one image of an able-bodied, nonethnicized, white man. Unlike every other figure in this commercial, he does not look up or in any way acknowledge the audience. The promise of the Internet to disembody would seem to be outside his concern or, more precisely, not something about which he needs to address the audience. Unlike the others in the ad, who declare that there are no races, genders, ages, or infirmities, he is raceless, genderless, ageless, and infirmity free. He is, perhaps, the very person typing those messages to us.

As construed by MCI, then, the Internet offers us the limited textual opportunity to *pass* as this *fictional,* unmarked, white male.[7] Through its presentation of regularly consumable yet unsatisfactory bodies, and this fleeting white male placeholder, MCI merges the "equality" that stems from mass consumption with the supposed subject of the bourgeois public sphere—a subject that writes and argues rather than merely consumes and is supposedly judged by his words and acts rather than his appearance. Jürgen Habermas condemns the laws of the market for destroying rational-critical debate by replacing it with consumption. In contrast, MCI offers a way to *buy* oneself back into the realm of rational-critical debate, which is now redefined as a *marketplace of ideas.*[8] This moment of consumer communion makes us most vulnerable to the ad's question: "Is this a great time, or what?"[9]

By conflating racial and technological empowerment, by rewriting the goals of the civil rights movement from the eradication of discrimination to the eradication of physical markers of difference, these commercials conflate color with technology blindness while also restricting empowerment to the Internet. These commercials posit racism as stemming from the visual recognition of race, so the solution is color blindness. This drive to blindness and individuality represents as empowering one of the most invasive and insecure forms of communications created to date. Glorifying the power of the mouse click, they effectively screen the ways in which the Internet operates by engaging machines in an unceasing and mainly involuntary exchange of information.

Digital Divides

To repeat, cyberpunk and the "Anthem" ads represented and still represent a virtual state of affairs. Again, little to nothing connects Gibson's cyberspace to the Internet besides the desire on the part of early net enthusiasts to make Gibson's fiction an end to the Internet. In 1997, Internet usage was just starting to explode, and Internet demographics did not coincide with "Anthem." As *Falling through the Net II*—a government report that analyzed telecommunications use in 1997—revealed, white households were more than twice as likely (40.8 percent) to own a computer than black (19.3 percent) or Hispanic (19.4 percent) households were.[10] These numbers, of course, do not reveal the whole story: black Americans, as Anna Everett argues, have been using the Internet for years—and not to declare there is no race.[11] Indeed, both scenes of empowerment and high-tech orientalism screen the ways in which people of color around the world have engaged, and been engaged in, computer technology: from Chinese women employed in semiconductor factories to Indian programmers and from African American digital sound artists to Asian American net activists.

Countering corporate scenes of empowerment with "digital divide" statistics is hardly effective, for seemingly contradictory narratives about digital empowerment and disempowerment coexist nicely. Cisco Systems ran its ads, in which people of color all around the world happily offer statistics about future Internet usage (claiming they are "ready") at the same time that it devoted corporate energy to battling the digital divide. These corporate scenes of empowerment did not seek to get more raced others on the Internet (after all, these others urge viewers to enter *their* utopia); rather, they sought to convince "the general public" (in particular, business investors—these commercials played nonstop during CNN's *Moneyline*) that the Internet was a safe and happy place. Films and news features portrayed the Internet as dangerous, the debate over cyberporn saturated public dialogue, and transmitting one's credit card number online was read as an invitation to identity theft. The e-commerce revolution began in 1998. Clearly, not everyone who viewed these commercials, optimistic news reports, and Supreme Court decisions believed the Internet was a virtually realized utopia, and these texts did not single-handedly change public perception. They did, however, help to transform the public debate over the net. After the "Net as Racial Utopia" explosion, the debate was recentered on the question "To what extent does the Internet allow for democratic exchange and equality?" rather than "To what extent is the Internet a pornographic badlands or lawless frontier?" The former encourages commercial transactions far more than the latter.[12]

Corporations have no problem with the digital divide because they use the disparity between potential and actual empowerment to insinuate that they are the solution. By defining technologically produced racial equality as the ideal, they argue for increased technology adaptation until such racial (consumer) equality is reached, effectively giving themselves an unending mandate. This mandate to eradicate inequality begs the question, "Why exactly is Internet *access* valuable?" Indeed, narratives of the digital divide and digital empowerment form a circle that circumvents questions about the value of information, or the value of access alone, since the Internet—redefined through issues of social justice—becomes inherently valuable.[13] Within the United States, solutions to the digital divide also concentrate on giving raced others access to the Internet, though not to the tools and skills needed to build Web sites and maintain servers, nor to the capital necessary to build and own part of the backbone, all of which are necessary for the decommodification of information. They concentrate on tactics to make the Web more attractive to middle-income people of color. So, whereas commercials such as MCI's insist on the irrelevance of race, corporate solutions to the digital divide reintroduce race through their advocacy of racially marked Web sites—and indeed race is proliferating on the Internet, not disappearing.

The Internet *proliferates* race as a consumer category. This proliferation also constructs race or ethnicity as a category to be consumed: it encourages one to celebrate, or identify with, another race by indulging in the same "authentic" pleasures. According to Jennifer Gonzalez, this form of consumption as "passing," where one takes on a racially marked body rather than an unmarked one, stereotypes and fetishizes.[14] In her reading of "virtual worlds," Gonzales argues that the fantasy of "taking on another body" merges the postmodern subject with the transcendent subject of old to create a new cosmopolitanism. Through this new cosmopolitanism, one avoids the complex subjectivity of the other: the postmodern (virtual) subject appends various racial features to itself in order to "pass" as the other, with no regard to historical specificity or social process. Importantly, this phenomenon is not limited to cyberspace. The most banal and prevalent example of this is consumer multiculturalism as a form of "taste testing" (e.g., "Honey, let's eat Chinese tonight").[15] This idea of consuming what the other consumes, or literally consuming the other, leads to the increasing presence of racial categories as pornographic ones. Race has not disappeared on the Internet, but rather has become entrenched as a pornographic category—though importantly not simply one. Race, like so many "details," has become a database category—one that reinforces user control through the display of others. A search on Google for "asian+woman" produces more pornographic sites in its top ten hits than one on "pornography."

Many English-language "Asian" porn sites are directed at those wishing to pass or playact as authentic ethnic subjects through fetishistic or exotic desires (or, in the terms of Gibson's fiction, to employ "simstim," a technology that enables one to inhabit the skin, if not the mind, of another). The sites continually emphasize the "exotic" or the "authentic" in their descriptions and address their users as "samurai" or "papa san."[16] For instance, the introduction to asiannudes.com encourages surfers to become a samurai.

> You are welcome to our dojo! Look no further, traveler. You have found the Clan of Asian Nudes, filled with gorgeous Asian women in complete submission. Take them by becoming a samurai. Our dojo houses the most incredible supermodels from Japan, Vietnam, China, Laos, and San Francisco's Chinatown! Their authentic, divine beauty will have you entranced nightly. New girls are added almost every day, their gifts blossoming before you on the screen.

Whether the viewer is Asian, Asian American, or non-Asian, the site seeks to make him or her feel like all-powerful samurai, all-powerful users—spectators rather than spectacles. This open invitation to "become samurai" reveals the mediated nature of identification since Asians and Asian Americans too must pass as samurai. (Given that most of the Hapa porn star Asia Carrera's fans are Asian or Asian American, a significant portion of these Web sites' visitors is probably the same.[17] This complicates any simplistic reading of the orientalism involved in these sites and of the significance of male white figures in them.) Clearly, passing as a samurai differs from passing as an invisible white male, but both require concurrent identification and misrecognition, as well as the objectification of others. If pornography in general, as Linda Williams has argued in *Hard Core,* is linked to the "frenzy of the visible"—the increasing desire to "see" and "know"—these Web sites reveal the link between pornography and the frenzied display of authentic ethnic knowledge. For instance, xxxasians.com claims that it has "Asian Sex Shows! Better Than Amsterdam. We hit the sides streets of Singapore and the remote hidden away places in Bangkok to find the best for you. . . . Asian Porn at it's best!! 100% legit Asian films. Don't be fooled by these other Asian / American sites. We have the best LEGIT Asian porn, shot straight from the backwoods of Asia." The privileged position of the viewer depends on the reduction of authentic others to flesh. The fantasy here, as in most mainstream pornography, is the fantasy of catching the authentic other unawares (in "the backwoods of Asia"!), so that it reveals its secrets to the viewing subject. These Asian porn sites, which, like all Web sites, endlessly circulate the *same* pictures, offer the lure of newness or breaking news. "Want something new?" asiannudes.com asks, "Having the largest Asian data base, we add new girls to our site every day! Other sites add pics weekly or monthly. But not here! At Asian Nudes, we present you with new girls every day, GUARANTEED!"

Although the content of pornographic Web sites may be intended to make their viewers seem all powerful, pornography's elucidation of visceral responses—the ways it moves its viewers—hardly enables "supercontrol." As well, porn sites are usually anything but empowering for the users who consume these images. They rewrite browser defaults through Java scripts so that new windows open when you try to close them, and your back button takes you to another porn site. They deluge your inbox, collect internet protocol (IP) information, and track their visitors. On pornographic sites (and commercial sites more generally), users experience the greatest disparity between their perceived and actual levels of control. In order to compensate for the ways in which interactivity breaches the self, in which the electronic self emerges through the call of another (a call that, unlike linguistic calls, cannot be read or heard), dreams of superagency emerge.[18]

Refusing Markets

Race may be a pornographic (consumer) database category, but this does not mean that all references to it on the Internet are racist, all pornography simply reinforces racism, or consumption is always racist. As Ernesto Laclau and Chantal Mouffe have argued,

> interpellated as equals in their capacity as consumers, ever more numerous groups are impelled to reject the real inequalities which continue to exist. This "democratic consumer culture" has undoubtedly stimulated the emergence of new struggles which have played an important part in the rejection of old forms of

subordination, as was the case in the United States with the struggle of the black movement for civil rights."[19]

Consumer equality—and the demand for autonomy both spurred on and denied by its promise—is part of the democratic adventure; it is an extension of the logic of equivalence beyond what has traditionally been considered the political and public. If "the public / private distinction constituted the separation between a space in which differences were erased through the universal equivalence of citizens, and a plurality of private spaces in which the full force of those differences were maintained," the demand for new social rights seeks to dissolve this distinction and explode the political by turning subordinate relationships into antagonistic ones.[20] Cyberpunk and the rhetoric of the Internet as a racial utopia seek to eradicate antagonism by offering a space of virtual equality and autonomy, reworking the antagonism so that domination stems from one's very body and making the political dissolve within the technological. In doing so, it makes one's body something to be consumed and makes one's race a commodity in order to erase it. This corporate hijacking of democratic logic works to ensure inequality. Thus, effective antiracist uses of the Internet must resist both the commodification and the erasure of race while taking advantage of the demand for equality embedded within consumer culture. They must also attack the separation of mind and body that drives the superuser construct and refuse to employ a "navigate by difference" technique that uses people of color to mark a dystopian future.

The noncyberpunk science fiction of Ted Chiang offers an interesting counterpoint to Gibson's Neuromancer. Given Chiang's background—a degree in computer science and employment as a technical writer for the computer industry—his fiction is surprisingly devoid of references to computers; it focuses instead on religion, aliens, mind-altering drugs, and mathematical dilemmas. Also, if Neuromancer described cyberspace as a means to escape one's flesh, Chiang's fiction insists on the indivisibility of mind and body and troubles the assertion that a "handicapped" or gendered body should naturally desire to be upgraded. In "Understand," the protagonist, Leon Greco, recovers from a coma after a dose of Hormone K, which also elevates his mental capacity. Choosing to become an experimental subject in order to receive more doses, Greco eventually outpaces the "simple" humans who wish to study or profit from him and begins to make sense of the patterns of everyday life: emotional responses move from mystery to logic.[21] This control over one's mind does not come at the cost of leaving the "meat" (the term for the body used by Gibson, which stems from the Meat Puppets) but rather enhances one's body: Hormone K restructures the brain and leads to greater physical agility. Greco begins to know his body afresh,

> as if it were an amputee's stump suddenly replaced by a watchmaker's hand. Controlling my voluntary muscles is trivial; I have inhuman coordination. Skills that normally require thousands of repetitions to develop, I can learn in two or three. I find a video with a shot of a pianist's hands playing, and before long I can duplicate his finger movement without a keyboard in front of me.[22]

Unlike cyberpunk, which separates mental from physical agility through virtual space, "Understand" denies the difference between simulation and actuality, software and hardware. In doing so, it makes the unremarkable white male body itself handicapped, revealing its vulnerability and incompleteness, and portrays the prosthesis as an effect of changes within the body. This control over one's body also leads to control over other people's emotions. The narrator boasts, "I've developed abilities reminiscent of the mind-control schemes offered by tabloid advertisements. My control over my somatic emanations now lets me provoke precise reactions in others. With pheromones and muscle tension, I can cause another person to respond with anger, fear, sympathy, or sexual arousal."[23] Thus, control is not linked to individual freedom but control over others: the self is not separate from others precisely because our actions stem from our reactions. This manipulation of others, this reduction of others and one's body to control systems, means that everyone is information—everyone is an artificial intelligence—and because of this everyone can be destroyed (in an odd parallel to *Neuromancer*, the narrator in the end self-destructs by intuiting "the Word").

Chiang's fiction similarly stresses the fact that discrimination does not stem from one's body but from the behavior of one's peers. In "Hell Is the Absence of God," Chiang's rewriting of the story of Job, in which he explores the ramifications of an unjust God, the world resembles the Old Testament: angels visit the earth, causing both grave injury and healing. The protagonist, Neil, is born with a "congenital abnormality that caused his left thigh to be externally rotated and several inches shorter than his right."[24] Although he wondered at times if his abnormality was a punishment from God, "most of the time he blamed his classmates for his unhappiness. Their nonchalant cruelty, their instinctive ability to locate the weaknesses in a victim's emotional armor, the way their own friendships were reinforced by their sadism: he recognized these as examples of human behavior, not divine."[25] (This separation between divine and human behavior, however, will be tried by the divine's unjust rejection of Neil). Another character, Janice, pretty, confident, and charismatic, and whose legless condition is the result of divine intervention, is miraculously cured but left with no purpose in life (she had been an inspirational speaker to those with disabilities, telling them to reach for the strength God has given them). In the same visitation that kills Neil, Janice is blinded and reduced to a dime-a-dozen blind witness to the power and love of God.

If Chiang's fiction explores physical abnormalities, it is surprisingly silent on the question of race and racial discrimination. His fiction, indeed, is curiously short on all physical description (except the descriptions of infirmities key to "Hell"). A surname dropped here and there, historical circumstances, and a chance reference to someone's blue eyes do reveal racial characteristics, and his future seems surprisingly un–Asian American. However, the fact that he declines to talk overtly about race does not mean he avoids it. Science fiction often addresses questions of race indirectly through stories of aliens and other implausible physical differences. Rather than addressing these here, I want to focus briefly on the story that comes closest to directly approaching questions of race, "Liking What You See: A Documentary." This story, formatted like a documentary transcript, follows campus debate over "lookism" and the mandatory adoption of "calliagnosia," a technology that negates the effects of beauty by blocking the neural pathways that respond to them. By setting the story as a debate over the adoption of "calli," Chiang portrays technology as not solving the political but rather as part of a political process. The upending of this process through malevolent corporations and their use of deceptive advertising techniques also nicely reveals the limits of the type of liberal debate idealized on college campuses.[26]

Calliagnosia enables one to recognize faces and facial attributes but blinds one to beauty, which, our resident neurologist explains, is surprisingly consistent across cultures. Beauty is so consistent because it is related to issues of evolutionary fitness: beauty approximates the mean of a population (the closer to the mean, the more genetically fit and therefore the more beautiful); it stresses symmetry, which implies resistance to environmental stressors; and it stresses good skin, "the single best indicator of youth and health."[27] Calliagnosia thus supposedly evens "the odds; it takes away the innate predisposition, the tendency for such discrimination to arise in the first place." Interestingly, although lookism can be prevented technologically, racism cannot. Attempts to use similar technology to induce race and ethnicity blindness have resulted in failure, with the test subjects unable to distinguish between similar-looking individuals. As the recurring neurologist explains, "There's no neural pathway that specifically handles resentment towards immigrants, any more than there's one for Marxist doctrine or foot fetishism. If we ever get to true mind programming, we'll be able to create 'race blindness,' but until then, education is our best hope."[28] As Thomas Foster has argued,

> This story complicates simplistic notions of race as either mere culture or mere physical. The story implies that these kinds of technologies could only produce race-blindness or neutrality if race were a purely natural phenomena, while it can leave racial perceptions untouched only if race is just a cultural construction. The story also implies, however, that either interpretation of race is unduly reductive.[29]

Foster also argues that the fact that Chiang links race and beauty through population "problematizes the sociobiological premise that the natural perception of facial beauty can be sharply distinguished from the cultural perception of racial difference."[30]

Chiang's separation of beauty from race, however complicated, raises several questions. Why is it that beauty is a *cause* and race is not? What is at stake in this elevation of supposedly evolutionary impulses and physical manifestations? Can racism be boiled down to "resentment against immigrants" inseparable from Marxist doctrine or foot fetishism? Positing racism as resentment against immigrants, as a form of xenophobia, once again focuses attention on the relationship between race and population and implies that once one sufficiently integrates a genetic population racism should fade. This threatens to naturalize racism within the United States against Asian Americans that stems from them being marked as forever immigrant, even though they have been part of the United States for over a century.[31] The biggest question Chiang's fiction poses is: What about the racial stereotypes that have been so key to the selling of computer technology and a certain type of future? Is there a way to address this question directly, perhaps by directly inhabiting stereotypes, by facing head-on the question of an Asian future?

The work of the Asian American filmmaker Greg Pak addresses these issues. His feature film *Robot Stories,* which is comprised of four shorts, presents a future inhabited by Asian Americans (but not for that reason terrifying) and explores the parallel between robots and Asians that lies at the core of high-tech orientalism. To follow the reductiveness of the promotional materials, which claim that "everything is changing . . . except for the human heart," the "message" of *Robot Stories* is encapsulated by the introductory credits, which begin with the now stereotypical stream of ones and zeroes. However, rather than these combining to produce the name of the actors and crew (as in *Ghost in the Shell* and *The Matrix*), the credits interrupt this diagonal stream (which mimics the path of the flying robots in "Robot Fixer," one of the film's segments). As well, little robots are revealed to be the source of the ones and zeroes. After they are revealed, one malfunctions, turns a different color, and produces a two. Soon all the robots follow, turn various colors, and produce all sorts of colorful base-ten numbers. Thus, in the end robots turn out to be colorful and to operate in the same manner as humans. The sound-track features a country and western song telling mama to let herself go free. Although the humanism and sentimentality seems relentless at times (perhaps compensated for in part by the fact that the first two shorts were submitted for a Mother's Day competition), Pak's humanism does have an edge. Through his stories, he both asserts Asian Americans as human through their opposition to robots *and* deconstructs the opposition between humans and robots. In "Robot Child," an Asian American couple takes care of a robot baby for a month in hopes of being given a real baby to adopt.[32] Taking care of a raceless robot, it is hoped, will make these stereotypically work-driven people human, especially the nonmaternal Marcia Ito, who is scarred by memories of her own mother; Roy Ito turns to his wife at the agency and says that this will make them "real" people, a "real" family. Although Roy seems to be the most committed to having a child and to nontraditional gender roles (the child and he bond quickly, and the child and Marcia reject each other's awkward gestures), he soon leaves for Japan, in proper husbandly fashion, to pursue a project that will secure the child's future. Turning to her father to find a software solution to the problem of baby care, Marcia returns home to a robot child gone mad. Deciding in the end not to return the robot and thus disappoint Roy by jeopardizing their chance of ever adopting, Marcia goes after the "little fucker," only to find it, like herself so many years ago, crying in a closet. Breaking down in tears herself as she identifies with the robot, the "mother" and robot finally bond.

In the next story, "Robot Fixer," a mother, wrought with grief, guilt, and anger over her son Wilson, who is in a comatose state after an accident, is driven to complete and repair his toy robot collection. Obsessively fixing these robots—showing them the care she felt her son was never able to give— becomes a way for the mother to deal with her son's accident and his failure to live up to her dreams. Through these robots, she comes to respect the interests and ways of her son, who seems to have been a bit of a robot himself: one coworker describes him as a "G9," an office robot, and as a child he played endlessly with these toys, perhaps dreamed of them. The mother becomes obsessed with one robot in particular, whose wingless condition stems from her carelessness while vacuuming. Stealing a rare female figure for her wings, she accidentally handicaps it as well. As the son's body parts are distributed to needy Asian Americans, the mother returns home, carrying a prized one-winged robot, which she no longer feels the need to fix. Insisting on the importance of parts, as both a human and a robot condition, this story, like "Robot Child," portrays Asian Americans as robots, as ideal workers, to break down the opposition between robot and human, Asian American and white.

The next story, "Robot Love," moves from this Asian American son who is "like" a G9 to a pair of G9 robots that are "like" Asian Americans. These G9 robot coders, raced Asian, are perfect workers (much better than their real Asian American counterparts, who play video games in their spare time), working continuously; following the commands of their bosses and their "inner" female voice, which reminds them "you have work"; and accepting sexual harassment (both male and female robots are objects of scopic desire). The male G9, Archie, attempts to interact with his human coworkers and is rebuked by all except a nerdy white sysop, Bob, who sympathizes and identifies with him. Bob allows Archie to call him by name (after Bob is teased by his coworkers). He also allows Archie to leave the building to pursue a female G9 after a coworker calls the pair of them "fucking freaks." The audience, too, is made to identify with Archie: not only are many shots taken from Archie's point of view, but the audience's view goes dark when Archie is turned off. This story brings out nicely the relationship between sexual exploitation and reduction and information brought about by high-tech orientalism. Its ending, in which the two explore robot sex by using the female plugs in their backs for other purposes, both reinforces and displaces heterosexual normativity.

Pak's melding of Asian American and human through his use of the science fiction genre, in which anything seems possible, seems to have worked: almost all the critics who reviewed *Robot Stories* emphasized its universal "human heart" angle and its differences from blockbuster sci-fi films rather than its status as an "ethnic film" or its relationship to other Asian American films. This silence on the question of race, however, is peculiar. Besides being in accord with the universal liberal values seemingly embodied by this film, it probably also stems from an unwillingness to explore Pak's film with negative stereotypes of Asian Americans (robotic workers, dragon ladies, etc.). Though perhaps excessive in its emphasis on Asian Americans as human (but importantly not the *only* humans), this is not a feel good movie in which hardworking Asian Americans overcome adversity in order to emerge as a model minority. At the same time, Pak's film is sanitized—*Robot Stories* does not address directly questions of oriental sexuality explored in his popular short piece *Asian Pride Porn!* (one of the top ten downloads from Atomfilms.com in 2003). As Thuy Linh Nguyen Tu has argued, *Asian Pride Porn!* is a hilarious infomercial send-up of the adult porn industry.[33] Featuring David Henry Hwang as a narrator, it begins with Hwang sampling the usual "Oriental Blossoms" type of pornography but then saying, "I don't need guilt over the sexual oppression of women of color and anger about the absence / emasculation of the Asian male in America media." His solution? *Asian Pride Porn!*—a collection of politically correct pornography featuring empowered Asian American women and sexy Asian American men that allows onanism to become a form of activism. Pak, in an interview with Tu, explains:

> "Sex films are *the* most successful films online," says Pak, "so I knew there would be an immediate audience for *Asian Pride Porn!*" Having "figured out that sex and jokes are what people use the Internet for," he decided to make a product that would cater to what they wanted, but would also send out "a little subversive message. . . . I figure I can bitch and moan about representations of Asian men and women, or I can make fun of it."[34]

By using the Internet to make fun of representations of Asian men and women, Pak seeks to reach a wide audience that may misread his short but would certainly never attend "a fist-raising lecture on the politics of representation."[35]

Audience reaction to *Asian Pride Porn!* has certainly been interesting. Although the majority of the reviews on Atomfilms.com have been positive (mostly because they view it as a great parody of representations of Asian Americans but sometimes because they view it as a send-up of political correctness), a substantial number of posters have given it the thumbs down, asking, "Where's the porn?" Most revealing have been responses such as those posted by Critic_Man on June 6, 2002—"Racial Slurs + Porn = Great Comedy! Well, at least it should. 'Asian Pride Porn' just isn't funny"—and by Anonymous on July 22, 2002—"If i were blind and deaf and this would be the only thing I would ever be able to see in all my days, I would stay blind and deaf not to ruin my perseption of the world." These responses expose the ways in which Pak's parody messes with normal expectations, forcing people to confront issues they would rather not confront and disturbing the usual formula of racist humor.

This use of technology to critique technology, to create a debate that moves beyond cultural and national borders, is also exemplified by the software art projects of a "digital collective" called Mongrel, which is based in the United Kingdom and Jamaica. The group's search engine, Natural Selection, for instance, ties antiracist Web sites to racist searches. As Graham Harwood, part of the Mongrel core, explains to Matthew Fuller,

> Well basically, it's the same as any other search engine. The user types in a series of characters that they wish to have searched for. The engine goes off and does this and then returns the results. If you're looking for sites on monocycles, that's what you get. If you're looking for sites on elephants, that's what you get. As soon as you start typing in words like "nigger" or "paki" or "white" you start getting dropped into a network of content that we have produced in collaboration with a vast network of demented maniacs strung out at the end of telephone wires all over the place. The idea is to pull the rug from underneath racist material on the net, and also to start eroding the perceived neutrality of information science type systems. If people can start to imagine that a good proportion of the net is faked then we might start getting somewhere.[36]

Natural Selection is an elegant hack on search engines: it uses another database to run its nonracialized queries, illustrating nicely Mongrel's tactic of "taking on the media by mounting it from the rear" (as does its commissioned reworking of the Tate Museum site, which loads behind the official one). Designed to dispel the specter of "neo-nazi and racist material on the web" through parody rather than censorship, Natural Selection highlights the duplicity of electronic communications: advertising Natural Selection as a way to "stop you smearing skin lightener on your computer," Mongrel and its associated network of "demented" content providers offer parodies of racist Web sites, such as Goldhorn's "Racially Motivated Fuck Fantasia," as well as By Bad Boy Byju's "Aryan Nations," which reveals how "pure English" was always overrun with the language of the colonized.[37] These sites attack the reliability and authenticity of online representations of raced others. If the user as super-agent emerged partly as a way to blind users to the constitutive duplicity and unreliability of "information," this attack belies the value of the "Information Superhighway" and offers an opportunity to rethink the Internet as a way to obtain publicity.

The Natural Selection Web sites are not simply antiracist. As Matthew Fuller explains, "If people are going to check it out, they need to be looking for more than a punchline, or a nice neat 'anti-racist' or 'multicultural' solution."[38] They should also be prepared, in some cases, to be confronted with pornographic images that expose the thin line between white supremacist fetishism and gay pornography, to listen to white supremacist punk spliced together with black nationalist rap, and to be interrogated by Java script alerts. To make race "hard to consume," the Natural Selection Web sites deny the "distance" needed for a color-blind subject to emerge. They also refuse to offer authentic images of others as a way to counter the racist stereotypes that are perpetuated online—they refuse to confess their (sexual or ethnic) "truth" to the user for the user's edification. As Rey Chow argued in "Gender and Representation," self-representations do not get us out of the bind of representation since they, too, operate as "voluntary, intimate confessions" that can buttress power.[39] Rather than presenting themselves as authentic amateurs "outside" representation, these sites interrupt the *pleasure* of knowledge, the pleasure and mastery of the user.

Dimela Yekwai's "antiviral" site, for instance, juxtaposes the words of "Venus-Fly-Killer" against the racist words of "Bombarded-Images."[40] Using pronouns such as *I* and *you*, these poems establish a personal relationship between these voices and the user, as well as between each other, setting up what Yekwai calls a "triple-consciousnessed Afrikan virus." The Venus-Fly-Killer section begins with: "Let me introduce myself / I am ≫ Venus Fly Killer ≪," whereas the "Bombarded-Images" poem begins with: "Let me introduce myself / you ≫ Black-bastard ≪."[41] In the "Venus-Fly-Killer" poem, the narrator's lyrics kill racism, which she figures as flies; in the "Bombarded-Images" section, the white male narrator bombards the user with racist epithets, explaining how the "blessed-race" used genetics to extinguish blacks and create a "lily-white" environment in which the remaining people live with bubbles on their heads.

In addition to these conflicting addresses, Yekwai's Java script alerts interrupt the user, highlighting "responsibility" (the call of the other precedes the "user" or self). The first alert informs the user and the narrator of "Bombarded-Images," "You can't get rid of me." Once the user clicks "OK," Yekwai's spinning head emerges in a small window on the upper-right-hand side of the monitor. The virus she protects against (her spinning head "accompanies" us throughout our travels) is racist information: "To / help you in your quest for / truth, For life itself, as I / have stated earlier, I will now / traverse the INTERNET with / you, The highway on which most / of these lies lurk, I can only / alert you to their hiding / places / Make the choice NOW! / YOU HAVE THE / POWER!!" ("Venus-Fly-Killer"). Once her head has emerged, more

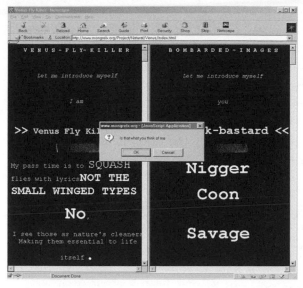

Dimela Yekwai's Web site uses Java script alerts to interrupt the user, controlling his or her interactions with the racist and anti-racist poems on the site.

alerts bombard would-be users. First, they are offered an epithet, such as "Lazy Bums"; in order to continue, they must click "OK." Then they must answer the question: "Is this what you think of me?" Using the default settings of Java, this alert offers two answers: "OK" or "Cancel." If you answer "OK," you are taken to the specific section in the "Venus-Fly-Killer" poem that addresses this racist epithet. If you answer "Cancel," you are taken to the section within the "Bombarded-Images" poem that perpetuates the racist term. These alerts leave no position for denial, no way to say no, no way of putting the site in the background. So, if you have the site in one window but are working in another, your operating system interrupts you and lets you know that Netscape Communicator needs your immediate attention. Yekwai's site is interactive but in a manner that belies interactivity as user controlled.

Another Mongrel project, National Heritage, confronts racism as a global national heritage. Describing National Selection as an "abortion" on "cyber-civilization," it wages "info-war against the racially-exclusive, US west coast eutopian nonsense" and seeks to take the "future" away from those "who left us out of the past."[42] By insisting on this "heritage," it historicizes and dissemi-nates images of raced others while at the same time refusing to offer users ethnographic images. National Heritage uses seemingly stereotypical or rep-resentative "amateur" racial specimens, which are in fact composites of numerous "friends" of Mongrel, drawn from their Colour Separation project. These images are also offered in a grid that depicts them in varying colors. In the National Heritage installation, the user must spit on these images by pressing a mouse button in order to persuade them to "tell" their stories (spitting on these images also changes and produces their masks). This spitting not only establishes these persons' experiences as bruised—and relationships in general as conflictual rather than peaceful—it also implicates the user as part of a racist society. However, through this spitting, understanding and mask changing can also emerge. Through this denial of indexicality, Mongrel seeks to show how

> constructions of race in the form of mental images are much more than simple indexes of biological or cultural sameness. They are the constructs of the social imagination, mapped onto geographical regions and technological sites.
>
> These fabrications of race have traceable links to historically specific relations, from those informing the experience of slavery, migrant labour, colonisation, to those affecting friendship and family life. Racial images are pregnant with the social and political processes from which they emerge and to which, in turn, they contribute, and images of different races articulate the political and economic relations of races in society.[43]

Through fabrications of "people that never existed," Mongrel insists on historical and economic context. By exposing the duplicity central to digital imaging, they expose the duplicity central to racial stereotyping. Mongrel attacks the premise of these supposedly authentic images, showing that such constructions can only be fabrications.

The mask portrays interactions as always mediated. According to Mervin Jarmin, another core member of Mongrel,

> I believe the mask to be one of the most defining aspects of the whole project in more ways than one; the mask represents the mask that I always have to wear at the point of entry into Britain, it represents the mask that I wear repeatedly as I go about my everyday activities in this lovely multicultural state. . . . And then it also represents the mask that mongrel has to wear in sourcing resources for the project. So you see the whole National Heritage project is a constitution of the mask.[44]

Rather than stereotypical raced selves, National Heritage reveals the mask—that is, the state of passing—as the default mode of using. Just as the figure of the mask reverses the relation between stereotype and passing, Mongrel's interfaces and software reverse the usual system of software design; they produce interfaces and content that are provocative—even offensive—in order to reveal the limits of choice, to reveal the fallacy of the all-powerful, race-free user. They also produce software tools, such as *Linker*, that are extremely easy to use and work with historically "unwired" communities to produce beautiful digital projects.

Mongrel's project of spreading critical literacy about the Web through projects that move along the same trajectory as racist terms, brilliant as it is, also runs into the problems associated with all parodies, namely, the question of audience. As with Pak's projects, there is no guarantee that readers will recognize Mongrel's sites as parody rather than the "real thing." This difficulty is exacerbated by the fact that people "surf" rather than "read" the net. How many users, for instance, will read Yekwai's entire poem? How many will recognize Critical Art Ensemble's bio.com's site as a parody (arguably, the "real" eugenics sites to which it links are the most terrifying)? Making Natural Selection accessible to its so-called target audience—those genuinely searching for racist terms—is complicated by the fact that Natural Selection is currently offline (search engines view it as a hack and refuse access). Regardless, other search engines do index these sites, and perhaps this indexing is the best way to ensure success. If a search of "asian+woman" on Google could bring up Goldhorn's "racially motivated fuck fantasia," then perhaps we would be getting somewhere. Kristina Sheryl Wong's site, Big Bad Chinese Mama, which satirizes mail-order bride and Asian porn sites, takes such an approach. As she explained to the *Village Voice,* Wong began copying porn sites' Meta tags (information tags that do not appear on the Web page, but are embedded within the source code) in order to rank higher on search engines: "They [Meta tags] were huge, and would be jammed full of search terms like 'blow job,' '69,' 'ass,' and 'dutch'—I don't even know what 'dutch' is. . . . Now I love to check my statistics and see what people typed in to find my site. One time, it was 'Eskimo-fucking Cambodian women.' "[45]

All of these sites, however, raise the question "What next?" Harwood, discussing the site Colour Separation, argues that "in this work as in the rest of society we perceive the demonic phantoms of other races. But these characters never existed just like the nigger bogeyman never existed. But sometimes . . . reluctantly we have to depict the invisible in order to make it disappear."[46] What remains to be made clear is how these depictions will make the invisible disappear. Clearly, the grid structure of Colour Separation, which shows the various transformations and their masks, troubles "natural" assumptions about race and makes the viewer pause, perhaps even pause in the ways that Mongrel intends. But, given the increasing tendency to view *culture*, rather than *biology*, as the term that creates irreconcilable differences, a type of racism Etienne Balibar calls "neoracism," the insistence on biological fluidity is not enough in and of itself.[47] Taken as a whole, Mongrel's projects interrogate both the biological and the cultural. The pertinent question then becomes "How can one highlight the whole given that surfers move from part to part?"

Further complicating this work is the question of reincorporation. The presence of Mongrel's Uncomfortable Proximity site behind the Tate site does mount the media from the rear, but it also becomes enfolded within the official site itself, revealing the incredible flexibility of what they call "bourgeois sensibility." Uncomfortable proximity can translate into uncomfortable incorporation, and the Internet exacerbates this tendency since it does not allow for "outsides"—everything becomes yet another window within the same screen. Mongrel's work is within the circuit, no matter how vehemently it may claim to be outside it. This is not a condemnation, for there are different ways of being "inside," but this fact does pose another problem to National Heritage: making users spit may expose our relation to another's pain, but it also flattens differences between users. Also, making the "faces" speak after being spit on exposes the ways in which the other speaks its truth in response to the demands of the would-be user or subject, but it forecloses the possibility of silence and refusal. It would be intriguing to have one face that could not speak, that refused to speak, no matter how much one spit. Such an intraface would bring out more clearly the violence associated with making one speak and would also explore the possibilities of silence.

Regardless, Mongrel's projects highlight the fact that the pornographizing of difference does not close the possibility of the Internet as public, as a new, more open means of textual communication with others. It offers us a point from which to begin an analysis of the Internet as a rigorously public medium. To begin this analysis, though, we must explore the consequences and possibilities behind intrusion and disembodiment (albeit disembodiment in a nontextual sense). Disembodiment—not disembodiment as empowerment—has always been part of representative democracy. As Claude Lefort observes, "It is at the very moment when popular sovereignty is assumed to manifest itself, when the people is assumed to actualize itself by expressing its will, that social interdependence breaks down and that the citizen is abstracted from all the networks in which his social life develops and becomes a mere statistic."[48]

Thus, democracy, rather than creating individual speakers fully in control of their actions and respected as individuals, reduces citizens to abstractions whose reactions are measured statistically. This same abstraction takes place in political discussions on the Internet. At the very moment when individuals are assumed to be engaging in public discussion, their opinions are abstracted and their texts compromised. During the 1998–99 debate over President Bill Clinton's impeachment, for instance, electronic communications enabled more contact between citizens and their representatives; sites such as Moveon.org and electronically forwarded e-mail petitions made contacting representatives as easy as clicking a mouse button. This arguably revealed that the Internet can lead to more meaningful participation by the citizenry—rather than simply registering a vote during elections, they were taking a more active and textual role in democracy (it was not simply a vote, it was an e-mail). On the other hand, the sheer number of e-mails sent guaranteed that they would remain largely unread, and they often crashed representatives' e-mail servers. Read or not, these e-mails served as a harassing message whose import was measured by *number*, just like votes. Furthermore, these e-mails inverted the relationship between header and body; given that many were forwarded, and thus identical, the subject header came to represent the message. Through the subject headers, these e-mails were quickly divided into pro- or anti-impeachment camps. Finally, e-mail eradicated the semblance of personal dialogue between representative and represented. Although a signed letter of acknowledgment tried to sustain the fiction of personal contact and concern, the automated e-mail "thank-you" exposed the mechanical nature of the entire interchange. Thus, as a public space, or a space for public discourse, cyberspace does not ensure that individuals will be able to fully explain, sell, and control their opinions. It does, however, offer a means by which their words—which are also citations of another's—can be compromised, acknowledged, ignored, and assessed.

Moreover, unread electronic texts still function. For instance, Electronic Disturbance Theatre's software Floodnet allows users to tie up servers (it takes advantage of the fact that most servers cannot handle many simultaneous requests). The group first unleashed its software during a "virtual sit-in" on the Mexican and U.S. governments' Web sites in response to the military suppression of the Zapatistas. After a similar attack was unveiled on CNN.com and Yahoo.com, such acts no longer qualified as civil disobedience and are now considered criminal offenses (a consequence of the Internet going "public" by being sold to private corporations). Such acts reveal how Internet communication can work to belie the marketplace of ideas or commodities. As well, the effects of circulating electronic texts are not limited to the Internet. Finally, the Internet's networked structure can be used productively to explore possibilities of alternate futures and different democracies. Natalie Bookchin's Agora and AgoraXchange, which bring together open source and open content, promise to pursue the (more conscious) democratic potential of the Internet.

Mongrel's projects also reveal the ways in which critical race studies are crucial for the study of software as such, for the question of the nonexistence yet effectiveness of racial bogeymen and related stereotypes coincides in important ways with the nonexistence of software itself. As Friedrich Kittler has argued, there is no software. Everything comes down in the end to voltage differences.

> Not only no program, but no underlying microprocessor system could ever start without the rather incredible autobooting faculty of some elementary functions that, for safety's sake, are burned into silicon and thus form part of the hardware. Any transformation of matter from entropy to information, from a million sleeping transistors into differences between electronic potentials, necessarily presupposes a material event called "reset."
>
> In principle, this kind of descent from software to hardware, from higher to lower levels of observation, could be continued over more and more decades. All code operations, despite their metaphoric faculties such as "call" or "return," come down to absolutely local string manipulations and that is, I am afraid, to signifiers of voltage differences.[49]

User control dwindles as one moves down the software stack; software itself dwindles, since everything reduces to voltage differences as signifiers. Although one codes software and, by using another software program, reads noncompiled code, one cannot see software—software cannot be physically separated from hardware, only ideologically.[50] Software persists as an ideological phenomenon or, to be more precise, as a phenomenon that mimics or simulates ideology.[51]

Mongrel's HeritageGold software highlights the relationship between software and ideology, software and race, beautifully. By rewriting the standard menus of Photoshop 1.0, they address the politics of changing color, of passing. For instance, under the "social class" image (in the original Photoshop) they translate "RGB" to "middle class" and "index" to "aspiring." So, in order to apply a social filter to the image ("assimilate," "add more cash"), one must first make the image middle class. The image channels are AAA (RGB), Aryan (Red),

Asian (Green), and Afro (Blue). To save one "births," to close one "kills." Page setup is "immigration setup," printing is "migrating," one opens "families" instead of "files," one copies and pastes skin and fills in flesh wounds, and one defines breeds and patrimonies instead of brushes and patterns (if the selected area is too big, one cannot define a breed because it is too big to be a ghetto). The site's "historical relations" option (which allows one to apply various masks to the images) is particularly insightful. The slavery function produces a new image by adding the image to itself using the Aryan (red) channel. This produces a duplicate, overexposed image in black and white. This simple hack of Photoshop insightfully and provocatively manipulates the resonances between race and software in order to make clear the costs and assumptions behind the rhetoric of the Internet as "race free." Making explicit the parallel between race and software enables a response to the simultaneous erasure and commodification of race and software.

Critical race studies are key to something like critical software studies, for conceiving race as skin deep has been central to viewing technology as screen deep. The message of the scenes of empowerment offered by MCI, for instance—that race is a form of bad visual knowledge that the Internet can supplant—portrays the Internet as screen deep, thus erasing both hardware and bodies. Race as bad visual knowledge posits race as false ideology, as a bad way of seeing (generated by genetic coding) that obscures the truth, but can be torn away—through bodily recoding, going online, or recoding society to "see" correctly. Even as it depends on the display of raced others, race, this argument stresses, does not exist. However—and this is a point that Asian American studies has been making repeatedly—race may not exist scientifically, it may not be absolutely categorized or described, yet it makes all the difference. It frames us in a logic of visibility and medical and cultural pathology; it is a bureaucratic categorization that we cannot avoid. Race and software are both nebulous entities yet solid everyday experiences. We are expected to be as blind to software as we are to race. Race and software both act and maintain visual knowledge in an age of waning indexicality. Both buttress notions of agency and choice that fly in the face of technology and biology. Both work to convince us that we are users.

Notes

1 See my "Orienting Orientalism or How to Map Cyberspace" and "Scenes of Empowerment." This chapter is a revision of the latter essay.

2 When Gibson's hero, Case, jacks into cyberspace—the so-called consensual hallucination—his is the only mind out there. Gibson's fiction orients the reader to a technology-overloaded present and future, portrayed as belonging to Japan or other Far Eastern countries (Kirin takes the place of Budweiser, Case jacks in and sees the neon cube representing the Mitsubishi Bank of America), by conflating information networks and Ninsei, Gibson's fictional depiction of Tokyo. In *Neuromancer*, cyberspace and Ninsei are both virtual spaces: if it is wasted enough, Ninsei becomes cyberspace; Ninsei and cyberspace are both dominated by neon; and cyberspace opens up for Case like a fluid origami trick.

3 Unlike the Internet of today, Gibson's cyberspace (and Neal Stephenson's Metaverse) is *navigable* and its breadth conceivable. Console cowboys in Gibson's Sprawl trilogy (*Neuromancer, Count Zero,* and *Mona Lisa Overdrive*) control their data paths as they *travel through* cyberspace; they move from graphic representation to graphic representation as though playing a video game (Stephenson's *Snow Crash* contains a high-speed chase in the Metaverse). Most important, in Gibson's fiction users can visualize cyberspace's size and scope, even if they cannot know its intimate details.

4 Gibson, *Neuromancer,* 51.

5 High-tech orientalism is not simply "a western style for dominating, restructuring, and having authority over the Orient" (Said, *Orientalism,* 2). If Said's groundbreaking interrogation of orientalism examined it in a period of colonialism, high-tech orientalism takes place in a period of anxiety and vulnerability. As David Morely and Kevin Robins argue in "Techno-Orientalism," it engages with the economic crises of the 1980s, which supposedly threatened to "emasculate" the United States and Europe (Japan became the world's largest creditor nation in 1985 and threatened to say no). Faced with a "Japanese future," high-tech orientalism resurrects the frontier—in a virtual form—in order to open space for America. As opposed to the openly racist science fiction of the early to mid–twentieth century, which warned against the "yellow peril," cyberpunk fiction does not advocate white supremacy or the resurrection of a strong United States of America. It rather offers representations of survivors, savvy navigators who can open closed spaces.

6 The commercial aired throughout 1997. This essay cites the short version. The long version contains two extra characters: an "ethnic" white male who speaks with a heavy Eastern European accent, and a white boy in a wheelchair.

7 This white male is the obverse of the naturalized queer subject Mimi Thi Nguyen describes in her "Queer Cyborgs and New Mutants."

8 See Habermas, "The Blurred Blueprint."

9 More progressive versions of this promise of fleeing the body are critiqued in Nguyen, "Queer Cyborgs and New Mutants."

10 National Telecommunications and Information Administration, *Falling through the Net II.*

11 Everett, "The Revolution Will Be Digitalized."

12 Commercial pornography, of course, played a huge role in the emergence of marketplaces on the Internet—a point I elaborate on in *Control and Freedom: Power and Paranoia in the Age of Fiber Optics.* Also, the net utopia explosion did not entirely dispel fears about the "pornographic" nature of the Internet but rather dislodged them temporarily. These two portrayals serve as the poles between which public perception of the net would swing. Both poles effectively screen the fact that vulnerability and publicity are *constitutive of* the system: one by claiming all vulnerability to be accidental and the other by displacing this vulnerability onto certain *content.*

13 Faced with the economic slowdown in 2001, members of the U.S. Congress looked to the digital divide for investment opportunities. Rep. Barbara Cubin, R-Wyo., for instance, introduced a bill in the spring of 2001 that would provide regulatory relief for all but the biggest telecommunications companies so they could build more broadband in rural areas.

14 Gonzalez, "The Appended Subject."

15 The most extraordinary example of this is the portrayal of Jeffrey Dahmer as a "multicultural" mass murderer because he killed and feasted on people of color (after he decided he was a cannibal) on a program broadcast on the television network A&E.

16 The introduction to http://www.xxxasians.com (accessed February 9, 2001) reads: "The Streets Of Beijing To The Red Light District Of Tokyo. We've Picked Out For You Only The Best Girls Doing The Hottest Nastiest Sex Acts. They Are All Waiting For 'YOU' Papasan, What More Could You Ask For?"

17 According to a study by NetValue, 8.49 million Asian Internet users visited adult Web sites in January 2001. See Shane Abrahams, "In Asia, Cyber-Porn Pulls a Crowd."

18 Mark Poster, in his analysis of "virtual ethnicity," argues that ethnicity is the product of many everyday practices and is itself constructed. Thus, comparisons between virtual ethnicity and real ethnicity, which portray real ethnicity as some-how fixed and lost, create ethnicity as fixed and lost. However, this does not mean that the two terms are equivalent; as opposed to "real life," the Internet allows an underdetermined" subject to emerge, a subject that is implicated within the circuit of the Internet and is not abstracted from technology because technology itself is not an object but rather a social place. This means that virtual ethnicity enables a far more fluid subject to emerge. Although this analysis is insightful, it ignores the ways in which the user's fluidity is compensated for by dreams of superagency. As well, it is not simply that analyses of virtual ethnicity perpetuate real ethnicity as solid but that representations of virtual ethnicity and the call to pass do so as well. See Poster, *What's the Matter with the Internet.*

19 Laclau and Mouffe, *Hegemony and Socialist Strategy,* 164.

20 Ibid., 181.

21 Patterns are also key in Gibson's fiction: Case reads the patterns in cyberspace, and Linda Lee represents the complex patterns of biological life.

22 Ted Chiang, *Stories of Your Life and Others,* 75. Greco also learns martial arts through this method rather than having this knowledge downloaded into his virtual representation as in the film *The Matrix* (dir. Andy Wachowski and Larry Wachowski, 1999).

23 Ibid., 78.

24 Ibid., 245.

25 Ibid., 246.

26 Chiang also explores the relationship between technology and politics in "Seventy-Two Letters," in ibid.

27 Chiang, *Stories of Your Life,* 284.

28 Ibid., 304–5.

29 Foster, "Ethnicity and Technicity."

30 Ibid.

31 Chiang's biologizing also leads him to make rather odd assertions about mother-daughter relationships, for example, "It'll be when you first learn to walk when I get daily demonstrations of the asymmetry in our relationship. . . . each time you walk into a door frame or scrape your knee, the pain feels like it's my own. It'll be like growing an errant limb, an extension of myself whose sensory nerves report pain just fine, but whose motor nerves don't convey my commands at all. It's so unfair: I'm going to give birth to an animated voodoo doll of myself" (*Stories of Your Life,* 149). In this passage, Chiang explores the downside of simstim and other technologies sold as pleasurable, but he does so by idealizing the relationship between mother and child, although his portrayals of women are certainly not limited to mothers (the narrator is also a university professor, as are others).

32 The race of the baby is unclear. The shot at the agency begins by focusing on a picture of a blond child. The "evaluators" at the agency are white.

33 See Tu, "Good Politics, Great Porn," 267–80.

34 Ibid., 274–75.

35 This widely diverse audience would probably not sit through Darrell Hamamoto's pro-Asian pornographic film *Skin on Skin* either. *Asian Pride Porn!* responds to projects such as Hamamoto's, as well as mainstream pornography. It brilliantly and hilariously points to the limitations of pornography as a means of activism.

36 Graham Harwood, interview with Matthew Fuller, in Fuller, "The Mouths of the Thames."

37 http://www.mongrelx.org/Project/Natural/StarSites/starsites.html (accessed February 26, 2001). As Matthew Fuller, an artist, programmer, and activist who worked with Harwood on Natural Selection, explains on the site: "Along with porn, one of the twin spectres of 'evil' on the internet is access to neo-nazi and racist material on the web. Successive governments have tried censorship and failed. This is another approach—ridicule."

38 Fuller, "The Mouths of the Thames."

39 Chow, "Gender and Representation," 46.

40 http://www.mongrelx.org/Project/Natural/Venus (accessed February 26, 2001).

41 Ibid.

42 http://www.mongrelx.org/Project/projects.html (accessed February 26, 2001).

43 Ibid.

44 Fuller, "The Mouths of the Thames."

45 See Hill and Tu, "Asian Artists Make Porn Sites Work for Them."

46 http://www.mongrelx.org/Project/projects.htm (accessed February 26, 2001).

47 See Balibar and Wallerstein, Race, Nation, Class.

48 Lefort, Democracy and Political Theory, 18–19.

49 Kittler, "There Is No Software."

50 Those seeking to archive software programs face this indivisibility all the time. Many old software programs cannot be run on current computers, although custom-built virtual computer simulations can get around these difficulties.

51 For more on this, see Chun, Control and Freedom.

Bibliography

Aaron, Charles. "What the White Boy Means When He Says Yo." *Spin*, November 1998.

Abrahams, Shane. "In Asia, Cyber-Porn Pulls a Crowd." *CNN.com*, http://www.cnn.com/2001/BUSINESS/asia/03/13/asia.cyberporn (accessed March 13, 2001).

Abu-Lughod, Lila. "The Interpretation of Culture(s) after Television." *Representations* 59 (summer 1997): 493–514.

Ake, David. *Jazz Cultures*. Berkeley: University of California Press, 2002.

Al-'Azm, Sadik Jalal. "Orientalism and Orientalism in Reverse." In *Orientalism: A Reader*, ed. Alexander Macfie. New York: New York University Press, 2000. 217–38.

Anderson, Benedict. *Imagined Communities*. New York: Verso, 1991.

Anderson, Iain. "Jazz outside the Marketplace: Free Improvisation and Nonprofit Sponsorship of the Arts, 1965–1980." *American Music* 20, no. 2 (summer 2002): 131–67.

Ansermet, Ernst-Alexandre. "Bechet and Jazz Visit Europe, 1919." In *Reading Jazz: A Gathering of Autobiography, Reportage, and Criticism from 1919 to Now*, ed. Robert Gottlieb. New York: Pantheon, 1996. 741–46.

Appadurai, Arjun. *Modernity at Large: Cultural Dimensions of Globalization*. Minneapolis: University of Minnesota Press, 1996.

Arnold, David, ed. *Imperial Medicine and Indigenous Societies*. Manchester: Manchester University Press, 1988.

Ashraf, Irshad. "Dear Weekend." *Guardian*, August 16, 2003.

Atkins, E. Taylor. *Blue Nippon: Authenticating Jazz in Japan*. Durham, N.C.: Duke University Press, 2001.

Auerbach, Brian. "Profile: United Front." *Down Beat*, February 1986, 46–47.

Bachman, Sarah. "Buy a Bindi—or Boycott?" *India Currents* 15, no. 3 (June 2001): 24–28.

Balibar, Etienne, and Immanuel Wallerstein. *Race, Nation, Class: Ambiguous Identities.* London: Verso, 1991.

Barlow, Tani. "International Feminism of the Future." In *Feminisms at a Millennium*, ed. Judith A. Howard and Carolyn Allen. Chicago: University of Chicago Press, 2000. 104–10.

Batra, Sumitra. *The Art of Mehndi.* New York: Penguin Studio, 1999.

Berger, Maurice. "Picturing Whiteness: Nikki S. Lee's Yuppie Project." *Art Journal* (winter 2001): 55–56.

Berlant, Lauren. "National Brands / National Body: Imitation of Life." In *The Phantom Public Sphere*, ed. Bruce Robbins. Minneapolis: University of Minnesota Press, 1993. 173–208.

———. *The Queen of America Goes to Washington City: Essays on Sex and Citizenship.* Durham, N.C.: Duke University Press, 1997.

Bobo, Jacqueline. "The Color Purple: Black Women as Cultural Readers." In *Female Spectators: Looking at Film and Television*, ed. D. Pribram. New York: Verso, 1988. 90–109.

Bose, Purnima, and Linta Varghese. "*Mississippi Masala*, South Asian Activism, and Agency." In *Haunting Violations: Feminist Criticism and the Crisis of the "Real,"* ed. Wendy Hessford and Wendy Kozol. Urbana-Champaign: University of Illinois Press, 2001. 137–69.

Brand, David. "The New Whiz Kids: Why Asian Americans Are Doing So Well and What It Costs Them." *Time*, August 31, 1987.

Breest, Norm. "Hiroshima: Bridging Music." *Jazz Review.* http://www.jazzreview.com/articledetails.cfm?ID=2026 (accessed August 2, 2003).

Butler, Judith. *Gender Trouble.* New York: Routledge, 1990.

———. "Performative Acts and Gender Constitution: An Essay in Phenomenology and Feminist Theory." In *Performing Feminisms: Feminist Critical Theory and Theatre*, ed. Sue-Ellen Case. Baltimore: Johns Hopkins University Press, 1990. 270–82.

Canclini, Nestor Garcia. *Consumers and Citizens: Globalization and Multicultural Conflicts.* Minneapolis: University of Minnesota Press, 2001.

Carr, C. "Icon Remix." *Village Voice*, November 29, 2000.

Carruthers, Ashley. "National Identity, Diasporic Anxiety, and Music Video Culture in Vietnam." In *House of Glass: Culture, Modernity, and the State in Southeast Asia*, ed. Yao Souchao and Pasir Panjang. Singapore: Institute of Southeast Asian Studies, 2000. 119–49.

Cartwright-Jones, Catherine. "The Henna Page." http://www.hennapage.com (accessed August 1999).

Çelik, Zeynep. "Speaking Back to Orientalist Discourse at the World's Columbian Exposition." In *Noble Dreams, Wicked Pleasures: Orientalism in America, 1870–1930*, ed. Holly Edwards. Princeton: Princeton University Press, 2000. 77–97.

Chan, Jachinson. *Chinese American Masculinities: From Fu Manchu to Bruce Lee.* New York: Routledge, 2001.

Chang, Jeff. "Race, Class, Conflict, and Empowerment: On Ice Cube's 'Black Korea.'" *Amerasia Journal* 19, no. 2. (1993): 87–107.

Chappell, Ben. "'Take a Little Trip with Me': Lowriding and the Poetics of Scale."

In *Technicolor: Race, Technology, and Everyday Life*, ed. Alondra Nelson and Thuy Linh N. Tu with Alicia Headlam Hines. New York: New York University Press, 2001. 100–120.

Chiang, Ted. *Stories of Your Life and Others*. New York: Orb, 2002.

Chiao, Hsuing-ping. "Bruce Lee: His Influence on the Evolution of the Kung Fu Genre." *Journal of Popular Film and Television* 9, no. 1 (spring 1981): 30–42.

Chin, Frank, and Jeffrey Paul Chan. "Racist Love." In *Seeing through the Shuck*, ed. Richard Kostelanetz. New York: Ballantine, 1972. 65–79.

Chomsky, Noam. "Free Trade and Free Practice: Pretense and Practice." In *The Cultures of Globalization*, ed. Fredric Jameson and Masoa Miyoshi. Durham, N.C.: Duke University Press, 1998. 356–70.

Chow, Rey. "Gender and Representation." In *Feminist Consequences*, ed. Elisabeth Bronfen and Misha Kavka. New York: Columbia University Press, 2000. 38–57.

Chuh, Kandice. *Imagine Otherwise: On Asian Americanist Critique*. Durham, N.C.: Duke University Press, 2003.

Chuh, Kandice, and Karen Shimakawa, eds. *Orientations: Mapping Studies in the Asian Diaspora*. Durham, N.C.: Duke University Press, 2001.

Chun, Wendy Hui Kyong. *Control and Freedom: Power and Paranoia in the Age of Fiber Optics*. Cambridge, Mass.: MIT Press, 2005.

——. "Orienting Orientalism or How to Map Cyberspace." In *Asian America.Net: Ethnicity, Nationalism, and Cyberspace*, ed. Rachel Lee and Sau-ling Cynthia Wong. New York: Routledge, 2003. 3–36.

——. "Scenes of Empowerment: Virtual Racial Diversity and Digital Divides." *New Formations* 45 (winter 2001–2002): 169–88.

Chung, Brian. "Hip Hop Asian America." *Evil Monito* 2, no. 11 (summer 2002). http://www.evilmonito.com / 011 / hiphopasiaamerica / hiphopasia.htm (accessed October 4, 2006).

Clancy, Tom. *Debt of Honor*. New York: Putnam, 1994.

Clark, Andrew, ed. *Riffs and Choruses: A New Jazz Anthology*. London: Continuum, 2001.

Clarke, John, Stuart Hall, Tony Jefferson, and Brian Roberts. "Subcultures, Cultures, and Class." In *The Subcultures Reader*, ed. Ken Gelder and Sarah Thornton. London: Routledge, 1997. 100–111.

Classen, Constance. *Worlds of Sense: Exploring the Senses in History and Across Cultures*. London: Routledge, 1993.

Classen, Constance, David Howes, and Anthony Synnott. *Aroma: The Cultural History of Smell*. London: Routledge, 1994.

Coates, Ta-Nehisi. "Just Another Quick-Witted, Egg-Roll-Joke-Making, Insult-Hurling Chinese-American Rapper." *New York Times Magazine*, November 21, 2004.

Cohen, Stanley. "Symbols of Trouble." In *The Subcultures Reader*, ed. Ken Gelder and Sarah Thornton. London: Routledge, 1997. 149–62.

Colburn, Judith. "Terror in Saigontown, U.S.A." *Mother Jones*, February–March 1983.

Connery, Christopher. "Pacific Rim Discourse: The U.S. Global Imaginary in the Late Cold War Years." In *Asia / Pacific as Space of Cultural Production*, ed. Rob Wilson and Arif Dirlik. Durham, N.C.: Duke University Press, 1995. 30–56.

Conroy, Marianne. "Discount Dreams: Factory Outlet Malls, Consumption, and the Performance of Middle-Class Identity." *Social Text* 54 (1998): 63–83.

Coombes, Rosemary. *The Cultural Life of Intellectual Properties: Authorship, Appropriation, and the Law*. Durham, N.C.: Duke University Press, 1998.

Corrigan, Maureen. "Beijing Body Count." *Washington Post Book World*, September 21, 1997.

Cowan, Peter. "Devils or Angels: Literacy and Discourse in Lowrider Culture." In *What They Don't Learn in School: Literacy in the Lives of Urban Youth*, ed. Jabari Mahiri. Oxford: Peter Lang, 2004. 47–74.

Crichton, Michael. *Rising Sun*. New York: Ballantine, 1993.

Crosby, Alfred W. *Germs, Seeds, and Animals: Studies in Ecological History*. Armonk, N.Y.: M. E. Sharpe, 1994.

Crouch, Stanley. "On the Corner: The Sellout of Miles Davis." *The All-American Skin Game, or the Decoy of Race: The Long and Short of It, 1990–1994*. New York: Pantheon, 1995. 166–85.

Cunningham, Stuart, and Tina Nguyen. "Popular Media of the Vietnamese Diaspora." In *Floating Lives: The Media and Asian Diasporas*, ed. Stuart Cunningham and John Sinclair. St. Lucia: University of Queensland Press, 2000. 91–135.

Cussler, Clive. *Dragon*. New York: Pocket Books, 1991.

Davis, Clive. "Has Jazz Gone Classical?" *Wilson Quarterly* 21 (1997): 56–63.

De Jong, Peter. "Fast Times in Stock Car Country." *National Geographic*, June 1998.

Del Barco, Mandalit. "Rap's Latino Sabor." In *Droppin' Science: Critical Essays on Rap Music and Hip Hop Culture*, ed. William Eric Perkins. Philadelphia: Temple University Press, 1996. 63–84.

DeVeaux, Scott. *The Birth of Bebop: A Social and Musical History*. Berkeley: University of California Press, 1997.

———. "Constructing the Jazz Tradition: Jazz Historiography." *Black American Literature Forum* 25, no. 3 (fall 1991): 525–60.

———. "What Did We Do to Be So Black and Blue?" *Musical Quarterly* 80, no. 3 (1996): 525–60.

Deutsch, Nathaniel. " 'The Asiatic Black Man': An African American Orientalism?" *Journal of Asian American Studies* 4, no. 3 (October 2001): 193–208.

Dirlik, Arif, ed. *What Is in a Rim? Critical Perspectives on the Pacific Region Idea*. Boulder: Westview, 1993.

Do, Anh. "Dazzling a Crowd: Vietnamese Singers Put Own Stamp on U.S. Tunes." *Orange County Register*, November 19, 1991.

Do, Hien Duc. "A Space of Their Own: Vietnamese Music Legends in America." Lecture, University of Michigan, November 2, 1998.

Dowling, William C. *Jameson, Althusser, Marx*. Ithaca, N.Y.: Cornell University Press, 1984.

Dyer, Richard. *Heavenly Bodies: Film Stars and Society*. London: British Film Institute, 1986.

Edelstein, Paula. "An Inventive Fusion of Music and Culture Has Hiroshima Building the Bridge." http://home.att.net/paula.edelstein/Hiroshima.html (accessed August 5, 2003).

Edwards, Holly "Curator's Preface." In *Noble Dreams, Wicked Pleasures: Orientalism in*

America, 1870–1930, ed. Holly Edwards. Princeton: Princeton University Press, 2000. vii–x.

——. "A Million and One Nights: Orientalism in Ameria, 1870–1930." In *Noble Dreams, Wicked Pleasures: Orientalism in America, 1870–1930*, ed. Holly Edwards. Princeton: Princeton University Press, 2000. 11–57.

——, ed. *Noble Dreams, Wicked Pleasures: Orientalism in America, 1870–1930*. Princeton: Princeton University Press, 2000.

Ellison, Ralph. *Invisible Man*. New York: Random House, 1952.

Emmiere, Dan. "Pacifics Interview 2001." *Asiatic Theory Online*, 2001. http://www.csu pomona.edu / dehadinata / asiatic / music_pacifics.htm (accessed December 8, 2001).

Engen, Trygg. *Odor Sensation and Memory*. New York: Praeger, 1991.

Espana-Maram, Linda. "Brown 'Hordes' in McIntosh Suits: Filipinos, Taxi Dance Halls, and Performing the Immigrant Body in Los Angeles, 1930s–1940s." In *Generations of Youth: Youth Culture and History in Twentieth Century America*, ed. Joe Austin. New York: New York University Press, 1998. 118–35.

Espiritu, Yen Le. *Asian American Panethnicity: Bridging Institutions and Identities*. Philadelphia: Temple University Press, 1992.

——. *Asian American Women and Men*. Thousand Oaks, Calif.: Sage Publications, 1996.

Evans, K., I. Taylor, and P. Fraiser. "Shop 'Til You Drop." In *The City Cultures Reader*, ed. Malcolm Miles. New York: Routledge, 2003. 158–62.

Everett, Anna. "The Revolution Will Be Digitized: Afrocentricity and the Digital Public Sphere." *Social Text* 20, no. 2 (summer 2002): 125–46.

Ewen, Stuart. *All-Consuming Images: The Politics of Style in Contemporary Culture*. New York: Basic Books, 1988.

Fabius, Carine. *Mehndi: The Art of Henna Body Painting*. New York: Three Rivers, 1998.

Fallows, James M. *More Like Us: Making America Great Again*. Boston: Houghton Mifflin, 1989.

Fang, Karen. "Sex God: Why *The Guru* Was the Most Important Bad Movie about Asian Men out This Year." *Jade* (winter 2002): 8.

Feng, Peter X. *Identities in Motion: Asian American Film and Video*. Durham, N.C.: Duke University Press, 2002.

——. "Recuperating Suzie Wong: A Fan's Nancy Kwan-dary." In *Countervisions: Asian American Film Criticism*, ed. Darrell Hamamoto and Sandra Liu. Philadelphia: Temple University Press, 2000. 40–58.

Feng, Theodric. "Akira Tana: Oct. 98." *AAMPlitude: Asian / Asian American Music*. http:// members.tripod.com / tfeng / int-tana.htm (accessed August 5, 2003).

Finkelpearl, Thomas. "The Western Mirror." In *Man + Space*. Gwangju: Gwangju Biennale Foundation, 2000. 156–67.

Flores, Juan. *From Bomba to Hip Hop*. New York: Columbia University Press, 2000.

——. "Puerto Rocks: New York Ricans Stake Their Claim." In *Droppin' Science: Critical Essays on Rap and Hip Hop Culture*, ed. William Eric Perkins. Philadelphia: Temple University Press, 1995. 85–116.

Florida, Richard. *The Rise of the Creative Class and How It's Transforming Work, Leisure, Community, and Everyday Life*. New York: Basic Books, 2002.

Fong, Timothy P. *The Contemporary Asian American Experience: Beyond the Model Minority.* Upper Saddle River, N.J.: Prentice Hall, 1998.

Forman, Murray. *The 'Hood Comes First: Race, Space, and Place in Rap and Hip Hop.* Middletown, Conn.: Wesleyan University Press, 2002.

Foster, Thomas. "Ethnicity and Technicity: Ted Chiang's 'Liking What You See: A Documentary.' " Paper presented at the conference Only Skin Deep: Changing Visions of the American Self, Columbia University, New York, February 7, 2004.

Foucault, Michel. *Discipline and Punish: The Birth of the Prison.* Trans. Alan Sheridan. New York: Pantheon, 1977.

——. *The History of Sexuality.* Vol. 1. New York: Vintage, [1978] 1990.

——. *Technologies of the Self: A Seminar with Michel Foucault,* ed. Luther H. Martin, Huck Gutman, and Patrick H. Hutton. Amherst: University of Massachusetts Press, 1988.

Francia, Luis H. "Memories of Overdevelopment." In *Memories of Overdevelopment,* ed. Wayne Baerwaldt. Winnipeg: Plug In Editions, 1997.

Freeman, James. *Hearts of Sorrow: Vietnamese-American Lives.* Stanford: Stanford University Press, 1989.

Fuller, Matthew. "The Mouths of the Thames: An Interview with Mongrel and Some of Their Collaborators." http://www.tate.org.uk/netart/mongrel/home/faqs/ns.htm (accessed February 26, 2001).

Fung, Richard. "Looking for My Penis: The Eroticized Asian in Gay Video Porn." In *How Do I Look? Queer Film and Video,* ed. Bad Object-Choices. Seattle: Bay, 1991. 145–60.

Funke, Karl, and Jason Mulroney. "Cover Car—Mister 2 Crazy." *Import Tuner,* April 2000.

Fusco, Coco. "At Your Service: Latina Women in the Global Information Network." In *The Bodies That Were Not Ours and Other Writings.* London and New York: Routledge with the Institute of International Visual Arts, 2001. 186–201.

——. *The Bodies That Were Not Ours and Other Writing.* London: Routledge, 2001.

——. *English Is Broken Here: Notes on Cultural Fusion in the Americas.* New York: New Press, 1995.

Gabaccia, Donna. *We Are What We Eat: Ethnic Food and the Making of Americans.* Cambridge, Mass.: Harvard University Press, 1998.

Gabbard, Krin. "Signifyin(g) the Phallus: 'Mo' Better Blues' and Representations of the Jazz Trumpet." *Representing Jazz,* ed. Krin Gabbard. Durham, N.C.: Duke University Press, 1995. 104–30.

Gaines, Jane. *Contested Culture: The Image, the Voice, and the Law.* London: BFI, 1992.

Gamson, Joshua. *Freaks Talk Back: Tabloid Talk Shows and Sexual Non-Conformity.* Chicago: University of Chicago Press, 1998.

Garelick, Jon. "Toys 'R' Murder," *New York Times,* October 17, 1999.

Gelder, Ken. "Introduction to Part Two." In *The Subcultures Reader,* ed. Ken Gelder and Sarah Thornton. London: Routledge, 1997. 83–89.

Geurts, Kathryn Linn. *Culture and the Senses: Bodily Ways of Knowing in an African Community.* Berkeley: University of California Press, 2002.

Ghosh, Amitav. *The Calcutta Chromosome.* New York: Avon, 1995.

Gibson, William. *Neuromancer.* New York: Ace, 1984.

Gilbert, David. "Urban Outfitting: The City and the Spaces of Fashion Culture." In

Fashion Cultures: Theories, Explorations, and Analysis, ed. Stella Bruzzi and Pamela C. Gibson. London: Routledge, 2000. 7–24.

Gilroy, Paul. *Black Atlantic: Modernity and Double Consciousness*. Cambridge, Mass.: Harvard University Press, [1993] 1999.

Golden, Thelma. "Mama said . . ." In *Words of Wisdom: A Curator's Vade Mecum on Contemporary Art*, ed. Carin Kuoni. New York: Independent Curators International, 2001. 72–74.

Gonzalez, Jennifer. "The Appended Subject: Race and Identity as Digital Assemblage." In *Race in Cyberspace*, ed. Beth E. Kolko, Lisa Nakamura, and Gilbert B. Rodman. New York: Routledge, 2000. 27–50.

Gonzalez, Vernadette V., and Robyn M. Rodriguez. "Filipina.com: Wives / Women / Whores on the Cyberfrontier." In *Asian America.Net: Ethnicity, Nationalism, and Cyberspace*, ed. Rachel Lee and Sau-ling Cynthia Wong. New York: Routledge, 2003. 215–314.

Goodman, Peter S. "A Letter from Hong Kong: Farewell to a Troubled Star and a City's High Times." *Washington Post*, April 5, 2003.

Gottlieb, Robert, ed. *Reading Jazz: A Gathering of Autobiography, Reportage, and Criticism from 1919 to Now*. New York: Pantheon, 1996.

Grewal, Inderpal. "The Postcolonial, Ethnic Studies, and the Diaspora: The Contexts of Ethnic Studies / Migrant Cultural Studies in the U.S." *Socialist Review* 24, no. 4 (fall 1994): 45–74.

———. "Traveling Barbie: Indian Transnationality and New Consumer Subjects." *positions: east asia cultures critique* 7, no. 3: 799–826.

Grewal, Inderpal, Akhil Gupta, and Aihwa Ong. "Introduction: Asian Transnationalities—Media, Markets, and Migration." *positions: east asia cultures critique* 7, no. 3 (winter 1999): 653–66.

Grewal, Inderpal, and Caren Kaplan. "Introduction: Transnationalism, Feminist Practices, and Questions of Postmodernity." In *Scattered Hegemonies: Postmodernity, and Transnational Feminist Practices*, ed. Inderpal Grewal and Caren Kaplan. Minneapolis: University of Minnesota, 1994. 1–33.

Gridley, Mark. *Jazz Styles: History and Analysis*. 7th ed. Upper Saddle River, N.J.: Prentice Hall, 2000 [1978].

Ha, K. Oanh. "Some Seeing Red over Videos." *Orange County Register*, December 27, 1997.

Habermas, Jürgen. "The Blurred Blueprint: Developmental Pathways in the Disintegration of the Bourgeois Public Sphere." In *The Structural Transformation of the Public Sphere: An Inquiry into the Category of Bourgeois Society*. Trans. Thomas Burger. Cambridge, Mass.: MIT Press, 1991. 175–80.

Hagedorn, Jessica, ed. *Charlie Chan Is Dead 2: At Home in the World (An Anthology of Contemporary Asian American Fiction)*. New York: Penguin, 2004.

Halberstam, Judith. *Female Masculinities*. Durham, N.C.: Duke University Press, 1998.

Hall, Stuart. "The Local and the Global: Globalization and Ethnicity." In *Dangerous Liaisons: Gender, Nation, and Postcolonial Perspectives*, ed. Anne McClintock, Aamir Mufti, and Ella Shohat. Minneapolis: University of Minnesota Press, 1997. 173–87.

———. "New Ethnicities." In *Stuart Hall: Dialogues in Cultural Studies*, ed. David Morley and Kuan-Hsing Chen. New York: Routledge, 1996. 441–49.

———. "What Is This Black in Black Popular Culture?" In *Black Popular Culture*, ed. Gina Dent. Seattle: Bay Press, 1994. 21–33.

Hamamoto, Darrell Y. *Monitored Peril: Asian Americans and the Politics of TV*. Minneapolis: University of Minnesota Press, 1994.

Hamamoto, Darrell Y., and Sandra Liu, eds. *Countervisions: Asian American Film Criticism*. Philadelphia: Temple University Press, 2000.

Hamilton, William L. "Dressing the Part Is Part of Her Art." *New York Times*, December 2, 2001.

Han, Darow. "Asian American Nation." *SF Weekly*, June 24, 1992.

Han, Ju Hui Judy, with Marie K. Morohoshi. "Creating, Curating, and Consuming Queer Asian American Cinema: An Interview with Marie K. Morohoshi." In *Q&A: Queer in Asian America*, ed. David L. Eng and Alice Y. Hom. Philadelphia: Temple University Press, 1998. 81–94.

Hanson, Ellis, ed. *Outtakes: Essays on Queer Theory and Film*. Durham, N.C.: Duke University Press, 1999.

Harvey, David. *The Condition of Postmodernity*. Cambridge: Blackwell, 1990.

Hebdige, Dick. *Subculture: The Meaning of Style*. London: Methuen, 1979.

———. "Subculture: The Meaning of Style." In *The Subcultures Reader*, ed. Ken Gelder and Sarah Thornton. London: Routledge, 1997. 130–43.

Heller, Skip. "Streetology: Joe Bataan's Rap on Latin Soul." *LA Weekly*, December 17, 1999.

Hill, Logan, and Thuy Linh Nguyen Tu. "Asian Artists Make Porn Sites Work for Them: Nude Japanese Schoolgirls! Lotus Blossoms! Radical Feminists?" *Village Voice*, August 22–28, 2001.

Hing, Bill Ong. "Reframing the Immigration Debate: An Overview." In *Reframing the Immigration Debate*, ed. Bill Ong Hing and Ronald Lee. Los Angeles: LEAP Asian Pacific American Public Policy Institute, 1996. 1–30.

Ho, Fred. "Beyond Asian American Jazz: My Musical and Political Changes in the Asian American Movement." *Leonardo Music Journal* 9 (1999): 45–51.

Ho, Fred, Carolyn Antonio, Diane Fujino, and Steve Yip, eds. *Legacy to Liberation: Politics and Culture of Revolutionary Asian Pacific America*. San Francisco and New York: AK and Big Red Media, 2000.

Hodeir, André. *Jazz: Its Evolution and Essence*. New York: Grove, 1980.

Holden, Stephen. "Using Ditsy Maxims for Erotic Self-Help." *New York Times*, January 31, 2003.

Hongo, Garrett, ed. *Under Western Eyes: Personal Essays from Asian America*. New York: Anchor, 1995.

Howes, David, ed. *The Varieties of Sensory Experience: A Sourcebook in the Anthropology of the Senses*. Toronto: University of Toronto Press, 1991.

Huggan, Graham. *The Postcolonial Exotic: Marketing the Margins*. London: Routledge, 2001.

Hutnyk, John. "Hybridity Saves? Authenticity and / or the Critique of Appropriation." *Amerasia Journal* 25, no. 3 (1999): 39–58.

———. "Magical Mystical Tourism." In *Travel Worlds: Journey in Contemporary Cultural Politics*, ed. Raminder Kaur and John Hutynk. London: Zed, 1999. 94–119.

Inden, Ronald. "Orientalist Constructions of India." In *Orientalism: A Reader*, ed. Alexander L. Macfie. New York: New York University Press, 2000. 277–84.

Inoue, Todd S. "The Stealth Asian Shall Inherit the Earth." *Metroactive*, April 23, 1998.

Iyer, Pico. "I'm Anyone I Choose to Be." *Daily Telegraph*, November 22, 2003.

Jameson, Fredric. *The Political Unconscious: Narrative as a Socially Symbolic Act*. Ithaca, N.Y.: Cornell University Press, 1981.

Jang, Jon. "88 Keys to Revolution." *East Wind* (winter / spring 1985): 34–35.

Jenkins, Henry, Tara McPherson, and Jane Shattuc, eds. *Hop on Pop: The Politics and Pleasure of Popular Culture I*. Durham, N.C.: Duke University Press, 2003.

Jiobu, Robert M. "Recent Asian Pacific Americans: The Demographic Background." In *Reframing the Immigration Debate*, ed. Bill Ong Hing and Ronald Lee. Los Angeles: LEAP Asian Pacific American Public Policy Institute, 1996. 35–57.

Johnson-Wright, Heidi. " 'Tale' Filled with 6 Days of Excitement, Intrigue." *Columbus Dispatch*, March 17, 1996.

Jones, Andrew F. *Yellow Music: Media Culture and Colonial Modernity in the Chinese Jazz Age*. Durham, N.C.: Duke University Press, 2001.

Jones, Carla, and Ann Marie Leshkowich. "Introduction: The Globalization of Asian Dress—Re-Orienting Fashion or Re-Orientalizing Asia?" In *Re-Orienting Fashion: The Globalization of Asian Dress*, ed. Sandra Niessen, Ann Marie Leshkowich, and Carla Jones. New York: Berg, 2003. 1–48.

Jones, LeRoi. *Black Music*. New York: Morrow, 1968.

———. *Blues People: Negro Music in White America*. New York: Morrow, 1963.

Kalra, Virinder, and John Hutnyk. "Brimful of Agitation, Authenticity, and Appropriation: Madonna's 'Asian Kool.' " *Postcolonial Studies: Culture, Politics, Economy* 1, no. 3 (1998): 339–55.

Kang, Laura Hyun Yi. *Compositional Subjects: Enfiguring Asian / American Women*. Durham, N.C.: Duke University Press, 2002.

———. "The Desiring of Asian Female Bodies: Interracial Romance and Cinematic Subjection." In *Screening Asian Americans*. Ed. Peter X. Feng. New Brunswick, N.J.: Rutgers University Press, 2002. 71–98.

Kaplan, Caren. "Resisting Autobiography: Out-law Genres and Transnational Feminist Subjects." In *Women, Autobiography, Theory: A Reader*, ed. Sidonie Smith and Julia Watson. Madison: University of Wisconsin Press, 1998. 208–16.

Kaplan, Marion A. *The Making of the Jewish Middle Class: Women, Family, and Identity in Imperial Germany*. Oxford: Oxford University Press, 1991.

Kapur, Shekhar. "The Asians Are Coming." *Guardian*, August 23, 2002.

Kelley, Robin D. G. "People in Me." *ColorLines* 1, no. 3 (1999): 5–7.

Kelly, Raegan. "Hip Hop Chicano." In *It's Not about a Salary: Rap, Race, and Resistance in Los Angeles*, ed. Brian Cross. New York: Verso, 1993. 65–76.

Kempley, Rita. "*The Guru:* Enlightened Goofiness." *Washington Post*, February 14, 2003.

Kerr, Merrily. "Li'l Nikki 'N' Friends." *New York Arts Magazine*, October 2001.

Khan, Naseem. "Asian Women's Dress: From Burqah to Bloggs—Changing Clothes for Changing Times." In *Chic Thrills: A Fashion Reader*, ed. Judith Ash and Elizabeth Wilson. Berkeley: University of California Press, 1992. 61–74.

Kim, Daniel Y. "The Strange Love of Frank Chin." In *Q&A: Queer in Asian America*, ed. David L. Eng and Alice Y. Hom. Philadelphia: Temple University Press, 1998. 270–303.

Kim, Elaine. "Introduction." In *Fresh Talk/Daring Gazes: Conversations on Asian American Art*, ed. Elaine Kim, Margo Machida, and Sharon Mizota. Berkeley: University of California Press, 2003. 1–50.

Kim, Elaine, and Lisa Lowe. "Guest Editors' Introduction." *positions: east asia cultures critique* 5, no. 2 (fall 1997): vi–xiv.

Kim, Jungwon. "Common Ground: Where Asian American and African American Cultures Merge." *A.*, February–March 1999.

Kim, Kevin. "Repping Chinatown." *Colorlines* 7, no. 4. (winter 2004–2005). http://www.colorlines.com/article.php?ID=48 (accessed October 4, 2006).

King, Richard. "Orientalism, Hinduism, and Feminism." In *Orientalism: A Reader*, ed. Alexander L. Macfie. New York: New York University Press, 2000. 335–42.

Kittler, Friedrich. "There Is No Software." *CTheory*, October 18, 1995.

Kolar-Panov, Dana. "Video and the Diasporic Imagination of Selfhood: A Case Study of the Croatians in Australia." *Cultural Studies* 10, no. 2 (1996): 288–314.

Koltyk, Jo Ann. "Telling Narratives through Home Videos: Hmong Refugees and Self-Documentation of Life in the Old and New Country." *Journal of American Folklore* 106, no. 422 (autumn 1993): 435–49.

Kondo, Dorinne. *About Face: Performing Race in Fashion and Theater*. New York: Routledge, 1997.

Koshy, Susan. "Morphing Race into Ethnicity: Asian American and Critical Transformations of Whiteness." *boundary 2* 28, no. 1. (2001): 153–94.

Kumar, Amitava. *Bombay—London—New York*. New York: Routledge, 2002.

Kwon, Miwon. "The Wrong Place." *Art Journal* 59, no. 1 (spring 2000): 33–44.

Kwon, Soo Ah. "Autoexoticizing: Asian American Youth and the Import Car Scene." *Journal of Asian American Studies* 7, no. 1 (February 2004): 1–26.

——. " 'Keeping It Real': An Exploration of Asian American Youth Import Subculture." MA thesis, Stanford University, 1999.

Laclau, Ernesto, and Chantal Mouffe. *Hegemony and Socialist Strategy: Towards a Radical Democratic Politics*, 2d ed. London and New York: Verso, 2001.

Lake, Max. *Scents and Sensuality: The Essence of Excitement*. London: John Murray, 1989.

Lane, Anthony. "Don of Creation." *New Yorker*, February 3, 2003.

Lau, Kimberly J. *New Age Capitalism: Making Money East of Eden*. Philadelphia: University of Pennsylvania Press, 2002.

Le Guerer, Annick. *Scent: The Mysterious and Essential Powers of Smell*. New York: Turtle Bay, 1992.

Lee, Gus. *Tiger's Tail*. New York: Ivy, 1996.

Lee, Rachel, and Sau-ling Cynthia Wong, eds. *Asian America.Net: Ethnicity, Nationalism, and Cyberspace*. New York: Routledge, 2003.

Lee, Josephine. *Performing Asian America: Race and Ethnicity on the Contemporary Stage*. Philadelphia: Temple University Press, 1997.

Lee, Robert. *Orientals: Asian Americans in Popular Culture*. Philadelphia: Temple University Press, 1999.

Lees, Gene. *Cats of Any Color: Jazz, Black, and White*. New York: Oxford, 1995.

Lefort, Claude. *Democracy and Political Theory*. Trans. David Macey. Minneapolis: University of Minnesota Press, 1988.

Leong, Russell, ed. *Moving the Image: Independent Asian Pacific American Media Arts*. Los Angeles: Asian American Studies Center, University of California, Los Angeles, 1991.

Lessinger, Johanna. *From the Ganges to the Hudson: Indian Immigrants in New York City*. Boston: Allyn and Bacon, 1995.

Lewis, Reina. *Gendering Orientalism: Race, Femininity, and Representation*. New York: Routledge, 1996.

Lhamon, W. T. *Raising Cain: Blackface Performance from Jim Crow to Hip Hop*. Cambridge, Mass.: Harvard University Press, 1998.

Lien, Pei-Te. *The Making of Asian America through Political Participation*. Philadelphia: Temple University Press, 2001.

Lieu, Nhi. "Overlapping Diasporas: Chinese Money, Little Saigon, and the Struggle to Define Vietnamese Identity in the United States." Unpublished paper, Program in American Culture, University of Michigan, Ann Arbor, 2001.

Ling, Amy. "Jamez Chang." In *Yellow Light: The Flowering of Asian American Arts*, ed. Amy Ling. Philadelphia: Temple University Press, 1999. 355–61.

———, ed. *Yellow Light: The Flowering of Asian American Arts*. Philadelphia: Temple University Press, 1999.

Ling, Peter J. *America and the Automobile: Technology, Reform, and Social Change*. Manchester: Manchester University Press, 1990.

Lipset, Seymour Martin. *American Exceptionalism: A Double-Edged Sword*. New York: Norton, 1996.

Lipsitz, George. *Dangerous Crossroads: Popular Music, Postmodernism, and the Poetics of Place*. New York: Verso, 1994.

Lipsitz, George, and David W. Noble. *Death of a Nation*. Minneapolis: University of Minnesota Press, 2002.

Liu, Cynthia W. "When Dragon Ladies Die, Do They Come Back as Butterflies? Reimagining Anna May Wong." In *Countervisions: Asian American Film Criticism*, ed. Darrell Hamamoto and Sandra Liu. Philadelphia: Temple University Press, 2000. 23–39.

Liu, William T. *Transition to Nowhere: Vietnamese Refugees in America*. Nashville: Charter House, 1979.

Lott, Eric. *Love and Theft: Blackface Minstrelsy and the American Working Class*. New York: Oxford University Press, 1995.

Lowe, Lisa. "Epistemological Shifts: National Ontology and the New Asian Immigrant." In *Orientations: Mapping Studies in the Asian Diaspora*, ed. Kandice Chuh and Karen Shimakawa. Duke University Press, 2001. 267–76.

———. *Immigrant Acts: On Asian American Cultural Productions*. Durham, N.C.: Duke University Press, 1996.

———. "Turkish Embassy Letters." In *Orientalism: A Reader*, ed. Alexander L. Macfie. New York: New York University Press, 2000. 324–25.

Lubiano, Wahneema. "A Symposium on Popular Culture and Political Correctness." *Social Text* 36 (fall 1993): 10–16.

Lyotard, Jean-François. *The Postmodern Condition*. Minneapolis: University of Minnesota Press, 1991.

Macfie, Alexander L., ed. *Orientalism: A Reader*. New York: New York University Press, 2000.

Machida, Margo. "Out of Asia: Negotiating Asian Identities in America." In *Asia / America: Identities in Contemporary Asian American Art*, ed. Margo Machida, Vishakha Desai, and John Tchen. New York: Asia Society Galleries, 1994. 65–110.

MacLeod, Roy, and Milton Lewis, eds. *Disease, Medicine, and Empire*. New York: Routledge, 1988.

Madsen, Deborah. *American Exceptionalism*. Jackson: University Press of Mississippi, 1998.

Magdoff, Harry. *Imperialism without Colonies*. New York: Monthly Review Press, 2003.

Maira, Sunaina. *Desis in the House: Indian American Youth Culture in New York City*. Philadelphia: Temple University Press, 2002.

——. "Desis Reprazent: Bhangra Remix and Hip Hop in New York City." *Postcolonial Studies* 1, no. 3 (1998): 357–70.

——. "Henna and Hip Hop: The Politics of Cultural Production and the Work of Cultural Studies." *Journal of Asian American Studies* 3, no. 3 (2000): 329–69.

——. "Identity Dub: The Paradoxes of an Indian American Subculture." *Cultural Anthropology* 14, no. 1 (1999): 29–60.

——. "Trance-Global-Nation: Orientalism, Cosmopolitanism, and Citizenship in Youth Culture." Paper presented at the American Studies Association annual conference, Washington, D.C., 2001.

Malkki, Liisa. "National Geographic: The Rooting of Peoples and the Territorialization of National Identity among Scholars and Refugees." In *Becoming National: A Reader*, ed. Geoff Eley and Ronald Grigot Suny. New York: Oxford University Press, 1996. 441–42.

Mankekar, Purnima. *Screening Culture, Viewing Politics: An Ethnography of Television, Womanhood, and Nation in Postcolonial India*. Durham, N.C.: Duke University Press, 1999.

Mannur, Anita. "Culinary Scapes: Contesting Food, Gender, and Nation in South Asia and Its Diaspora." PhD diss., University of Massachusetts, Amherst, 2002.

Marchetti, Gina. *Romance and the "Yellow Peril": Race, Sex, and Discursive Strategies in Hollywood Fiction*. Berkeley: University of California Press, 1993.

Marks, Laura U. *The Skin of Film: Intercultural Cinema, Embodiment, and the Senses*. Durham, N.C.: Duke University Press, 2000.

Marshall, P. David. *Celebrity and Power: Fame in Contemporary Culture*. Minneapolis: University of Minnesota Press, 1997.

Marti, J. "Context Marketing: The 'Honey-Pot' Approach to Segmentation Strategy." *Quarterly Review of Marketing* (autumn 1987): 7–12.

McClintock, Anne. "Soft-Soaping Empire: Commodity Racism and Imperial Advertising." In *The Gender and Consumer Culture Reader*, ed. Jennifer Scanlon. New York: New York University Press, 2000. 129–52.

McLeod, Kembrew. "Authenticity within Hip Hop and Other Cultures Threatened with Assimilation." *Journal of Communication* 49, no. 4 (autumn 1999): 134–50.

McRobbie, Angela. *Feminism and Youth Culture: From Jackie to Just Seventeen*. Boston: Unwin Hyman, 1991.

Mercer, Kobena. "Black Hair/Style Politics." In *Out There: Marginalization and Contemporary Cultures*, ed. Russell Ferguson, Martha Gever, Trinh T. Minh-Ha, and Cornell West. Cambridge, Mass.: MIT Press, 1990. 247–64.

——. "Black Masculinity and the Sexual Politics of Race." In *Welcome to the Jungle: New Positions in Black Cultural Studies*. New York and London: Routledge, 1994. 131–70.

——. *Welcome to the Jungle*. New York: Routledge, 1994.

Miller, Daniel. "Consumption and the Vanguard of History." In *Acknowledging Consumption: A Review of New Studies*, ed. Daniel Miller. London: Routledge, 1995. 1–57.

Miller, Toby. "Culture and the Global Economy." In *Performing Hybridity*, ed. May Joseph and Jennifer Natalya Fink. Minneapolis: University of Minnesota Press, 1999. 35–45.

Misir, Deborah N. "The Murder of Navroze Mody: Race, Violence and the Search for Order." *Amerasia Journal* 22, no. 2 (1996): 55–75.

Mitchell, Tony, ed. *Global Noise: Rap and Hip-hop Outside the USA*. Middletown, Conn.: Wesleyan University Press, 2002.

Modleski, Tania. *Loving with a Vengeance: Mass-Produced Fantasies for Women*. Hamden, Conn.: Archon, 1982.

Monson, Ingrid. "The Problem with White Hipness: Race, Gender, and Cultural Conceptions in Jazz Historical Discourse." *Journal of the American Musicological Society* 48 (fall 1995): 396–422.

Morely, David, and Kevin Robins. "Techno-Orientalism: Futures, Foreigners, and Phobias." *New Formations* 16 (spring 1992): 136–56.

Mort, Frank. "Boulevards for the Fashionable and Famous." In *The City Cultures Reader*, ed. Malcom Miles, Tim Hall, and Iain Borden. London: Routledge, 2000. 180–84.

Moy, James. *Marginal Sights: Staging the Chinese in America*. Iowa City: University of Iowa Press, 1993.

Mui, Ylan Q. "Culture on Rewind: Vietnamese Video Series Links a Far-Flung People to Their Past." *Washington Post*, July 12, 2001.

Murray, Albert. *Stomping the Blues*. New York: Da Capo, 1976.

Naficy, Hamid. *The Making of Exile Cultures*. Minneapolis: University of Minnesota Press, 1992.

Nash, Jesse W. "Confucius and the VCR: Vietnamese Values Find a Haven in the Electronic Age." *Natural History* 97, no. 5 (May 1988): 28–31.

National Telecommunications and Information Administration (NTIA). *Falling through the Net II: New Data on the Digital Divide*, July 1998, http://www.ntia.doc.gov/ntiahome/net2/falling.html (accessed February 26, 2001).

Nguyen, Mimi Thi. "Drag Kings and Democracy." *Punk Planet* 56 (July–August 2003). http://www.worsethanqueer.com/slander/pp56.html (accessed October 9, 2006).

——. "Queer Cyborgs and New Mutants: Race, Sexuality, and Prosthetic Sociality in Digital Space." In *AsianAmerica.Net: Ethnicity, Nationalism, and Cyberspace*, ed. Rachel Lee and Sau-Ling Cynthia Wong. New York: Routledge, 2003. 281–305.

Nguyen Tan Hoang. "The Resurrection of Brandon Lee: The Making of a Gay Asian American Porn Star." In *Porn Studies*, ed. Linda Williams. Durham, N.C.: Duke University Press, 2004. 223–70.

Nimbark, Ashakant. "Hinduism in New York City." In *New York Glory: Religions in the City*, ed. Tony Carnes and Anna Karpathakis. New York: New York University Press, 2001. 88–100.

Oishi, Eve. "Bad Asians: New Film and Video by Queer Asian American Artists." In *Countervisions: Asian American Film Criticism*, ed. Darrell Hamamoto and Sandra Liu. Philadelphia: Temple University Press, 2002. 221–44.

———. "Bad Asians, the Sequel: Continuing Trends in Queer API Film and Video." *Millennium Film Journal* 41 (fall 2003): 34–41.

Okihiro, Gary. *Margins and Mainstreams: Asians in American History and Culture*. Seattle: University of Washington Press, 1994.

Omi, Michael, and Howard Winant. *Racial Formations in the United States: From the 1960s to 1990s*. New York: Routledge, 1994.

Ouellette, Dan. "The Question Is . . ." *Down Beat*, September 2003.

Paine, Jeffrey. *Father India*. New Delhi: Penguin, 1998.

Palumbo-Liu, David. *Asian / American: Historical Crossings of a Racial Frontier*. Stanford: Stanford University Press, 1999.

Panassié, Hugues. *The Real Jazz*. Trans. Anne Sorelle Williams. New York: Smith and Durrell, 1942.

Pannish, Jon. *The Color of Jazz: Race and Representation in Postwar American Culture*. Jackson: University Press of Mississippi, 1997.

Parcellin, Paul. "In Focus: Nikki S. Lee." Retro-rocket.com. http://www.retro-rocket .com / archive / nikki_lee.html (accessed August 31, 2001).

Parker, Eric. "Golden Child." *XXL*, September 2002, 158–62.

Pement, Eric. "Louis Farrakhan and the Nation of Islam, Part Two." *Cornerstone* 26, no. 112 (1997). http://www.cornerstonemag.com / pages / show_page.asp?315 (accessed October 4, 2006).

Perkins, William Eric. "Youth's Global Village: An Epilogue." In *Droppin' Science: Critical Essays in Rap and Hip Hop Culture*, ed. William Eric Perkins. Philadelphia: Temple University Press, 1995. 258–71.

Perry, Imani. *Prophets of the Hood: Politics and Poetics in Hip Hop*. Durham, N.C.: Duke University Press, 2004.

Pfeiffer, Paul. "Quod nomen mihi est? Excerpts from a Conversation with Satan." *Felix: A Journal of Media Arts* 5 (2000). http://www.e-felix.org / issue5 / pfeiffer.html (accessed October 4, 2006).

Pollock, Sheldon. "Indology, Power, and the Case of Germany." In *Orientalism: A Reader*, ed. Alexander L. Macfie. New York: New York University Press, 2000. 306–12.

Poster, Mark. *What's the Matter with the Internet?* Minneapolis: University of Minnesota Press, 2001.

Prashad, Vijay. *Everybody Was Kung Fu Fighting: Afro-Asian Connections and the Myth of Cultural Purity*. New York: Beacon, 2001.

———. *The Karma of Brown Folk*. Minneapolis: University of Minnesota Press, 2000.

Prestowitz, Clyde, Jr., *Trading Places*. New York: Basic Books, 1989.

Procter, James. *Dwelling Places: Postwar Black British Writing*. Manchester: Manchester University Press, 2003.

Radway, Janice. *Reading the Romance: Women, Patriarchy, and Popular Literature*. Chapel Hill: University of North Carolina Press, 1984.

Ray, Krishnendu. "Meals, Migration, Modernity: Domestic Cooking and Bengali Ethnicity in the United States." *Amerasia Journal* 24, no. 1 (1998): 105–27.

Reyes, Adelaida. *Songs of the Caged, Songs of the Free: Music and the Vietnamese Refugee Experience*. Philadelphia: Temple University Press, 1999.

Rivera, Raquel Z. *New York Ricans from the Hip Hop Zone*. New York: Palgrave Macmillan, 2003.

Rodaway, Paul. *Sensuous Geographies: Body, Sense, and Place*. London: Routledge, 1994.

Rogin, Michael. *Blackface, White Noise: Jewish Immigrants in the Hollywood Melting Pot*. Berkeley: University of California Press, 1996.

——. " 'Make My Day!' Spectacle as Amnesia in Imperial Politics [and] the Sequel." In *Cultures of United States Imperialism*, ed. Amy Kaplan and Donald E. Pease. Durham, N.C.: Duke University Press, 1993. 499–534.

Romero, D. James. "A Turbocharged Obsession." *Los Angeles Times*, January 22, 1997.

Roome, Loretta. *Mehndi: The Timeless Art of Body Painting*. New York: St. Martin's, 1998.

Rose, Tricia. *Black Noise: Rap Music and Black Culture in Contemporary America*. Hanover, N.H.: University Press of New England, 1994.

Rosen, Marjorie. "Wrap Artist." *New York Times Magazine*, February 20, 2000. "Fashions of the Times" special issue, pt. 2.

Rosenzweig, Ilene. "Attack of the Killer Yogis." *New York Times*, January 7, 2001.

Ross, Andrew. "Tribalism in Effect." In *On Fashion*, ed. Shari Benstock and Suzanne Ferris. New Brunswick, N.J.: Rutgers University Press, 1997. 284–99.

Ruark, Jennifer K. "A Place at the Table." *Chronicle of Higher Education*, July 9, 1999.

Rutledge, James. *The Vietnamese Experience in America*. Bloomington: Indiana University Press, 1992.

Said, Edward W. *Orientalism*. New York: Vintage, 1978.

Sales, Grover. *Jazz: America's Classical Music*. New York: Prentice Hall, [1984] 1988.

Sassen, Saskia. *Losing Control? Sovereignty in the Age of Globalization*. Berkeley: University of California Press, 1998.

Schein, Louisa. "Forged Transnationality and Oppositional Cosmopolitanism." In *Cultural Compass: Ethnographic Explorations of Asian America*, ed. Martin Manalansan. Philadelphia: Temple University Press, 2000. 199–215.

Schramm, Adelaida Reyes. "From Refugee to Immigrant: The Music of Vietnamese in the New York and New Jersey Metropolitan Area." In *New Perspectives on Vietnamese Music: Six Essays*, ed. Phong T. Nguyen. New Haven: Yale Center for International and Area Studies, 1992. 90–102.

Schuller, Gunther. *Early Jazz*. New York: Oxford University Press, 1968.

——. *The Swing Era*. New York: Oxford University Press, 1989.

Sedlmayr, Hans. "Preface." In Alois Riegl, *Gesammelte Aufsäzte*. Augsburg: B. Filser, 1929.

See, Lisa. *The Interior*. New York: Harper Collins, 1999.

Sengupta, Somini. "Beyond Yoga, Curry and Nehru Jackets Into Film, Publishing and Body Painting." *New York Times*, August 30, 1997.

Sengupta, Somini, and Vivian S. Toy. "United Ethnically, and by an Assault." *New York Times*, October 7, 1998.

Shah, Nayan. *Contagious Divides: Epidemics and Race in San Francisco's Chinatown*. Berkeley: University of California Press, 2001.

Shatz, Adam. "New Seekers in Jazz Look to the East." *New York Times*, November 23, 1997.

Shimakawa, Karen. *National Abjection: The Asian American Body Onstage*. Durham, N.C.: Duke University Press, 2002.

Shoemaker, Bill. "East Meets Left: Politics, Culture, and Asian-American Jazz." *JazzTimes*, September 2003, 82–87.

Shohat, Ella. "Gender and Culture of Empire: Toward a Feminist Ethnography of the Cinema." In *Visions of the East: Orientalism in Film*, ed. Matthew Bernstein and Gaylyn Studlar. New Brunswick, N.J.: Rutgers University Press, 1997. 52–57.

Shohat, Ella, and Robert Stam. *Unthinking Eurocentrism: Multiculturalism and the Media*. London: Routledge, 1994.

Silverman, Deborah. *Selling Culture: Bloomingdale's, Diana Vreeland, and the New Aristocracy of Taste in Reagan's America*. New York: Pantheon, 1986.

Silverstein, Alvin, Virginia Silverstein, and Robert Silverstein. *Smell, the Subtle Sense*. New York: Morrow Junior Books, 1992.

Sklair, Leslie. "Social Movements and Capitalism." In *The Cultures of Globalization*, ed. Fredric Jameson and Masoa Miyoshi. Durham, N.C.: Duke University Press, 1998. 291–311.

Slotkin, Richard. *Gunfighter Nation: The Myth of the Frontier in Twentieth-Century America*. New York: Atheneum, 1992.

——. *Regeneration through Violence: The Mythology of the American Frontier, 1600–1860*. Middletown, Conn.: Wesleyan University Press, 1973.

Small, Christopher. *Musicking: The Meanings of Performing and Listening*. Hanover, N.H.: University Press of New England, 1998.

Smith, Baldwin. Interview with Dan and June Kuramoto. *Jazz Nation*, http://www.jazz nation.com/spotlight/hiroshima/hiroshima.htm (accessed August 10, 2003).

Smith, Danyel. "Ain't a Damn Thing Changed: Why Women Rappers Don't Sell." In *Rap on Rap: Straight-Up Talk on Hip Hop Culture*, ed. Adam Sexton. New York: Delta Trade, 1995. 125–28.

Smith, Mark Chalon. "The Big Mix: Little Saigon's Video Kicks." *Los Angeles Times*, February 5, 1989.

Smyth, Cherry. "Trash Femme Cocktail." *Sight and Sound*, September 1992.

Sobel, Robert. *Car Wars: The Untold Story*. New York: Dutton, 1984.

Spero, Donald M. "Patent Protection or Piracy: A CEO Views Japan." *Harvard Business Review* 68, no. 5 (September 1990): 58–67.

Stein, Barry. "Occupational Adjustment of Refugees: The Vietnamese in the United States." *International Migration Review* 13, no. 1 (spring 1979): 25–45.

Stoller, Paul. *Sensuous Scholarship*. Philadelphia: University of Pennsylvania Press, 1997.

——. *The Taste of Ethnographic Things: The Senses in Anthropology*. Philadelphia: University of Pennsylvania Press, 1989.

Strong, Nolan. "Jin Says Rap Career Is Over, Records 'I Quit.'" *Allhiphop.com*, http://www.allhiphop.com/hiphopnews/?ID=4412 (accessed May 20, 2005).

Sudhalter, Richard. *Lost Chords: White Musicians and Their Contributions to Jazz, 1915–1945*. New York: Oxford University Press, 1999.

Sutton, David. *Remembrance of Repasts: An Anthropology of Food and Memory*. New York: Berg, 2001.

Takaki, Ronald. *Strangers from a Different Shore: A History of Asian Americans*. Boston: Little, Brown, [1989] 1998.

Tam, Christina. "Jin and Juice." *New York Post*, October 17, 2004.

Tan, Amy. *The Joy Luck Club*. New York: Putnam, 1989.

Tasker, Yvonne. "Fists of Fury: Discourses of Race and Masculinity in the Martial Arts Cinema." In *Race and the Subject of Masculinities*, ed. Harry Stecopoulos and Michael Uebel. Durham, N.C.: Duke University Press, 1997. 315–36.

Taylor, Charles. "The Guru." *Salon.com*. http://archive.salon.com/ent/movies/review/2003/02/05/guru/print.html (accessed March 2003).

Taylor, Juval, ed. *The Future of Jazz*. New York: A Capella, 2002.

Tinkcom, Matthew. *Working Like a Homosexual: Camp, Capital, Cinema*. Durham, N.C.: Duke University Press, 2002.

Tongson, Karen. "JJ Chinois' Oriental Express; or How a Suburban Heartthrob Seduced Red America." *Social Text* 84–85 (2005): 193–217.

Tran, De. "Songwriters Return to Love." *San Jose Mercury News*, December 20, 1993.

Troka, Donna, Kathleen LeBesco, and Jean Noble, eds. *The Drag King Anthology*. New York: Harrington Park, 2003.

Truong, Sydney. "Paris by Night: Phenom or Phizz?" *Vietnow*, March–April 1996.

Tsai, Ming. *Blue Ginger: East Meets West Cooking*. New York: Random House, 1999.

Tseng, Judy. "Asian American Rap: Expression through Alternate Forms." Unpublished paper, Georgetown University Law Center, Washington, D.C., 1998.

Tu, Thuy Linh Nguyen. "Good Politics, Great Porn." In *AsianAmerica.Net: Ethnicity, Nationalism, and Cyberspace*, ed. Rachel Lee and Sau-Ling Cynthia Wong. New York: Routledge, 2003. 267–80.

——. "Outside In: Immigration and Popular Culture in Asian New York." PhD diss., New York University, 2003.

Tuan, Mia. "On Asian American Ice Queens and Multigeneration Asian Ethics." *Amerasia Journal* 25, no. 1 (1999): 181–86.

Tucker, Sherrie. *Swing Shift: "All-Girl" Bands of the 1940s*. Durham, N.C.: Duke University Press, 2000.

U.S. Bureau of the Census. 2000 Annual City Census, Northampton Board of Registrars. U.S. Census Bureau: Census 2000; http://censtats.census.gov/data/MA/1602546330.pdf#search='City%20Census%20Northampton%202000' (accessed November 2001).

Vicario, Gilbert. "Conversation with Nikki S. Lee." In *Nikki S. Lee: Projects*, ed. Lesley A. Martin. Osfildern-Ruit: Hatje Cantz, 2001. 95–110.

Vidhani, V. "Wake up Bollywood." *Daily Mail* (Islamabad), September 22, 2003.

Wald, Gayle. "'I Want It That Way': Teenybopper Music and the Girling of Boy Bands."

Genders 35 (2002). http://www.genders.org/g35/g35_wald.html (accessed October 4, 2006).

Wang, Dorothy. Review of *Orientations: Mapping Studies in the Asian Diaspora*. *Journal of Asian American Studies* 5, no. 3 (October 2002): 269–77.

Wang, Oliver. "Between the Notes: Finding Asian America in Popular Music." *American Music* 19, no. 4 (winter 2001): 439–65.

Weiss, Andrea. *Vampires and Violets: Lesbians in Film*. New York: Penguin, 1992.

Weston, Kath. "Do Clothes Make the Woman? Gender, Performance Theory, and Lesbian Eroticism." *Genders* 16 (1993): 1–21.

White-Parks, Annette. *Sui Sin Far/Edith Maude Eaton: A Literary Biography*. Urbana-Champaign: University of Illinois Press, 1995.

Wilson, Ernest J., III. "Orientalism: A Black Perspective." In *Orientalism: A Reader*, ed. Alexander L. Macfie. New York: New York University Press, 2000. 239–48.

Wimsatt, William Upski. *Bomb the Suburbs*. New York: Soft Skull, 2000.

———. "We Use Words Like Mackadocious." In *Bomb the Suburbs*. New York: Soft Skull Press, 1994. 22–41.

Won, Joseph. "Yellowface Minstrelsy: Asian Martial Arts and the American Popular Imaginary." PhD diss., University of Michigan, 1996.

Wong, Deborah. "The Asian American Body in Performance." In *Music and the Racial Imagination*, ed. Ronald Radano and Philip V. Bohlman. Chicago: University of Chicago Press, 2000. 57–94.

———. *Speak It Louder: Asian Americans Making Music*. New York: Routledge, 2004.

Wong, Sau-ling Cynthia. " 'Asian for the Man!' Stereotypes, Identity, and Self-Empowerment in Asian American Rap." Unpublished paper, 1996.

———. "Denationalization Reconsidered: Asian American Cultural Criticism at a Crossroads," *Amerasia Journal* 21, nos. 1–2 (1995): 1–27.

———. "The Invisible Man Syndrome: Politics of Representation in Asian American Rap." Unpublished paper, 1996.

———. "The Politics and Poetics of Folksong Reading: Literary Portrayals of Life under Exclusion." In *Entry Denied: Exclusion and the Chinese Community in America, 1882–1943*, ed. Sucheng Chan. Philadelphia: Temple University Press, 1991. 246–67.

———. *Reading Asian American Literature: From Necessity to Extravagance*. Princeton: Princeton University Press, 1993.

———. " 'We Define Ourselves!': The Negotiation of Power and Identity for Asian Americans in Hip Hop." Unpublished paper, 1996.

Wong, Shawn Hsu. "Good Luck, Happiness, and Long Life." In *Counterpoint: Perspectives on Asian America*. Los Angeles: Asian American Studies Center, University of California, Los Angeles, 1976. 464–70.

Yang, Alice. "Asian American Exhibitions Reconsidered." In *Why Asia?*, ed. Jonathan Hay and Mimi Young. New York: New York University Press, 1998. 94–98.

Yegenoglu, Meyda. *Colonial Fantasies: Towards a Feminist Reading of Colonialism*. Cambridge: Cambridge University Press, 1998.

Yokota, Ryan Masaaki. "Key Kool: Nikkei on the Down Side." *Pacific Ties*, October 1994.

Yoshida, George. *Reminiscing in Swing Time: Japanese Americans in American Popular Music, 1925–1960*. San Francisco: National Japanese American Historical Society, 1997.

Yoshikawa, Yoko. "The Heat Is on Miss Saigon Coalition: Organizing across Race and Sexuality." In *Q&A: Queer in Asian America*, ed. David L. Eng and Alice Y. Hom. Philadelphia: Temple University Press, 1998. 41–56.

Yu, Henry. *Thinking Orientals: Migration, Contact, and Exoticism in Modern America*. New York: Oxford University Press, 2001.

Yudice, George. *The Expediency of Culture: Uses of Culture in the Global Era*. Durham, N.C.: Duke University Press, 2004.

Yun, Grace, ed. *A Look beyond the Model Minority Image: Critical Issues in Asian America*. New York: Minority Rights Group, 1989.

Zia, Helen. *Asian American Dreams: The Emergence of an American People*. New York: Farrar, Straus, and Giroux, 2000.

——. "To Market, To Market, New York Style." In *Asian American Dreams: The Emergence of an American People*. New York: Farrar, Straus, and Giroux, 2001. 82–108.

Contributors

Wendy Hui Kyong Chun is an associate professor of modern culture and media at Brown University. She has studied both systems design engineering and English literature, which she combines and mutates in her current work on digital media. She is the author of *Control and Freedom: Power and Paranoia in the Age of Fiber Optics* (2005) and the coeditor, with Thomas Keenan, of *New Media, Old Media: A History and Theory Reader* (2005). She is currently preparing a manuscript on the relationship between race and code entitled "Programmed Visions: Software, DNA, Race." She has been a fellow at the Radcliffe Institute for Advanced Study at Harvard University and the recipient of a Henry Merritt Wriston fellowship at Brown.

Kevin Fellezs is an assistant professor of art in the School of Social Sciences, Humanities and Arts at the University of California, Merced. His primary research interest is twentieth-century popular music and popular culture writ large, focusing particularly on Asian American and African American contexts. He also has a scholarly interest in Hawai'ian musical culture. He received his PhD (with a parenthetical in American Studies) from the History of Consciousness program at the University of California, Santa Cruz.

Vernadette Vicuña Gonzalez is an assistant professor of American studies at the University of Hawai'i, Manoa. Her research connects transnational feminisms, tourism, and militarism, primarily in the Asia-Pacific region. She is currently writing on the overlaps between cultures and technologies of militarism and tourism in the Philippines and Hawaii and starting a new research project on the transnational networks formed between missionary projects and the cultures and economies of tourism in the Asia-Pacific region.

Joan Kee is an art historian based in Seoul and Tokyo. She guest edited a special issue of *positions: east asia cultures critique* on contemporary art in East Asia. Other publications have appeared in *Third Text, Oxford Art Journal,* and *Yishu: The Journal of Contemporary Chinese Art.*

Nhi T. Lieu is an assistant professor of American studies and Asian American studies at the University of Texas, Austin. She received her PhD in American culture at the University of Michigan. Her current book project, entitled "Private Desires on Public Display: Vietnamese American Pursuits of Leisure and the American Dream," explores multiple sites of diasporic Vietnamese niche media and cultural production and their relationship to the formation of contemporary Vietnamese American identities.

Sunaina Maira is an associate professor of Asian American studies at the University of California, Davis. Her research focuses on youth culture, popular culture, immigration and transnationalism, citizenship, and empire. She is the author of *Desis in the House: Indian American Youth Culture in New York City* (2002). She coedited an anthology, *Contours of the Heart: South Asians Map North America* (1997), which received the American Book Award from the Before Columbus Foundation, and is coeditor of *Youthscapes: Popular Culture, National Ideologies, Global Markets* (2004). She received a grant from the Russell Sage Foundation to conduct an ethnographic study of South Asian Muslim immigrant youths in the United States and their notions of cultural citizenship after September 11, 2001, which is the basis of her current book project.

Martin F. Manalansan IV is an associate professor of anthropology at the University of Illinois, Urbana-Champaign. He has appointments in the Unit for Criticism and Theory, the Asian American Studies Program, and the Program for Gender and Women's Studies. He edited a collection of essays entitled *Cultural Compass: Ethnographic Explorations of Asian America* (2000) and coedited, with Arnaldo Cruz-Malavé, an anthology entitled *Queer Globalizations: Citizenship and the Afterlife of Colonialism* (2002). His *Global Divas: Filipino Gay Men in the Diaspora* was published by Duke University Press in 2003 and was awarded the Ruth Benedict Prize by the Society of Lesbian and Gay Anthropologists. His essays on sexuality, gender, immigration, and transnationalism have been published in several journals, including *glq* and *positions: east asia cultures critique.* His present projects include an ethnographic study of Filipino American and Filipino Canadian repatriates in the Philippine entertainment industry and an investigation of the politics of the senses and Asian American culinary cultures in New York City.

Mimi Thi Nguyen is an assistant professor in the programs of Gender and Women's Studies and Asian American Studies at the University of Illinois, Urbana-Champaign. She is currently completing her first book, which examines the uses of the refugee figure and its affect in mobilizing, and sometimes deferring, claims to historical justice. She continues to situate her work within transnational feminist cultural studies in her next project, focusing on fashion, citizenship, and transnationality. She is the author of multiple essays on Asian American, queer, and punk subcultures; digital technologies; and Vietnamese diasporic culture published in academic collections, online publications, and popular magazines.

Robyn Magalit Rodriguez is an assistant professor in the department of sociology at Rutgers University, New Brunswick–Piscataway. Her dissertation, "The Labor Brokering State: The Global Production of Philippine Citizen-Workers," examines the processes by which the Philippine state produces, distributes, and regulates gendered and racialized labor for the global economy. She has several publications related to her dissertation topic and has worked collaboratively with Vernadette Vicuña Gonzalez on several projects. Most recently, she has published on the topic of race and citizenship post–9/11. She is also a founding member of the Critical Filipino/a Studies Collective.

Sukhdev Sandhu is an assistant professor of Asian/Pacific/American studies and English literature at New York University. He writes regularly for the London Review of Books and Modern Painters. He is the chief film critic for the Daily Telegraph in London and a contributing editor at Granta. His books include the first volume of Slavery, Abolition, and Emancipation: Writings in the British Romantic Period (1999) and London Calling: How Black and Asian Writers Imagined a City (2003).

Christopher A. Shinn is an assistant professor of English at Florida State University and specializes in the study of world literature, cultural studies, and postcolonial theory and criticism. He was awarded a Fulbright Grant in 2002 and conducted research on the discourse on "race" and miscegenation in Brazil. He is currently working on a book project entitled Black Dragon: Towards an Afro-Asiatic Imagination, which examines the cross-cultural exchanges, entangled diasporic histories, and world decolonization movements of Asian and African peoples.

Indigo Som is a visual artist and writer based in the San Francisco Bay Area. Her work addresses a wide range of concerns: "American" identity; place, landscape, and architecture; text, language, and folklore; repetition and accretion; and the mundane. In various projects, she has deconstructed gingham fabric, stacked common office paper from floor to ceiling, stitched illegible handwriting on silk, and drawn grammatical diagrams of pop lyrics. Perhaps her best-known work is her long-term project investigating relationships between Chinese restaurants and American identity, for which she received a Creative Work Fund grant to photograph Chinese restaurants in the American South. Some of the resulting works are included in the group exhibition One Way or Another: Asian American Art Now, which began its national tour at the Asia Society Museum (New York City) in fall 2006. Widely exhibited in group and solo shows at diverse venues, her artwork has been collected by the Museum of Modern Art and the Getty Center, among other institutions and collectors internationally, and throughout the United States. She has also been awarded several residency grants. Her work has received critical attention in such publications as the New York Times, Sculpture, the San Francisco Chronicle, Artweek, and Giant Robot. Her writing has been published in numerous journals and anthologies. More information is available on her Web site, www.indigosom.com.

Thuy Linh Nguyen Tu is an assistant professor of art history and Asian American studies at Cornell University. She is the coeditor of Technicolor: Race, Technology, and Everyday Life (2001) and is currently completing a manuscript on Asian American cultural labors.

Contributors

Oliver Wang is an assistant professor of sociology at California State University, Long Beach, specializing in popular culture, race, and ethnicity. He writes extensively on popular music and film for *Vibe*, the *Oakland Tribune*, *Wax Poetics*, and the *San Francisco Bay Guardian*, and his commentaries can be heard on National Public Radio's *Morning Edition*. He is the editor and coauthor of *Classic Material: The Hip-Hop Album Guide* (2003). More information can be found at the Web site www.o-dub.com.

Contributors

Index

Dalena, 211, 213
Days of Being Dumb, 52–53
Deleuze, Gilles, 163
Delinquent Chacha, 169
DeVeaux, Scott, 71
Diaspora, 21, 88, 140, 194–95, 234; diasporic consciousness, 25; diasporic media, 203, 214; diasporic subject, 26, 196; Vietnamese, 202, 213, 214, 217
"Digital divide," 310
Dil Se, 167
Disease, associated with native other, 118
Drag, 29, 274, 278–79, 282, 283, 301 n. 36
Dragon: A Bruce Lee Story, 272, 273
Dragon Bones, 112
Du Bois, W. E. B., 44
Dyer, Richard, 288

East Is East, 171
East Meets West, 184–85, 186
Ecology of form, 135, 146, 149 n. 14
Economics, 13
Elizabeth (film), 168
Ellison, Ralph, 112
Embodiment, 25; as method, 191; race and, 182
Eminem, 56, 60
Espiritu, Yen Le, 40
Essentialism, 134–35
Ethnicity, 13, 40, 212, 255; ethnic experience, 133, 134, 148, 181, 191–92; ethnic subject, 113; food and, 180; performance and, 210
Ewen, Stuart, 277
Exile, 205

Fang, Karen, 163
Fans, 291; fan labor, 276, 297
Fantasy, 3, 9, 180, 202, 206, 292; heterosexist, 266
Fashion, 223, 225
Fast and the Furious, The, 247
Femininity, 25, 208, 249, 279

Feminism, 21, 26, 222
Feng, Peter X., 24
Film, 137, 161–74, 213, 286; Chinese, 200; Hindi, 168; martial arts, 290
Fingers and Kisses, 21
Fists of Fury, 42–43
Florida, Richard, 12
Flower Net, 112
Food, 19, 179; Chinese restaurants and, 22, 150–60; cultural studies and, 181; fusion cuisine, 184, 186–88; nationality and, 185; senses and, 188
Fordism, 249–50
Foster, Thomas, 317
Foucault, Michel, 24, 113
Four Feathers, The, 168
Francia, Luis H., 141
Francisco, Rich, 41–42
Fresh Talk / Daring Gazes, 134
Fuller, Matthew, 321
Fun-Da-Mental, 172
Fung, Richard, 291
Fusco, Coco, 17

Gender, 207–8, 214, 249, 262–63. *See also* Drag; Femininity; Masculinity
Ghatak, Ritwik, 166
Ghosh, Amitav, 111–12, 118–21
Ghost World, 167
Giant Robot, 20
Gilroy, Paul, 76, 101 n. 25
Globalization, 21–22, 26, 115, 134, 135, 162, 237, 240; capitalism and, 117, 119, 236; global social control and, 113; markets and, 116, 162–64, 259; place and, 23, 162
Golden, Thelma, 133, 148 n. 2
Gonzalez, Jennifer, 311
Goonies, The, 1, 4, 30
Grewal, Inderpal, 21, 262, 263
Grewel, Shani, 169
Guattari, Félix, 163
Gung Ho, 28
Gupta, Sanjay, 168

Mimi Thi Nguyen is an assistant professor in the programs of gender and women's studies and Asian American studies at the University of Illinois, Urbana-Champaign.

Thuy Linh Nguyen Tu is an assistant professor of art history and Asian American studies at Cornell University. She is the coeditor of *Technicolor: Race, Technology, and Everyday Life* (2001).

Library of Congress Cataloging-in-Publication Data

Alien encounters : popular culture in Asian America /
Mimi Thi Nguyen and Thuy Linh Nguyen Tu, editors.
   p. cm.
Includes bibliographical references and index.
   ISBN-13: 978-0-8223-3910-6 (cloth : alk. paper)
   ISBN-13: 978-0-8223-3922-9 (pbk. : alk. paper)
1. Asian Americans—Intellectual life. 2. Asian Americans—Ethnic identity. 3. Asian Americans—Social life and customs. 4. Asian Americans—Study and teaching. 5. Popular culture—United States. 6. United States—Intellectual life. 7. United States—Social life and customs. 8. United States—Ethnic relations. I. Nguyen, Mimi Thi. II. Tu, Thuy Linh N.
   E184.A75A45 2007
   305.895'073—dc22   2006034549